E█████

Verbs

And a Review of Standard English Usage

Fourth Edition

by
Vincent F. Hopper

Former Professor of English
New York University, NY

and

George Ehrenhaft

Former Chairman, English Department
Mamaroneck High School, NY

BARRON'S

BARRON'S EDUCATIONAL SERIES, INC.

© Copyright 2012, 2004, 1991, 1975 by Barron's Educational Series, Inc.

All inquiries should be addressed to:
Barron's Educational Series, Inc.
250 Wireless Boulevard
Hauppauge, New York 11788
www.barronseduc.com

ISBN: 978-0-7641-4785-2

Library of Congress Control Number: 2012936059

PRINTED IN CHINA
9 8 7 6 5 4 3 2 1

aid, aide	*Aid* can mean "assistance" or "to assist," but *aide* is always a noun meaning an assistant.
almost, most	*Almost* means *nearly:* "He was *almost* ready when we called for him." "*Almost* every girl in the class had long hair." *Most* as an adjective or adverb means *in the greatest degree:* "A *most* difficult problem was presented." "*Most* people prefer sunny climates." *Most* as a noun means the largest number or the greatest quantity: "The *most* I can give you is $2."
all ready, already	*All ready* (two words) is used in such sentences as "They are *all ready* to go." *Already* is an adverb meaning *previously:* "We ran to catch the train but it had *already* left."
all right, alright	*Alright* is illiterate for *all right.* Do not confuse the spelling with words like *almost, already, altogether.*
a lot, allot	*Allot* is a verb meaning *to apportion, to share out.* When speaking of a large quantity, use *a lot.* Never write it as a single word (*alot*). There is no such word in standard English.
altogether, all together	*All together* (two words) is used in such sentences as "They were *all together* in the same room." *Altogether* is an adverb, meaning *completely:* "You are *altogether* wrong in your assumption."
allusion, illusion, delusion	*Allusion* means reference to: "She made an *allusion* to last week's meeting." *Illusion* is an unreality: "That a pair of railroad tracks seems to meet in the distance is an optical *illusion.*" *Delusion* is a false belief: "Convinced that he was the King of Spain, Tom lived in a *delusion.*"
alternative, alternate	*Alternative* means a choice in a situation where a choice must be made between two possibilities: "If you can't take the test on Thursday, your only *alternative* is to take it next week." *Alternate* means substitute, as in: "Because the main road was under construction, they took an *alternate* route to town."
alumnus, alumna, alumni, alumnae	An *alumnus* is a male graduate. *Alumni* is the plural. An *alumna* is a female graduate. *Alumnae* is the plural. *Alumni* is used for male and female combined.
among, between	*Between* is used in connection with two persons or things: "He divided the money *between* his two children." *Among* is used for more than two. "He divided the money *among* his three children." EXCEPTIONS: If more than two are involved in a united situation, *between* is used: "*Between* the four of us we raised a thousand dollars." If a comparison or an opposition is involved,

	between is used: "There was great rivalry *between* the three colleges. It was difficult to choose *between* them."
amount, number	*Amount* refers to bulk or quantity: *amount* of sugar, grain, flour, money. *Number* refers to objects that are thought of as individual units: *number* of oranges, children, diamonds. Notice that most words following *amount* are singular (*coal*, *butter*, *water*) and that most words following *number* are plural (*apples*, *bottles*, *glasses*).
and/or	Although this usage is becoming common, it is unnecessary and should be avoided. *Or* alone carries the same meaning.
ante- anti-	These similar prefixes carry different meanings. *Ante-* means "before" and *anti-* means "against" or "opposed to." Notice *antebellum* (before the war) and *antiwar* (against war).
any one, anyone	*Any one* means any single person or thing of a group: "*Any one* of the students in the class was capable of passing the course." *Anyone* is an indefinite pronoun meaning *anybody:* "*Anyone* can tell that you are not as stupid as you pretend."
appraise, apprise	*Appraise* means to make an estimate: "Will you *appraise* the value of this ring?" *Apprise* means *inform* (usually in a formal sense): "He was *apprised* by registered mail that his lease would not be renewed."
apt, liable, likely	*Apt* refers to a habitual disposition: "Having a good brain, he is *apt* to get good grades." *Likely* merely expresses probability: "It is *likely* to rain." *Liable* implies the probability of something unfortunate: "The firm is *liable* to fail."
as . . . as, so . . . as	*As . . . as* is used for affirmative comparisons. "He was *as* tall *as* his father." *So . . . as* is used for negative comparisons: She was not *so* tall *as* her mother."
as, like	When used as a preposition, *like* should never introduce a clause (NOT *like I was saying*). When introducing a clause, *as* is used (*as I was saying*) even if some of the words of the clause are implied: "He did it as well *as* I [did]."
beside, besides	*Beside* means *by the side of*: "Ask him to sit *beside* me." *Besides* means *in addition*: "She was an expert secretary. *Besides*, she had a wonderful disposition."
bimonthly, semimonthly	*Bimonthly* magazines are published once every two months. *Semimonthly* ones are published twice a month.
bring, take	*Bring* refers to movement toward the speaker: "*Bring* me a ham sandwich, please." *Take* refers to movement away from the speaker: "*Take* this book over to the shelf near the window."

can, may	*Can* implies ability: "*Can* you (are you able to) lift that heavy box?" *May* denotes permission: "*May* I (Have I permission to) swim in your pool?"
cite, site	To *cite* is to make a reference to a source in a term paper. The noun *site* refers to a space of ground, as in "the *site* of a new dormitory."
claim, assert	*Claim* refers to a justified demand or legal right: "I *claim* this piece of property." "I *claim* the prize." It should not be used when only an assertion is intended: "He *asserted* (not *claimed*) that his demands were reasonable."
common, mutual	*Common* means shared by two or more people or things: "The classmates had a *common* admiration for their school." "All the houses in the development had a big recreation area in *common*." *Mutual* means *reciprocal*: "The classmates had a *mutual* admiration for each other."
compare to, compare with	*Compare to* is used to indicate a definite resemblance: "He *compared* the railroad *to* a highway." *Compare with* is used to indicate an examination of similarities and dissimilarities: "He *compared* the middle ages *with* modern times."
complement, compliment	*Complement* as a verb means *complete*: "He needed a typewriter to *complement* his office equipment." As a noun *complement* means whatever is needed for completion: "I am sending you fifty books as a *complement* to your law library." It can also mean whatever is needed to complete an operation: "The officers and crew are the *complement* of a ship." *Compliment* is a noun meaning an expression of admiration: "He paid her the *compliment* of saying that she had exquisite taste in clothes."
confidant, confident	A *confidant* (*confidante*, if female) is a trusted friend in whom one can "confide." *Confident* is an adjective meaning you are certain, e.g., you are *confident* he or she will not betray your trust.
consul, council, counsel	A *consul* is a government agent who lives in a foreign country to protect the interests of the citizens of his own country: "When I lost my passport, I went immediately to the *consul*." *Council* is a *group* of individuals who act in an advisory capacity or who meet for the purposes of discussion or decision-making: "The mayor met with the *council*." "They called a *council* to make plans for the future." *Counsel* as a noun means *advice*, or, in legal parlance, a lawyer or lawyers: "He sought my *counsel*." "He retained *counsel* to represent him at the trial." As a verb *counsel* means *advise*: "I would *counsel* you to accept his offer."

Glossary of Troublesome Words and Phrases

contemptuous,   *Contemptuous* means showing contempt: "My teacher was
contemptible   *contemptuous* of my performance." *Contemptible* means
                deserving of contempt: "His rude behavior at the wedding was
                contemptible."

continual,   *Continual* means *constantly with interruptions*: "She smoked
continuous   *continually*." *Continuous* means *without interruptions*: "The
                water flows *continuously* over Niagara Falls."

councilor,   A *councilor* is a member of a council. A *counselor* is an adviser.
counselor   The term is also used to denote a leader, guardian, or super-
                visor of children or young people as at a summer camp.

credible,   *Credible* means *believable*: "His story was entirely *credible*."
creditable,   *Creditable* means *meritorious*, *praiseworthy*—but not
credulous   outstanding: "His performance was *creditable*, but I wouldn't
                pay admission to hear him again." *Credulous* means *ready to
                believe*: "Being a *credulous* person, he believed everything he
                read."

different from, *Different from* is the correct idiom, NOT *different than*.
differ from,   *Differ from* applies to differences between one person or thing
differ with   and another or others: "My car *differs from* his because it is a
                newer model." *Differ with* means to have a difference in opinion:
                "I *differ with* him in his views about government."

discreet,   *Discreet* means careful in avoiding mistakes, as in "He was
discrete   *discreet* in his habits." *Discrete* means separate, or detached, as
                in "Each grain of rice was *discrete*, not clinging to the rest in a
                glutinous mass."

disinterested, *Disinterested* means impartial: "The two sides chose a
uninterested   *disinterested* party to settle the dispute between them." *Uninteres-
                ted* means apathetic: "Some people are *uninterested* in modern art."

dominate,   *Dominate* means to rule over: "He *dominated* the audience
domineer   with his oratory." *Domineer* means to rule tyrannically: "One of
                his daughters *domineered* over the entire family."

don't   *Don't* is the contraction of *do not*: *I don't, you don't, we don't,
                they don't*. Do not confuse it with *doesn't*, the contraction of *does
                not*: *He doesn't, she doesn't, it doesn't*.

dual, duel   *Dual* means *double*: "Since he was born in England of American
                parents, he could lay claim to *dual* citizenship." A *duel* is a
                combat between two men: "He challenged his enemy to a *duel*
                with pistols."

due to   *Due to* acts grammatically as an adjective and must therefore
                modify a specific noun or pronoun: "The flood was *due to* the
                rapid spring thaw." If there is no specific noun or pronoun for
                due to modify, use the phrase *because of*: "He was late *because*

of an accident." Or rephrase the sentence: "His *lateness* [noun] was *due to* an accident."

elicit,
illicit

Elicit means to draw or bring forth: "After hours of questioning, they *elicited* the truth from him." *Illicit* is an adjective meaning not permitted or illegal: "Traffic in drugs is *illicit*."

emigrant,
immigrant

A *migrant* is a member of a mass movement of people from one region to another. A migrant who leaves a country or place of residence is called an *emigrant*; one who comes in is an *immigrant*.

eminent,
imminent

Eminent means famous or prominent; *imminent* means soon to take place: "The Christmas season is *imminent*."

famous,
infamous

Famous means well-known: "After medical school, she became a *famous* surgeon." *Infamous* also means well-known but for a negative reason: "He participated in the *infamous* art theft at the museum."

fewer, less

Fewer is used in connection with people or with objects which are thought of as individual units: *fewer oranges, fewer children, fewer books, fewer dollars. Less* is used in connection with the concept of bulk: *less money, less coal, less weight, less grain.* Notice that most words following *fewer* are plural (*oranges, books, dollars*); most words following *less* are singular (*money, coal, weight*).

flaunt, flout

Flaunt means to display in an ostentatious fashion: "He *flaunted* his learning before his friends." *Flout* means to treat with contempt: "They *flouted* the law by parking in front of a hydrant."

forcible,
forceful

Forcible means effected by force, no matter how much or how little force is used: "Since the key wouldn't fit, they made a *forcible* entry into the house by breaking a window." *Forceful* means full of force: "He was a very *forceful* speaker."

former,
latter

Former and *latter* are used to designate one of two persons or things: "Of the two possibilities, I prefer the *former* to the *latter*." If more than two persons or things are involved, *first* or *first named* and *last* or *last named* are used: "He had a choice of yellow, rose, pink, and brown. He preferred the *first* and *last* to the others."

formerly,
formally

Formerly means at an earlier time: "He is a rich man, but he was *formerly* poor." *Formally* means done in a very correct manner: "He was *formally* inducted into the lodge."

fortuitous,
fortunate

That which is *fortuitous* happens by accident and may or may not be a favorable event. The word is often misused as a synonym for *fortunate*, but it does not have this meaning.

Glossary of Troublesome Words and Phrases

had ought	*Ought* is known as a defective verb because it has only one form and cannot be used with an auxiliary: "They *ought* (NOT *had ought*) to have told her."
hanged, hung	*Hanged* is used in connection with executions: "He was condemned to be *hanged* by the neck until dead." *Hung* is the past tense of *hang* and denotes any other kind of suspension: "The pictures were *hung* on the wall."
hardly	Like *barely* and *scarcely*, *hardly* should not be used with a negative. "He was *hardly* (*barely*, *scarcely*) able to do it." (NOT *not hardly, barely, scarcely*.)
healthful, healthy	*Healthful* means *health-giving:* a *healthful* climate. *Healthy* means *in a state of health*: "She was a *healthy* young girl."
imply, infer	*Imply* means to throw out a hint or suggestion: "She *implied* by her manner that she was unhappy." *Infer* means to take in a hint or suggestion: "I *inferred* from her manner that she was unhappy."
in, into	*In* means within or inside: "Old correspondence is stored *in* this file." *Into* refers to motion from outside to inside: "Put the pickles *into* the glass jar."
indict, indite	*Indict* means to make a formal charge of an offense as a means of bringing a suspect to trial: "He was *indicted* for evasion of income tax." *Indite* means to compose a formal or literary work: "Robert Frost *indited* many poems about New England."
ingenious, ingenuous	*Ingenious* means possessing unusual powers of invention when applied to a person and showing the result of clever inventiveness when applied to a thing: "The *ingenious* inventor perfected a most *ingenious* mechanical toy." *Ingenuity* is the noun. *Ingenuous* means naive or unsophisticated: "He was so *ingenuous* that he believed everything he read."
its, it's	*Its* (no apostrophe) is the possessive case of *it*: "The pig suckled *its* young." *It's* is the contraction of *it is*: "*It's* too late to go to church."
kind, sort, type, variety	When these words are singular in number, they should never be prefaced by plural modifiers: *This kind of book* (Not *these kind of book*). If you want a plural construction, you must make sure all parts are plural: *These kinds of books*.
kind of, sort of, type of, variety of	Never place an article after these expressions: *This kind of pistol* (NOT this kind of *a* pistol).

Contents

Contents

Infinitive: to be written   *Present Participle:* being written
Perfect Infinitive: to have been written   *Past Participle:* been written

INDICATIVE MOOD

Pres.	I am written	we are written
	you are written	you are written
	he (she, it) is written	they are written
Pres. Prog.	I am being written	we are being written
	you are being written	you are being written
	he (she, it) is being written	they are being written
Pres. Int.	I do get written	we do get written
	you do get written	you do get written
	he (she, it) does get written	they do get written
Fut.	I shall be written	we shall be written
	you will be written	you will be written
	he (she, it) will be written	they will be written
Fut.	I will be written *(P)*	we will be written *(P)*
	you shall be written *(C)*	you shall be written *(C)*
	he (she, it) shall be written *(C)*	they shall be written *(C)*
Past	I was written	we were written
	you were written	you were written
	he (she, it) was written	they were written
Past Prog.	I was being written	we were being written
	you were being written	you were being written
	he (she, it) was being written	they were being written
Past Int.	I did get written	we did get written
	you did get written	you did get written
	he (she, it) did get written	they did get written
Pres. Perf.	I have been written	we have been written
	you have been written	you have been written
	he (she, it) has been written	they have been written
Past Perf.	I had been written	we have been written
	you had been written	you had been written
	he (she, it) had been written	they had been written
Fut. Perf.	I shall have been written	we shall have been written
	you will have been written	you will have been written
	he (she, it) will have been written	they will have been written

IMPERATIVE MOOD
be written

SUBJUNCTIVE MOOD

Pres.	if I be written	if we be written
	if you be written	if you be written
	if he (she, it) be written	if they be written
Past	if I were written	if we were written
	if you were written	if you were written
	if he (she, it) were written	if they were written
Fut.	if I should be written	if we should be written
	if you should be written	if you should be written
	if he (she, it) should be written	if they should be written

to write (active voice)   *Principal Parts:* write, writing, wrote, written

---

Infinitive: to write   *Present Participle:* writing
Perfect Infinitive: to have written   *Past Participle:* written

INDICATIVE MOOD

Pres.	I write	we write
	you write	you write
	he (she, it) writes	they write
Pres.	I am writing	we are writing
Prog.	you are writing	you are writing
	he (she, it) is writing	they are writing
Pres.	I do write	we do write
Int.	you do write	you do write
	he (she, it) does write	they do write
Fut.	I shall write	we shall write
	you will write	you will write
	he (she, it) will write	they will write
Fut.	I will write *(P)*	we will write *(P)*
	you shall write *(C)*	you shall write *(C)*
	he (she, it) shall write *(C)*	they shall write *(C)*
Past	I wrote	we wrote
	you wrote	you wrote
	he (she, it) wrote	they wrote
Past	I was writing	we were writing
Prog.	you were writing	you were writing
	he (she, it) was writing	they were writing
Past	I did write	we did write
Int.	you did write	you did write
	he (she, it) did write	they did write
Pres.	I have written	we have written
Perf.	you have written	you have written
	he (she, it) has written	they have written
Past	I had written	we had written
Perf.	you had written	you had written
	he (she, it) had written	they had written
Fut.	I shall have written	we shall have written
Perf.	you will have written	you will have written
	he (she, it) will have written	they will have written

IMPERATIVE MOOD
write

SUBJUNCTIVE MOOD

Pres.	if I write	if we write
	if you writo	if you writə
	if he (she, it) write	if they write
Past	if I wrote	if we wrote
	if you wrote	if you wrote
	if he (she, it) wrote	if they wrote
Fut.	if I should write	if we should write
	if you should write	if they should write
	if he (she, it) should write	if you should write

ADJECTIVE	ADVERB
a *fast* train [modifies *train*]	He ran *fast*. [modifies *ran*]
a *slow* watch [modifies *watch*]	Go *slow*. [modifies *go*]
an *early* bird [modifies *bird*]	She came *early*. [modifies *came*]
the *late* student [modifies *student*]	They slept *late*. [modifies *slept*]
a *well* child [modifies *child*]	She played *well*. [modifies *played*]

Good, along with some other adjectives, sometimes causes trouble when used after a verb. Because *good* should not be used after most verbs, avoid *talks good*, *drives good*, *writes good*, and so on. *Good*, as well as other adjectives, however, may be used after some verbs, called *linking verbs*, such as *look*, *smell*, *taste*, *feel*, *appear*, *stay*, *seem*, *remain*, *grow*, *become*, and all forms of *to be*. Thus, it is correct to say *sounds good*, *feels good*, *is good*, and so forth. (Notice that many, but not all, linking verbs refer to the senses.)

Occasionally linking verbs are used as active verbs. *Look*, for instance, is a linking verb when referring to someone's health or to the appearance of things, as in *The day looks good for a picnic*. But it is an active verb when it refers to the act of looking, as in *Mary looked proudly at her son*. To check whether a verb is a linking verb or an active verb, substitute a form of the verb *to be* in its place. If the sentence retains its basic meaning, the verb is probably a linking verb. For example:

> The pizza *tastes* good. The pizza *is* good.
> She will *stay* asleep until noon. She *will be* asleep until noon.

In both examples, the substitute verb maintains the essential meaning of the sentence. Therefore, *tastes* and *stay* are linking verbs and may be followed by any adjective you choose: *sour*, *sweet*, *tart*, *spoiled*, *happy*, *satisfied*, *cool*, *depressed*, and many, many others.

Adverbs usually describe, or modify, verbs, adjectives, or other adverbs. They often give answers to such questions as How? When? How much? Where? In what sequence? To what extent? In what manner?

> How does Richard run? Richard runs *well*. (The adverb *well* modifies the verb *run*.)
> When should Martha go to the store? Martha should go *now*. (The adverb *now* modifies the verb *go*.)
> How much did it rain last night? It rained *enough* to flood the basement. (The adverb *enough* modifies the verb *rain*.)
> In what manner did Juan sit down? Juan sat down *quickly*. (The adverb *quickly* modifies the verb *sat*.)

Adjectives and Adverbs

Review: Whenever a choice must be made between an adjective or an adverb, determine whether the verb is a linking verb. If it is, use the adjective. If it isn't, use the adverb. Also, if the word modifies an adjective or another adverb, you must use the adverb. If it modifies a noun or pronoun, use the adjective. Most errors involving adjective/adverb usage occur when no clear distinction is evident between the linking verbs and the active verbs being modified.

Use adverbs to modify active verbs:

> The dancer spun swiftly around the stage. (*Swiftly* is an adverb; it explains how the dancer spun; therefore, *swiftly* modifies, or clarifies, the active verb *spun*.)

When the verb is clearly active, it must be followed by an adverb, never by an adjective. But when the verb is a linking verb, use an adjective:

> Onion soup tastes good. (*Good* is an adjective; it describes the soup. If *tastes* were an active verb, the adverb *well* would be needed. To say that the soup tastes *well* is nonsense, however.)

The first word of a sentence is always capitalized.

The pronoun *I* is always capitalized: "John and *I* are good friends."

Proper nouns are always capitalized. The individual title of any person, place, or thing is a proper noun. A good dictionary indicates proper nouns by capitalizing them. Some examples of proper nouns are: *James Madison High School, The Pine Tree Tavern, Hamilton College, Florida, Crescent City, New York State, African, France, Mary Roberts Rinehart, Second Avenue, Mr. Smith, Judge Black, Elm Street.* Notice that words like *school* and *city* are capitalized when they are part of the title. So are honorary or distinguishing titles (whether abbreviated or not) when placed before names: *Miss Halpern, Mrs. Smith, Doctor Johnson, Dr. Johnson, Capt. Darcy, Professor Edwards, Prof. Edwards.* Remember that titles are not capitalized when they come after the person's name: *Jonathan Edwards, professor of theology; Martha Johnson, doctor of pediatric cardiology.*

Titles of books, plays, poems, themes, essays, etc., are capitalized. The first word of the title is always capitalized and all other words except the articles (*a, an, the*) and short prepositions and conjunctions (like *and, but, in, of*). The last word of the title is always capitalized: *The Phantom of the Opera, Back to the Future, A Rose for Emily, For Whom the Bell Tolls.*

The names of geographical regions are capitalized: the *Southwest*, the *South*. Such words are not capitalized when they merely indicate direction: "He went *west*." BUT "He settled in the *West*."

Days of the week, months of the year, holidays are capitalized: *Monday, Tuesday, January, February, Easter, Martin Luther King's Birthday*. But names of the seasons are not capitalized: *spring, autumn, fall, winter.*

Common nouns are capitalized when they become proper nouns by being used to identify a specific person, place, or thing. For example, *history* is a common noun. But *History of the United States* or *History 201* might be names of academic courses. *Mother* is a common noun in a phrase like *my mother*. But in the sentence *I will ask Mother*, the absence of the identifying word *my* makes *Mother* the identification of one specific person. In similar identifications like *Uncle John* or *President Smith*, the nouns *uncle* and *president* become proper nouns because they are part of the identifications of specific people.

Abbreviations of titles, usually placed after a name, are capitalized: *John Larkin, M.D., Frank Loeser, Jr., James Donovan, Ph.D.*

The first word of a line of verse is usually capitalized.

The word or opening and closing words used for the salutation of a letter are capitalized: *Gentlemen: Dear Madam: Dear Sir: My dear Mrs. Smith: Dear Fred, Dear Mr. Strong,.*

The opening word of the complimentary close of a letter is capitalized: *Sincerely, Sincerely yours, Yours very truly, Cordially yours,.*

Conjunctions

Coordinating Conjunctions

Coordinating conjunctions are the glue that ties words, phrases, and clauses of equal value together. The conjunction that does more gluing than any other is the word *and*, which can join two nouns (ham *and* eggs), two adjectives (black *and* blue), two verbs (pick *and* choose), and more, including:

PREPOSITIONAL PHRASES: Of the people, for the people *and* by the people

SENTENCES: The President came to town, *and* he gave a speech.

DEPENDENT CLAUSES: The ferry that sank *and* that had sailed without a permit changed maritime law in the Mediterranean.

ADVERBIAL CLAUSES: The film won an award because of its director *and* because it broke new ground in special effects.

In formal speech and writing, it's best to avoid starting a sentence with *and* or its close companion, *but*. Yet, in more casual communication it's done all the time. Don't do it too often, however, for it can get monotonous.

Both *and* and *but* belong to a group of seven coordinating conjunctions. The others are *or, yet, for, nor,* and *so.* (The word *whereas*, found most often in the legal speech and writing, is also a coordinating conjunction, but many people who are not lawyers happily pass through life using it only rarely.)

> **TIP**
> To remember the coordinating conjunctions, keep in mind the acronym BOYFANS:
>
> > **B**ut
> > **O**r
> > **Y**et
> > **F**or
> > **A**nd
> > **N**or
> > **S**o

Coordinating conjunctions earn their name from their function—joining grammatically equivalent words, phrases, and clauses. Each item in a series of words, phrases, or clauses must be equal, or parallel, in both function and form.

Consider this sentence, for example:

> *Last weekend, Rex listened to music, played his guitar,*
> *and writing a song.*

Two of Rex's actions—*listened* and *played*—are stated with verbs in the simple past tense. The third verb—*writing*—is in the past participle form. Although the meaning is clear, standard English calls for the third verb to be parallel to the other two. It should be *wrote*, the simple past tense of the verb *to write*.

This principle of parallelism applies to all words, phrases, clauses, and sentences joined by coordinating conjunctions.

and	He likes bread and butter.
	She bought a black-and-white dress.
	He did it quickly and well.
	Over the fence and into the woods went the ball.
	They sang and danced all night.
	The crowds were inside and outside the church.
	Drinking too much and eating too little was bad for him.
	Mary prepared the salad, and Jane made the cake.
but	(As a preposition it means *except*.)
	He did it quickly but well.
	Over the net but into the woods went the ball.
	They did not sing but danced all night.
	The crowd was angry but not ready to take action.
	Drinking too much but eating too title was bad for him.
	Mary prepared the salad, but Jane made the cake.
for	They decided to leave, for they could see that a storm was coming.
nor	He didn't mind leaving the party, nor would anyone miss him.
or	Do you want tea or coffee?
	I want a red or a green dress.
	Do it immediately or not at all.
	I will do it quickly or carefully, whichever you please.
	Put it on the table or on the counter.
	They sang or danced all night long.
	Are you for or against this proposal?
	Eating too much or drinking too much was bad for him.
	Get dressed quickly, or I won't wait for you.
so	The driver explained the reason for the delay, so everybody was willing to wait patiently.

Conjunctions

whereas   (formal usage)

Whereas the council has deliberated this matter for several weeks, be it resolved that no sensible action can be taken.

yet   She was a pretty, yet not very attractive girl.

She did it quickly, yet well.

He heard the clock strike, yet did not pay attention to the time.

Speaking with apparent frankness, yet concealing his inner thoughts, he swayed the crowd.

Again and again he cried for help, yet nobody paid any attention to him.

Correlative Conjunctions

Correlative conjunctions are pairs of words used to join sentence elements of equal importance. The most common pairs are *neither-nor, either-or, not only-but also, whether-or not, both-and*. Some pairs are virtually inseparable. You'll rarely find *either* without *or* and *neither* without *nor*.

> I'll *either* go for a walk *or* go to sleep when I get home.
> *Neither* rain *nor* sleet will keep me from seeing you tonight.

as	The tree was as tall as the house.
... as	He did it as well as he could.
both	Both the men and the women took part in the sports.
... and	He was both older and wiser as a result of long experience.
either	Either John or Fred is at home.
... or	Either John or his sisters are at home.
	Either his sisters or John is at home.
	We can either walk or ride to the picnic.
neither	Neither John nor Fred is at home.
... nor	Neither John nor his sisters are at home.
	Neither his sisters nor John is at home.
	We can neither walk nor ride to the picnic.
not only	He played not only jazz but also classical music.
... but also	He not only worked hard, but he also played hard.
so	He was not so tall as his sister.
... as	He was not so happy as he pretended to be.

NOTE: *So ... as* is used after a negative construction instead of *as ... as*.

Subordinating Conjunctions

Subordinating conjunctions join sentence elements of unequal rank.

> Justin finally married his sweetheart, *and* he ordered a latte at Starbucks.

In spite of rumors to the contrary, getting married and drinking a latte are not equivalent actions unless the sentence was meant to get a laugh. A subordinating conjunction will fix the incongruity.

> *After* finally marrying his sweetheart, Justin ordered a latte at Starbucks.

By using the subordinating conjunction *after*, the sentence now makes slightly more sense.

Here's another example. Say that you wanted to convey two seemingly unrelated facts: 1) Jody rushed to school, and 2) Jody put on mascara. The link between these two statements can quickly be clarified with a subordinating conjunction. Let's use *while*:

> *While* she rushed to school, Jody put on mascara.

Or the sentence might have been stated as follows:

> *While* she put on mascara, Jody rushed to school.

In each sentence the less important idea (that is, the *subordinate* idea) is contained in the subordinate clause, that section of the sentence that starts with the subordinating conjunction.

In addition to *after* and *while*, other common subordinating conjunctions include *as, although, because, if, since, that, though, unless, until, when, whenever, where,* and *whether.* It's useful to keep in mind that subordinate clauses, also called **dependent clauses**, cannot stand alone as complete sentences. In other words, they depend grammatically on **independent clauses**.

> He whistled *while* he worked.

A few words like *after* can function both as prepositions and conjunctions.

> He came *after* me. [preposition]
> He came *after* I did. [conjunction]

The conjunctions *as* and *than* are sometimes confused with prepositions because they frequently introduce elliptical clauses (clauses where words are omitted because the meaning is clear without them).

> He worked as rapidly *as* I [worked].
> I worked more rapidly *than* he [worked].
> She disliked him as much *as* [she disliked] me.
> The rain soaked him more *than* [it soaked] me.

Conjunctions

The relative pronouns (*who, which, that*) frequently act as subordinating conjunctions.

> John, *who* was ill, recovered.
> He did not know *which* of the girls he liked best.
> The cake *that* she made was good.

When indicating a causal relationship, the conjunctions *because, since,* and *as* are preferable in that order. *Since* is weaker than *because,* for it also refers to time (*She has been unhappy since she left the city.*). *As* is the weakest because it also refers both to time and comparison (*He tackled each problem as he came to it. He played as hard as he worked.*).

Most of the subordinating conjunctions frequently introduce participial phrases.

> *After* cleaning the house, she took a nap.
> He read the paper *while* eating his breakfast.
> *Although* driven to the wall, he kept calm.

Conjunctive Adverbs

A few adverbs, like *consequently, furthermore, however, moreover, nevertheless, then, therefore,* function with the effect of conjunctions because they refer to the subject matter of the preceding sentence. They are not actually conjunctions because they may not be used to join sentence elements of either equal or unequal value.

> He was sick. *Consequently,* he did not go to work.
> It costs more than it's worth. *Furthermore,* I don't need it.
> He was not poor. He was glad, *however,* to inherit the money.
> He was tired from lack of sleep. *Moreover,* he had a bad cold.
> She hated the town. *Nevertheless,* she was willing to live there.

As its name suggests, a *contraction* combines two words into one by eliminating one or more letters. An apostrophe is inserted where letters have been removed, as in:

> *We've* (we have) never taken the train to the city.
> Antonia said *she'll* (she will) mop the floor.
> He *hasn't* (has not) replied to my text message.

aren't	are not	shan't	shall not
can't	cannot	she'd	she would, she had
couldn't	could not	she'll	she will
didn't	did not	she's	she is, she has
doesn't	does not	shouldn't	should not
don't	do not	they'd	they would, they had
hadn't	had not	they'll	they will
hasn't	has not	they're	they are
haven't	have not	wasn't	was not
he'd	he would, he had	we'd	we would, we had
he'll	he will	we're	we are
he's	he is, he has	weren't	were not
I'd	I would, I had	we've	we have
I'll	I shall, I will	won't	will not
I'm	I am	wouldn't	would not
I've	I have	you'd	you would, you had
isn't	is not	you'll	you will
it's	it is	you're	you are
mightn't	might not	you've	you have
mustn't	must not		

Contractions are used mostly in casual speech and writing. In conversation the contraction *n't* is more frequently used than *not*. There's no law against using contractions in a formal context, however, as you might have noticed in the sentence you're now reading. If in doubt, steer clear of contractions unless you need them to create a special effect.

> **TIP**
> Don't confuse the apostrophes
> found in contractions with those
> used in possessive nouns.

Glossary of Troublesome Words and Phrases

Diction

Diction means word choice. Faulty diction occurs when a word is used that means something other than what is intended (*e.g.*, *infer* instead of *imply*, or *eminent* instead of *imminent*). Faulty word choice also occurs when an inappropriate word is used (*e.g.*, a slang expression like *chill out* or *you guys* in a formal context), or when a grammatically incorrect word is used (*e.g.*, *good* instead of *well* after a certain verb, or *where* instead of *when*, as in "the time where you lost your wallet").

a, an	Use *a* before words beginning with a consonant sound: *a book*, *a unique ring*. Use *an* before words beginning with a vowel sound: *an apple*, *an urchin*.
accept, except	*Accept* means to *receive*: "Please *accept* my offer." The verb *except* means to leave out or omit: "Will you *except* the last provision of the contract?"
adapt, adopt	*Adapt* means to modify and make suitable; *adopt* is to choose or select, as in "We adopted a style of play that had been adapted from one used by the New York Giants."
adverse, averse	*Adverse* means *opposing: adverse circumstances*. *Averse* means *opposed to:* "He was *averse* to my proposal." *Adverse* usually relates to actions or things. *Averse* usually applies to people (who have an aversion).
advert, avert	*Advert* means *refer:* "The speaker *adverted* to an earlier talk he had given." *Avert* means *ward off:* "He narrowly *averted* a bad fall."
advice, advise	*Advice* is a noun meaning recommendation concerning an action or decision: "Few people will take my *advice* when I give it to them." *Advise* is a verb: "I *advise* you to take fewer courses next year."
affect, effect	*Affect* means to *influence:* "His attitude in class *affected* his grade." *Affect* is never used as a noun except in psychological terminology. *Effect* as a noun means *result:* "The *effect* of the explosion was disastrous." *Effect* as a verb means to *accomplish:* "The new machinery *effected* a decided improvement in the product."
aggravate	Do not use *aggravate* to mean *irritate*. *Aggravate* means to make a bad situation worse: "I was *irritated* by his behavior when he came in, but he *aggravated* the situation when he slammed the door when he went out."
aggravation	*Aggravation* means an act or circumstance that increases the gravity or seriousness of a situation: "His job was difficult enough in itself without the unexpected *aggravation* of the addition of overtime work."

last, latest
: *Last* means that which comes at the end: "It is the *last* game of the season." *Latest* is the last in time, but not necessarily the final occurrence: "That was the *latest* insult in a series of indignities."

lay, lie
: *Lay, laid, laid* are the principal parts of the transitive verb which means *to put down*: "I shall *lay* the rug." "I *laid* the rug." "I have *laid* the rug." "I *am laying* the rug." *Lie, lay, lain* are the principal parts of the intransitive verb (it cannot take an object) which means *to recline* or *repose*: "She will *lie* in the hammock." "She *lay* in the hammock yesterday." "She *has lain* there all afternoon." "She *is lying* in the hammock."

lead, led
: When pronounced alike, the noun *lead* is the metal; *led* is the past tense and past participle of the verb *to lead* (*pronounced leed*).

learn, teach
: *Learn* means to acquire information or knowledge: "I *learned* my lesson." *Teach* means to impart information or knowledge: "I intend to *teach* him as much as he *taught* me."

liable
: See *apt*.

like
: See *as*.

likely
: See *apt*.

loose, lose
: *Loose* is an adjective meaning *not completely attached*: "The screw is *loose*." *Lose* is a verb meaning *to be deprived of*: "I *lost* a lot of money at the race track and I don't intend to *lose* any more."

majority, plurality
: In voting, *majority* means the number of votes constituting more than half of the total number cast. "Since fifty-one of the one hundred members voted for Jane, she won by a *majority*." *Plurality* is used when there are three or more candidates. It means the excess of votes received by the leading candidate over those received by the next most popular candidate: "The results of the ballot are as follows: Smith, 254; Jones, 250; Marshall, 243; Edwards, 23. Therefore Smith won by a *plurality* of 4. *Plurality* is also used to mean the largest number of votes received by a single candidate: "In the results listed above, Smith received a *plurality* but not a *majority*."

mean, median
: *Mean* is the middle point between extremes (computed mathematically by dividing the sum of the quantities in a set by the number of terms in the set). *Median* refers to the middle value in a series of numbers, ranged from smallest to largest.

militate, mitigate
: *Militate* (connected with *military*) means to have a strong influence for or against, usually against: "His grouchy manner

Glossary of Troublesome Words and Phrases

militated against his success as a salesman." *Mitigate* means to lessen: "The cold compress on his leg *mitigated* the pain."

miner, minor   A *miner* is one who extracts minerals from the earth. When used as a noun a *minor* means one who is under age. As an adjective *minor* means *unimportant*. "Since he was a *minor*, the judge let him off with a *minor* penalty."

moral, morale   *Moral* is an adjective meaning pertaining to the accepted customs of a society with reference to right or wrong: "I know that he didn't steal my book because he is a very *moral* young man." *Morality* is the noun. *Morale* means *a state of well being*: "The *morale* of the employees was very good."

myself   *Myself* (like *yourself, himself, herself, itself, yourselves, themselves*) is an intensive and reflexive pronoun. It should never be used in a sentence without its corresponding noun or pronoun: "*I myself* will do it." "*I* hurt *myself*." "They sent for John and *me* (NOT *myself*)."

nauseated, nauseous   *Nauseated* means sick: "After the roller coaster ride, Susan felt *nauseated*." *Nauseous* refers to something that evokes disgust: "The rotten eggs left a *nauseous* odor in the refrigerator."

personal, personnel   *Personal* is an adjective meaning *pertaining to an individual*: "The watch was his *personal* property." *Personnel* is a noun meaning the group of people employed in an organization: "The *personnel* manager is in charge of the welfare of the *personnel* of the firm."

plain, plane   *Plain* is an adjective meaning *simple* or *unadorned*: "Carl Sandburg loved the *plain* people." *Plain* is also a noun meaning flat country. *Plane* is a noun meaning *a flat surface*. It is also a tool used to make a flat surface smooth. It is also an accepted abbreviation for *airplane*. "When he went by *plane* to the great *plain* between the mountains, he took several *planes* with him along with his other carpenter's tools."

plurality   See *majority*.

practicable, practical   *Practicable* means capable of being put into practice: "He found a *practicable* way of depositing money without going to the bank." *Practical* means *useful* or *related to actual experience* as opposed to *theoretical*: "The *practical* nurse knew several *practical* methods to stop the flow of blood."

principal, principle   *Principal* is usually an adjective meaning *main*: *principal* cities, *principal* people. It has become a noun in a few usages where the noun it formerly modified is understood. "He was the *principal* (teacher) of the school." "I withdrew the

principal (amount) and interest from my savings account." "He acted as the *principal* (person) rather than as an agent." The noun *principle* means a *basic law* or *doctrine*: "The country was founded on the *principle* that all men are created free and equal."

prone, supine *Prone* means reclining with the face downward: "He slept in a *prone* position to keep the sun out of his eyes." *Supine* means reclining with the face upward (note the word *up* in *supine*): "He lay *supine* on the ground all morning watching the clouds."

quiet, quite *Quiet* means free from noise: "*Quiet* must be preserved in the library." *Quite* means either *fully* or *to a considerable extent*, depending on the sense of the sentence: "By the time the doctor arrived, the mother was *quite* upset because she thought her child was *quite* ill."

rare, scarce *Rare* and *scarce* refer to hard-to-find items in short supply. *Rare* usually implies exceptional quality, as in a "*rare* book." *Scarce* can be applied to ordinary things like potatoes that are usually abundant.

reason is, because The words *reason is* (*was*, etc.) should be followed by a statement of the reason: "The *reason* for his failure *was* illness." "The *reason* for the strict rules *is* to enforce discipline." Similar statements can be made by using *because*: "He failed *because* of illness." "The rules are strict *because* it is necessary to enforce discipline." *Reason* and *because* convey the same sense. It is illogical to use both words to indicate the same meaning.

recommend, refer *Recommend* means *to present as worthy of confidence*: "Do you know any doctor you could *recommend* to me?" *Refer* means *to direct attention to*: "Can you *refer* me to a good doctor?"

regardless, irregardless *Regardless* means in spite of: "*Regardless* of the strike, they will go to work." *Irregardless* is a non-standard synonym for regardless and should not be used.

same Do not use *same* as a pronoun: "I have your order and will send it (NOT will send *same*)."

sensory, sensuous, sensual *Sensory* pertains to one or more of the five senses: "Walking through the rose garden was a *sensory* delight." *Sensuous* means gratifying to the senses: "A vase with a *sensuous* shape stood on the shelf." *Sensual* refers to the pleasures of the senses, especially the pleasures of the flesh: "It is clearly wrong to broadcast *sensual* advertisements during Saturday morning cartoons."

Glossary of Troublesome Words and Phrases

stationary,
stationery

Stationary is an adjective meaning *fixed* or *attached*: "The benches are *stationary* because they are fastened to the floor." *Stationery* is writing paper used in correspondence: "He bought a box of *stationery* at the *stationery* store so that he could write to his friends." Notice that the *er* in *stationery* corresponds to the *er* in *paper*.

terse, trite

Terse means *concise*: "Francis Bacon wrote in a very *terse* style." *Trite* means *hackneyed, worn out from overuse*: "*As different as night and day* is a *trite* expression."

than, then

Than is a conjunction: "She was wealthier *than* her sister." *Then* is an adverb denoting time, past or future: "She remembered her youth because her sister was richer *then*. But *then* she herself fell heir to a fortune."

their, there

Be careful to distinguish the spelling of the possessive case of the pronoun *their* (*their* books) from the spelling of the adverb and expletive *there*. "I got *there* before I knew it." "*There* are forty oranges in the crate."

therefor,
therefore

Therefor means *for that, for it, for them*: "I sent the manuscript by registered mail and have the receipt *therefor*." *Therefore* means for that reason: "He was sick. *Therefore*, he did not go to work."

to, too, two

To is a preposition meaning *direction toward*: "Take this package *to* the store." It is used to make the infinitive when combined with the root of a verb: *to eat, to sing*. *Too* is an adverb meaning *more than enough*: "He was *too* tired to eat." *Two* is the number 2.

tortuous,
torturous

Tortuous means full of twists or bends: "The car was moving too fast for such a *tortuous*, crooked road." *Torturous* means inflicting great pain in a cruel manner.

unique

Unique means the only one of its kind: "His was a *unique* personality." It cannot logically be used in a comparative or superlative form. Something may be more or most odd, rare, unusual, peculiar, remarkable, etc., but NOT more or most *unique*.

verbal, oral

Verbal means *pertaining to words*; *oral* means *pertaining to spoken words*: "She nodded assent, but gave no *verbal* confirmation, either written or *oral*."

waist, waste

Waist is the middle section of the body. "He wore a belt around his *waist*." As a verb *waste* means *to squander*; as a noun it means *that which is squandered or useless*: "He *wasted* his money." "Reading that stupid novel was a *waste* of time."

who's, whose   *Who's* is the contraction for *who is* and *who has*: "I don't know *who's* coming." "*Who's* taken my matches?" *Whose* is the possessive form of *who*: "We knew the family *whose* house was robbed."

your, you're   *Your* is the possessive case of *you*: "I have read *your* notes." *You're* is the contraction of *you are*: "*You're* sure to be there on time if you leave now."

Avoiding Errors in Diction

When in doubt about a correct word choice, consult a dictionary. A comprehensive dictionary will not only define each word but illustrate its use in a sentence or phrase. The famous *Oxford English Dictionary* is the most complete dictionary in existence, but other, more modest, dictionaries will serve most people equally well.

Be wary of a dictionary or thesaurus of synonyms found in most computer word-processing programs. The dictionary will check spelling but won't differentiate among misused words. The thesaurus will offer a list of synonyms. But use the thesaurus cautiously because many words only approximate the meaning of other words. Don't be misguided into thinking that any word listed as a synonym will be the equivalent of any other word. In the previous sentence, take the word *misguided*, for example. The thesaurus in Microsoft Word lists the following as synonyms: *mistaken, foolish, ill-advised, unwise, erroneous, injudicious, imprudent*, and *wrong*. All these words come close to the key word *misguided*, but not one of these so-called synonyms can properly serve as a substitute in the given sentence—not without making another revision to eliminate an awkward use of the word. Keep this caution in mind whenever you use the thesaurus for help.

Every language has its own idioms. An idiom usually consists of a group of words that is either meaningless or absurd if the words are understood to mean what they usually do. For example, *catch* is a simple and common word in such sentences as "He will catch a fish" and "He will catch the ball." But in English it is commonplace to say, "He will catch the train," meaning that he will be at the station in time to board the train before it leaves. Similarly, a common English idiom for suffering from a common winter ailment is "to catch cold." People are not being proud of their abilities when they say, "I caught a bad cold." Actually, the cold caught them.

The list of common idioms that begins on page 24 is arranged alphabetically according to the key word in the idiom. The usual meaning of the key word can be found in any dictionary. Only the idiomatic meanings are described in this section.

Idioms

Idioms

ABOUT

The store is *about* five miles from here. (approximately)

I was *about to invite* you to the party. (on the verge of inviting)

It is *about* time you decided to pay back what you owe me. (certainly)

AFRAID

My sister would like to join us, but *I'm afraid* she has another engagement. (I regret that it is likely that)

AFTER

Who will *look after* the dog while we are on vacation? (take care of)

John won't be able to join us *after all*. (in spite of previous expectation)

Nellie asked *after you* when I saw her yesterday. (about you)

BACK

The mayor *backed* my brother for councilman. (supported)

The councilman had the mayor's *backing*. (support)

The tree stood *in back of* the house. (behind)

BALL

Stop loafing and *get on the ball*. (become efficient)

The noisy teenagers were having *a ball*. (a good time)

After losing his money, John found himself *behind the eight ball*. (in serious trouble)

BLUE

The departure of her friend left Mary feeling *blue*. (depressed, melancholy)

BUCK

It is foolish to try to *buck* an established system. (battle against)

BRIGHT

All *bright* young people should go to college. (intelligent)

CAR

The entire family went for a long ride in the *car*. (automobile)

CATCH

Take off your wet shoes and socks before you *catch cold*. (become ill from a cold)

They were late in leaving the house, but they *caught* the train. (arrived in time to board it before it left)

CHISEL

> The dishonest storekeeper tried to *chisel* the customer. (cheat)
>
> The storekeeper had the reputation of being a *chiseler*. (cheater)

COME

> Father *came to grief* when he invested in real estate that lost its value. (suffered misfortune)
>
> The skeptical employee finally *came to believe* in the business. (acquired faith)
>
> The dogmatic professor got *his comeuppance* when he was proved to be entirely wrong. (what he deserved)
>
> Yellow tomatoes are *hard to come by*. (difficult to find)

COOL

> Only a few of the people *kept cool* during the panic. (remained unexcited)
>
> After his friend's apology, John *cooled down*. (lost his anger)
>
> The labor arbitrator ordered *a cooling-off period*. (time to think calmly)
>
> *Cool off* with a glass of cold beer. (lower body temperature)

DEAD

> They were startled by the sound of sirens in the *dead of night*. (darkest hours)
>
> I should have taken Fred's advice; he was *dead right*. (entirely)
>
> The bus came to a *dead stop* at the railroad crossing. (complete)

DESERT

> The judge gave the convicted criminal his *just deserts*. (justified punishment)

DISH

> Mother asked me to *dish up* the peas. (serve from a bowl or pot)
>
> The dean's job is to *dish out* punishment to students who misbehave. (give)

DO

> Good morning, my friend. How *do you do*? (are you)
>
> Will you please *do up* my package? (wrap)
>
> The soldiers *did away with* their prisoner. (killed)
>
> Numbers *have to do* with arithmetic. (are connected)
>
> Thank you. That *will do*. (is enough, is satisfactory)
>
> I have eaten so much that I *can do without* dessert. (am willing to omit)
>
> That steak is really *well done*. (thoroughly cooked)
>
> The job was *well done* by the efficient clerk. (excellently completed)
>
> It is time for us to *have done with* childish toys. (abandon)
>
> Most missionaries are *do-gooders* at heart. (determined to help others)

Idioms

DOWN

Fearing the dark, my mother hoped to arrive by *sundown*. (dusk)

Amy went *downtown* to buy some new clothes. (business section or southern part of a town or city)

I made a *down* payment on the car and will pay the rest in installments. (first, initial)

I paid $500 *down* and will pay $10 a week for three years. (as a first payment)

DRIVE

After taking lessons, she learned to *drive* our car. (operate)

The entire family has gone out for *a drive*. (an automobile ride)

I don't understand what you are *driving at*. (trying to convey)

The vigorous young woman had lots of *drive*. (energy and determination)

DROP

Drop in (by) to see me some day. (make a casual visit)

The dull-eyed boy was a *high school dropout*. (left school before graduating)

EYE

The detective *eyed* the shopper suspiciously. (scrutinized)

The pretty girl *gave me the eye*. (flirted with me)

My shrewd friend *has his eyes open*. (isn't easily fooled)

My little daughter was *all eyes* when she saw her birthday presents. (amazed and delighted)

My father and I hardly ever *see eye to eye*. (agree)

That decaying old building is certainly *an eyesore*. (ugly)

The plane flew into the *eye* of the hurricane. (center)

FACE

Let him *face up to* his mistakes. (admit)

If he does, he will have to *face the music*. (be responsible for past errors)

Your explanation puts a new *face on* the matter. (interpretation of)

Most pompous people are apt to be *two-faced*. (hypocritical)

FALL

John and Mary *fell in love*. (became enamoured of each other)

The baby will soon *fall* asleep. (be)

FIRE

The employee was *fired* because of his inefficiency. (dismissed)

FIX

The automobile mechanic *fixed* our car. (repaired)
I was really in a *fix* when I lost my job. (difficult predicament)

FOOT

John was so naive that he was always *putting his foot in it*. (making embarrassing blunders)
Our wealthy friend offered to *foot* the bill at the hotel. (pay)

GET

The patient is feeling better and will soon *get* well. (become)
There are so many clouds that it is *getting* dark. (becoming)
Please try to *get along* with what you have. (manage)
It will be difficult, but we will try to *get along* without you. (manage)
Instead of talking so much, let's *get on with it*. (make progress)
The cheated customer *got even with* the salesman by calling the police. (avenged himself on)
Not knowing that he was being observed, the student expected to *get away with* his cheating. (evade discovery of)

GIVE

After several useless attempts, they *gave up*. (stopped trying)
During the earthquake a corner of the building *gave way*. (broke off)

GO

Tomorrow I *am going to* finish my work. (shall)
My energetic wife is always *on the go*. (active)
The mediator of the dispute acted as a *go-between*. (intermediary)
I believe the baby is *going to sleep*. (will soon be asleep)
It *goes without saying* that winters are cold in the north. (is self-evident)
The new fall styles are *all the go*. (popular)
The manufacturing company is a *going* concern. (thriving)
If you were only older, I could *go for* you. (fall in love with)
The job may be difficult, but let's *have a go at* it. (attempt)
We tried to finish the job, but it was *no go*. (unsuccessful)

HARD

The feeble old man was *hard of hearing*. (partially deaf)
The planning expert was a *hard-headed* man. (clear thinking)
The boss was too *hard-hearted* to raise my salary. (unsympathetic)
Being paid so little, I was always *hard up*. (poor)

Idioms

HAVE

The construction workers *have to* be careful. (must)

The *haves and* the *have-nots* have been studied by sociologists. (rich and poor)

HEART

Agnes *learned* the entire poem *by heart*. (memorized)

When his friend deserted him, he *took it to heart*. (was deeply troubled)

Mother couldn't resist a beggar, because she was *all heart*. (emotionally generous)

HIGH

After several cocktails our guests became quite *high*. (intoxicated)

The professor was very *high-handed* in assigning grades. (arrogant and arbitrary)

Emerson was a *high-minded* American author. (idealistic)

It is *high time* for all of us to go to bed. (latest reasonable time)

His experiences in the war left him very *high strung*. (nervous and hypersensitive)

The *highbrows* usually scorn the ordinary lowbrow people. (intellectuals)

After being awarded the Nobel prize, he became very *high hat*. (snobbish)

I'll meet you at the station at *high noon*. (on the dot of 12 noon)

HOLD

The lecturer *held forth* on the subject for nearly an hour. (orated)

How long can the enemy *hold out*? (endure)

The bandits *held up* the train. (stopped and robbed)

KNOW

Max was *in the know about* his sister's plans. (acquainted with)

After forty years in his firm, he had a lot of *know-how*. (expert knowledge)

LOOK

She gave him an angry *look*. (stare)

The boys like her because of her *good looks*. (attractive appearance)

That is another way of saying that she is *good looking*. (pleasant to look at)

Please *look after* my dog while I am away. (take care of)

Please *take a look at my oil*. (verify the level on the oil gauge)

It *looks like rain*. (appears as if rain was imminent)

LONG

The people at the beach basked in the sunshine *all day long*. (the entire day)

On vacation my brother had nothing to do *all the livelong day*. (the entire day)

MAKE

The shy young man was too timid to *try to make love* to her. (attempt sexual advances)

After their lover's quarrel, they kissed and *made up*. (were reconciled)

If we don't really have a good time, let's *make believe* it was fun. (pretend)

This hammer isn't really satisfactory, but I'll try to *make do* with it. (serve my purpose)

The salesman *made good* on the defective merchandise he sold us. (corrected the defect either by refunding money or substituting a satisfactory product)

I hearby *make it known* that I have divorced my wife. (publish the fact)

Let us eat, drink, and *make merry*. (have a good time)

After finishing college, he had to *make his way* in the world. (succeed)

The three men who robbed the bank *made off with* nearly a million dollars. (ran away with)

She *made up to* the professor, hoping that she would pass the course. (flattered)

MOUTH

He was so nervous at the meeting that he *mouthed his words*. (talked indistinctly)

I didn't read it in the newspaper; I heard it *by word of mouth*. (orally)

My brother was really *down in the mouth* after his house was robbed. (depressed)

OUT

The new book on outer space has just *come out*. (been published)

Mary and Jane quarreled a week ago; they are still *on the outs*. (unfriendly)

I never believe what he says because he is an *out-and-out* liar. (complete)

Your outrageous demands are *out of the question*. (impossible to fulfill)

I'll mend your rug tomorrow; I can't do it *out of hand*. (immediately or without preparation)

The Chinese have been growing rice since *time out of mind*. (extremely remote past)

Idioms

PASS

His grandfather *passed away* six months ago. (died)

One of the guests became so drunk that he *passed out*. (became unconscious)

The counterfeiter tried to *pass* one of his bills at the bank. (have it accepted)

It *came to pass* that there was a new prophet in Israel. (happened)

The clever actor *passed himself off as* a woman. (convinced the public that he was)

Things will come to a *pretty pass* if we don't act immediately. (critical situation)

PRETTY

After several months of practice, he became *pretty* good at golf. (quite)

Considering the short time he studied, he learned the lesson *pretty* well. (quite)

After her wealthy husband died, she found herself *sitting pretty*. (in an affluent position)

PUT

James was very much *put out* when the bank refused to give him a loan. (annoyed)

I can't believe you; you must be *putting me on*. (fooling me)

It is so late now that we will have to *put up with* this miserable hotel. (tolerate)

"*Put up or shut up*," said my partner when I argued about my share of the business. (Produce or be quiet.)

RED

The young man *saw red* when he was evicted from his room. (became very angry)

There is too much *red tape* involved in registering for this course. (tiresome details)

The thief was caught *red-handed* as he exited from the bank. (in the act)

He threw a *red herring* into the case by pretending deafness. (misleading clue)

REST

Rest assured that I will do everything I can to help you. (Be)

RUN

When my father became ill, I had to *run* the establishment. (manage)

I believe that we will succeed *in the long run*. (over an extended period of time)

Our competitor is not exactly thriving, but he is still *in the running*. (competitive)

The splinter on the chair caused a *run* in Mary's stocking. (long vertical tear)

Don't you dare *run down* my achievement. (deprecate)

He *ran up* a big bill at the hotel. (accumulated)

The old building on the corner is in a *run-down* condition. (deteriorating)

The gambler decided to give his friend a *run* for his money. (contest)

SET

Early in the morning, they *set off* for the country. (departed)

The angry heirs had a real *set-to* about dividing the estate. (dispute)

SHARP

The millionaire was very *sharp* in running his business. (shrewd, clever)

With your new suit, you are really looking *sharp*. (well-groomed)

SHORT

I'll pay you tomorrow when I won't be so *short of* funds. (lacking in)

The business operation was *short-handed* during vacation periods. (deficient in number of employees)

He left the main road and took a *shortcut* to his house. (shorter way)

It never pays to be *shortsighted*. (remiss in foreseeing the future)

SHUT

"Shut up," said the angry father to his argumentative son. (Be quiet)

SMALL

I hate to go to the store with nothing but *small change* in my pocket. (pennies, nickels, dimes)

Bothered by his many worries, he stayed awake during the *small hours* of the night. (1, 2, 3 A.M.)

STAND

In spite of strong opposition, he took a firm *stand* on the matter. (position)

He left home because he couldn't *stand* his wife's friend. (endure)

Don't stand on ceremony; take off your jackets. (Be informal)

Throughout the entire trial, the attorney *stood up for* his client. (supported)

He asserted his rights and *stood up to* the boss. (was firm in his attitude toward)

The snow was so heavy that everything came to a *standstill*. (complete stop)

The *standing* committee gave its annual report. (permanent)

STICK

Our best plan to avoid trouble is for all of us to *stick* together. (stay)

There is no point in *sticking at* trifles. (making an issue of)

TAKE

I expect to *take a train* to Boston. (go on a train)

It doesn't seem sensible to *take* the time to pack. (use)

The strange dog *took to* me right away. (liked)

Both of the children *take after* their mother. (resemble)

I am so tired of this job that I think I'll *take off*. (leave)

It is impossible to *take* you seriously when you talk so wildly. (consider)

TIE

At 8 to 8 the score was *tied*. It was a *tie* score. (even)

The busy executive was *tied up* at the office. (too busy to leave)

The ballplayer was *fit to be tied* when the umpire ruled against him. (extremely angry)

TIME

It isn't a perfect job, but it will do for the *time being*. (present)

If the plane isn't *on time*, we will have to wait. (punctual in arriving)

Once upon a time, there was a fairy princess. (in the remote past)

EXPRESSIONS OF TIME

8:30   Eight-thirty, half-past eight
9:15   Nine-fifteen, a quarter after (past) nine
10:45 Ten-forty-five, a quarter to eleven
2:50   Two-fifty, ten of (to) three
4:20   Four-twenty, twenty minutes past four, twenty after four

TRY

The tailor asked me to *try on* the suit. (put it on for fitting and appearance)

I met so many difficult customers that I had a *trying* day. (nerve-wracking)

TURN

He did me a *good turn* by mowing my lawn when I was away. (favor)

The old car *turned out* to be in good condition. (was actually)

I *turned over* my account to another bank. (transferred)

Our whole success in this undertaking *turns* on his ability. (depends)

Appearing so suddenly, you gave me quite a *turn*. (fright)

USE

I *used to enjoy* drinking milk, but now I prefer coffee. (formerly enjoyed)

The new stove is very difficult to *get used to*. (become adjusted to)

WEATHER

It is raining, snowing, hailing, thundering and lightning, fair, warm, dry, humid, etc.

It *looks like* rain, snow, etc. (appears likely that it will rain, etc.)

It has been a rainy, snowy, etc., day.

Interjections

The word *interjection* means *thrown in*. Interjections are words that either stand alone or are thrown into sentences, often to heighten emotion or express feelings. *Uh oh!* is an interjection. So are *alas, well, oh, wow, good grief, shhh!, for Pete's sake, damn!,* and a host of other expressions, including any number of expletives that can't be printed here.

Sometimes interjections are used to greet people (*hello, hi, ciao*) or to bid adieu (*good-bye, so long*) or to answer questions (*Yes,* let's meet at three o'clock).

Since interjections are not properly parts of sentence structure, they either stand alone or are separated from the remainder of the sentence by commas.

> *Hello.* How are you?
> *No! Please!* Don't say it!
> *Yes,* I'll come with you.
> *Oh,* you can't mean it!
> I was resigned, *alas,* to failing the course.
> *Wow,* that is terrific news.

TIP

When you write, use interjections sparingly—with or without exclamation points.

No and *not* are the usual words to express negation.

> He has *no* money left.
> They have *not* done what was expected of them.

CONTRACTION	NEGATIVE	EXAMPLE
aren't	are not	They *aren't* able to come.
can't	cannot	They *can't* come.
couldn't	could not	He *couldn't* care less about his future.
doesn't	does not	He *doesn't* want to join the club.
don't	do not	They *don't* want to join the club.
hasn't	has not	He *hasn't* any money.
hadn't	had not	He *hadn't* enough time to pack before the train came.
haven't	have not	We *haven't* anything in the house for dessert.
isn't	is not	He *isn't* interested in her.
mustn't	must not	They *mustn't* think that we avoided them.
shan't	shall not	He *shan't* get any of my money.
shouldn't	should not	He *shouldn't* expect the impossible.
wasn't	was not	She *wasn't* able to complete her assignment.
weren't	were not	They *weren't* expecting him to come.
wouldn't	would not	He insisted that he *wouldn't* do the job.
won't	will not	She *won't* come even if you beg her to be agreeable.

Double Negatives

In some languages two negative words reinforce the negative sense; in standard English two negatives may not be used in the same statement.

> They *didn't* do *nothing* wrong.

Because both *didn't* and *nothing* are negatives, the sense of the sentence is the reverse of what was probably intended. Accurately stated:

> They *didn't* do anything wrong. or
> They did *nothing* wrong.

In some constructions, particularly when *not* modifies an adjective with a negative prefix such as *un*, *in*, and *im*, a double negative pairs words to make a positive statement:

> It was *not uncommon* for Lilah to wake up before dawn.
> For the train to arrive on time is *not impossible*.
> The schedule was *not* at all *incomplete*.

Negatives in English

Be vigilant for words like *hardly* and *scarcely*. They, too, are considered negative words.

You *can't hardly* tell one tree from another without a guidebook.

Both *can't* and *hardly* are negative words.

Likewise, stay alert for negative words followed by *but*, a word that is also regarded as negative. An expression like *can't help but* violates the double-negative rule. Therefore, "Harvey *can't help but* tell everyone what to do" should properly be "Harvey *can't help* telling everyone what to do."

Nouns are the names of things, the labels we apply to everything we can see, touch, taste, and feel. They name the places we go (*work, mall, bus stop*), our means of getting there (*subway, SUV, bicycle*), and what we pass by, pass through, and pass over (*station, park, Eads Bridge*) on our way. Nouns name the solid, concrete, and tactile things of the world—the infrastructure, so to speak. But they also name:

- people (*Louise, mail carrier*)
- activites (*swimming, texting*)
- concepts (*love, afterlife*)
- conditions (*confusion, poverty*)
- events (*9/11, marathon*)
- groups (*Google.com, SADD*)
- feelings (*enthusiasm, reluctance*)
- times (*morning, curfew*)

Some nouns such as *Detroit* and *Facebook* are capitalized. Those are **proper nouns** and refer to specific places, groups, titles, events, and so on. The nouns that begin with lower-case letters go by the name **common nouns**.

All the nouns listed above are singular. That is, they name only one person, one place, one activity, and so forth.

Plurals

	SINGULAR	PLURAL
Most nouns form their plurals by adding *s* to the singular.	son	sons
	house	houses
Nouns ending in *s*, *sh*, *x*, or *z* add *es* to the singular.	boss	bosses
	gas	gases
	dish	dishes
	tax	taxes
	waltz	waltzes
Many nouns ending in *f* or *fe* change the *f* to *v* when forming their plurals.	half	halves
	wife	wives
Nouns ending in *y* preceded by a consonant change the *y* to *i* and add *es*.	penny	pennies
	laboratory	laboratories

Nouns

	SINGULAR	PLURAL
The following nouns ending in *o* add *es* when forming their plurals.	buffalo	buffaloes
	calico	calicoes
	cargo	cargoes
	desperado	desperadoes
	domino	dominoes
	embargo	embargoes
	hero	heroes
	mosquito	mosquitoes

Nouns With Irregular Plurals

SINGULAR	PLURAL	SINGULAR	PLURAL
addendum	addenda	knife	knives
alumna (fem.)	alumnae	leaf	leaves
alumnus (masc.)	alumni	life	lives
analysis	analyses	loaf	loaves
antithesis	antitheses	louse	lice
appendix	appendices	man	men
axis	axes	maximum	maxima
bacterium	bacteria	metamorphosis	metamorphoses
basis	bases	minimum	minima
beef	beeves	mouse	mice
cannon	cannon	oasis	oases
cherub	cherubim	ourself	ourselves
child	children	ox	oxen
curriculum	curricula	parenthesis	parentheses
die	dice	phenomenon	phenomena
elf	elves	radius	radii
ellipsis	ellipses	self	selves
emphasis	emphases	seraph	seraphim
fish	fish (*fishes*— different kinds)	sheaf	sheaves
		sheep	sheep
focus	foci	swine	swine
foot	feet	synopsis	synopses
fungus	fungi	synthesis	syntheses
goose	geese	terminus	termini
half	halves	thesis	theses
hoof	hooves	thief	thieves
hypothesis	hypotheses	tooth	teeth

SINGULAR	PLURAL	SINGULAR	PLURAL
vertebra	vertebrae	wife	wives
virtuoso	virtuosi	wolf	wolves
yourself	yourselves	woman	women

Several nouns are the same in both singular and plural forms, among them *deer/deer, scissors/scissors,* and *moose/moose,* as well as a handful of nouns with Latin endings, such as *data* and *media,* which are technically plural but have become singular through constant repetition.

English also contains nouns that come only in singular form. These include *news, garbage, happiness, information, physics, air, laryngitis,* and *honesty.*

Possessive Nouns

The possessive case of nouns, meaning *belonging to,* is usually formed by adding the apostrophe and *s* to the word, in such phrases as the <u>*boy's*</u> *desk* and the <u>*children's*</u> *school.* If the noun ends with an *s* or a *z* sound, however, add only the apostrophe, as in <u>*Dickens'*</u> *novels* and the *World* <u>*Series'*</u> *first game.*

EXCEPTION: In singular one-syllable nouns ending in the *s* or *z* sound, add the apostrophe and *s* and pronounce the word as though it ended is *es,* as in <u>*class's morale.*</u>

When a noun is plural and ends in *s,* put the apostrophe after the *s,* as in <u>*leaves'*</u> *color* and <u>*horses'*</u> *stable.*

To be certain about the correct placing of the apostrophe, remember that it always means belonging to whatever immediately precedes it:

the boy's suit	belonging to a boy
the boys' room	belonging to the boys
the boss's office	belonging to the boss
the bosses' office	belonging to the bosses
the women's department	belonging to the women

When possession is shared by two or more nouns, this fact is indicated by using the possessive case for the last noun in the series: *John, Fred, and Edward's canoe.* They all own the same canoe. If each one separately owns a canoe, each name is placed in the possessive case: *John's, Fred's, and Edward's canoes.*

Inanimate objects are not capable of possession. The relationship meaning *a part of* is indicated by the use of the preposition *of*:

the wall of the castle NOT *the castle's wall*

EXCEPTIONS: Objects which are personified, such as ships and airplanes, may use the possessive case: *the ship's compass, the plane's gyroscope.* Idiomatic usage also allows the possessive case for time and money: *a day's work, a dollar's worth, three years' time.* In such instances be careful in placing the apostrophe to observe whether the noun is singular or plural: *a month's vacation, two months' vacation.*

Short phrases consisting of verbs plus adverbs or prepositions are called *phrasals*. Each word in a phrasal has a meaning unto itself, but when combined into a unit can convey a meaning far different from the individual words. Consider the verb *hang*, for example. The dictionary lists a dozen or more definitions, most related to raising up and suspending in the air. Yet the phrasal *hang in* has nothing to do with curtains or bridges or gallows. Rather, it means to persevere, as in:

> Although he's exhausted, Trent will *hang in* there until he reaches the finish line.

Phrasals enrich our language. Linking a verb to a preposition or adverb not only expands the meaning of the verb, it puts at our disposal many more choices for expressing ourselves in speech and writing.

Abide by: comply with, conform to
> *You should abide by your parents' wishes.*

Act out: dramatize
> *John and Sara acted out the dialogue.*

Act up: misbehave
> *Joe continues to act up during class.*

Act up: begin to bother
> *My old war injury started to act up again.*

Add up: be logical, make sense
> *Their main points in the discussion simply did not add up.*

Add up to be: amount to
> *Their arguments all added up to be a reasonable conclusion.*

Allow for: make provision for
> *We allowed for a slight overage in our calculations.*

Ask after: inquire about someone
> *He asked after you last evening.*

Ask for it (trouble): continue an action in spite of likely punishment
> *The kids were finally punished by their mother, who simply said: "They asked for it."*

Ask out: invite (as on a date)
> *I'm so happy that George asked me out to the prom.*

Be about: occupy self with
> *You should be about your business.*

*From *501 English Verbs,* by Thomas R. Beyer, Jr., Barron's Educational Series, Inc., 2007.

Phrasal Verbs

Bear down: apply maximum effort
> *It's time for us to bear down and get this job completed.*

Bear down on: harm
> *The financial pressures are already beginning to bear down on him.*

Bear out: confirm
> *The results of the experiment bore out our worst fears.*

Bear up: withstand the pressure
> *Given all of the commotion, it is a wonder how well he is bearing up.*

Bear with: endure, persevere
> *Bear with me for just a minute as I try to explain.*

Beat off: repel
> *They ultimately beat off their attackers.*

Beat it: leave quickly
> *He beat it when the police arrived.*

Beat out: arrive first
> *He beat out the other candidate by just two votes.*

Become of: happen to
> *What becomes of a broken heart?*

Beg off: ask to be excused
> *Given the constraints on his time, he begged off the assignment.*

Bid up: force a price higher
> *They bid up the price of the painting to over a million dollars.*

Bind over: to hold someone on bail or bond
> *The prisoner was bound over for trial.*

Blow away: overwhelm
> *His performance blew me away.*

Blow off: release
> *Let him blow off some steam.*

Blow out: extinguish
> *Please don't forget to blow out the candles.*

Blow over: pass by (like a storm)
> *We're hoping the controversy will blow over with time.*

Blow up: enlarge
> *Can you blow up these photos?*

Blow up: explode
> *If you're not careful, you'll blow up the whole neighborhood with that explosive charge.*

Boot up: turn on a computer.
> *After you boot up, open the program.*

Break down: cause to collapse
> *The elevator is always breaking down.*

Break down: become distressed
> *When confronted with the evidence the suspect broke down and cried.*

Break even: gain back the original investment
> *After many years of hard work they finally broke even.*

Break in: train
> *They were trying to break in the new horse.*

Break in: adapt for a purpose
> *He used the oil to break in his new baseball glove.*

Break in: enter illegally
> *The burglars broke in last evening.*

Break in/into: interrupt
> *The secretary broke into our conversation with an important message.*

Break into: enter a profession
> *He broke into the major leagues in 1947.*

Break off: cease
> *They broke off negotiations after the last round of talks.*

Break out: skin eruption
> *He broke out in a rash after eating just a few peanuts.*

Break out: escape
> *Last evening two criminals broke out of a maximum security prison.*

Break out: begin
> *Fighting broke out in the streets of Jerusalem.*

Break up: separate
> *The couple broke up after the argument on their last date.*

Bring around: convince one to adopt an opinion
> *The shop foreman finally brought the workers around to management's point of view.*

Bring around: restore to consciousness
> *They used smelling salts to bring her around.*

Bring back: recall to mind
> *Those songs bring back such fond memories.*

Bring down: **cause to fall**
The Russian Revolution brought down the Romanov dynasty.
Bring forth: **propose**
They brought forth a series of new proposals at our meeting this morning.
Bring forth: **give birth**
And she brought forth a son.
Bring in: **render a verdict**
The jury brought in a verdict of "not guilty."
Bring off: **accomplish**
I don't see how we can bring that off without help.
Bring on: **cause to appear**
You can bring on the dancers.
Bring out: **reveal or expose**
The lecture brought out the best and worst in him.
Bring to: **restore to consciousness**
The doctor brought him to.
Bring up: **raise**
I didn't want to bring this up, but since you mentioned it, I feel I must.

Build in: **include as an integral part**
The car stereo is built in.
Build on: **use as a basis**
These proposals finally give us something to build on.
Build up: **increase gradually**
The errors continued to build up until they harmed his performance.

Burn out: **wear out from exhaustion**
Toward the end of the race he felt like he was burning out.
Burn up: **make very angry**
Your attitude really burns me up.

Burst out: **begin suddenly**
They burst out laughing at the speaker.

Buy into: **buy a stock of**
I bought into IBM when it was just beginning.
Buy into: **give credence to**
He never bought into the company's philosophy.
Buy off: **bribe**
They bought off the politician with a large contribution to her campaign.

Buy out: purchase all the shares
The larger company bought them out.
Buy up: purchase all that is available
The speculator keeps buying up the plots in that old neighborhood.

Call back: ask to return
The workers were called back to the job as the strike vote was being counted.
Call for: arrive to meet
The young gentlemen called for his new found friend.
Call for: requires
That calls for a celebration.
Call forth: evoke
Their attack called forth an immediate response.
Call in: summon
A heart specialist was called in to review the diagnosis.
Call in: use the telephone to communicate
Has the salesman called in yet?
Call off: cancel
The ball game was called off on account of rain.
Call up: summon to military duty
The reserves were called up during the Gulf War.
Call upon: require
I call upon you to take up your arms in the defense of liberty.
Call upon: visit
When can I call upon you to discuss this matter?

Care for: provide for
I cared for the children while their Mom was away.

Carry away: excite
She was carried away by the sound of his voice.
Carry off: cause the death of
The entire population of the village was carried off by a new strain of the virus.
Carry on: continue
The officer was pleased with the inspection and told his men to carry on with their duties.
Carry out: put into practice
They carried out his orders without hesitation.

Phrasal Verbs

Carry through: persevere to a goal or conclusion
> *He rarely carries through on his promises.*

Cast about: search for
> *He kept casting about for the answers.*

Cast around: search about for something
> *She was casting around for a friend.*

Cast off: throw away
> *She loves to cast off last year's fashions.*

Cast off: launch a boat
> *They cast off for the next destination.*

Cast out: expel
> *An exorcist casts out devils.*

Catch on: become popular
> *It didn't take long for colored hair to catch on with the younger generation.*

Catch up: overtake from behind
> *How do you ever expect me to catch up if you walk so fast?*

Change off: alternate performing tasks
> *We can change off in an hour or so if you get tired.*

Close down: discontinue, go out of business
> *The clothing store closed down after the Christmas season.*

Close in: advance, surround
> *The enemy used the darkness of night to close in on our positions.*

Close up: block up or shut down
> *They closed up the entrance to the cave.*

Close out: dispose, terminate
> *We must close out this particular product at the end of the month.*

Come about: happen
> *It just came about.*

Come across: find, meet
> *I was lucky to come across just the perfect gift.*

Come along: go with someone else
> *You may come along if you wish.*

Come around (round): regain consciousness
> *The boxer finally came around in the dressing room.*

Come at: approach
> *You can come at that problem from a number of angles.*

Come back: regain past state
>   *He came back quickly after the knee operation.*

Come by: acquire
>   *How did you come by this money?*

Come down: lose position, money, standing
>   *He has certainly come down in the opinion polls.*

Come in: arrive
>   *The new spring fashions have just come in.*

Come into: acquire or inherit
>   *My brother recently came into a small fortune.*

Come off: happen, occur
>   *The concert came off without any problems.*

Come on: show an interest in
>   *He came on to her all evening at the party.*

Come out: make known
>   *They finally came out with the official statement.*

Come through: deliver on a promise
>   *I am so happy he finally came through with his contribution.*

Come to: regain consciousness
>   *He came to an hour after the operation.*

Come over: drop by for a visit
>   *Why don't you come over this evening?*

Come to pass: happen
>   *And so it came to pass that they parted as friends.*

Come up: appear
>   *Everything is coming up on the screen as we expected.*

Come upon: discover
>   *I came upon the evidence quite by accident.*

Cover up: conceal after the fact
>   *They tried to cover up their wrongdoing.*

Cry down: belittle someone
>   *The speaker was cried down by the unruly audience.*

Cry out: exclaim
>   *The wounded soldier cried out in pain.*

Cut back: reduce
>   *We are cutting back production as of next Monday.*

Cut down: kill
>   *He was cut down by a stray bullet on the street last evening.*

Phrasal Verbs

Cut down: reduce
> *You should cut down on the amount of fat in your diet.*

Cut in: break into a line
> *It is rude to cut in, when we have been standing here over an hour.*

Cut off: stop
> *I am afraid that I must cut off this discussion right now.*

Cut off: separate
> *They were cut off from the exit by the progress of the fire.*

Cut out: form or shape by cutting
> *Little children love to cut out paper dolls.*

Cut out: exclude
> *Let's cut her out of the final decision.*

Cut out: suited for
> *He is not cut out to be a doctor.*

Cut short: interrupt
> *Our trip was cut short by my wife's accident.*

Cut up: clown about
> *The little boy loves to cut up when the teacher turns his back.*

Cut up: destroy completely
> *The division was cut up by the air attack.*

Dial in: access by telephone or modem
> *He often dials in from home to check his e-mail.*

Dial out: access a telephone line for a phone call
> *How can I dial out from this phone?*

Die down: subside
> *The controversy died down after a month.*

Die off: decline dramatically
> *The tribal members died off.*

Die out: become extinct
> *The tigers in India are dying out.*

Dig in: hold on stubbornly
> *Let's dig in and meet the challenge.*

Dig in: begin to eat
> *Let's dig in, guys. I'm so hungry I could eat a horse.*

Do in: ruin or kill
> *He was done in by his fellow inmates.*

Do up: dress elaborately
> *The little girl was all done up for her school play.*

Do without: manage in spite of a lack of something
The kids can't do without television.

Drag on: go on for a long time
The hours seem to drag on endlessly.

Drag out: extend
I can't understand why they are dragging this matter out so long.

Draw away: pull ahead
We must continue drawing away from the other colleges.

Draw back: retreat
Let's draw back and regroup.

Draw down: deplete resources
We will have to draw down on our grain supplies.

Draw out: prolong
Just how long can she draw out the committee meeting?

Draw up: compose
Let's just draw up a contract.

Dream up: invent
Who dreamed up that idea?

Drink in: listen closely
He drank in her every word.

Drink to: raise a toast
Let's drink to days gone by.

Drive at: hint, lead in a direction
What are you driving at?

Drop behind: fall behind
The little kids kept dropping behind their parents on the walk.

Drop by: stop in for a visit
Don't forget to drop by when you are in town.

Drop off: go to sleep
I finally dropped off at midnight.

Drop out: withdraw from school
Continue your studies. Don't drop out of school.

Dwell on/upon: write, speak, or think at length
We have been dwelling on this topic for over a week.

Phrasal Verbs

Eat into: deplete
> *The number of returns began to eat into their profits.*

Eat out: dine in a restaurant
> *Do you eat out often?*

Eat up: enjoy enormously
> *She ate up the evening's entertainment.*

End up: reach a place
> *I don't know how, but I ended up in Cleveland.*

Enter into: take an active role in
> *He entered into politics late in life.*

Enter on/upon: set out, begin
> *Today we enter on the new phase of our project.*

Explain away: minimize
> *He kept trying to explain away the illegal contributions.*

Face down: confront and overcome
> *He faced down his opponent in the first match.*

Face off: start or resume play in hockey, lacrosse, and other games
> *They faced off in their opponents' zone.*

Face off: take sides against one another
> *The two warring factions had faced off at the first meeting.*

Face up: deal with an issue
> *It's time for you to face up to your obligations.*

Fall apart: break down
> *After his wife's death he completely fell apart.*

Fall back: lag behind
> *The others fell back after the first mile of the hike.*

Fall back on: rely on
> *What can I fall back on if this doesn't work?*

Fall behind: fail to pay on time
> *When he lost his job, they fell behind in their mortgage payments.*

Fall down: fail to meet expectations
> *Unfortunately the new boss fell down on the job.*

Fall for: succumb to, fall in love
> *He fell for her at first glance.*

Fall for: be deceived
> *He fell for the con artist's scam.*

Fall in: take a place
> *All of the principal investors fell in after the initial presentation.*

Fall off: decrease
> *The interest in foreign languages has been gradually falling off.*

Fall on: attack
> *Those waiting in ambush fell on the unsuspecting soldiers.*

Fall out: leave military formation
> *The sergeant roared, "Company, fall out!"*

Fall through: fail
> *The deal fell through at the last moment.*

Fall to: approach energetically
> *The new maid fell to the cleaning.*

Fall short: fail to obtain
> *His efforts to earn a million dollars fell short.*

Feel like: wish or want to
> *I feel like taking a walk.*

Feel out: try to find out something indirectly
> *Could you feel out the opposition before we meet next week?*

Feel up to: be prepared for
> *I don't really feel up to a five mile run.*

Fight back: suppress one's feeling
> *He fought back tears at the announcement.*

Fight off: repel an attack
> *They fought off the attackers until their ammunition ran out.*

Figure in: include
> *Be sure to figure in the extra expenses.*

Figure on: depend upon someone
> *I never thought we could figure on their support.*

Figure on: consider
> *Figure on at least a one-hour delay in your flight.*

Figure out: resolve
> *Now how are we going to figure that out?*

Fill in: provide with new information
> *Could you fill me in on the latest news?*

Fill in: substitute for
> *He filled in for her when she was on vacation.*

Fill out: complete a form or application
> *Be sure to fill out both sides of the form.*

Phrasal Verbs

Find out: learn or discover
>*Let's see what we can find out about tigers.*

Finish off: end or complete
>*Let's finish off for the evening.*

Finish off: destroy or kill
>*He finished them off with a hunting knife.*

Finish up: conclude, bring to an end
>*He finished up at midnight.*

Fit in: be compatible
>*He doesn't fit in with that crowd.*

Fly at: attack someone
>*He flew at him in a rage.*

Follow along: move in unison with
>*The others just followed along with the song.*

Follow through: pursue something to completion
>*We simply have to follow through on our commitments.*

Follow through: complete the motion of a baseball, golf, or tennis swing
>*When you hit the ball, be sure to follow through.*

Follow out: comply with
>*They followed out his instructions precisely.*

Follow up: check the progress
>*Did you ever follow up on those sales leads?*

Freeze out: exclude
>*They froze him out of the negotiations.*

Get about: walk again
>*It was a week before he could get about.*

Get across: make something comprehensible
>*I keep trying to get the same point across to you.*

Get after: encourage, follow up
>*It's time to get after those kids again.*

Get along: co-exist
>*Can't you find a way to get along with one another?*

Get around: avoid
>*There is no way we can get around this situation.*

Get at: reach successfully
>*Put the cookies where the children can't get at them.*

Get at: suggest
>*What are you trying to get at with that question?*

Get back: receive
>*Did you ever get your money back?*

Get back at: exact revenge
>*He tried unsuccessfully to get back at his enemies.*

Get by: go past
>*Excuse me, can I get by here?*

Get by: barely succeed
>*He did just enough homework to get by.*

Get down: descend
>*Please get down from the table.*

Get down: devote your attention
>*Let's get down to work.*

Get down: discourage
>*Don't let her criticism get you down.*

Get in: enter
>*We were lucky to get in before they closed the doors.*

Get in: succeed in accomplishing
>*They got the game in before the rain.*

Get into: become involved
>*I really can get into this assignment.*

Get off: depart
>*Did he ever get off last evening?*

Get off: fire a shot
>*Try to get off a shot if he appears.*

Get off: send a message
>*He got off a quick note before he left the office.*

Get off: escape punishment
>*He got off with only two years.*

Get off: finish the work day
>*When do you get off?*

Get on: continue on good terms
>*They seem to be getting on well together.*

Get on: make progress
>*Let's get on with it. Time is money.*

Get out: escape
>*How did the bird get out of its cage?*

Get out: publish a newspaper
>*They got the paper out last evening.*

Phrasal Verbs

Get over: prevail
> *How will they ever get over the loss of their home?*

Get over: recover from difficult experience
> *He never got over the death of his son.*

Get through: make contact
> *I tried calling, but I couldn't get through.*

Get to: make contact with
> *How can we get to the head of the corporation?*

Get to: affect
> *The strain of the job finally got to him.*

Get together: gather
> *We should all get together on Friday morning.*

Get up: arise from bed
> *It's six o'clock and time to get up.*

Get up: initiate
> *He got up a petition against the property tax.*

Give away: present at a wedding
> *The father gave his daughter away with a tear in his eye.*

Give away: reveal accidentally
> *He gave away the secret in the press conference.*

Give back: return
> *Don't forget to give me the book back.*

Give in: surrender
> *Don't give in—regardless of the pressure.*

Give of: devote
> *He gave generously of himself in the cause of peace.*

Give off: emit
> *The lawn mower was giving off strange smells.*

Give out: distribute
> *The company representative was giving out free samples.*

Give out: stop functioning
> *His heart gave out last night.*

Give over: place in another's care
> *He gave over his assets to his attorney for safekeeping.*

Give over: devote oneself
> *He gave himself over to helping humanity.*

Give over: surrender oneself
> *He gave himself over to her with his heart and soul.*

Give up: surrender, desist, lose hope
> *Don't give up, try again.*

Go about: continue
    He should go about his business.
Go along: agree
    They will go along with whatever we suggest.
Go at: attack
    He went at his opponent determined to prevail.
Go at: approach
    How many ways can we go at this problem?
Go by: elapse
    As time goes by we grow wiser.
Go by: pay a short visit
    They went by the new neighbors' house to say hello.
Go down: set
    The sun goes down very early in winter.
Go down: fall to ground
    The boxer went down after being hit on the chin.
Go down: lose
    They went down to defeat.
Go down: be recorded
    This will go down as a very important event of the decade.
Go for: like, have an urge for
    I could go for an ice cream.
Go in for: participate
    He goes in for tennis and swimming.
Go off: explode
    The bomb went off on a deserted street.
Go off: depart
    He went off to the navy after high school.
Go on: happen
    What's going on here?
Go on: continue
    Life goes on.
Go on: keep on doing
    He went on reading even after the sun went down.
Go out: become extinguished
    The fire went out.
Go out: go outdoors
    Mommy, can we go out?
Go out: partake in social life
    Since her husband died, she never goes out anymore.

Phrasal Verbs

Go over: review
> *Can we go over these figures one more time?*

Go over: gain acceptance
> *The presentation went over very well.*

Go through: examine carefully
> *We have to go through the clothes and papers.*

Go through: experience
> *I hope I never have to go through that again.*

Go through: perform
> *He went through his lines like a professional actor.*

Go under: fail
> *The business went under after only six months of mismanagement.*

Go under: lose consciousness to anesthesia
> *The patient wanted to see her before he went under.*

Go with: date regularly
> *Sally has been going with John since eighth grade.*

Grind out: produce by hard work
> *He keeps grinding out those articles for the newspaper.*

Grow into: develop
> *He is growing into a handsome young man.*

Grow on: become acceptable
> *That music grows on you.*

Grow out of: become too mature for something
> *He grew out of those children's books.*

Grow out of: come into existence
> *This project grew out of preliminary discussions last year.*

Grow up: become an adult
> *When will you grow up?*

Hang around: loiter
> *Why does he hang around with those kids every afternoon?*

Hang back: hold back
> *Be sure to hang back at the start of the match.*

Hang in: persevere
> *You just have to hang in there with him.*

Hang on: persevere
> *We must hang on until the rescue helicopter arrives.*

Hang together: be united
> *Let's hang together in the salary negotiations.*

Hang up: end a telephone conversation
>   *Don't you dare hang up on me.*
Hang up: hinder
>   *What's hanging up the parade?*

Have on: wear
>   *What did he have on when you saw him?*
Have to: must
>   *I just have to see that movie.*

Hear from: be notified
>   *When will we hear from you about the application?*
Hear from: be reprimanded
>   *He certainly will hear from his superiors about that error.*
Hear of: be aware of
>   *Have you heard of the new family in town?*
Hear out: listen fully
>   *I would like you to hear me out on this matter before you proceed.*

Heave to: turn into the wind or to the seas before a storm
>   *With the storm approaching, the captain gave the order to heave to.*

Hide out: conceal yourself
>   *He hid out for two months in the hills.*

Hold back: restrain oneself
>   *All evening I held back my applause.*
Hold down: restrict
>   *Please hold down the noise.*
Hold forth: talk at length
>   *The president held forth on international relations all during dinner.*
Hold off: withstand
>   *Can anyone hold off the invaders?*
Hold on: persist
>   *We will just hold on until our wish is granted.*
Hold out: last
>   *The supplies held out for two months.*
Hold over: delay
>   *The sale has been held over one more week.*
Hold to: remain loyal
>   *He held to his promises.*

Phrasal Verbs

Hold up: delay
> *What is holding up the construction?*

Hold up: rob
> *He held up a bank in Chicago.*

Hold with: agree
> *No one seriously holds with his opinions.*

Join in: participate
> *They joined in at the end of the first verse.*

Keep at: persevere
> *Just keep at it and you'll succeed.*

Keep down: restrain
> *They kept the cost of college education down as long as they could.*

Keep off: stay away from
> *Keep off the grass!*

Keep to: stay with
> *Let's keep to the main idea.*

Keep up: maintain properly
> *You must keep up your dues to remain a member in good standing.*

Kill off: eliminate
> *All the rats were killed off by the poison.*

Knock around: be rough with someone
> *You won't be able to knock her around any more.*

Knock around: travel
> *They knocked around California for a month.*

Knock back: gulp down
> *They both knocked back the vodka in true Russian style.*

Knock down: topple
> *The little girl knocked down the sand castle her father had just completed.*

Knock off: stop work
> *Let's knock off today at four.*

Knock off: kill
> *They knocked off the drug dealer in a back alley.*

Knock out: render unconscious
> *That last punch knocked him out for two minutes.*

Knock out: be confined by illness or injury
> *The flu really knocked him out for a week.*

Knock together: make something quickly
>   *Let's see if we can knock this table together before evening.*
Knock up: wake or summon by knocking at the door (British English)
>   *Don't forget to knock me up tomorrow.*
Knock up: make pregnant (American English—crude and vulgar)

Lay aside: give up
>   *Lay aside your arms and come out.*
Lay away: reserve for the future
>   *Be sure to lay away some extra funds for a vacation.*
Lay in: store for the future
>   *It's time to lay in some seed for the spring.*
Lay into: reprimand
>   *The boss is really laying into the new employee.*
Lay off: terminate one's employment
>   *Ten thousand people are scheduled to be laid off tomorrow.*
Lay on: prepare
>   *They laid on a reception for fifty people.*
Lay out: present
>   *Can you lay out your intentions for us?*
Lay out: clothe a corpse
>   *She was laid out in her finest dress.*
Lay over: make a stopover
>   *We will have to lay over in Moscow enroute to Siberia.*

Lead off: start
>   *Johnny will lead off the discussion.*
Lead on: entice, encourage, deceive
>   *The young man led her on for almost two years.*

Lean on: apply pressure
>   *I want you to lean on him until his performance improves.*

Leave alone: refrain from disturbing
>   *Please leave me alone. I'm busy.*
Leave go: relax one's grasp
>   *She left go of the girl's hand.*
Leave off: cease doing something
>   *She left off in the middle of the sentence.*
Leave out: omit
>   *She left out two answers.*

Phrasal Verbs

Lend itself to: be suitable for
That story lends itself well to a screen adaptation.

Let down: disappoint
In the end his friends let him down.

Let on: admit knowing
We finally had to let on to the fact that we had known all along.

Let out: end
School let out at 2:00 PM.

Let up: diminish
The rain did not let up for two hours.

Lie down: do little
He keeps lying down on the job.

Lie with: depend upon
The final word lies with you.

Light into: attack
Did you see how she lit into him?

Light out: depart hastily
He certainly lit out after work.

Light up: become animated
Whenever he started talking, her face lit up.

Light up: start smoking
They both lit up after the play.

Listen in: eavesdrop
The teacher tried to listen in to the conversation at the next table.

Listen in: tune in to a radio broadcast
They listened in to the show every Sunday morning.

Live down: overcome the shame
Can he ever live down that disgraceful performance?

Live it up: enjoy life in an extravagant fashion
After we won the lottery, we lived it up for a year.

Live out: go through a period of time
They lived out their days in peace.

Live with: resign oneself to
He learned to live with his limitations.

Live up to: achieve
How can you live up to your parents' expectations?

Look after: take care of
She will look after you while I'm gone.
Look down on: despise
They always looked down on the new students.
Look for: expect
What can we look for in the new year?
Look for: search
Look for tea in the coffee aisle of the supermarket.
Look forward to: await with great anticipation
I am looking forward to our meeting
Look like: appear as
It looks like rain.
Look on/upon: regard
They looked upon him with skepticism.
Look out: be careful
Look out. It's a dangerous crossing.
Look to: expect from
We looked to you for guidance.
Look up: search and find
What words do you have to look up in a dictionary?
Look up to: admire
She really looks up to her daddy.

Lose out: fail to achieve
Those who came late lost out on a golden opportunity.

Make for: promote, lead to, results in
That approach makes for better productivity.
Make off: depart hastily
The thieves made off with their jewelry.
Make out: discern
Without my glasses I can't make out this note.
Make out: understand
I can't make out what he means.
Make out: compose
Have you made out a will?
Make out: get along with
How did you make out with the new eyeglasses?
Make over: redo
She was completely made over for the new part.

Make up: **construct**
> *Let's make up a new proposal.*

Make up: **alter appearance**
> *They made her up to be an old woman for the play.*

Make up: **apply cosmetics**
> *She always makes herself up before she goes out.*

Make up: **resolve a quarrel**
> *After an hour they decided to make up and start over again.*

Make up: **take an exam later**
> *The student who had been ill had a chance to make up the math exam.*

Mark down: **decrease the price**
> *They marked down the toys after the Christmas holidays.*

Mark out: **plan something**
> *He marked out a course of action.*

Mark up: **deface**
> *They marked up the subway car with spray paint.*

Mark up: **increase the price**
> *As soon as the New Year came they marked up the new car models.*

Measure up: **match requirements**
> *He just didn't measure up to our qualifications.*

Meet with: **be received**
> *The outline of the plan met with his approval.*

Mete out: **allot**
> *It is the responsibility of the judge to mete out punishment.*

Move in/into: **occupy a place**
> *We are moving into the new offices next week.*

Move on: **begin a passage**
> *It's time to move on and try something new.*

Move out: **leave a place**
> *When will they be moving out of their apartment?*

Mow down: **destroy (as in cutting grass)**
> *Every time the enemy soldiers attacked, they were mowed down by the machine gun.*

Open up: unfold
> *She opened up the letter with mixed emotions.*

Open up: begin the business day
> *We open up at 7:00 A.M. on Sundays.*

Open up: speak candidly
> *Only after we became good friends did she begin to open up.*

Open up: start
> *They opened up the newsstand as soon as the dawn came.*

Pass away: die
> *He passed away last year.*

Pass off: offer an imitation as the original
> *He tried to pass it off as a Picasso painting.*

Pass out: lose consciousness
> *After drinking ten bottles of beer he passed out.*

Pass over: omit
> *They passed over the difficult items on the agenda.*

Pass over: skip
> *He was passed over for promotion.*

Pass up: miss an opportunity
> *He passed up a chance to sing with the Beatles.*

Pay off: pay the full amount
> *He paid off the mortgage last year.*

Pay off: return a profit
> *Their investment in real estate paid off handsomely.*

Pay out: spend
> *He paid out twenty dollars for the gift.*

Pay up: give the requested amount
> *He paid up his bar tab on Friday evening.*

Pick apart: refute by careful analysis
> *He picked apart the prosecution's argument in front of the jury.*

Pick at: pluck with fingers
> *He picked at the guitar strings before playing a song.*

Pick on: tease
> *You shouldn't pick on your baby sister.*

Pick out: select
> *Pick out a nice tie for me.*

Pick out: distinguish in a large group
> *He could always pick her out in a crowd.*

Phrasal Verbs

Pick up: retrieve by hand
He picked up a newspaper on the way to work.
Pick up: organize, clean
Let's pick up this room right now.

Play at: take half-heartedly
He only played at being the boss.
Play back: replay
We played back the tape.
Play down: minimize
We want to play down the weakest aspects of our proposal.
Play on: take advantage of
He often played on her fears.
Play out: exhaust
This type of approach played itself out long ago.
Play up: emphasize
They played up her good looks.

Pull away: withdraw
They pulled away from the attack.
Pull away: move ahead
He pulled away in the public opinion polls.
Pull back: withdraw
Let's pull back and regroup.
Pull in: arrive at destination
The train pulled in at 10:00 PM.
Pull out: depart
The train pulled out on time.
Pull over: bring a vehicle to a stop
The policeman asked him to pull over.
Pull through: endure and emerge successfully
He finally pulled through after much extra work.
Pull up: bring to a halt
The riders pulled up at the gate.

Put across: make comprehensible
He was able to put across his main points.
Put away: renounce
They put away their thoughts of revolution.
Put down: write down
He put down his thoughts on paper.

Put down: **to end**
We must put down the revolt.
Put down: **criticize**
Someone was always putting her down.
Put forth: **exert**
He put forth his best effort in the race.
Put forward: **propose**
He put forward his ideas in his presentation.
Put in: **apply**
He put in for the new position at his office.
Put in: **spend time**
He put in ten extra hours last week.
Put off: **postpone**
They put off the meeting until after the harvest.
Put on: **clothe oneself**
Put on a hat.
Put out: **extinguish**
He put out the fire.
Put out: **publish**
She put out a small literary journal.
Put over on: **get across deceptively**
He tried to put over his schemes on the people.
Put through: **bring to a successful end**
He put the bill through in the Senate.
Put together: **construct**
She put together the model airplane with her dad.
Put upon: **imposed**
He was often put upon by friends.

Read out: **read aloud**
The teacher read out the names at the beginning of class.
Read up: **learn or study by reading**
I'll have to read up on my history for the exam.
Read out of: **be expelled from**
He was read out of the party organization.

Ride out: **survive**
They rode out the latest dip in the stock market.

Phrasal Verbs

Ring up: record a sale
I can ring those items up at this register.
Ring up: extend out a series
They rang up ten victories without a loss.

Rip into: criticize
She certainly ripped into him for that performance.
Rip off: steal from, defraud
Several customers felt they had been ripped off at the sale.

Rise above: be superior to
You must rise above these petty squabbles.

Run across: find by chance
They simply ran across each other at the shopping mall.
Run after: seek attention
Stop running after her and maybe she'll pay you more attention.
Run against: encounter
He kept running against new obstacles.
Run against: oppose
He ran against the incumbent senator.
Run along: leave
Run along now, children.
Run away: flee
The prisoners tried to run away.
Run down: stop because of lack of power
The tractor simply ran down.
Run down: tire
He was very run down after the basketball season.
Run down: collide with
They ran down that poor little dog.
Run down: chase and capture
They ran him down in Philadelphia.
Run down: review
Let's run down the list of our options.
Run in: take into legal custody
He was run in by the two officers.
Run into: meet by chance
I ran into my wife at the post office.
Run into: amount to
This could run into millions of dollars.

Run off: print, duplicate
> *He ran off a hundred copies.*

Run off: escape
> *He ran off with all their money.*

Run off: flow or drain away
> *The water ran off the roof.*

Run off: decide a contest
> *They are running off the tie vote today.*

Run on: continue to talk
> *How he runs on when he gets to the podium.*

Run out: deplete
> *I never want to run out of money.*

Run over: knock down
> *Who ran over the dog?*

Run over: review quickly
> *I ran over my notes before the speech.*

Run over: overflow
> *My cup runneth over.*

Run over: exceed the limit
> *I don't want any of you to run over budget this month.*

Run through: pierce
> *He ran the knife through the butter.*

Run through: use up quickly
> *We have run through all our copy paper.*

Run through: rehearse
> *Let's run through the play one more time.*

Run through: go over main points
> *Let's run through the first two points.*

Run up: make larger
> *He ran up a huge bar bill.*

Run with: adopt an idea
> *Let's run with this idea for the time being.*

See after: take care of
> *She will see after you until I return.*

See off: take leave of
> *They saw the children off at the airport.*

See out: escort to the door
> *Judy will see you out. Please come again.*

See through: understand the true nature
> *I can see through his plans.*

Phrasal Verbs

See through: continue
> *I will see this deal through until they sign on the bottom line.*

See through: support in difficult times
> *My dad saw us through financially the first few years.*

See to: attend to
> *See to the new patient and I'll find his chart.*

Sell off: get rid of at discount prices
> *We will be selling off any leftover items at the end of the month.*

Sell out: dispose of all
> *The tickets were all sold out by mid-morning.*

Send for: summon
> *They sent for the police.*

Send in: cause to arrive
> *They sent in dozens of e-mail messages.*

Send out: order from
> *They sent out for two pizzas and some beer.*

Send up: confined to jail
> *He was sent up for five years on a drug charge.*

Set about: begin
> *They set about their business.*

Set apart: distinguish
> *Her qualifications clearly set her apart from the other candidates.*

Set aside: reserve
> *Can you set aside two tickets for us?*

Set aside: reject
> *Their claim was set aside by the service manager.*

Set at: attack
> *The dogs set at the two little boys throwing stones.*

Set back: slow down
> *The family was severely set back by the flood.*

Set back: cost a lot
> *That new part for the car set me back one hundred dollars.*

Set down: seat someone
> *They set the baby down at the table.*

Set down: put in writing
> *He wanted to set down his thoughts before the meeting.*

Set down: land a plane
> *The pilot set down in a grassy field.*

Set forth: express
>   *He set forth his principles in his campaign speech.*

Set forth: propose
>   *The attorneys set forth the necessary conditions of the tentative agreement.*

Set in: insert
>   *His last words are set in stone.*

Set in: begin happening
>   *The storm set in overnight.*

Set off: initiate
>   *His words set off a rally on Wall Street.*

Set off: explode
>   *He set off the bomb.*

Set out: undertake
>   *He set out to conquer the world.*

Set out: lay out graphically
>   *He set out the new plans for the museum.*

Set to: begin
>   *Can we set to work?*

Set up: put forward, select
>   *He was set up as the group's leader.*

Set up: assemble
>   *He set up the train set in the living room.*

Set up: establish business
>   *What do we still need to set up production?*

Set up: arrange
>   *Please set up the glasses on the rear shelf of the cabinet.*

Set upon: attack violently
>   *The dogs set upon the cat.*

Sew up: complete successfully
>   *We finally sewed up the deal.*

Shake down: subject to search
>   *I want you to shake down his apartment for evidence in the case.*

Shake hands: greet by clasping one another's hands
>   *Americans often shake hands when they meet one another.*

Shake off: dismiss
>   *He shook off the injury and continued to play.*

Shake off: get rid of
>   *How can I shake off this cold?*

Phrasal Verbs

Shake up: upset
> *The death of his father really shook him up.*

Shake up: rearrange drastically.
> *He will really shake up the industry.*

Shape up: develop
> *This is shaping up to be a close contest.*

Shape up: improve to the standard.
> *He will have to shape up or he'll be fired.*

Shoot down: bring down
> *They shot down the enemy aircraft.*

Shoot for: aspire
> *You ought to shoot for the top job.*

Shoot up: increase dramatically
> *The stock prices shot up toward the end of the day.*

Shoot up: damage or terrorize a town
> *The guerrillas shot up the entire village.*

Shoot straight: be truthful
> *I love someone who shoots straight in negotiations.*

Shop around: look for bargains
> *The girls love to shop around at the discount stores.*

Shop around: look for something better, like a job.
> *We decided to shop around for a while, before we make a career decision.*

Show around: act as a guide
> *My daughter can show you around the city if you have time.*

Show off: display
> *The goods were shown off to their best advantage.*

Show off: behave ostentatiously
> *He always likes to show off in front of his friends.*

Show up: be visible
> *The cancer showed up clearly on the X-ray.*

Show up: arrive
> *Will they ever show up?*

Shut down: stop something from operating
> *They shut the plant down.*

Shut off: stop the flow
> *Shut off the electricity before you work on the outlet.*

Shut off: isolate
>   *He was shut off from all news for two months.*

Shut out: prevent from scoring
>   *We were able to shut them out in the last inning of the game.*

Shut up: silence, be silent
>   *You should shut up before you get in more trouble.*

Sing out: cry out
>   *He sang out from the rear of the crowd.*

Sit down: take a seat
>   *Please sit down until you are called.*

Sit in: participate
>   *They sat in on the discussions.*

Sit in: participate in a sit-in demonstration
>   *The demonstrators intend to sit in at the plant gates tomorrow.*

Sit on: consider
>   *Can we sit on this for a day or two and then give you our response?*

Sit on: suppress
>   *The defense attorneys sat on the new evidence.*

Sit out: stay to the end
>   *We will sit this out until it is over.*

Sit out: not participate
>   *I sat out the second match and let my brother play.*

Sit up: rise from lying to sitting position
>   *After his nap he sat up in bed.*

Sit up: sit with spine erect
>   *Mothers always want you to sit up straight.*

Sit up: stay up late
>   *They sat up until past midnight waiting for their daughter to come home.*

Sit up: become suddenly alert
>   *He sat up at the sound of shots.*

Sleep in: sleep late
>   *I like to sleep in on Sundays.*

Sleep out: sleep away from one's home
>   *The parents are sleeping out this weekend.*

Sleep over: spend the night at another home
>   *The girls slept over at their friend's house.*

Phrasal Verbs

Sleep with: have sexual relations
>*He slept with her for the first time on their vacation.*

Slip away: depart without taking one's leave
>*They just slipped away from the party.*

Slip out: depart unnoticed
>*He slipped out for a cigarette break.*

Smell out: discover through investigation
>*They smelled out the criminal after years of investigation.*

Sound off: express an opinion
>*He sounded off about taxes at the town meeting.*

Sound out: elicit an opinion
>*Sound out the board on this matter before Monday.*

Speak out: talk freely
>*He spoke out at our weekly meeting.*

Speak up: talk loud enough to be heard
>*We can't hear you. Would you please speak up?*

Speak up: talk without fear
>*You must learn to speak up for your rights.*

Spell out: read slowly
>*Try to spell it out if you can't understand the meaning.*

Spell out: make clear
>*Would you please spell out your specific objections?*

Spell out: decipher
>*Let's see if we can spell out the new proposal and write a response.*

Spin off: develop from an existing project
>*They spun off two shows from the original.*

Spin out: rotate out of control
>*The car spun out on the ice when he hit the brakes.*

Split up: part company
>*After ten years of marriage they decided to split up.*

Stand by: be ready
>*Stand by for the commercial.*

Stand by: remain uninvolved
> *He just stood by and watched.*

Stand by: remain loyal
> *She stood by me in my time of trouble.*

Stand down: withdraw, cease work
> *The soldiers on duty stood down at midnight.*

Stand for: represent
> *What do you stand for?*

Stand for: put up with
> *I don't know why I stand for this nonsense.*

Stand in: replace
> *She stood in for the sick actress.*

Stand off: stay at a distance
> *They stood off and observed from afar.*

Stand on: be based on
> *These findings stand on my previous calculations.*

Stand on: insist on
> *There are times when you must stand on ceremony.*

Stand out: be conspicuous
> *She really stood out in the green dress.*

Stand out: refuse compliance
> *He is going to stand out against the tax people.*

Stand over: supervise
> *She stood over him the entire test.*

Stand to: prepare to act
> *The police were ordered to stand to.*

Stand up: remain valid
> *His conclusions stood up to various attacks.*

Stand up: miss an appointment
> *She stood him up again last evening.*

Stand up for: defend
> *I stood up for you in my meeting with the school board.*

Start out: begin a trip
> *They started out for Miami at dawn.*

Stave off: prevent
> *They staved off the attackers countless times.*

Stay put: remain in place
> *Now you kids stay put until I get the ice cream.*

Stay up: remain awake
> *They stayed up all night talking about old times.*

Stick around: remain
> *He stuck around for an hour after the press conference to sign autographs.*

Stick out: be prominent
> *He really sticks out in a crowd.*

Stick up: to rob at gunpoint
> *They were stuck up twice in six months.*

Stick up for: defend
> *He always sticks up for his kid brother.*

Stop by: visit
> *They stopped by for coffee after the theater.*

Stop off: interrupt a trip
> *They stopped off in Rome for two days.*

Strike down: fell with a blow
> *He was struck down by a lightning bolt.*

Strike out for: begin a course of action
> *He struck out for California on his own.*

Strike out: fail in one's attempts
> *He struck out in his attempts to get approval for the highway.*

Strike up: start
> *Strike up the band!*

String along: entice by giving false hope
> *They strung him along for a few weeks before telling him they had hired someone else.*

String out: prolong
> *How long can we string out these talks?*

String up: hang someone
> *They strung him up without a trial.*

Swear at: verbally abuse
> *She swore at them like a sailor.*

Swear by: rely on
> *I swear by these calculations.*

Swear by: take an oath
Do you swear by the Bible?
Swear in: administer a legal oath
He was sworn in as Governor.
Swear off: renounce
I have sworn off cigarettes.
Swear out: process
The detectives swore out a warrant for his arrest.

Sweat out: await anxiously
Some students sweated out the two weeks before grades were mailed home.

Take after: follow the example of, resemble
She takes after her father.
Take apart: separate
He took the motor apart in an afternoon.
Take back: retract
I take back my original comments.
Take down: lower
He was taken down a notch or two by the negative fitness report.
Take down: record in writing
He took down the minutes of the meeting.
Take for: regard
What do you take me for?
Take in: grant admittance
She was taken in as a member of the law firm.
Take in: reduce
She took in his new slacks at the waist.
Take in: include
This article takes in all of the existing information.
Take in: deceive
He was taken in by her flashy business card.
Take in: observe thoroughly
He took in the entire scene with a single glance.
Take off: remove
Take off your hat indoors.
Take off: depart by aircraft
Our flight to Madrid took off on schedule.
Take off: deduct
He took off ten percent from the marked price.

Phrasal Verbs

Take on: hire
> *We took him on temporarily for the job.*

Take on: accept
> *We took on the new responsibilities cheerfully.*

Take on: oppose
> *He took on the taller man in a fistfight.*

Take out: secure a license
> *I took out a hunting license.*

Take out: escort
> *I took out our guests for a look at the city.*

Take out: vent
> *He took out his anger on the punching bag.*

Take out: kill
> *He took out the enemy sniper with his first shot.*

Take over: assume control
> *I am taking over here as of today.*

Take to: develop habit or ability
> *He took to swimming at an early age.*

Take to: escape
> *The escapees took to the hills.*

Take up: assume
> *He took up the burden of his family's debts.*

Take up: reduce
> *She took up the dress a full inch.*

Take up: use time
> *It took up all morning.*

Talk around: persuade
> *He tried to talk me around to his point of view.*

Talk around: avoid
> *He tried talking his way around the parking ticket.*

Talk at: address
> *He talked at the rotary club.*

Talk back: reply rudely
> *Don't talk back to your parents.*

Talk down: deprecate
> *He loves to talk down to his secretary.*

Talk down: silence
> *By the end of the meeting he had successfully talked down all the dissenting voices.*

Talk out: resolve
> *Can we not talk this out in a friendly fashion?*

Talk over: consider
> *We talked it over before deciding.*

Talk over: persuade
> *They talked her over by the end of the day.*

Talk up: promote, exaggerate
> *Let's talk up our accomplishments.*

Tear at: attack like an animal
> *They tore at the package like wild animals.*

Tear at: distress oneself
> *Stop tearing at yourself.*

Tear down: vilify
> *They love to tear other people down.*

Tear down: demolish
> *They love to tear down the walls that separate the people in our community.*

Tear into: attack vigorously
> *They tore into their opponents.*

Tear up: destroy
> *We tore up the lease.*

Tell off: reprimand
> *They certainly told him off.*

Throw away: get rid of
> *We throw the boxes away.*

Throw away: waste
> *She threw away her life's savings in Las Vegas.*

Throw away: fail to take advantage
> *They threw away their chance.*

Throw back: hinder the progress
> *They were completely thrown back by his critical comments.*

Throw back: revert
> *They were thrown back to the beginning by the new discovery.*

Throw in: insert
> *Throw in your opinions whenever ready.*

Throw off: rid oneself
> *They threw the dogs off their scent by crossing a stream.*

Phrasal Verbs

Throw off: emit
> *The new plant throws off a foul odor.*

Throw off: divert
> *They were thrown off course by a faulty computer.*

Throw open: make accessible
> *We must throw open our doors to every deserving student.*

Throw out: emit
> *It throws out a powerful signal to other countries.*

Throw out: reject
> *The new design was thrown out by the board of directors.*

Throw out: force to leave
> *Throw the bum out.*

Throw over: overturn
> *They threw over the leftist government in the sixties.*

Throw over: reject
> *The new tax laws were thrown over by the voters in a special vote.*

Throw up: vomit
> *I was so sick I threw up twice.*

Throw up: abandon
> *She threw up her attempts to gain the money.*

Throw up: refer to something repeatedly
> *He kept throwing up her name.*

Throw up: construct hastily
> *Those buildings were thrown up in a matter of months.*

Throw up: project
> *Please throw that image up on the screen.*

Tie in: connect
> *Can we tie in these findings with our previous data?*

Tie into: attack
> *He tied into her.*

Tie up: block
> *They tied up traffic for hours.*

Tie up: occupy
> *I was tied up in the office all last week.*

Try on: check out clothes for size
> *Try on the shoes before you buy them.*

Try out: undergo a competitive qualifying exam
> *He must try out for the soccer team.*

Try out: test or examine
> *Can I try out these new glasses before I purchase a pair?*

Turn away: dismiss
> *They were turned away at the hotel because it was full.*

Turn away: reject
> *They were turned away at the last moment by a violent counterattack.*

Turn back: reverse direction
> *Can you turn back time?*

Turn back: halt advance
> *The invaders were turned back by the courageous citizens of the village.*

Turn down: reject
> *She was turned down by the police department.*

Turn down: fold down
> *The bed was turned down by the chambermaid before they returned last evening.*

Turn in: give over
> *Turn in your papers at the end of class.*

Turn in: inform on
> *They turned in their own brother to the authorities.*

Turn off: stop operation
> *Turn off the electricity.*

Turn off: offend
> *He was turned off by their use of profanity.*

Turn off: cease paying attention
> *He turned them off and played all by himself.*

Turn on: begin operation
> *Turn on the television.*

Turn on: alter the mind with drugs
> *In the sixties people were eager to turn on.*

Turn on: interest
> *That course turned him on.*

Turn out: produce
> *They turn out dozens of autos an hour.*

Turn out: gather
> *Hundreds turned out for his speech.*

Turn out: develop
> *The cake turned out wonderfully.*

Turn over: shift position
> *Turn over on your side if you snore.*

Turn over: reflect upon
> *He turned the request over and over in his mind for a long time.*

Phrasal Verbs

Turn over: transfer to another
> *The papers were turned over to the judge.*

Turn over: sell
> *How many of these cars can we turn over by the end of the month?*

Turn to: seek assistance
> *Whom can I turn to?*

Turn to: begin
> *He turned his attention to the new project.*

Turn up: increase volume
> *Turn up the radio. I want to hear the weather report.*

Turn up: find
> *Where did you turn up the missing wallet?*

Turn up: appear, be found
> *The ring turned up among her dirty socks.*

Turn up: just happen
> *In every translation, some new difficulty turns up.*

Use up: exhaust the supply
> *He used up all the sugar for the cake.*

Wait on/upon: attend to
> *She waited on him day and night.*

Wait out: endure
> *We will have to wait out the storm in a hotel.*

Wait up: postpone sleep
> *Daddy still waits up for his daughters even though they are grown up.*

Walk out: go on strike
> *The workers walked out at midnight without a contract.*

Walk out: leave suddenly
> *He just got up and walked out.*

Walk over: gain easy victory
> *They walked all over their opponents.*

Walk over: treat poorly
> *They walk all over the staff.*

Walk through: perform
> *They walked through their lines for the last time.*

Watch out: be careful
> *Watch out, it's very slippery.*

Watch over: be in charge of
> *I was told to watch over him until the doctor came.*

Watch it: be careful
> *I'm telling you, you'd better watch it, or there will be trouble.*

Wear down: exhaust by continuous pressure
> *They finally wore him down by constant interrogation.*

Wear off: diminish gradually
> *The paint has worn off the siding.*

Wear out: become unusable
> *These jeans will never wear out.*

Win out: prevail
> *He finally won out over his competitors.*

Win over: persuade
> *He won them over with his charm.*

Wind down: relax
> *After work they wound down for an hour in the hot tub.*

Wind up: end
> *They wound up the party at midnight.*

Work in: insert
> *They worked in an hour of relaxation.*

Work off: rid by effort
> *She worked off ten pounds at the gym.*

Work out: accomplish
> *That worked out well.*

Work out: develop
> *They worked out a satisfactory arrangement for them both.*

Work out: engage in strenuous activity
> *She works out every afternoon for two hours.*

Work over: repeat, revise
> *They are working over their papers for submission on Monday.*

Work up: get excited
> *She got all worked up over her grade.*

Work up: increase ability or capacity
> *She worked her way up to ten pages an hour.*

Phrasal Verbs

Wrap up: complete
> *Let's wrap up the meeting and go home.*

Wrap up: summarize
> *Can you wrap up the presentation with your main points?*

Wrap up: intensely involved
> *She's all wrapped up in her schoolwork.*

Write down: record
> *She wrote down the assignment.*

Write in: insert
> *She wrote in a new opening scene for the main actress.*

Write in: submit name of candidate not on the ballot
> *They wrote her in for the post of treasurer.*

Write in: write to organization
> *They wrote in to the maker of the toy with their complaint.*

Write off: dismiss
> *They wrote her off even before the tryouts.*

Write out: write in full
> *She had to write out the complete sentence.*

Write up: report
> *She wrote up the minutes of the meeting.*

Zero in: concentrate on
> *They zeroed in on their long-term goals during the afternoon session.*

Zip up: close, enclose
> *Please zip up your files before sending them to me.*

Prepositions function as connecting words. They show the relationship of one word to another—a vague definition, to be sure, but one that can be clarified by the following scenario: In your mind's eye, picture a flying airplane and a puffy cloud. The airplane can fly *to* the cloud, *through* the cloud, *above* the cloud, *under* the cloud, and so forth. All the words in italics—*to, through, above,* and *under*— are prepositions, serving to show the relative position of one object, the airplane, to another, the cloud. (Notice the word *position* within the word *preposition*.)

English contains dozens of other prepositions that more or less refer to location, for example, *at, off, between, among, over, beside, near, onto, out, past, toward, with, within, behind,* and *across.*

Another group of prepositions enables you to express the relative time when events took place, for example, *before, after, during, since, until.*

Still other prepositions serve to connect and compare objects and ideas, as in:

Julia cooks *like* a master chef, *unlike* Max, who cooks *like* a beginner.
No one is as good *as* you at making a salad.
Except *for* Marion, no one at the meeting wanted to be there.
Because of you, my life is now worthwhile.

Prepositions are always attached to nouns or pronouns in what are known as **prepositional phrases**: *to* the country, *after* the ball, *concerning* this book, *in accordance with* her wishes. Grammatically speaking, the noun or pronoun in a prepositional phrase is called the **object of the preposition**, which means, at least for pronouns, that they must be in the objective case. That is why the phrase *between you and I* is not grammatically correct (because *I* is in the nominative case and it shouldn't be used in this context). Instead, say *between you and me,* because *me* is in the objective case. (For details on the case of pronouns, turn to page 86.)

> **TIP**
> A pronoun serving as the object of a preposition must be in the objective case. Therefore, say *between you and me,* not *between you and I.*

Likewise:

NONSTANDARD: The toll collector argued *with* Harry and *I.*
STANDARD: The toll collector argued *with* Harry and *me.*

Take note of these four additional guidelines involving the use of prepositions:

- **When to use *like* and when to use *as***

The word *like* can be a verb, a noun, an adjective, and an adverb. It can also be a preposition used for making comparisons, as in:

> Maria looks *like* a princess tonight.
> My dog looks *like* me.

The word *as* (along with *as if* and *as though*) is a *conjunction* that introduces clauses and is followed by a verb.

| NONSTANDARD: | Alice does *like* her father says. |
| STANDARD: | Alice does *as* her father says. |

| NONSTANDARD: | Do *like* I say, not *like* I do. |
| STANDARD: | Do *as* I say, not *as* I do. |

When you are uncertain whether to use *like* or whether to use *as*, check whether a verb is used after the preposition. If a verb follows, use *as*, as in:

> He acts *as if* (preposition) he *had seen* (verb) a ghost.

If no verb follows, use *like*, as in:

> The child acts *like* (preposition) her mother (no verb).

In comparisons using *as* or *than*, the verb may sometimes be left out to avoid wordiness. So stay alert for usages in which the verb is optional. Supply the omitted word (in brackets below) in your mind.

> Melissa loves the city as much *as* I [do].
> Harold likes me more *than* [he likes] Maude.

- **When to use *between* and when to use *among***

Use the preposition *between* to refer to anything split into two or divided by two, such as the money that a pair of bank robbers divided *between* them. Use *among* for a division by more than two, say, the five famished hikers who divided a bag of chips *among* themselves.

- **Ending a sentence with a preposition**

English teachers have fought hard to keep students from ending sentences with prepositions. It's a losing battle, however, because the rule forces you to use antiquated language, as in:

> After the test, we had many things *about* which to talk.

In the twenty-first century, it's far more natural to say:

> After the test, we had many things to talk *about*.

Yet, the restriction against sentence-ending prepositions should be respected. Therefore, a reasonable rule of thumb to follow is: Avoid sentence-ending prepositions unless by doing so you'll end up sounding phony or pompous.

- **The idiomatic use of prepositions**
  Many words go hand in hand with certain prepositions. That's why *wait for the bus* is standard English, whereas *wait on the bus* is not. Yet, you can *wait for a table* or *wait on a table*, depending on whether you intend to eat lunch or serve it. In short, there is no consistent logic why certain words go with certain prepositions. Customary English language simply obliges you to choose your prepositions according to common usage.

  | NONSTANDARD: | Maude stepped *in* a puddle. |
  | STANDARD: | Maude stepped *into* a puddle. |

  | NONSTANDARD: | I sympathize *on* your loss. |
  | STANDARD: | I sympathize *with* your loss. |

Pronouns

Personal Pronouns

Personal pronouns are categorized according to four attributes:

    I. Case
    II. Person
    III. Number
    IV. Gender

I. CASE

A personal pronoun is a word used as a substitute for a common or a proper noun. *He, she,* and *him,* along with *I, me, her, it, they, them, we, us,* and *you* are examples. Most of the time, your ear tells you which pronoun to use. For example, you'd never say to the bus driver, "Let *I* off at the corner." Rather, you'd use *me* without even thinking about it.

Unfortunately, pronoun choice isn't always that simple. For instance, which pronoun—*I* or *me*—should complete this sentence?

> Philip is friendlier than _____ .

Half the people who speak English would probably say *I,* the other half *me.* Which half is correct? Read on, and you'll learn how to figure it out.

When you can't depend on what sounds right, it helps to know that personal pronouns fall into two groups.

Group 1	Group 2
I	me
he	him
she	her
they	them
we	us
you	you

Group 1 words are called subject pronouns and are in the *nominative case.* Group 2 words are called object pronouns and are in the *objective case.* The two types of pronouns are labelled differently because they play different roles in sentences.

1. Nominative case pronouns often serve as sentence subjects—hence, their name *subject pronouns.* They name the people, places, or things that are described by the sentence, as in:

> *She* is wealthy.

They may also refer to the performer of some sort of action, as in:

> *He* turned out the light.

(For details about sentence subjects, turn to page 107.)

It happens that the verbs used in both sample sentences are forms of the verb *to be*, a fact worth noting because *being verbs*—sometimes called **linking** verbs—such as *is, was, were, has been, had been, will be,* and so on, are always paired with subject pronouns, never with object pronouns, even when the pronoun is not the subject of the sentence, as in:

The instructors (subject of sentence) in the course *were* (verb) Donald and *he* (pronoun). *Object* pronouns don't work as sentence subjects because you'll end up saying something like "*Them* are going to be late" or "*Him* and *me* walked to the diner."

2. In contrast to subject pronouns, *object* pronouns refer to people, places, or things being acted upon:

The music carried *them* (object pronoun) away.

He asked *her* (object pronoun) to call him (object pronoun) on his cell phone.

Object pronouns are also used in prepositional phrases—that is, phrases that begin with prepositions, as in: *between you and <u>me</u>, to Sherry and <u>her</u>,* and *from <u>them</u>.*

Using pronouns in comparisons

To find the correct pronoun in a comparison that uses *than* or *as,* complete the comparison by inserting the verb that would follow naturally. [Say the bracketed words silently to yourself.]

Jackie runs faster than *she* [runs].

My brother has bigger feet than *I* [do].

Carol is as tough as *he* [is].

A woman such as *I* [am] could solve the problem.

By now it should be clear which pronoun (*I* or *me*) to use in the sentence

Philip is friendlier than _____

Why is *I* the correct answer? First, because the sentence uses the being verb *is,* and second, a pronoun in the nominative case is needed because the sentence has no purpose other than to describe the speaker. In other words, the speaker is not being acted upon. Therefore, an objective case pronoun—in this case, *me*—is ungrammatical.

Possessive pronouns

Some pronouns, labeled *possessive pronouns,* fall into a third case, called the *possessive* case. Possessive pronouns—*my, mine, his, her, hers, your, yours, our, ours, their,* and *theirs*—indicate ownership, as in *my* hair, *your* sister, *his* house, *their* party, and so on. Such pronouns always answer the question "whose?"

> "Whose cat is that?"
> "It is *hers* (possessive pronoun)."
> "Are you sure?"
> "Well, no, maybe it is *theirs* (possessive pronoun)."

Unlike possessive nouns, possessive pronouns are spelled without apostrophes. Therefore, never write *her's, their's, your's.* And don't confuse the possessive pronoun *its* with its look-alike cousin *it's,* a contraction meaning *it is.*

II. PERSON

Personal pronouns also fall into three additional groups—first person, second person, and third person.

> *First-person* pronouns—*I, we, me, us, mine, our, our*—refer to the speaker(s) or writer(s).

> *Second-person* pronouns—*you, your, yours*—refer to the person, singular or plural, being addressed in speech or writing.

> *Third-person* pronouns—*she, he, it, one, they, him, her, them, his, her, hers, its, their, theirs*—refer to people and things being written or spoken about.

Third-person pronouns also include *indefinite pronouns* such as *all, any, anyone, each, none, nothing, one, several, many,* and others.

III. NUMBER

Still another way to classify pronouns is by their number. Some pronouns are singular: *he, she, it, him, her,* one, etc. Some are plural: *they, them, their,* etc. Still others, such as *you* and *yours,* are sometimes singular and sometimes plural, depending on the context.

IV. GENDER

> Masculine pronouns: *he, his, him*
> Feminine pronouns: *she, her, hers*
> Neuter pronouns: *it, its, they ,their, theirs, them*

Until now, these pages have focused on *personal pronouns*. But pronouns also come in other varieties:

> Relative pronouns
> Reflexive pronouns
> Interrogative pronouns
> Demonstrative pronouns
> Indefinite pronouns

Relative Pronouns

Like all other pronouns, *relative pronouns* (*which*, *that*, *who*, *whom*, *whose*, and *what*) refer to nouns or other pronouns, as in:

> Those are the dishes *that* I washed this morning.

Here the relative pronoun *that* refers to *dishes*. Simple, right? Yes, but that's not quite the end of the story. If you study the sentence some more, you'll see that the word *that* comes before the words *I washed yesterday*—words that describe the dishes. That is, the dishes are not just any dishes but specifically those dishes that the speaker washed yesterday—a detail to keep in mind when choosing between *that* and *which*, two relative pronouns often used interchangeably. Use *that* when the subsequent words define or describe something essential to the meaning of the sentence, as in:

> Those are the dishes *that* need to be put away.

On the other hand, use *which* if the words that follow give information that isn't crucial to the meaning of the sentence as in:

> Those dishes, *which* once belonged to my grandmother, need to be put away.

Here, the fact that the dishes once belonged to the speaker's grandmother is of secondary importance to the main purpose of the sentence.

You should also know that the words that come after relative pronouns are called *relative clauses*. Or, put another way, *relative pronouns* introduce *relative clauses*. For example, here are two sentences with their relative clauses underlined:

1. The store *that* sold used bikes went out of business.
2. The backpack, *which* Belinda takes to school, disappeared.

Notice that sentence 1 contains no punctuation, while sentence 2 uses a comma both before and after the relative clause. The difference is a clue to the importance of the clause to the meaning of the sentence. In the comma-free sentence the clause is essential, but in the other sentence it's not. How a sentence is punctuated, then, indicates whether the relative clause is essential or not to the

meaning of the sentence. If ever you're torn between choosing *that* or *which*, determine whether the relative clause needs to be punctuated with a comma. If so, use *which*; if not, use *that*.

> **TIP**
> Commas precede relative clauses starting with *which* (or one of the other relative pronouns), but not before relative clauses starting with *that*.

Who or *Whom*?
Use the relative pronoun *who* as the grammatical subject of a sentence or as a pronoun that stands for the subject, as in:

> *Who* (subject) ordered a pizza?
> That (subject) is the woman *who* (subject stand-in) ordered it.

Use *whom* following a preposition or when it functions as the object of a verb, as in:

> To (preposition) *whom* should this fish be given?
> The detective found (verb) the thief *whom* he'd been seeking.

While weighing the use of *who* or *whom*, ask yourself whether the pronoun is performing an action. If so, use *who*. If the pronoun is being acted upon, use *whom*. Also, you can depend on prepositions as clues toward correct usage because they are always followed by *whom*, as in *with whom*, *in whom*, *before whom*, *around whom*, *between whom*, and so on.

Who, That, or *Which*?
1. Use *who* and *whom* to refer to people.
2. Use *that* to refer to things, animals, and people, but use *who* when referring to a specific person, as in:

> This is Corporal Powder, *who* fought in the Iraq War.

Either *who* or *that*, however, may be used for more general references, as in:

> Those are the pilots *who* flew the plane./Those are the pilots *that* flew the plane.

Take your pick; both sentences are valid.
3. Use *which* to refer to things and non-human creatures, but never to people.

Reflexive Pronouns

Reflexive pronouns stand out among all other pronouns because they end with *self* (singular form) or *selves* (plural form):

> First person: *myself/ourselves*
> Second person: *yourself/yourselves*
> Third person: *herself, himself, itself/themselves*

Reflexive pronouns refer to the noun or pronoun that is the grammatical subject of the sentence in which they appear:

> We will be going to the city by ourselves.

In this sentence the reflexive pronoun *ourselves* refers to the subject *We*. Because both the subject and the reflexive pronoun must be present in the same sentence, reflexive pronouns can't be subjects:

NONSTANDARD: *Myself* wrote every word of the paper.
STANDARD: *I* (subject) wrote every word of the paper by *myself*.

Nor can they be object pronouns:

NONSTANDARD: Mimi served lunch to Margie and *myself*.
STANDARD: Mimi served lunch to Margie and *me*.

Reflexive pronouns are sometimes called *intensive pronouns* because they are used to emphasize, or intensify, an idea:

Intensive usage: I *myself* will do it. He *himself* was the culprit.
Reflexive usage: I hurt *myself*. They fooled *themselves*.

Interrogative Pronouns

Interrogative pronouns are often called question pronouns. Their antecedents are the answers to whatever question is asked.

> Who is the presiding officer? Answer: Joan (the antecedent).
> What is he carrying? Answer: a suitcase (the antecedent).

Who as an interrogative pronoun is distinguished by case.

Nominative: Who is coming to dinner?
Objective: Whom were you talking to? (object of the preposition)
Possessive: Whose gloves are these?

Demonstrative Pronouns

Demonstrative pronouns, such as *this, these, that*, and *those* also get their name from their function. They point like arrows to nouns, phrases, clauses, and even whole sentences. The pronoun *this* points out an object close by in space (*this notebook*), time (*this year*), and thought, (*this idea of yours*). The pronoun *that*, on the other hand, points to distant objects (*that star, that time, that theory*).

Pronouns

Like other pronouns, demonstrative pronouns need to point to clear antecedents. When a writer or speaker expects too much from the demonstrative pronoun, ambiguity results:

> The zoo features more than 1,500 mammals, reptiles, and birds kept in tiny cages. In the primate area, eleven species of monkeys, gorillas, and apes live in small space no bigger than your average schoolroom. All the animals are fed only twice a day, even though some require nourishment several times in 24 hours. *This* bothers me.

What does *this* refer to? The irregular feeding of some animals? The conditions described throughout the paragraph? It's hard to tell. Fix the problem with a new pronoun and a more specific antecedent:

These (pronoun) conditions (antecedent) bother me.

Indefinite Pronouns

The *indefinite pronouns* are so named because their antecedents are vague or unknown. They are such words as *each, all, either, anyone, everyone, everybody, somebody, nobody*.

Indefinite pronouns and antecedents should agree in number and gender. Yet, the practice of using plural pronouns to refer to singular antecedents is so common, that flouting the rule has almost become the norm:

> Everybody (singular) is sticking to *their* (plural) side of the story.
> Anybody (singular) can be successful if *they* (plural) work hard.
> Neither (singular) candidate plans to change *their* (plural) position on immigration.
> If *someone* (singular) breaks the law, *they* (plural) should be prepared to pay the consequences.

Such agreement errors occur because indefinite pronouns sound plural. But they are and always have been singular. Grammatically worded, therefore, the sentences should be:

> Everybody is sticking to *his* side of the story.
> Anybody can be successful if *he* works hard.
> Neither candidate plans to change *his* position on immigration.
> If *someone* breaks the law, *he* should be prepared to pay the consequences.

Note: Some people object to the use of male pronouns when referring to people who might be of either sex. They prefer the more politically correct phrase "*he or she*," but because seasoned writers regard that usage ungraceful they use gender-neutral plural pronouns, as in:

AWKWARD: During a college interview, a *student* should avoid criticizing *his or her* high school teachers.

REVISED: During a college interview, *students* should avoid criticizing *their* high school teachers.

Or they might simply restructure their sentences to avoid the problem altogether:

A college interview is not a place to criticize high school teachers.

SINGULAR PRONOUNS AFTER TWO OR MORE SINGULAR ANTECEDENTS JOINED BY *or* OR *nor:* When the pronoun refers to only one of two or more from which a selection is to be made, the pronoun is singular.

CORRECT: Either Jack or Pearl is bound to forget *his* appointment.

CORRECT: Neither the train nor the plane can be expected to keep *its* schedule.

SINGULAR PRONOUNS AFTER COLLECTIVE NOUNS THE SENSE OF WHICH IS SINGULAR: Many nouns like *army, class, committee, group,* refer to more than one person, place, or thing. When such a group is considered as a single unit, as is usual, pronouns referring to the unit should be singular, neuter in gender.

CORRECT: The class elected *its* officers at the end of the term.

CORRECT: An army marches on *its* stomach.

Only when a group is thought of as made up of many individuals should a plural pronoun be used.

CORRECT: The choir sang *their* different parts perfectly.

FEMININE PRONOUNS FOR SOME NEUTER ANTECEDENTS: Traditionally, a few inanimate and actually sexless things have been referred to as feminine: ships, airplanes, nations, colleges. Hurricanes are now both masculine and feminine. Neuter pronouns are correct when referring to such antecedents, but feminine pronouns are sometimes used.

CORRECT: The plane took off for *its* second flight that day.

CORRECT: The plane took off for *her* second flight that day.

AN IMPOSSIBLE SITUATION: SINGULAR AND PLURAL ANTECEDENTS JOINED BY *or* OR *nor:* When there are two possible antecedents, one of which is singular and the other plural, English offers no grammatical solution.

EXAMPLE: Either the *boy* or his *parents* have lost *his? their?* mind.

The only escape from such a dilemma is to recast the sentence.

SOLUTION: Either the *boy* has lost *his* mind or his *parents* are out of *their* wits.

Pronouns

Pronoun Reference Problems

Since a pronoun has no meaning without an antecedent, it is important that the antecedent of every pronoun be clearly stated and unmistakable. Apart from such obvious idiomatic usage as "*It* is raining" or the deliberate indefiniteness of "*They* say . . ." or the lazy vagueness of "Why don't *they* repair this sidewalk?" or a conversational situation where the antecedent is obvious ("It won't start."), the exact antecedent of every pronoun must be made clear.

AVOID AMBIGUOUS REFERENCE: Be sure that a pronoun cannot be taken to refer to more than one possible antecedent.

AMBIGUOUS: My mother told our maid that *she* had made a mistake.
QUESTION: Who made a mistake? *She* could refer to *mother* or *maid*.
SOLUTION: My mother scolded our maid for making a mistake.
SOLUTION: My mother said to our maid, "You have made a mistake."

AVOID REMOTE REFERENCE: Be sure that a pronoun is reasonably close to its antecedent.

REMOTE: The curtain rose on *Carmen* which is a very popular opera with lively music, a colorful cast of characters, and a large chorus. *It* is made of a heavy brocade.
PROBLEM: The *it* is so far from its antecedent *curtain* that the reader is put to unnecessary effort in clarifying the meaning of the pronoun.
SOLUTION: The *curtain, which* is made of a heavy brocade, rose . . .

AVOID INDEFINITE REFERENCE: Be sure that a pronoun has a definite antecedent instead of a vague idea.

VAGUE: He played golf all morning and tennis all afternoon *which* was probably bad for his health.
SOLUTION: He played golf all morning and tennis all afternoon. So much exertion was bad for his health.
VAGUE: They asked me to join them at six o'clock in the morning, but *this* is something I can't stand.
SOLUTION: They asked me to join them at six o'clock in the morning, but early rising is something I can't stand.

AVOID REFERENCE TO A NOUN IN THE POSSESSIVE CASE: However clear such reference may be, usage of this kind constitutes slovenly English.

EXAMPLE: Goethe's *Faust* has been called the epic of modern man. *He* was particularly fitted to write such an epic because of his extraordinarily broad experiences.
SOLUTION: Goethe's *Faust* has been called the epic of modern man. *Goethe* was particularly . . .

Commas

MAXIM: *When in doubt, leave it out.* This well-known maxim makes relatively good sense because most uncertain punctuators annoy their readers by scattering commas at random through their writings.

A BETTER MAXIM: *Master the few definite principles of correct comma usage.*

COMMAS TO SEPARATE PARTS OF A SERIES: When the parts of a series are not joined by a connecting word like *and* or *or*, commas keep the parts of the series apart.

She was tall, young, beautiful.

The last term of any series is usually preceded by the conjunction *and* or *or*. The conjunction takes the place of a comma, but since it is not unusual for an *and* to occur within one element of the series, careful writers place a comma before the final *and* or *or* to indicate the termination of the series.

A SERIES WITH *and*'s:	For breakfast he had orange juice, ham and eggs, toast and butter, and coffee.
A SERIES WITH *or*'s:	When he invested his money, he had choices of buying common or preferred stock, safe or speculative stock, or corporate or municipal bonds.
A SERIES OF WORDS:	This bus goes to Trenton, Baltimore, and Washington.
A SERIES OF PHRASES:	They ran into the house, through the living room, and up to his room.
A SERIES OF VERBS:	He combed his hair, put on a clean shirt, and went to the party.
A SERIES OF CLAUSES:	The food was good, the service was excellent, and the dinner-music was enchanting.
A SERIES OF ADJECTIVES:	It was a big, ugly, unfriendly dog.

NOTE: Frequently a single adjective modifying a noun is so much a part of the identification that the adjective-noun is thought of as a single word: *oak tree, dress shirt, straw hat*. Whenever such combinations are thought of as units, no comma is required to separate a preceding adjective: *tall oak tree, dirty dress shirt, old straw hat*. Similarly, when an adjective is used only for identification, it is felt to be part of the noun: She wore her old *red dress*. If the intention is to emphasize the color of the dress instead of merely identifying it, a comma is used: *her old, red dress*.

COMMA TO SEPARATE THE CLAUSES OF A COMPOUND SENTENCE: In a compound sentence all but very short clauses joined by a coordinating conjunction are separated by a comma immediately preceding the conjunction (*and, but, or, nor, for, yet, so, whereas*).

COMPOUND SENTENCE:	My father was born and raised on a large farm in New England, and I learned a great deal about rural life from him.
COMPOUND SENTENCE:	I have been studying French for the last seven years, so I am sure that I shall feel at home in Paris.
SHORT CLAUSES:	He wrote to me and I answered his letter.

COMMA TO SEPARATE AN INTERJECTION OR TERM OF DIRECT ADDRESS: When a word or phrase is clearly not a part of the structure of a sentence, separate it from the sentence by a comma; by two commas if necessary.

INTERJECTION:	*Hello*, I didn't expect to see you.
INTERJECTION:	*Oh no*, you can't expect me to do that!
INTERJECTION:	He's going to be late again, *darn it!*
DIRECT ADDRESS:	*John*, come over here at once!
DIRECT ADDRESS:	That vegetable soup, *Mother*, is delicious!

COMMA TO SET OFF A SENTENCE MODIFIER: Instead of modifying a single word, a sentence modifier modifies the whole sentence in which it occurs because it usually refers the sense of the entire sentence to something preceding that sentence. Common sentence modifiers are *however, moreover, therefore, nevertheless, furthermore, in addition, on the other hand, on the contrary.*

> He made no effort to take care of his health. *Nevertheless*, he was never sick.
> She cooked all the meals, kept the house clean, and raised four children. *In addition*, she was a member of three clubs.
> Banks observe a shorter business day than almost any other kind of commercial operation. Bankers, *on the other hand*, often work longer than other businessmen.

Another kind of sentence modifier is the absolute phrase, made up of a noun or pronoun and a participle.

ABSOLUTE PHRASE:	*The sun having risen*, we set forth on our journey.
ABSOLUTE PHRASE:	It seemed entirely reasonable, *things being what they were*, to expect a disastrous outcome of the affair.

COMMA AFTER A LONG PHRASE OR A CLAUSE PRECEDING THE SUBJECT: Since the subject of a sentence is usually expected at the beginning, any phrase or clause of more than five words which precedes the subject is ended with a comma to assist the reader in determining the subject.

LONG PHRASE:	*After a long afternoon of tedious debate*, the meeting was adjourned.

LONG CLAUSE: *When I think of all the things I might have done*, I feel very discouraged.

COMMAS TO INDICATE INTERRUPTIONS OF NORMAL WORD ORDER: When unexpected or interrupted word order occurs, commas are very helpful to the reader.

UNEXPECTED: The chaplain, loved and respected by all, went to his rest.

COMMENT: Adjectives (*loved*, *respected*) usually precede the word they modify.

INTERRUPTION: The price of the eggs, *ninety cents a dozen*, was exhorbitant.

INTERRUPTION: He was lazy and shiftless and, *to put it bluntly*, untrustworthy.

COMMAS TO SET OFF NONRESTRICTIVE ELEMENTS: Any word, phrase, or clause that is not essential to the meaning of a sentence is called nonrestrictive. Such elements may be highly informative, but the fact that they are not essential is indicated by setting them off with commas.

RESTRICTIVE: Fielding's novel *Tom Jones* was made into a motion picture.

COMMENT: Since Fielding wrote more than one novel, the title, *Tom Jones*, is essential in this sentence.

NONRESTRICTIVE: Dante's epic, *The Divine Comedy*, is an undisputed masterpiece.

COMMENT: Dante wrote only one epic. Supplying its name is useful but not essential.

RESTRICTIVE: The people *who came by train* missed the first race.

COMMENT: No commas because *who came by train* is obviously essential to the meaning.

NONRESTRICTIVE: The people, *who came by train*, enjoyed their vacations at the summer resort.

NOTE: By the use of commas, the writer makes clear whether the word, phrase, or clause in question is intended to be restrictive or not. The preceding sentence implies that everybody came by train. The information is added but it is not essential. If some people came by other means of transportation and only the people who came by train enjoyed their vacations, the commas should not be used.

COMMAS TO EMPHASIZE CONTRASTS: If one part of the meaning of a sentence is in contrast to the other, a comma emphasizes the contrast.

CONTRAST: She was beautifully, yet inexpensively dressed.

CONTRAST: The singing was noisy, not melodious.

CONTRAST: They ran to the dock, but found that the boat had left.

COMMAS TO PREVENT MISREADING: Occasionally, a comma is used when none of the above principles is involved, but when it is helpful to avoid possible confusion on the part of the reader.

MOMENTARY POSSIBLE CONFUSION:	"Whatever is, is right."
COMMENT:	If Pope had omitted the comma from this famous quotation, the reader might have been momentarily troubled by the repetition of *is*.
MOMENTARY CONFUSION:	During the winter nights become longer.
INSTANTLY CLARIFIED:	During the winter, nights become longer.

Conventional Comma Usages

There are a few comma usages that have been established by convention. These are entirely arbitrary.

After the salutation of an informal letter: *Dear John,   Dear Mr. Smith, Dear Mrs. Jones,*

After the complimentary close of a letter: *Yours truly,   Sincerely, With love,*

Separating dates of the month from the year: *July 16, 1948*

Separating parts of an address: *Mrs. Andrew Clark,   142 South Street, New Lebanon, Indiana, 10765*

Separating numbered or lettered divisions or subdivisions: *Book VII, Canto 42, Stanza 17; Section B, 4, d*

Separating distinguishing titles from names: *John J. Darcy, Jr. Jacob Elson, M.D.*

Separating thousands in large figures: *7,639,420*

Placed before introductory words and abbreviations such as i.e., e.g.:   *Some colleges are coeducational, for example, Cornell. Some books need to be digested, i.e., they must be read slowly and thoughtfully.*

Pitfalls in Comma Usage

THE COMMA SPLICE: Don't separate two sentences or two independent clauses by using a comma.

INCORRECT:	The robins came early that spring, the weather was unusually warm.
CORRECT:	The robins came early that spring. The weather was unusually warm.

CORRECT: The robins came early that spring; the weather was unusually warm.

THE COMMA INTERRUPTER: Don't interrupt a natural flow of thought with a comma.

INCORRECT: The many hours of painstaking effort that she spent in completing her term paper, were rewarded when it was highly praised.

CORRECT: The many hours of painstaking effort that she spent in completing her term paper were rewarded when it was highly praised.

INCORRECT: He said, that he was anxious to see me.

CORRECT: He said that he was anxious to see me.

THE MISPLACED COMMA: Place a comma before, not after, the coordinating conjunction in a compound sentence.

INCORRECT: The architects drew excellent plans for the building but, the builder was unwilling to follow them.

CORRECT: The architects drew excellent plans for the building, but the builder was unwilling to follow them.

THE MISTAKEN COMMA: Do not mistake a compound predicate for a compound sentence. A compound predicate does not require a comma.

INCORRECT: The doctor spent the entire day driving about town, and was able to visit nearly all his patients.

CORRECT: The doctor spent the entire day driving about town and was able to visit nearly all his patients.

CORRECT: The doctor spent the entire day driving about town, and he was able to visit nearly all his patients. [compound sentence]

Terminal Punctuation

THE PERIOD: If a sentence is not a question or an exclamation, it should always be terminated by a period.

> There are forty students in the room. [statement]
> I asked if she was ready. [indirect question]
> Please write to me. [request or command]

Even when a sentence is not involved, the period is used for terminal purposes.

> Hello. I am delighted to see you.

In an enumerated list:

1. The Manager
2. The Foremen
3. The Workers

The period is used to terminate most abbreviations: *Mr.*, *Mrs.*, *Rev.*, *Mass.*, *i.e.*, *etc.*

Three spaced periods are used to indicate the omission of one or more words or sentences in a quotation:

"In the beginning God created . . . the earth."

When the omission occurs after the end of a sentence, the three spaced periods are added after the period which terminates the sentence.

"The Lord is my shepherd. . . . Surely, goodness and mercy . . ."

THE QUESTION MARK: The question mark is used to terminate a direct question:

Where are you going? Why? You are? May I come with you?

The question mark enclosed in parentheses is used to indicate uncertainty or doubt.

He was born in 1914 (?) and died in 1967.

THE EXCLAMATION MARK: The exclamation mark is used to emphasize a strong expression of feeling.

Never! I will never sign that document!
Don't you dare take the car without my permission!

Semicolons and Colons

The semicolon is used to separate the clauses in a compound sentence when they are not joined by a coordinating conjunction.

The judge instructed the jury; the jurors listened patiently.
The professor was an expert in his subject; nevertheless, he was a dull lecturer.

Since the semicolon is a stronger punctuation mark than the comma, it is sometimes used to separate parts of a series when commas are included within one or more of the parts.

She bought a rib roast of beef, ten lamb chops, and a pound of liver at the butcher shop; potatoes, apples, and oranges at the grocery store; and tooth paste and hand lotion at the drug store.

The colon is usually the signal for introducing a list. It is frequently used after such words as *as follows* or *following*.

> The following members of the committee were present: James Anderson, Mary Montgomery, Nelson Danforth, John Winters, and Sarah Dunn.

> The most important rules of this organization are:

> 1. Attendance is required at two-thirds of the regular meetings.
> 2. Dues must be paid during the first month of every year.
> 3. All members must be willing to serve on committees.

The colon is used after the salutation of a business letter: *Gentlemen*: *Dear Sirs*: *My dear Mr. Holstead*:

The colon is used to divide subdivisions from major divisions when indicating the time of day [7:25], or when making references to Biblical passages [Genesis 12:2].

Dashes, Hyphens, and Apostrophes

THE DASH: The dash indicates a sudden, and usually unexpected, break in the anticipated sequence of thought. Printing a dash requires clicking "insert," then "symbol," then "special characters," and "insert" on "em dash." Often, to avoid this time-consuming procedure, two connected hyphens are used (- -).

> I believed that my country—but why should I have believed it?—was always right.

The dash can be used to indicate hesitation or a suspension or breaking off of thought.

> I always wanted to—. But it's too late now to want anything.

The dash sometimes separates parenthetical material from the main body of a sentence.

> His hopeless condition—it seemed hopeless at the time—caused his wife intolerable anguish.

The dash is useful to indicate that a remark at the end of a sentence has been inserted as an afterthought, sometimes with ironic effect.

> The president of the firm was a man of absolute integrity—or so it seemed to the stockholders before the firm collapsed.

The dash is used for lists in apposition to avoid confusion.

> She invited her cousins—Albert, Arthur, and Englebert—for a visit.

Punctuation

THE HYPHEN: The hyphen is used to make a compound word out of two or more words that are to be thought of as a single unit.

> The 1990–91 academic year
> The Princeton-Yale game
> A blue-green dress
> He played a better-than-average game.

The hyphen is used where a word must be broken (hyphenated) at the end of a line because there is not enough space to write, type, or print all of it. Words must not be divided arbitrarily; they may be hyphenated only between syllables. Syllables are the parts of a word that are pronounced as units. When in doubt about correct hyphenation, consult a good dictionary.

> Samuel Johnson, who was an outstanding literary figure of the eighteenth century in England, was known as the great lexicographer. He compiled the first real English dictionary.

The hyphen is sometimes required to eliminate misreading when a prefix ends with the same letter as the initial letter of the word to which it is added.

> re-estimate   co-ownership   de-escalate

The hyphen is used in compound numbers from twenty-one to ninety-nine.

The hyphen is used to separate dates of birth and death: James Finch (1714–1778); scores of games: Princeton-Dartmouth, 78–67; and similar opposing or terminal relationships: Nearly everything goes in pairs: sun-moon, day-night, man-woman, winter-summer.

THE APOSTROPHE: The apostrophe is used to indicate the possessive case of a noun. Add the apostrophe and *s* to words that do not end with an *s* or *z* sound. Add only the apostrophe to words that end with an *s* or *z* sound:

> *the boy's room*   *the children's school*
> *the boys' room*   *Dickens' novels*

EXCEPTION: In singular one-syllable nouns ending in the *s* or *z* sound, it is customary to add the apostrophe and *s* and to pronounce the possessive as if it ended in *es: the boss's hat.*

The apostrophe is used to indicate missing letters in a contraction:

> *He's* ready to join us. [He is]
> Martha *can't* be with us. [cannot]

The apostrophe is used to form plurals of letters or symbols when simply adding an *s* could cause confusion.

> Remember to dot your i's.

Parentheses and Brackets

Parentheses ( ) and brackets [ ] are both used to exclude extraneous or inter-rupting material from a sentence or from a paragraph.

PARENTHESES: Parentheses are used to enclose anything that interrupts the sense of what is being written.

> I was born in 1906. (That was the year of the San Francisco earthquake.)
> I met my future wife (my first date, incidentally) at a high school dance.
> The dam was built (1) to provide water for irrigation, (2) to prevent flooding, and (3) to provide power for the generation of electricity.
> His seventh novel, *The Errant Wife* (1836), was a failure.

BRACKETS: Brackets are used only to enclose additions by an editor of any kind of quoted material.

> "The composer [Brahms] was frequently entertained by the nobility."
> "Jonathan Swift [1667–1745] lived during the War of the Spanish Succession."

Quotation Marks

QUOTATION MARKS TO INDICATE TITLES: Quotation marks should enclose titles of short pieces such as essays, articles in magazines, chapters in books, short stories, one-act plays, short musical compositions, short poems, etc.

> "The Afternoon of a Faun" [short musical composition]
> "The Killers" [short story]
> "Ode to the West Wind" [short poem]

NOTE: Titles of lengthier works are placed in italics, indicated by underlining in typed or handwritten material: Shakespeare's *Macbeth*.

DIRECT QUOTATIONS: The exact words of a quotation, spoken or written, should be placed in quotation marks. A paraphrase of what someone spoke or wrote (indi-rect quotation) does not require and should not be indicated by quotation marks.

DIRECT:	She said, "I am not going to wait for my husband."
INDIRECT:	She said that she wasn't going to wait for her husband.
DIRECT:	Dickens introduces his novel *David Copperfield* by saying, "Whether I shall turn out to be the hero of my own life, or whether that station will be held by anybody else, these pages must show."

INDIRECT: Dickens introduces his novel *David Copperfield* by saying that the pages that follow will show whether he will be the hero of his own life or whether that position will be held by somebody else.

OTHER PUNCTUATION MARKS WITH DIRECT QUOTATIONS: In the reporting of speech or dialogue, reference to the speaker (*I said, he answered*) are separated from the quotation by a comma. Two commas are required if the reference to the speaker is inserted within the quotation.

> "Let me know where I can reach you," I said.
> "I'm not at all sure," she replied, "that I want you to reach me."
> I answered abruptly, "Then don't bother."

The comma is omitted if a question mark or an exclamation mark is required where the comma would ordinarily be placed.

> "Why can't you finish your dinner?" I asked.
> "I refuse to see anybody!" he shouted.

If the quotation consists of more than one sentence, only one sentence is joined by a comma to the reference to the speaker.

> "I have come home after a long journey," he said. "I want to rest."

QUOTATIONS OTHER THAN DIALOGUE: When quoting printed or written subject-matter, reproduce the punctuation and capitalization of what is quoted exactly as it originally appeared.

> Benjamin Franklin believed that "A penny saved is a penny earned."
> The author expressed "a sinking feeling about our domestic problems."

If the quotation is longer than one paragraph, no end-quotation marks are placed at the conclusion of the first paragraph. All succeeding paragraphs are prefaced by quotation marks, but only the final paragraph is concluded with end-quotation marks.

In the following excerpt from Cervantes' *Don Quixote*, notice that only at the end of the third paragraph are the end-quotation marks used.

> "While Don Quixote was singing a ballad about the noble Marquis of Mantua, a neighbor from his own village happened to come along. Amazed at the appearance of Don Quixote and wondering about the sadness of his song, he asked what was the matter with him.
>
> "Don Quixote was firmly persuaded that this was the Marquis of Mantua so his only answer was to go on singing his ballad.

"The neighbor was amazed at such nonsense, and taking off Don Quixote's helmet, he recognized him as Senor Don Quixada which had been his real name when he was still possessed of his senses."

Long quotations (five lines or more) from writings are not usually enclosed in quotation marks. They are indicated as quotations by being indented at both right and left sides. Smaller typeface is customary for printed matter and single spacing for typescript.

Charles Dickens' *Child's History of England* is written in a very simple and vivid style. As a way of delineating the character of Oliver Cromwell, Dickens describes Cromwell's leadership of the Irish campaign:

> Oliver had been appointed by the Parliament to command the army in Ireland, where he took a terrible vengeance for the sanguinary rebellion, and made tremendous havoc, particularly in the siege of Drogheda, where no quarter was given, and where he found at least a thousand of the inhabitants shut up together in the great church, every one of whom was killed by his soldiers, usually known as Oliver's Ironsides. There were numbers of friars and priests among them; and Oliver gruffly wrote home in his dispatch that these were "knocked on the head" like the rest.

QUOTATIONS WITHIN QUOTATIONS: Single quotation marks are used to set off a quotation within another quotation.

"Have you read Poe's 'Ulalume' lately?" I asked.
At the trial the star witness testified, "On the night of the murder I distinctly heard Mrs. Knox say, 'I would give anything to get him out of the way.'"

QUOTATION MARKS RELATED TO OTHER PUNCTUATION: Without regard to logic, periods and commas are always placed inside quotation marks; colons and semicolons are always placed outside quotation marks.

"They insisted that I go with them," she said. "So I did."
There are four characters in the Brome "Abraham and Isaac": God, the angel, Abraham, and Isaac.
He glanced rapidly through Frost's "Mending Wall"; he was in a hurry to finish his assignment.

Other punctuation marks are placed where they logically belong: inside the quotation marks if they punctuate the quotation, outside if they punctuate the entire sentence of which the quotation is a part.

What is the theme of Longfellow's "Excelsior"?
She inquired, "Is this the road to Denver?"
Don't let me catch you reading "The Love Song of Alfred Prufrock"!
As he fell off the dock, the child screamed, "Help!"

PUNCTUATION OF DIALOGUE: When a dialogue between two or more persons is set down (usually in a story or novel), a new paragraph is used for each new speaker. Descriptive or other matter relevant to the speaker is placed in the same paragraph as the quotation. When only two speakers are involved, the alternation of paragraphs makes it unnecessary to identify the speaker every time and so permits the dialogue to proceed more rapidly and without interruption.

"Herbert," said I, after a short silence, in a hurried way, "can you see me best by the light of the window, or the light of the fire?"

"By the firelight," answered Herbert, coming close again.

"Look at me."

"I do look at you, my dear boy."

"Touch me."

"I do touch you, my dear boy."

"You are not afraid that I am in any fever, or that my head is much disordered by the accident of last night?"

"N-no, my dear boy," said Herbert, after taking time to examine me. "You are rather excited, but you are quite yourself."

—Charles Dickens, *Great Expectations*

A sentence is a group of words that makes sense. It says something definite. It must contain a verb because the verb is the asserting word. It ends with a period (.), a question mark (?), or an exclamation mark (!). A sentence can be made of only one word if that word is a verb: *Go!* On the other hand, many words even if they are related to each other cannot form a sentence without a verb: *all the friends of my family in their best clothes and on their best behavior.* What *about* all the friends of my family, etc., etc.?

THE SUBJECT: The subject is what is being talked or written about.

> *She* is sick.
> *The clever student* completed the test before all the others.

The simple subject is the basic word, usually a noun or a pronoun. The complete subject is the simple subject together with any modifiers it may have. In the sentence above, *student* is the simple subject; *the clever student* is the complete subject. In the following sentence *dispute* is the simple subject; the complete subject is italicized:

> *A lengthy dispute about wages and hours of employment* led to a strike.

In an interrogative sentence, the subject is the person, place, or thing about whom or which the question is being asked.

> Is *my book* lying on the table?

If in doubt, you can usually find the subject of such a sentence by answering the question: *My book* is lying on the table.

When talking directly to another person or persons (*you*), the subject is frequently omitted because it is understood.

> [You] Come to the table. Dinner is getting cold.

A compound subject contains two or more subjects joined by coordinating or correlative conjunctions.

> *The boys* and *the girls* played nicely together.
> *Dogs, cats, goats,* and *mules* were all over the street.
> Neither *an apartment in the city* nor *a house in the country* could serve to keep him happy.

THE PREDICATE: Everything in a sentence besides the complete subject is the predicate. It says whatever there is to be said about the subject. In an interrogative sentence it asks the question.

> The house *was falling apart because nobody lived in it any longer.*
> *Why is* the house *falling apart?*

The simple predicate is the principal verb of the sentence (*was falling*). All the other words except the complete subject constitute the complete predicate.

A compound predicate contains two or more predicates joined by coordinating or correlative conjunctions.

> He *eats* and *drinks* heartily every day.
>
> My friends either *go to Europe on their vacations* or *stay at home in their air-conditioned apartments.*

PHRASES: Phrases are closely joined groups of words that function in sentences as single parts of speech.

A prepositional phrase contains a preposition, the object of the preposition, and often modifiers of the object. The whole phrase functions as an adjective or an adverb.

> The man *in the blue suit* worked *at the bank.*

In this sentence, *in the blue suit* is an adjective phrase modifying *man*; *at the bank* is an adverbial phrase modifying *worked.*

A participial phrase contains a participle and either a complement or one or more modifiers or both.

> *Happily singing an old familiar song*, he wandered down the country road.

This is a present participial phrase used as an adjective to modify *he*. *Singing* is the present participle. *Happily* is an adverb modifying *singing*. The remainder of the phrase is the complement of *singing*.

> *Driven into a corner by the dog*, the cat hissed defiance.

This is a past participial phrase used as an adjective to modify *cat*. *Driven* is the past participle. *Into the corner* and *by the dog* are prepositional phrases modifying *driven.*

An infinitive phrase contains an infinitive and possible modifiers or an object or both. It functions as a noun, an adjective, or an adverb.

> *To live a good life* was his only ambition.

Functioning as a noun, this phrase is the subject of the verb *was*. *To live* is the infinitive. *Life* is the object of the infinitive. A and *good* are adjectives modifying *life.*

> She had a lifetime ambition *to live in style.*

This is an adjective phrase modifying *ambition* (describing her ambition). *In style* is an adverbial prepositional phrase modifying the infinitive.

> It was much too cold *to go outdoors.*

This is an adverbial phrase modifying the adjective *cold*. *Outdoors* is an adverb modifying the infinitive.

A verb phrase is any group of verbal units that functions as a single verb.

I *can do* it.   You *should be* happily *married*.

A gerund phrase is introduced by a gerund and acts as a noun.

Flying a kite is easy at the seashore.

Flying is the gerund. *Kite* is its object. The phrase is the subject of the sentence.

CLAUSES: A clause is a group of words containing a subject and a predicate. It is not a sentence only because it is part of a sentence and so is not complete in itself. An independent clause (sometimes called a main clause) is one that could stand by itself and be written as a sentence.

I am always late to dinner because the bus is so slow.

A dependent (or subordinate) clause cannot stand alone because it depends on something else in the complete sentence.

I am always late to dinner *because the bus is so slow*.

Since they depend on something else in the sentence, dependent clauses function as nouns, adjectives, or adverbs.

Noun Clauses

He hoped *that he would pass the course*. (object of verb *hoped*)
Why he did it was not clear to anybody. (subject of verb *was*)

Adjective Clauses

The money *that I lost* was quickly replaced. (modifies noun *money*)
I admire a person *who knows his way around*. (modifies noun *person*)

Adverbial Clauses

He was pleased *that he could master the problem*. (modifies adjective *pleased*)
She cried *when he went away*. (modifies verb *cried*)

TYPES OF SENTENCES: A simple sentence is the same as an independent clause standing alone. It actually contains no clauses:

They all enjoyed their trip to Canada.

A complex sentence is composed of one independent clause and one or more dependent clauses. The dependent clauses are italicized in the following complex sentences:

The opera, *which was written by Wagner*, didn't end until midnight.
While I was waiting for the train, an old man *who reminded me of my grandfather* entertained me with stories of people *who had lived in the neighborhood years ago*.

A compound sentence contains two or more independent clauses and no dependent clauses. Numbers in parentheses indicate the beginnings of the clauses in the following sentences:

(1) The flowers were blooming, (2) the birds were singing, (3) and spring was in the air.
(1) There is one important rule in this factory: (2) haste makes waste.
(1) Lord Gladstone rose to speak; (2) the house listened attentively.

A compound-complex sentence contains two or more independent clauses and one or more dependent clauses. In the following sentences, the dependent clauses are italicized:

Men *who are wise* are often mistaken, and fools are sometimes right.
The captain, *who was standing on the bridge*, thought he saw a shape looming ahead in the fog, but it turned out to be only an illusion *that fooled his tired eyes*.

Sentences that ask questions are *interrogative*.

PRESENT TENSE:	*Is* he *coming* to dinner?
	Does he *know* the way?
	May I *borrow* your eraser?
	What *do* they *have* for breakfast?
FUTURE TENSE:	*Will* he *come* to dinner?
	What *will* they *have* for breakfast?
PAST TENSE:	*Was* he *eating* his dinner?
	Did he *know* the way?
	What *did* they *have* for breakfast?
PRESENT PERFECT TENSE:	*Has* he *eaten* his dinner?
	Have I *finished* the assignment?
PAST PERFECT TENSE:	*Had* he *eaten* his dinner?
	Had I *finished* the assignment?
FUTURE PERFECT TENSE:	*Will* he *have eaten* his dinner?
	Shall I *have finished* the assignment?

Idiomatic question after statement:

He won't be here after all, *will he*?
They have all gone to the movies, *haven't they*?

In phrasing a question, put the subject after the verb.

Have *you* any money?	(subject of verb *have*)
Was the *train* on time?	(subject of verb *was*)
Is there a *doctor* in the house?	(subject of verb *is*)

A declarative sentence used as a question is so indicated by a rising voice inflection in speaking or by a question mark in writing.

> You believe that I am not telling the truth?

Sometimes a declarative sentence is followed by a question phrased in the negative.

> She has a lovely voice, hasn't she?
> The shirt is very dirty, isn't it?

Pitfalls in Sentence Construction

Do not write a "sentence" without a finite verb.

WRONG: All the little children miserable and poor and hungry.
CORRECT: All the little children *were* miserable and poor and hungry.

Do not omit any part of a finite verb.

WRONG: All the little children singing and dancing in the garden.
CORRECT: All the little children *were* singing and dancing in the garden.

Do not write a dependent clause without a complete independent clause in the same sentence.

WRONG: No point in doing anything if nothing could be done about it.
CORRECT: *There was* no point in doing anything if nothing could be done about it.

Do not consider an infinitive phrase to be a complete sentence.

WRONG: To visit every famous museum in the world and take my time in every one.
CORRECT: To visit every famous museum in the world and take my time in every one *is my ambition*.

Do not mistake a prepositional phrase for a complete sentence.

WRONG: Over the hills and dales and mountains and valleys.
CORRECT: He roamed over the hills and dales and mountains and valleys.

Do not separate one part of a compound predicate from the sentence in which it belongs.

WRONG: The weary clerk finally completed the tally of all his accounts. And then went home for a good meal and a long night's sleep.

CORRECT: The weary clerk finally completed the tally of all his accounts and then went home for a good meal and a long night's sleep.

Do not combine two sentences into one by attempting to make a single word do double duty.

WRONG: It is difficult to explain what he came for he was extremely bewildered about everything.

CORRECT: It is difficult to explain what he came for. For he was extremely bewildered about everything.

BETTER: It is difficult to explain what he came for because he was extremely bewildered about everything.

Agreement of Subject and Verb

A singular subject requires a singular form of the verb.
A plural subject requires a plural form of the verb.

SINGULAR PRONOUNS: Even when the sense of the subject seems to be plural, the following pronouns are singular: *each, every, everybody, anybody, anyone, nobody, no one, someone, either, neither.*

CORRECT: Everybody *is coming* to the party.
   Neither of the two sisters *is* really attractive.

With *some, most,* and *none,* a singular verb is used when the sense is a single quantity. Use a plural verb when a number of individual units seem to be implied.

CORRECT: Most of the sugar *is* stored in the warehouse.
   Most of the apples *are* rotten.
   None of the cereal *has* been eaten.
   None of the guests *are* going to stay all night.

COMPOUND SUBJECTS: When the parts of a compound subject are joined by *and,* the verb must be plural because at least two subjects are involved.

CORRECT: The house and the barn *are* for sale.
CORRECT: The captain and his men *are* ready to set sail.
CORRECT: The men and their captain *are* ready to set sail.

When the parts of a compound subject are joined by *either... or* or *neither... nor*, the verb agrees with the part of the compound subject which is nearest to it.

CORRECT: Either the whole engine or some of its parts *are* defective.

CORRECT: Neither the students nor the instructor *agrees* with the principal.

NOTE: The sentence usually sounds better if the plural noun is second, allowing a plural verb.

PROBLEMS WITH SINGULAR-PLURAL NOUNS AS SUBJECTS: Some nouns like *committee, crew, jury, club* are sometimes singular and sometimes plural in meaning. Use a singular verb if all the members of the named group are acting as a unit. Use a plural verb if they are being thought of as individuals.

CORRECT: The club *meets* every Friday.

CORRECT: The jury *find* themselves in disagreement.

As a general principle, use a singular verb if the form of the noun is singular. If the sense is plural, it is usually less awkward to substitute another noun.

CORRECT: The *jurors* find themselves in disagreement.

CORRECT: The *members of the jury* find themselves in disagreement.

SUBJECTS SEPARATED FROM OR FOLLOWING VERBS: Use special care when the subject does not immediately precede the verb. Be sure the verb agrees with the subject wherever it appears in the sentence.

WRONG: The *house* which is surrounded by junkyards and filling stations *are* going to be sold.

CORRECT: The *house*, which is surrounded by junkyards and filling stations, *is* going to be sold.

WRONG: The *leader* together with his twenty followers *are* approaching the town.

CORRECT: The *leader*, together with his twenty followers, *is* approaching the town.

WRONG: How many coats, shoes, and dresses *do she* own?

CORRECT: How many coats, shoes, and dresses *does she* own?

WRONG: There *is* too many *cars* in the city streets.

CORRECT: There *are* too many *cars* in the city streets.

NOTE: *There* is called an expletive. It is not to be confused with the subject although it usually immediately precedes the verb. When a sentence is introduced by *there*, the verb nearly always precedes the subject.

THE PROBLEM WITH NUMBER WHEN A PREDICATE NOMINATIVE IS INVOLVED: On rare occasions the subject of a sentence and the predicate nominative may not agree in number. Nevertheless, the verb must agree with the subject in number. The sentence generally sounds better if the plural noun is used as the subject.

CORRECT: Our greatest *asset is* the many loyal customers who buy regularly from us.

BETTER: Our many loyal *customers are* our greatest asset.

Clarity in Sentence Construction

A good sentence is a tightly constructed sentence where the meaning is unmistakably clear. To avoid flabby sentences keep all modifiers close to the words they modify and be sure that no modifier is left without a definite word to modify.

WATCH OUT FOR DANGLING PHRASES: Such phrases are called *dangling* because they are connected to nothing. The writer knows what they refer to and the reader can usually guess, but the reader will know that he is reading the work of an inept writer.

DANGLING: Driving through the rain, the street lights were scarcely visible.

AMUSED READER: Were the street lights driving a car or a bus?

TIGHTENED: Driving through the rain, I could hardly see the street lights.

DANGLING: To learn how to care for pets, hamsters are ideal to begin with.

AMUSED READER: I didn't know that hamsters had pets.

TIGHTENED: To learn how to care for pets, children should begin with hamsters.

WATCH OUT FOR REMOTE MODIFIERS:

REMOTE: He said that he was willing to sign the contract *yesterday*.

COMMENT: Clear if *yesterday* is meant to apply to the signing of the contract, but misleading if the intended meaning was that he made the remark *yesterday*.

TIGHTENED: He said yesterday that he was willing to sign the contract.

REMOTE: He took two aspirin tablets to cure his headache which made him feel much better.

COMMENT: If his headache made him feel much better, why did he want to cure it?

TIGHTENED: To cure his headache, he took two aspirin tablets that made him feel much better.

WATCH OUT FOR AMBIGUOUS MODIFIERS: Avoid placing modifiers in such a position in a sentence that they may apply to either a preceding or following word.

AMBIGUOUS: We decided *in the morning* to pack the car and take a long trip.

QUESTION: Was the decision made in the morning or is the packing planned for the morning?

SOLUTION: In the morning, we decided to pack the car and take a long trip.

SOLUTION: We decided to pack the car in the morning and take a long trip.

MEANINGLESS REPETITION: If a connecting word has already been used, don't repeat it even though it seems to come naturally.

REPEATED: He had so many friends that there were scores of people *to* whom he thought he could appeal *to* for advice.

CORRECTION: He had so many friends that there were scores of people *to* whom he thought he could appeal for advice.

MIXED VERB TENSES: Don't mix verb tenses without reason. Keep all verbs in the same tense in relating a sequence of events.

MIXED TENSES: John *ran* to the store, *bought* a bag of oranges, and *walked* slowly home. The grocer *noticed* that he *had* a Canadian nickel in his till and *wonders* if he *had gotten* it from John.

CORRECTION: *wonders* should be *wondered*.

COMMENT: *had gotten* is past perfect tense because the event occurred before he wondered.

MIXED CLAUSE STRUCTURE: Don't combine clauses that make a statement with clauses that ask a question.

MIXED CLAUSES: They asked me [declarative] would I run for councilman [interrogative].

CORRECTED: They asked me if I would run for councilman.

OMISSION OF *other*:   Do not omit *other* after *than* when comparing two members of the same class.

OMITTED: She was taller than any girl in her club.

QUESTION: Taller even than herself? She was a member of the club.

CORRECTED: She was taller than any *other* girl in her club.

INCONSISTENT COMPARISONS: Even though the meaning is understandable, do not compare things that are not really comparable.

INCONSISTENT:	The motor in the Elixir Vacuum Cleaner is more powerful than any other cleaner.
QUESTION:	A motor is more powerful than a cleaner?
SOLUTION:	The motor in the Elixir Vacuum Cleaner is more powerful than *that* of any other cleaner.

COMPARATIVE FOR TWO; SUPERLATIVE FOR THREE OR MORE: Do not use the comparative form to compare more than two; do not use the superlative form to compare fewer than three.

INCORRECT COMPARATIVE:	He is the *oldest* of the two brothers.
CORRECT COMPARATIVE:	He is the *older* of the two brothers.
INCORRECT SUPERLATIVE:	She is the *older* of the three sisters.
CORRECT SUPERLATIVE:	She is the *oldest* of the three sisters.

OMISSION OF NECESSARY ARTICLES OR POSSESSIVE PRONOUNS: When two or more terms are in parallel construction and refer to separate people or things, be sure to supply an article or appropriate possessive pronoun for each of the terms.

OMITTED ARTICLE:	He bought a brown and gray coat.
COMMENT:	This is correct if the same coat was brown and gray.
SUPPLIED ARTICLE:	He bought a brown and *a* gray coat.
OMITTED PRONOUN:	She always consulted her maid and accountant about her income tax.
COMMENT:	This is correct if the maid was her accountant.
SUPPLIED PRONOUN:	She always consulted her maid and *her* accountant about her income tax.

OMISSION OF NECESSARY PREPOSITIONS: Usually it is sufficient to use a single preposition to connect two parallel words to the object of the preposition, but occasionally because of idiomatic prepositional usage, the same preposition is not suitable to both of the parallel words.

CORRECT:	She spoke about her love and admiration *for* her father.
COMMENT:	*Love for her father* and *admiration for her father* are both correct.
INCOMPLETE:	She spoke of her confidence and love *for* her father.
COMMENT:	The idiom is *confidence in*, not *confidence for*.
COMPLETE:	She spoke of her confidence *in* and love for her father.

To the Reader

This book is meant to help both native English speakers and those learning English as a second language to avoid many common pitfalls of English grammar and usage. Many requirements of so-called "standard" written English are described and illustrated within these pages. Spoken language is, of course, less formal than written discourse. Readers should note, therefore, that usages considered incorrect in writing are often perfectly acceptable in casual conversation.

It is assumed that readers are somewhat familiar with grammatical terms common to most languages: for example, the parts of speech, such as nouns, adjectives, and conjunctions, as well as such concepts as plural and singular, verb tenses, idioms, sentence structure, and punctuation.

To use the book efficiently, review the Table of Contents, which lists major topics in alphabetical order, from Adjectives to Verbs. Afterward, keep the book by your side as a convenient guide to using correct English while speaking and especially while writing. When in doubt about correct usage, let the book steer you to the proper choice.

Adjectives and adverbs are descriptive words like *sweet*, *big*, *ripe*, *tender* (adjectives); *sweetly*, *beautifully*, *softly*, *tenderly* (adverbs).

> Adjectives modify nouns or pronouns: *sweet* Sue. (describes Sue)
> Adjective: *sweet*
> Adverbs modify verbs: She *sang* sweetly. (how she sang)
> Adverb: *sweetly*
> Or adjectives: very *sweet* Sue. (how sweet)
> Adverb: *very*
> Or other adverbs: She sang very *sweetly*. (how sweetly)
> Adverb: *very*
> Adverbs usually describe how, why, when, or where.

Adjectives and adverbs are said to limit or modify the meaning of the words they describe, and they usually do in the sense that the word *woman* applies to all females while the addition of an adjective like *beautiful* limits the noun *woman* by excluding all the women who are not beautiful.

Comparison of Adjectives

POSITIVE	COMPARATIVE	SUPERLATIVE

Most one-syllable adjectives add *er* for the comparative form and *est* for the superlative form.

| sweet | sweeter | sweetest |
| rich | richer | richest |

One-syllable adjectives ending in *e* add *r* for the comparative form and *st* for the superlative form.

| late | later | latest |
| bright | brighter | brightest |

Two-syllable adjectives ending in *e*—if the accent is on the first syllable—add *r* for the comparative form and *st* for the superlative form.

| little | littler | littlest |
| gentle | gentler | gentlest |

Two-syllable adjectives ending in *y* preceded by a consonant change the *y* to *i* before adding *er* or *est*.

| pretty | prettier | prettiest |
| handy | handier | handiest |

Most other adjectives of two or more syllables form the comparative and superlative by the use of the auxiliary adverbs *more* and *most*.

| sedate | more sedate | most sedate |
| beautiful | more beautiful | most beautiful |

IRREGULAR FORMS

bad	worse	worst
ill	worse	worst
good	better	best
much	more	most

Predicate Adjectives

Adjectives usually precede the words they describe or modify: *deep* river; *efficient, intelligent* woman. To make statements or sentences out of these phrases, place the adjectives after copulative verbs such as *is*.

The river is *deep*.	(Adjective modifies *river*.)
The woman is *efficient* and *intelligent*.	(Adjectives modify *woman*.)
She is *efficient* and *intelligent*.	(Adjectives modify *She*.)

Articles

The most commonly used adjectives are the articles, *a*, *an*, and *the*.

A and *an* are known as indefinite articles because they refer to any single member of the class specified by whatever noun they modify: *a* tree, *an* apple.

The is the definite article. It calls attention to a specific person, place, or thing: *the* boy, *the* city, *the* iPod.

Use *a* before words beginning with a consonant sound: *a* cat, *a* train.

Use *an* before words beginning with a vowel sound: *an* artist, *an* elephant.
NOTE: It is the sound, not the letter, which determines whether *a* or *an* should be used: *a* uniform, *an* L-shaped room, *an* 80-year-old man.

Adverbs are frequently formed from adjectives by adding *ly* to the adjective.

careful	*carefully*
quick	*quickly*

BUT many adjectives also end in *ly* (*lovely, elderly*). A common error, therefore, occurs when an adjective is used where an adverb is required. The reverse—using an adverb in place of an adjective—also occurs, but less often.

Several principles govern the choice between adjectives and adverbs:

Most adverbs form the comparative and superlative by the use of the auxiliaries more and most: *more quickly, most quickly*.

A few words like *fast, slow, early, late,* and *well* function as either adverbs or adjectives depending on what they modify or, occasionally, on what they mean. For example, when *well* means *healthy*, it is always an adjective, and when *late* means *no longer alive*, it is always an adjective.

OMISSION OF PART OF A VERB PHRASE: When two parts of a compound verb are in different tenses, be sure that each tense is completely expressed.

> INCOMPLETE: It will probably rain for the annual picnic because it always has.
>
> COMPLETE: It will probably rain for the annual picnic because it always has *rained*.
>
> INCOMPLETE: Many of our clients have and probably will be unable to pay their bills.
>
> COMPLETE: Many of our clients have *been* and probably will be unable to pay their bills.

OMISSION OF *that* AFTER CERTAIN VERBS. When verbs like *saying, thinking, hoping, feeling, wishing* introduce a dependent noun clause as object of the verb, the dependent clause should be introduced by *that* to avoid possible confusion.

> OMITTED: She felt her husband was not good enough for her.
>
> CORRECTED: She felt *that* her husband was not good enough for her.
>
> OMITTED: He believed his friend would not desert him.
>
> CORRECTED: He believed *that* his friend would not desert him.

Normal English Word Order

Normal sentence word order in English is subject—verb—complement.

> John ate *dinner*. (object of verb *ate*)
> John is *boss*. (predicate noun)
> John is *sick*. (predicate adjective)

Indirect objects usually precede direct objects.

> We gave *him* the check. (gave the check to him)

The expletives *here* and *there* usually precede the verb that is followed by the subject.

> Here is your *hat*. (subject in italics)
> There are *dozens* of roses in the garden. (subject in italics)

Modifiers are placed as close as possible to the words they modify. Adjectives usually precede the words they modify.

> the *tall* building   the *sick old* man

Adjective phrases or clauses usually follow the words they modify.

> The man *in the dark suit* (adjective phrase)
> The woman *who was in the grocery store* (adjective clause)

Adverbs usually follow the verbs they modify.

She ran *rapidly*.	(adverb)
She ran *into the house*.	(adverbial phrase)
She ran *when she saw her mother coming*.	(adverbial clause)

Single adverbs sometimes precede the verbs they modify.

They *rapidly* took advantage of the situation.

Single adverbs are usually inserted after the first element of a verb phrase.

They *will* really *have* trouble.	(verb phrase in italics)
He *has* certainly *been trying* hard.	(verb phrase in italics)

Single adverbs modifying adjectives or other adverbs precede the words they modify.

His uncle was *very* rich.	(modifies adjective *rich*)
The train was *extraordinarily* fast.	(modifies adjective *fast*)
He finished his work *more* quickly than the others.	(modifies adverb *quickly*)

EXAMPLE OF A DECLARATIVE SENTENCE WITH MODIFIERS: The strong smell of gas, which pervaded all the rooms of the house, quickly drove the guests at the party out into the street.

For variety of sentence structure, or for emphasis, dependent phrases and clauses frequently precede the subject.

In the late afternoon, Father usually took a nap.   (dependent phrase)
When they discovered their mistake, the workmen tried to correct it. (dependent clause)

The Power of Verbs

The remainder of this book focuses on verbs. Why verbs, you may ask. The answer lies in the importance of verbs in our language.

Verbs serve as the backbone of written and spoken language. Every sentence contains at least one verb. Many writers assert that no other part of speech carries as much power as verbs. The author Maria Padian, for instance, claims "I can name the author, book, chapter, page number and every sentence responsible for transforming me into an Ardent Believer in Verbs." On page 254 of *The Shipping News*, a novel by E. Annie Proulx, Padian came upon a description of a rainy wharf: "Rain sluiced over the upturned [boat] bottom, pattered on the stones. . . . A man leaning in a doorframe, hands draining into his pockets. . ." Inside the offices of The Shipping News, ". . . Billy Pretty's voice seesawed. Nutbeam snapped up alertly."

Her eyes widened in awe, Padian realizes that

> Proulx's rain didn't fall: it sluiced and pattered. Hands weren't thrust into pockets: they drained. Voices didn't get louder and softer: they seesawed.
>
> Assertively and efficiently, the author employed verbs not only to tell me what her characters were doing, but also how things looked and how they sounded. She was also telling me a little about how her characters felt: a man whose hands are draining into his pockets is in a different state of mind from a man whose hands are balled into fists and jammed into his pockets.
>
> Then . . . one of the main characters (Tert Card) approached a deli platter, and my writing life changed: "He plucked at the plastic wrap, seized a handful of ham, and shoved it into his mouth."
>
> I stopped, I reread. I counted: plucked, seized, shoved. In three verbs and one line, Proulx told me all about Tert Card's state of mind and foreshadowed the brutish events to follow. No adjectives, no physical descriptions, no annoying adverbs. Just simple, unequivocal language.

Verbs

Indeed, verbs are the asserting words. They name actions: *drink, speak, laugh, criticize, despair, cheer, flutter, facilitate, fantasize.* The list goes on and on. Without verbs it is impossible to make sentences. Without verbs, we'd end up uttering such things as:

> Brian on May 28th
> In which aisle sugar?
> If it, the game.

With verbs we can turn such nonsensical utterances into sentences that others will actually understand:

> Brian *graduates* on May 28th.
> In which aisle *can* sugar *be found*?
> If it *rains*, the game *will be cancelled*.

Not every verb involves actions like drinking, speaking, or laughing. Some simply express a state of being that tell you what the subject is (Titanium *is* a metal). State-of-being verbs also enable you to make a statement (Water *was* plentiful) or ask a question (*Are* you happy?).

The primary state of being verb in English is *to be*. Forms of *to be* include *are, am, was, were, will be, has been, had been, have been,* and *will have been.*

Verb Tenses

The tense of all verbs—both action and state-of-being verbs—provides information about when an action occurred. The verb *talked*, for example, has an *-ed* ending that signifies **past tense**, indicating that the action occurred at a time before the present moment, as in:

> The doctor *talked* to the patient.

If the verb had been *talks*, the *-s* ending would signify the **present tense** and indicate action taking place right now, although in another context it could mean that talking to patients is part of the doctor's present routine, as in:

> The doctor *talks* to the patient at the end of every physical examination.

When linked to singular nouns or third-person pronouns (*he/she/it*), some present-tense verbs end with *-es*, as in *marches* and *finishes*, *goes*, and *does*. Similarly, verbs ending in *-y* when linked to singular nouns or third-person pronouns are formed by changing the *y* to *i* and adding *-es*, as in *clarifies* and *denies*.

To make clear that an action is occurring at this very moment, the English language also provides the **present progressive** tense (also called the *present participle*), formed by adding *-ing* to the verb, as in:

> The doctor is *talking* to the patient.

A Handy Guide to Spelling Some Regular Verbs

Regular verbs ending in a consonant (push, cook, float):

> form the present participle by adding *ing* (pushing, cooking, floating).

> form the past tense and past participle by adding *ed* (pushed, cooked, floated).

Regular verbs ending in a vowel (veto):

> form the present participle by adding *ing* (vetoing).

> form the past tense and past participle by adding *ed* (vetoed).

BUT

Regular verbs ending in *e* preceded by a single consonant (make, smoke):

> form the present participle by dropping the *e* before adding *ing* (making, smoking).

> form the past tense and past participle by adding only *d* (raked, smoked).

Regular verbs ending in a single consonant preceded by a single vowel (drop, grip):

> double the final consonant before adding *ing* or *ed* (dropping, dropped, gripping, gripped).

Regular verbs ending in *y* preceded by a consonant (try, hurry):

> change the *y* to *i* before adding *ed* (tried, hurried).

> change the *y* to *i* for third person singular (tries, hurries).

Changing the tenses of regular active verbs often involves altering endings. But tense changes can also involve the addition of a so-called *auxiliary* verb (also called *helping* verb), such as *has, had, have, shall, will, shall have,* and *will have.* The verbs *am, is,* and *are* function as auxiliary verbs, too, as in:

> The doctor *is talking* to the patient.
> I *am talking* to the patient.
> The doctors *are talking* to the patient.

Principal Auxiliary Verbs		
PRONOUN	PRES. TENSE	PAST TENSE
I, you, he, she, it, we, they	can	could
I, you, we, they	do	did
he, she, it	does	did
I, you, we, they	have	had
he, she, it	has	had
I, you, he, she, it, we, they	may	might
I, you, he, she, it, we, they	must	had to
I, you, he, she, it, we, they	ought	should have
I, we	shall (future)	
I, you, he, she, it, we, they	should	should have
you, he, she, it, they	will (future)	
I, you, he, she, it, we, they	would	would have

PRINCIPAL PARTS OF VERBS: The essential forms of a verb are known as its principal parts:

Infinitive:	to go OR go
Present Tense:	go
Past Tense:	went
Present Participle:	going
Past Participle:	gone

NUMBER AND PERSON RELATED TO VERBS: Most English verbs have very easy conjugations because for nearly all verbs the forms for number (singular and plural) are the same. For example:

Singular: I sing   Plural: We sing

Person alludes to the subject of the verb.

First person is the person speaking or writing:

Singular: I   Plural: we

Second person is the person spoken or written to:

Singular: you   Plural: you

Third person is anybody or anything else:

Singular: he, she, it   Plural: they
street   streets
beauty   beauties

In nearly all verbs the only change of form occurs in the third person singular of the present and present perfect tenses and in the first person of the future and future perfect tenses. For example:

PRESENT TENSE:	I, you, we, they *go* BUT he, she, it *goes*.
PRESENT PERFECT TENSE:	I, you, we, they *have gone* BUT he, she, it *has gone*.
FUTURE TENSE:	you, he, she, it, they *will go* BUT I, *we shall go*.
FUTURE PERFECT TENSE:	you, he, she, it, they *will have gone* BUT I, we *shall have gone*.
PAST TENSE *(no change)*:	I, you, he, she, it, we, they *went*.
PAST PERFECT TENSE *(no change)*:	I, you, he, it, we, they *had gone*.

EXCEPTION: Various forms of the verb *to be*.

To illustrate the variety of endings and auxiliary verbs used to express the time when actions take place, what follows is the conjugation of the regular verb *to push*.

to push (active voice)

Principal Parts: push, pushing, pushed, pushed

Infinitive: to push, push

Perfect Infinitive: to have pushed

Present Participle: pushing

Past Participle: pushed

INDICATIVE MOOD

Pres.	I push	we push
	you push	you push
	he (she, it) pushes	they push
Pres. Prog.	I am pushing	we are pushing
	you are pushing	you are pushing
	he (she, it) is pushing	they are pushing
Pres. Int.	I do push	we do push
	you do push	you do push
	he (she, it) does push	they do push
Fut.	I shall push	we shall push
	you will push	you will push
	he (she, it) will push	they will push
Fut.	I will push *(P)*	we will push *(P)*
	you shall push *(C)*	you shall push *(C)*
	he (she, it) shall push *(C)*	they shall push *(C)*
Past	I pushed	we pushed
	you pushed	you pushed
	he (she, it) pushed	they pushed
Past Prog.	I was pushing	we were pushing
	you were pushing	you were pushing
	he (she, it) was pushing	they were pushing

Verbs

Past *Int.*	I did push you did push he (she, it) did push		we did push you did push they did push
Pres. *Perf.*	I have pushed you have pushed he (she, it) has pushed		we have pushed you have pushed they are pushed
Past *Perf.*	I had pushed you had pushed he (she, it) had pushed		we had pushed you had pushed they had pushed
Fut. *Perf.*	I shall have pushed you will have pushed he (she, it) will have pushed		we shall have pushed you will have pushed they will have pushed

IMPERATIVE MOOD

push

SUBJUNCTIVE MOOD

Pres.	if I push if you push if he (she, it) push		if we push if you push if they push
Past	if I pushed if you pushed if he (she, it) pushed		if we pushed if you pushed if they pushed
Fut.	if I should push if you should push if he (she, it) should push		if we should push if you should push if they should push

(passive voice)

Infinitive: to be pushed, be pushed   *Present Participle:* being pushed
Perfect Infinitive: to have been pushed   *Past Participle:* been pushed

INDICATIVE MOOD

Pres.	I am pushed you are pushed he (she, it) is pushed	we are pushed you are pushed they are pushed
Pres. *Prog.*	I am being pushed you are being pushed he (she, it) is being pushed	we are being pushed you are being pushed they are being pushed
Pres. *Int.*	I do get pushed you do get pushed he (she, it) does get pushed	we do get pushed you do get pushed they do get pushed
Fut.	I shall be pushed you will be pushed he (she, it) will be pushed	we shall be pushed you will be pushed they will be pushed
Fut.	I will be pushed *(P)* you shall be pushed *(C)* he (she, it) shall be pushed *(C)*	we will be pushed *(P)* you shall be pushed *(C)* they shall be pushed *(C)*
Past	I was pushed you were pushed he (she, it) was pushed	we were pushed you were pushed they were pushed
Past	I was being pushed	we were being pushed

Prog.	you were being pushed		you were being pushed
	he (she, it) was being pushing		they were being pushed
Past	I did get pushed		we did get pushed
Int.	you did get pushed		you did get pushed
	he (she, it) did get pushed		they did get pushed
Pres.	I have been pushed		we have been pushed
Perf.	you have been pushed		you have been pushed
	he (she, it) has been pushed		they have been pushed
Past	I had been pushed		we had been pushed
Perf.	you had been pushed		you had been pushed
	he (she, it) had been pushed		they had been pushed
Fut.	I shall have been pushed		we shall have been pushed
Perf.	you will have been pushed		you will have been pushed
	he (she, it) will have been pushed		they will have been pushed

IMPERATIVE MOOD
be pushed

SUBJUNCTIVE MOOD

Pres.	if I be pushed		if we be pushed
	if you be pushed		if you be pushed
	if he (she, it) be pushed		if they be pushed
Past	if I were pushed		if we were pushed
	if you were pushed		if you were pushed
	if he (she, it) were pushed		if they were pushed
Fut.	if I should be pushed		if we should be pushed
	if you should be pushed		if you should be pushed
	if he (she, it) should be pushed		if they should be pushed

Observe that the regular verb *to push* changes only slightly between tenses and persons or when shifting between singular and plural. As previously stated, an *-s* (or in this case *-es*) is added when the verb changes from first or second person to third person in the present tense. An *-ed* is added in shifts from present to past in the second person, and so on. Such changes follow a regular pattern. Hence, most verbs in English are given the designation *regular* verbs.

THE PRESENT TENSE: Use the present tense to indicate that something is so at the moment of speaking or writing.

> He *is* sorry.
> That *looks* like an expensive dress.

Use the present tense to describe something that is true regardless of time.

> Justice *is* important.
> Bees *sting*.

The present tense is frequently used to refer to artistic productions that exist in the present even though they were created in the past and to make statements about artists (in the sense that they continue to live because of their works). Similarly, synopses of plots are usually given in the present tense.

In *Romeo and Juliet*, Shakespeare's verse *has* a lyric quality.

Verdi *is* one of the greatest composers of all time.

At the beginning of *The Divine Comedy*, Dante *is* lost in a forest.

He *attempts* to climb a nearby hill.

Use the progressive form of the present tense to indicate a continuing action or situation.

The clock *is striking.*

The organ *is playing.*

The people *are listening.*

When the progressive form is not used for such continuing events, a dramatic effect is produced.

The clock *strikes,* the organ *plays,* the people *listen.*

Use the intensive form of the present tense to secure emphasis.

I *do work* hard.

He *does dress* well.

They *do understand* you.

THE FUTURE TENSE: English offers a number of ways to predict future happenings. Many people use only the auxiliary verb *will* for all persons, or else they use contractions.

I (we) will do it.   I'll do it.   We'll do it.

You will do it.   You'll do it.

He (she, it, they) will do it.   He'll, she'll, they'll do it.

In highly formal usage or in British English, *shall* is often used in place of *will* in the first person, although not in the second or third:

I (we) *shall* respond promptly.

I (we) *shall* write.

You *will* write.

He (she, it, they) *will* write.

To indicate intensity, implying a promise or determination, reverse the above formal usage by using *will* in the first person and *shall* in the second and third.

I (we) *will* succeed.

You *shall* succeed.

He (she, it, they) *shall* succeed.

A statement about the future can also be made by using either the present tense or the present progressive tense:

The World Series *begins* (present) next Tuesday.

Britain's royal wedding *is being televised* (present progressive) tomorrow morning starting at 5:00.

THE PAST TENSE: Use the past tense to refer to something that occurred at a definite time in the past.

He *opened* a bank account two years ago.

Use the progressive form of the past tense to indicate that the event in the past continued over a period of time.

When he was seven years old, he *was learning* to write.

Use the intensive form of the past tense to secure emphasis.

It took a long time, but he *did learn* to write.

THE PRESENT PERFECT TENSE: Use the present perfect tense when the emphasis is on the fact that something that occurred once or several times in the past is considered from a present point of view. "I *have been* in London" gives no indication of when the event occurred or even how many times it occurred except that it happened in the past. The emphasis is on the fact that at the present time a trip to London is a part of the speaker's or writer's experience.

Use the present perfect tense to describe an event that began at some time in the past and that has just been completed.

I *have finished* my homework.

Use the progressive form of the present perfect tense to indicate a continuing action.

I *have been looking* all over for you.

THE PAST PERFECT TENSE: Use the past perfect tense to refer to an event that was terminated prior to some definite time in the past.

She *had finished* her work before she went to bed.

Since the past perfect tense implies a past event before another past event, it is usually accompanied by another verb in the past tense (*went* in the example above) though not necessarily in the same sentence.

He *caught* a bad cold.
He *had been* out in the rain all day.

Use the progressive form of the past perfect tense to indicate a continuing action.

He *had been waiting* a long time when the train came.

Verbs

THE FUTURE PERFECT TENSE: Use the future perfect tense to indicate that something will be completed before some definite time in the future.

> By the time she gets married, she *will have learned* to cook.

The use of *shall* and *will* in forming the future perfect tense is the same as in the future tense.

Use the progressive form of the future perfect tense to indicate a continuing action.

> When we reach the top of the mountain, we *shall have been climbing* for more than seven hours.

Verbals

Verbals are words that are derived from verbs but that function as other parts of speech. Unlike finite verbs they do not have tense nor are they limited by person and number.

INFINITIVES:

Present Infinitive:	*to be, to go*
Perfect Infinitive:	*to have been, to have gone*
Progressive Forms:	*to be going, to have been going*

The *to* is sometimes omitted because of idiomatic usage: *Let him go.* (*Ask him to go.*)

Infinitives usually function as nouns. In the sentence *To die is common*, the infinitive *to die* could be replaced by the noun *death*. But since infinitives are nouns and verbs at the same time, they may also, like verbs, have modifiers and complements:

> *To sing* beautifully was her ambition.

[The adverb *beautifully* modifies *to sing; to sing* is the subject of *was.*]

> He loved *to eat* candy.

[*Candy* is the object of *to eat; to eat candy* is the object of *loved.*]

THE GERUND: A gerund is a present participle that functions as a noun. It is the name of an action or state of being. Like the infinitive it may have modifiers and complements.

> He enjoyed *driving* the car.
> Heavy *drinking* was his only bad habit.
> *Being* sensible was difficult for him.
> She enjoyed *cooking* on her new stove.

PRESENT AND PRESENT PERFECT PARTICIPLES: With or without complements or modifiers, present and present perfect participles function as adjectives.

> The *sinking* ship.
> The *rising* sun. [modify *ship* and *sun*]
> *Having lost* his notebook, he failed the test. [modifies *he*]

PAST AND PAST PERFECT PARTICIPLES: Past and past perfect participles (with or without complements or modifiers) also function as adjectives, but they describe an action happening *to* the noun or pronoun being modified.

> The robber, *shot* by the police, was in critical condition. [modifies *robber*]
> The lobsters, *flown* in from the ocean, were delicious. [modifies *lobsters*]
> *Having been drenched* by the rain, he caught a cold. [modifies *he*]

MOOD OF VERBS: Differences in the intention of the speaker or writer are shown by mood.

Indicative Mood: The indicative mood is used to make a statement or ask a question.

> The old man *walked* slowly down the street.
> Why *do* you *eat* so rapidly?

Conjugations of English verbs are usually in the indicative mood.

Imperative Mood: The imperative mood of English verbs is identical with the infinitive (without the *to*): *be, work, eat, run.*

It is used for commands, requests, or directions:

> COMMAND: *Sit* down and *eat* your supper.
> REQUEST: Please *be* on time, and *bring* your lunch.
> DIRECTION: *Fold* the paper vertically and *put* your name at the top.

Subjunctive Mood: The subjunctive mood is used occasionally in everyday English, most often to express a condition that is contrary to fact. It is usually found in a clause that starts with the word *if*, as in:

> If I *were* in good physical shape, I would run a marathon.

Ordinarily, a singular verb follows a singular pronoun (*I, he, she, it, you*) or any singular noun. Standard English usage, however, requires that sentences cast in the subjunctive mood (*i.e.*, with an *if* clause) use verbs in the plural form, as in:

> NOT STANDARD: If I *was* you, I'd accept the job offer.
> STANDARD: If I *were* you, I'd accept the job offer.

> NOT STANDARD: If the teacher *was* here, you'd behave differently.
> STANDARD: If the teacher *were* here, you'd behave differently.

Verbs

NOT STANDARD:	The book could be a best-seller, but only if it *was* published before the election.
STANDARD:	The book could be a best-seller, but only if it *were* published before the election.

Similarly, a sentence that expresses a wish is also cast in the subjunctive mood and therefore requires the plural form of the verb:

WISH: I wish I *were* as healthy as I used to be.

Another use of the subjunctive occurs in a dependent clause after a verb that expresses determination or conveys a command or a request:

DETERMINATION:	Mr. Conlan insists that he *meet* me at the bank.
COMMAND:	The admiral commanded that all sailors *be* in dress uniform.
REQUEST:	Long *live* the king.

Several additional verbs are typically followed by clauses that take the subjunctive. Such verbs include *ask, demand, insist, move, order, pray, prefer, recommend, regret, require,* and *suggest.*

Examples:

> He asked that we *be* patient.
> The landlord demanded that the tenant *pay* the rent immediately.
> Sophia insisted that she *be* given the key to the auditorium.
> We suggested that she *take* the Q-10 bus to the station.

The same form of the subjunctive is used in formal parliamentary procedure to introduce a motion or resolution.

Senator Briggs moved that this resolution *be* adopted: "*Be* it resolved that the Senate *go* on record as endorsing Article Seven of the Constitution."

Keep in mind that no difference exists between subjunctive and indicative verb forms except for present tense third person singular verbs (e.g., he *walks/walk*, she *passes/pass*, it *gathers/gather*), and for the verb *to be*). In other words, the subjunctive for the present tense third person singular omits the *-s* or *-es*, making the verb look and sound like the present tense for everything else. As for the subjunctive of the verb *to be*, use *be* in the present tense (If this *be* the whole story, it's not worth telling.).

TRANSITIVE AND INTRANSITIVE VERBS: The distinction between transitive and intransitive verbs is useful principally for the grammatical purpose of determining the case of a pronoun that follows a verb. Is it correct to say "It is I" or "It is me"? The answer is *I* because *is* is an intransitive verb. Transitive verbs are followed by the objective case (*me*); intransitive verbs are followed by the nominative case (*I*).

When a verb indicates a motion or a passing over from one person or thing to another, it is called *transitive*: He *hit* the ball. She *ate* her dinner. Usually, something is being done to something or somebody.

Many verbs are both transitive and intransitive, depending on the meaning of the sentence in which they are used. "He *is* still *breathing*" means that he is alive. "He *is breathing* the fresh air of the seashore" implies that he is having a fine vacation. The first *is breathing* is intransitive; the action is self-contained. The second *is breathing* is a transitive verb because the sense of the verb requires the object *air*.

A simple test for a transitive verb is to find out if the sentence can be reversed by being stated in the passive voice, since only transitive verbs have a passive voice:

ACTIVE VOICE: He is breathing the air.
PASSIVE VOICE: The air is being breathed by him.

If the object of the verb (*air*) cannot be made the subject and the subject expressed in a "by-phrase" (*by him*), the verb is not transitive.

An intransitive verb makes an assertion without requiring any object.

> The bell *rings*.
> The church *stands* on the top of a little hill.
> The books *are* on the desk.

This distinction is important grammatically only for one small class of intransitive verbs known as *linking*, or *copulative*, verbs. Such verbs link a sentence subject to a noun, pronoun, or adjective in the predicate. *To be* is the most frequently used linking verb. Pronouns following linking verbs should be in the nominative case.

> It is *I, we, you, he, she, it, they.*

Adjectives, not adverbs, follow linking verbs in the predicate.

> He is *tall, good, bad, weak, sick, strong.*

Besides *to be*, the most frequently used linking verbs are *become, seem, smell, look, grow, feel, sound, get, taste, appear.*

> The food smells bad.   (not *badly*)
> The orchestra sounded *good.*   (not *well*)
> I feel *well.*   (*Well* is here an adjective meaning "not sick.")
> I feel *good.*   (in good spirits)

Verbs

WARNING: The subject and object of an infinitive—even the infinitive *to be*—are always in the objective case.

At the masquerade they all believed *him* to be *me*.

VOICE OF VERBS: Transitive verbs—and only transitive verbs—depend on voice to indicate whether the emphasis in a sentence should be placed on the actor or the receiver of the action stated by the verb.

ACTIVE VOICE emphasizes the doer.

Andrew plays the piano.

The sentence implies that one of Andrew's talents is piano playing since *Andrew* is the subject of the transitive verb *plays* in the active voice. *Piano* is the object of the verb.

PASSIVE VOICE emphasizes the receiver of the action.

The piano is played by Andrew.

This sentence implies that someone has asked, "Who plays the piano?" probably referring to part of the furniture of a room. Therefore, *piano* is the subject of the sentence. But the piano isn't doing anything; something is being done to it. Therefore the passive form *is played* of the transitive verb *play* is followed by the prepositional phrase *by Andrew* to explain the use of the piano.

The passive voice is necessary on occasions where the actor is unknown or where it is preferable that he remain anonymous.

The wine was spilled on the floor.
The curtain was raised at precisely 8 P.M.

It is also used when the doer is of no importance or when his identity is already known, or on occasions where the performer of the action is obvious.

The programs were distributed during the concert.
The cellar was flooded.

CONJUGATIONS OF
IRREGULAR VERBS

Between two- and three-hundred English verbs refuse to conform to the patterns of regular verbs. Hence, their label: *irregular verbs*. Some irregular verbs change in ways that seem to defy logic, but their distinctiveness may be rooted in the historical fact that words from several different languages have found their way into English. Thus, the unusual conjugations of such everyday verbs *as sleep/slept, ride/rode, swim/swam, is/was, are/were, go/went, catch/caught*, can be explained.

Native speakers of English become attuned to irregular verb forms as they learn to talk, although some verbs like *lie/lay* (to recline) and *lie/laid* (to place) remain a lifelong mystery for some.

The pages that follow are composed of conjugations of many, but not all, of the irregular verbs in our language. Some conjugations shown in these pages may be more hypothetical than real. That is, their structure gives them the potential to be used in a particular context. The fact is, however, that they might never be found in actual speech or writing.

In the conjugations of the future tense, (P) indicates forms that imply a promise, and (C) indicates forms that imply a command. Note that the verb *shall* is now rare in conversation, though it is still used in formal written English.

Conjugation of Irregular Verbs

to arise (active voice)

Infinitive: to arise

Perfect Infinitive: to have arisen

Principal Parts: arise, arising, arose, arisen

Present Participle: arising **Past Participle:** arisen

INDICATIVE MOOD

Pres.	I arise	we arise
	you arise	you arise
	he (she, it) arises	they arise
Prog.	I am arising	we are arising
	you are arising	you are arising
	he (she, it) is arising	they are arising
Int.	I do arise	we do arise
	you do arise	you do arise
	he (she, it) does arise	they do arise
Fut.	I shall arise	we shall arise
	you will arise	you will arise
	he (she, it) will arise	they will arise
Fut.	I will arise (P)	we will arise (P)
	you shall arise (C)	you shall arise (C)
	he (she, it) shall arise (C)	they shall arise (C)
Past	I arose	we arose
	you arose	you arose
	he (she, it) arose	they arose
Past Prog.	I was arising	we were arising
	you were arising	you were arising
	he (she, it) was arising	they were arising
Past Int.	I did arise	we did arise
	you did arise	you did arise
	he (she, it) did arise	they did arise
Pres. Perf.	I have arisen	we have arisen
	you have arisen	you have arisen
	he (she, it) has arisen	they have arisen
Past Perf.	I had arisen	we had arisen
	you had arisen	you had arisen
	he (she, it) had arisen	they had arisen
Fut. Perf.	I shall have arisen	we shall have arisen
	you will have arisen	you will have arisen
	he (she, it) will have arisen	they will have arisen

IMPERATIVE MOOD

arise

SUBJUNCTIVE MOOD

Pres.	if I arise	if we arise
	if you arise	if you arise
	if he (she, it) arise	if they arise
Past	if I arose	if we arose
	if you arose	if you arose
	if he (she, it) arose	if they arose
Fut.	if I should arise	if we should arise
	If you should arise	if you should arise
	if he (she, it) should arise	if they should arise

Infinitive: to be, be   *Present Participle:* being
Perfect Infinitive: to have been   *Past Participle:* been

INDICATIVE MOOD

Pres.	I am	we are
	you are	you are
	he (she, it) is	they are
Fut.	I shall be	we shall be
	you will be	you will be
	he (she, it) will be	they will be
Fut.	I will be *(P)*	we will be *(P)*
	you shall be *(C)*	you shall be *(C)*
	he (she, it) shall be *(C)*	they shall be *(C)*
Past	I was	we were
	you were	you were
	he (she, it) was	they were
Pres. Perf.	I have been	we have been
	you have been	you have been
	he (she, it) has been	they have been
Past Perf.	I had been	we had been
	you had been	you had been
	he (she, it) had been	they had been
Fut. Perf.	I shall have been	we shall have been
	you will have been	you will have been
	he (she, it) will have been	they will have been

IMPERATIVE MOOD
be

SUBJUNCTIVE MOOD

Pres.	if I be	if we be
	if you be	if you be
	if he (she, it) be	if they be
Past	if I were	if we were
	if you were	if you were
	if he (she, it) were	if they were
Fut.	if I should be	if we should be
	if you should be	if you should be
	if he (she, it) should be	if they should be

Common Uses of *To Be*

The basic meaning of *to be* is *to exist* as in Hamlet's well-known soliloquy "To be or not to be: that is the question."

The principal use of *to be* is to make an assertion. An observation like "cold ice" becomes an assertion by adding the appropriate form of the verb *to be:* Ice *is* cold.

To be is called a copulative verb because it joins many kinds of sentence elements: nouns as in "Mr. Price *is* the mayor," nouns and predicate adjectives as in "The girl *was* beautiful," infinitives and predicate adjectives as in "To err *is* human," expletives and phrases as in "There *would be* many more people in the hall tonight if it *were* not raining," etc.

To be is also used to create the progressive forms of other verbs: "The water *is flowing*" as well as the passive voice: "I *was beaten*."

Infinitive: to bear *Present Participle:* bearing
Perfect Infinitive: to have borne *Past Participle:* borne

INDICATIVE MOOD

Pres.	I bear	we bear
	you bear	you bear
	he (she, it) bears	they bear

Pres. Prog.	I am bearing	we are bearing
	you are bearing	you are bearing
	he (she, it) is bearing	they are bearing

Pres. Int.	I do bear	we do bear
	you do bear	you do bear
	he (she, it) does bear	they do bear

Fut.	I shall bear	we shall bear
	you will bear	you will bear
	he (she, it) will bear	they will bear

Fut.	I will bear *(P)*	we will bear *(P)*
	you shall bear *(C)*	you shall bear *(C)*
	he (she, it) shall bear *(C)*	they shall bear *(C)*

Past	I bore	we bore
	you bore	you bore
	he (she, it) bore	they bore

Past Prog.	I was bearing	we were bearing
	you were bearing	you were bearing
	he (she, it) was bearing	they were bearing

Past Int.	I did bear	we did bear
	you did bear	you did bear
	he (she, it) did bear	they did bear

Pres. Perf.	I have borne	we have borne
	you have borne	you have borne
	he (she, it) had borne	they had borne

Past Perf.	I had borne	we had borne
	you had borne	you had borne
	he (she, it) had borne	they had borne

Fut. Perf.	I shall have borne	we shall have borne
	you will have borne	you will have borne
	he (she, it) will have borne	they will have bone

IMPERATIVE MOOD
bear

SUBJUNCTIVE MOOD

Pres.	if I bear	if we bear
	if you bear	if you bear
	if he (she, it) bear	if they bear

Past	if I bore	if we bore
	if you bore	if you bore
	if he (she, it) bore	if they bore

Fut.	if I should bear	if we should bear
	if you should bear	if you should bear
	if he (she, it) should bear	if they should bear

Infinitive: to be borne, to be born
Perfect Infinitive: to have been borne,
to have been born

Present Participle: being borne,
being born
Past Participle: been borne,
been born

INDICATIVE MOOD

Pres.	I am borne, born	we are borne, born
	you are borne, born	you are borne, born
	he (she, it) is borne, born	they are borne, born
Pres. Prog.	I am being borne, born	we are being borne, born
	you are being borne, born	you are being borne, born
	he (she, it) is being borne, born	they are being borne, born
Pres. Int.	I do get borne, born	we do get borne, born
	you do get borne, born	you do get borne, born
	he (she, it) does get borne, born	they do get borne, born
Fut.	I shall be borne, born	we shall be borne, born
	you will be borne, born	you will be borne, born
	he (she, it) will be borne, born	they will be borne, born
Fut.	I will be borne, born *(P)*	we will be borne, born *(P)*
	you shall be borne, born *(C)*	you shall be borne, born *(C)*
	he (she, it) shall be borne, born *(C)*	they shall be borne, born *(C)*
Past	I was borne, born	we were borne, born
	you were borne, born	you were borne, horn
	he (she, it) were borne, born	they were borne, born
Past Prog.	I was being borne, born	we were being borne, born
	you were being borne, born	you were being borne, born
	he (she, it) was being borne, born	they were being borne, born
Past Int.	I did get borne, born	we did get borne, born
	you did get borne, born	you did get borne, born
	he (she, it) did get borne, born	they did get borne, born
Pres. Perf.	I have been borne, born	we have been borne, born
	you have been borne, born	you have been borne, born
	he (she, it) had been borne, born	they had been borne, born
Past Perf.	I had been borne, born	we had been borne, born
	you had been borne, born	you had been borne, born
	he (she, it) had been borne, born	they had been borne, born
Fut. Perf.	I shall have been borne, born	we shall have been borne, born
	you will have been borne, born	you will have been borne, born
	he (she, it) will have been borne, born	they will have been borne, born

IMPERATIVE MOOD
be borne, be born

SUBJUNCTIVE MOOD

Pres.	if I be borne, born	if we be borne, born
	if you be borne, born	if you be borne, born
	if he (she, it) be borne, born	if they be borne, born
Past	if I were borne, born	if we were borne, born
	if you were borne, born	if you were borne, born
	if he (she, it) were borne, born	if they were borne, born
Fut.	if I should be borne, born	if we should be borne, born
	if you should be borne, born	if you should be borne, born
	if he (she, it) should be borne, born	if they should be borne, born

139

to beat (active voice)

Principal Parts: beat, beating, beat, beaten

Infinitive: to beat	*Present Participle:* beating
Perfect Infinitive: to have beaten	*Past Participle:* beaten

INDICATIVE MOOD

Pres.	I beat	we beat
	you beat	you beat
	he (she, it) beats	they beat
Prog. Pres.	I am beating	we are beating
	you are beating	you are beating
	he (she, it) is beating	they are beating
Int. Pres.	I do beat	we do beat
	you do beat	you do beat
	he (she, it) does beat	they do beat
Fut.	I shall beat	we shall beat
	you will beat	you will beat
	he (she, it) will beat	they will beat
Fut.	I will beat (P)	we will beat (P)
	you shall beat (C)	you shall beat (C)
	he (she, it) shall beat (C)	they shall beat (C)
Past	I beat	we beat
	you beat	you beat
	he (she, it) beat	they beat
Past Prog.	I was beating	we were beating
	you were beating	you were beating
	he (she, it) was beating	they were beating
Past Int.	I did beat	we did beat
	you did beat	you did beat
	he (she, it) did beat	they did beat
Pres. Perf.	I have beaten	we have beaten
	you have beaten	you have beaten
	he (she, it) have beaten	they have beaten
Past Perf.	I had beaten	we had beaten
	you had beaten	you had beaten
	he (she, it) had beaten	they had beaten
Fut. Perf.	I shall have beaten	we shall have beaten
	you will have beaten	you will have beaten
	he (she, it) will have beaten	they will have beaten

IMPERATIVE MOOD

beat

SUBJUNCTIVE MOOD

Pres.	if I beat	if we beat
	if you beat	if you beat
	if he (she, it) beat	if they beat
Past	if I beat	if we beat
	if you beat	if you beat
	if he (she, it) beat	if they beat
Fut.	if I should beat	if we should beat
	if you should beat	if you should beat
	if he (she, it) should beat	if they should beat

(passive voice)

Infinitive: to be beaten
Perfect Infinitive: to have been beaten

Present Participle: being beaten
Past Participle: been beaten

INDICATIVE MOOD

Singular

Pres. I am beaten
he (she, it) is beaten
you are beaten

Prog. I am being beaten
he (she, it) is being beaten

Pres. I do get beaten
you do get beaten
he (she, it) does get beaten

Fut. I shall be beaten
you will be beaten
he (she, it) will be beaten

Fut. I will be beaten (P)
you shall be beaten (C)
he (she, it) shall be beaten (C)

Past I was beaten
you were beaten
he (she, it) was beaten

Prog. I was being beaten
you were being beaten
he (she, it) was being beaten

Int. I did get beaten
you did get beaten
he (she, it) did get beaten

Perf. I have been beaten
you have been beaten
he (she, it) has been beaten

Perf. I had been beaten
you had been beaten
he (she, it) had been beaten

Fut. I shall have been beaten
you will have been beaten
he (she, it) will have been beaten

Plural

Pres. we are beaten
you are beaten
they are beaten

Pres. we are being beaten
they are being beaten

Pres. we do get beaten
you do get beaten
they do get beaten

Fut. we shall be beaten
you will be beaten
they will be beaten

Fut. we will be beaten (P)
you shall be beaten (C)
they shall be beaten (C)

Past we were beaten
you were beaten
they were beaten

Prog. we were being beaten
you were being beaten
they were being beaten

Past we did get beaten
you did get beaten
they did get beaten

Perf. we have been beaten
you have been beaten
they have been beaten

Perf. we had been beaten
you had been beaten
they had been beaten

Perf. we shall have been beaten
you will have been beaten
they will have been beaten

IMPERATIVE MOOD

be beaten

SUBJUNCTIVE MOOD

Pres. if I be beaten
if he (she, it) be beaten
if you be beaten
if we be beaten
if they be beaten

Past if I were beaten
if he (she, it) were beaten
if you were beaten
if we were beaten
if you were beaten
if they were beaten

Fut. if I should be beaten
if you should be beaten
if he (she, it) should be beaten
if we should be beaten
if you should be beaten
if they should be beaten

to begin (active voice)

Principal Parts: begin, beginning, began, begun

Infinitive: to begin   *Perfect Infinitive:* to have begun

Present Participle: beginning   *Past Participle:* begun

INDICATIVE MOOD

Pres.
I begin   we begin
you begin   you begin
he (she, it) begins   they begin

Pres. Prog.
I am beginning   we are beginning
you are beginning   you are beginning
he (she, it) is beginning   they are beginning

Pres. Int.
I do begin   we do begin
you do begin   you do begin
he (she, it) does begin   they do begin

Fut.
I shall begin   we shall begin
you will begin   you will begin
he (she, it) will begin   they will begin

Fut.
I will begin (P)   we will begin (P)
you shall begin (C)   you shall begin (C)
he (she, it) shall begin (C)   they shall begin (C)

Past
I began   we began
you began   you began
he (she, it) began   they began

Past Prog.
I was beginning   we were beginning
you were beginning   you were beginning
he (she, it) was beginning   they were beginning

Past Int.
I did begin   we did begin
you did begin   you did begin
he (she, it) did begin   they did begin

Perf. (Pres.)
I have begun   we have begun
you have begun   you have begun
he (she, it) has begun   they have begun

Perf. (Past)
I had begun   we had begun
you had begun   you had begun
he (she, it) had begun   they had begun

Perf. (Fut.)
I shall have begun   we shall have begun
you will have begun   you will have begun
he (she, it) will have begun   they will have begun

IMPERATIVE MOOD

begin

SUBJUNCTIVE MOOD

Pres.
if I begin   if we begin
if you begin   if you begin
if he (she, it) begin   if they begin

Past
if I began   if we began
if you began   if you began
if he (she, it) began   if they began

Fut.
if I should begin   if we should begin
if you should begin   if you should begin
if he (she, it) should begin   if they should begin

Infinitive: to be begun   *Present Participle:* being begun
Perfect Infinitive: to have been begun   *Past Participle:* been begun

INDICATIVE MOOD

Pres.	I am begun		we are begun
	you are begun		you are begun
	he (she, it) is begun		they are begun

Pres.
Prog.
I am being begun   we are being begun
you are being begun   you are being begun
he (she, it) is being begun   they are being begun

Pres.
Int.
I do get begun   we do get begun
you do get begun   you do get begun
he (she, it) does get begun   they do get begun

Fut.
I shall be begun   we shall be begun
you will be begun   you will be begun
he (she, it) will be begun   they will be begun

Fut.
I will be begun *(P)*   we will be begun *(P)*
you shall be begun *(C)*   you shall be begun *(C)*
he (she, it) shall be begun *(C)*   they shall be begun *(C)*

Past
I was begun   we were begun
you were begun   you were begun
he (she, it) was begun   they were begun

Past
Prog.
I was being begun   we were being begun
you were being begun   you were being begun
he (she, it) was being begun   they were being begun

Past
Int.
I did get begun   we did get begun
you did get begun   you did get begun
he (she, it) did get begun   they did get begun

Pres.
Perf.
I have been begun   we have been begun
you have been begun   you have been begun
he (she, it) has been begun   they have been begun

Past
Perf.
I had been begun   we had been begun
you had been begun   you had been begun
he (she, it) had been begun   they had been begun

Fut.
Perf.
I shall have been begun   we shall have been begun
you will have been begun   you will have been begun
he (she, it) will have been begun   they will have been begun

IMPERATIVE MOOD
be begun

SUBJUNCTIVE MOOD

Pres.
if I be begun   if we be begun
if you be begun   if you be begun
if he (she, it) be begun   if they be begun

Past
if I were begun   if we were begun
if you were begun   if you were begun
if he (she, it) were begun   if they were begun

Fut.
if I should be begun   if we should be begun
if you should be begun   if you should be begun
if he (she, it) should be begun   if they should be begun

to bend (active voice)

Principal Parts: bend, bending, bent, bent

Infinitive: to bend	*Perfect Infinitive:* to have bent
Present Participle: bending	*Past Participle:* bent

INDICATIVE MOOD

Pres. I bend	we bend
you bend	you bend
he (she, it) bends	they bend
Pres. I am bending	we are bending
Prog. you are bending	you are bending
he (she, it) is bending	they are bending
Pres. I do bend	we do bend
Int. you do bend	you do bend
he (she, it) does bend	they do bend
Fut. I shall bend	we shall bend
you will bend	they will bend
he (she, it) will bend	you will bend
Fut. I will bend (P)	we will bend (P)
you shall bend (C)	you shall bend (C)
he (she, it) shall bend (C)	they shall bend (C)
Past I bent	we bent
you bent	you bent
he (she, it) bent	they bent
Past I was bending	we were bending
Prog. you were bending	you were bending
he (she, it) was bending	they were bending
Past I did bend	we did bend
Int. you did bend	you did bend
he (she, it) did bend	they did bend
Pres. I have bent	we have bent
Perf. you have bent	you have bent
he (she, it) has bent	they have bent
Past I had bent	we had bent
Perf. you had bent	you had bent
he (she, it) had bent	they had bent
Fut. I shall have bent	we shall have bent
Perf. you will have bent	you will have bent
he (she, it) will have bent	they will have bent

IMPERATIVE MOOD

bend

SUBJUNCTIVE MOOD

Pres. if I bend	if we bend
if you bend	if you bend
if he (she, it) bend	if they bend
Past if I bent	if we bent
if you bent	if you bent
if he (she, it) bent	if they bent
Fut. if I should bend	if we should bend
if you should bend	if you should bend
if he (she, it) should bend	if they should bend

Infinitive: to be bent   *Present Participle:* being bent
Perfect Infinitive: to have been bent   *Past Participle:* been bent

INDICATIVE MOOD

Pres.	I am bent	we are bent
	you are bent	you are bent
	he (she, it) is bent	they are bent
Pres.	I am being bent	we are being bent
Prog.	you are being bent	you are being bent
	he (she, it) is being bent	they are being bent
Pres.	I do get bent	we do get bent
Int.	you do get bent	you do get bent
	he (she, it) does get bent	they do get bent
Fut.	I shall be bent	we shall be bent
	you will be bent	you will be bent
	he (she, it) will be bent	they will be bent
Fut.	I will be bent *(P)*	we will be bent *(P)*
	you shall be bent *(C)*	you shall be bent *(C)*
	he (she, it) shall be bent *(C)*	they shall be bent *(C)*
Past	I was bent	we were bent
	you were bent	you were bent
	he (she, it) was bent	they were bent
Past	I was being bent	we were being bent
Prog.	you were being bent	you were being bent
	he (she, it) was being bent	they were being bent
Past	I did get bent	we did get bent
Int.	you did get bent	you did get bent
	he (she, it) did get bent	they did get bent
Pres.	I have been bent	we have been bent
Perf.	you have been bent	you have been bent
	he (she, it) has been bent	they have been bent
Past	I had been bent	we had been bent
Perf.	you had been bent	you had been bent
	he (she, it) had been bent	they had been bent
Fut.	I shall have been bent	we shall have been bent
Perf.	you will have been bent	you will have been bent
	he (she, it) will have been bent	they will have been bent

IMPERATIVE MOOD
be bent

SUBJUNCTIVE MOOD

Pres.	if I be bent	if we be bent
	if you be bent	if you be bent
	if he (she, it) be bent	if they be bent
Past	if I were bent	if we were bent
	if you were bent	if you were bent
	if he (she, it) were bent	if they were bent
Fut.	if I should be bent	if we should be bent
	if you should be bent	if you should be bent
	if he (she, it) should be bent	if they should be bent

to bid (active voice)

Infinitive: to bid   *Present Participle:* bidding
Perfect Infinitive: to have bid   *Past Participle:* bid

INDICATIVE MOOD

Pres.	I bid	we bid
	you bid	you bid
	he (she, it) bids	they bid
Pres. *Prog.*	I am bidding	we are bidding
	you are bidding	you are bidding
	he (she, it) is bidding	they are bidding
Pres. *Int.*	I do bid	we do bid
	you do bid	you do bid
	he (she, it) does bid	they do bid
Fut.	I shall bid	we shall bid
	you will bid	you will bid
	he (she, it) will bid	they will bid
Fut.	I will bid *(P)*	we will bid *(P)*
	you shall bid *(C)*	you shall bid *(C)*
	he (she, it) shall bid *(C)*	they shall bid *(C)*
Past	I bid	we bid
	you bid	you bid
	he (she, it) bid	they bid
Past *Prog.*	I was bidding	we were bidding
	you were bidding	you were bidding
	he (she, it) was bidding	they were bidding
Past *Int.*	I did bid	we did bid
	you did bid	you did bid
	he (she, it) did bid	they did bid
Pres. *Perf.*	I have bid	we have bid
	you have bid	you have bid
	he (she, it) has bid	they have bid
Past *Perf.*	I had bid	we had bid
	you had bid	you had bid
	he (she, it) had bid	they had bid
Fut. *Perf.*	I shall have bid	we shall have bid
	you will have bid	you will have bid
	he (she, it) will have bid	they will have bid

IMPERATIVE MOOD
bid

SUBJUNCTIVE MOOD

Pres.	if I bid	if we bid
	if you bid	if you bid
	if he (she, it) bid	if they bid
Past	if I bid	if we bid
	if you bid	if you bid
	if he (she, it) bid	if they bid
Fut.	if I should bid	if we should bid
	if you should bid	if you should bid
	if he (she, it) should bid	if they should bid

(passive voice)

Infinitive: to be bid *Present Participle:* being bid
Perfect Infinitive: to have been bid *Past Participle:* been bid

INDICATIVE MOOD

Pres.	I am bid	we are bid
	you are bid	you are bid
	he (she, it) is bid	they are bid
Prog.	I am being bid	we are being bid
Pres.	you are being bid	you are being bid
	he (she, it) is being bid	they are being bid
Pres.	I do get bid	we do get bid
Int.	you do get bid	you do get bid
	he (she, it) does get bid	they do get bid
Fut.	I shall be bid	we shall be bid
	you will be bid	you will be bid
	he (she, it) will be bid	they will be bid
Fut.	I will be bid (P)	we will be bid (P)
	you shall be bid (C)	you shall be bid (C)
	he (she, it) shall be bid (C)	they shall be bid (C)
Past	I was bid	we were bid
	you were bid	you were bid
	he (she, it) was bid	they were bid
Past	I was being bid	we were being bid
Prog.	you were being bid	you were being bid
	he (she, it) was being bid	they were being bid
Past	I did get bid	we did get bid
Int.	you did get bid	you did get bid
	he (she, it) did get bid	they did get bid
Pres.	I have been bid	we have been bid
Perf.	you have been bid	you have been bid
	he (she, it) has been bid	they have been bid
Past	I had been bid	we had been bid
Perf.	you had been bid	you had been bid
	he (she, it) had been bid	they had been bid
Fut.	I shall have been bid	we shall have been bid
Perf.	you will have been bid	you will have been bid
	he (she, it) will have been bid	they will have been bid

IMPERATIVE MOOD

be bid

SUBJUNCTIVE MOOD

Pres.	if I be bid	if we be bid
	if you be bid	if you be bid
	if he (she, it) be bid	if they be bid
Past	if I were bid	if we were bid
	if you were bid	if you were bid
	if he (she, it) were bid	if they were bid
Fut.	if I should be bid	if we should be bid
	if you should be bid	if you should be bid
	if he (she, it) should be bid	if they should be bid

to bid (active voice)   *Principal Parts:* bid, bidding, bade, bidden
(order or command)

Infinitive: to bid   *Present Participle:* bidding
Perfect Infinitive: to have bidden   *Past Participle:* bidden

INDICATIVE MOOD

Pres.	I bid	we bid
	you bid	you bid
	he (she, it) bids	they bid
Pres.	I am bidding	we are bidding
Prog.	you are bidding	you are bidding
	he (she, it) is bidding	they are bidding
Pres.	I do bid	we do bid
Int.	you do bid	you do bid
	he (she, it) does bid	they do bid
Fut.	I shall bid	we shall bid
	you will bid	you will bid
	he (she, it) will bid	they will bid
Fut.	I will bid *(P)*	we will bid *(P)*
	you shall bid *(C)*	you shall bid *(C)*
	he (she, it) shall bid *(C)*	they shall bid *(C)*
Past	I bade	we bade
	you bade	you bade
	he (she, it) bade	they bade
Past	I was bidding	we were bidding
Prog.	you were bidding	you were bidding
	he (she, it) was bidding	they were bidding
Past	I did bid	we did bid
Int.	you did bid	you did bid
	he (she, it) did bid	they did bid
Pres.	I have bid	we have bid
Perf.	you have bid	you have bid
	he (she, it) has bid	they have bid
Past	I had bid	we had bid
Perf.	you had bid	you had bid
	he (she, it) had bid	they had bid
Fut.	I shall have bid	we shall have bid
Perf.	you will have bid	you will have bid
	he (she, it) will have bid	they will have bid

IMPERATIVE MOOD
bid

SUBJUNCTIVE MOOD

Pres.	if I bid	if we bid
	if you bid	if you bid
	if he (she, it) bid	if they bid
Past	if I bade	if we bade
	if you bade	if you bade
	if he (she, it) bade	if they bade
Fut.	if I should bid	if we should bid
	if you should bid	if you should bid
	if he (she, it) should bid	if they should bid

(passive voice)

Infinitive: to be bidden   *Present Participle:* being bidden
Perfect Infinitive: to have been bidden   *Past Participle:* been bidden

INDICATIVE MOOD

Pres. I am bidden / you are bidden / he (she, it) is bidden — we are bidden / you are bidden / they are bidden

Pres. Prog. I am being bidden / you are being bidden / he (she, it) is being bidden — we are being bidden / you are being bidden / they are being bidden

Pres. Int. I do get bidden / you do get bidden / he (she, it) does get bidden — we do get bidden / you do get bidden / they do get bidden

Fut. I shall be bidden / you will be bidden / he (she, it) will be bidden — we shall be bidden / you will be bidden / they will be bidden

Fut. I will be bidden *(P)* / you shall be bidden *(C)* / he (she, it) shall be bidden *(C)* — we will be bidden *(P)* / you shall be bidden *(C)* / they shall be bidden *(C)*

Past I was bidden / you were bidden / he (she, it) was bidden — we were bidden / you were bidden / they were bidden

Past Prog. I was being bidden / you were being bidden / he (she, it) was being bidden — we were being bidden / you were being bidden / they were being bidden

Past Int. I did get bidden / you did get bidden / he (she, it) did get bidden — we did get bidden / you did get bidden / they did get bidden

Pres. Perf. I have been bidden / you have been bidden / he (she, it) has been bidden — we have been bidden / you have been bidden / they have been bidden

Past Perf. I had been bidden / you had been bidden / he (she, it) had been bidden — we had been bidden / you had been bidden / they had been bidden

Fut. Perf. I shall have been bidden / you will have been bidden / he (she, it) will have been bidden — we shall have been bidden / you will have been bidden / they will have been bidden

IMPERATIVE MOOD
be bidden

SUBJUNCTIVE MOOD

Pres. if I be bidden / if you be bidden / if he (she, it) be bidden — if we be bidden / if you be bidden / if they be bidden

Past if I were bidden / if you were bidden / if he (she, it) were bidden — if we were bidden / if you were bidden / if they were bidden

Fut. if I should be bidden / if you should be bidden / if he (she, it) should be bidden — if we should be bidden / if you should be bidden / if they should be bidden

to bind (active voice)   *Principal Parts:* bind, binding, bound, bound

Infinitive: to bind   *Present Participle:* binding
Perfect Infinitive: to have bound   *Past Participle:* bound

INDICATIVE MOOD

Pres.	I bind	we bind
	you bind	you bind
	he (she, it) binds	they bind
Pres.	I am binding	we are binding
Prog.	you are binding	you are binding
	he (she, it) is binding	they are binding
Pres.	I do bind	we do bind
Int.	you do bind	you do bind
	he (she, it) does bind	they do bind
Fut.	I shall bind	we shall bind
	you will bind	you will bind
	he (she, it) will bind	they will bind
Fut.	I will bind *(P)*	we will bind *(P)*
	you shall bind *(C)*	you shall bind *(C)*
	he (she, it) shall bind *(C)*	they shall bind *(C)*
Past	I bound	we bound
	you bound	you bound
	he (she, it) bound	they bound
Past	I was binding	we were binding
Prog.	you were binding	you were binding
	he (she, it) was binding	they were binding
Past	I did bind	we did bind
Int.	you did bind	you did bind
	he (she, it) did bind	they did bind
Pres.	I have bound	we have bound
Perf.	you have bound	you have bound
	he (she, it) has bound	they have bound
Past	I had bound	we had bound
Perf.	you had bound	you had bound
	he (she, it) had bound	they had bound
Fut.	I shall have bound	we shall have bound
Perf.	you will have bound	you will have bound
	he (she, it) will have bound	they will have bound

IMPERATIVE MOOD
bind

SUBJUNCTIVE MOOD

Pres.	if I bind	if we bind
	if you bind	if you bind
	if he (she, it) bind	if they bind
Past	if I bound	if we bound
	if you bound	if you bound
	if he (she, it) bound	if they bound
Fut.	if I should bind	if we should bind
	if you should bind	if you should bind
	if he (she, it) should bind	if they should bind

150

Infinitive: to be bound   *Present Participle:* being bound
Perfect Infinitive: to have been bound   *Past Participle:* been bound

INDICATIVE MOOD

Pres.	I am bound	we are bound
	you are bound	you are bound
	he (she, it) is bound	they are bound
Pres.	I am being bound	we are being bound
Prog.	you are being bound	you are being bound
	he (she, it) is being bound	they are being bound
Pres.	I do get bound	we do get bound
Int.	you do get bound	you do get bound
	he (she, it) does get bound	they do get bound
Fut.	I shall be bound	we shall be bound
	you will be bound	you will be bound
	he (she, it) will be bound	they will be bound
Fut.	I will be bound *(P)*	we will be bound *(P)*
	you shall be bound *(C)*	you shall be bound *(C)*
	he (she, it) shall be bound *(C)*	they shall be bound *(C)*
Past	I was bound	we were bound
	you were bound	you were bound
	he (she, it) was bound	they were bound
Past	I was being bound	we were being bound
Prog.	you were being bound	you were being bound
	he (she, it) was being bound	they were being bound
Past	I did get bound	we did get bound
Int.	you did get bound	you did get bound
	he (she, it) did get bound	they did get bound
Pres.	I have been bound	we have been bound
Perf.	you have been bound	you have been bound
	he (she, it) has been bound	they have been bound
Past	I had been bound	we had been bound
Perf.	you had been bound	you had been bound
	he (she, it) had been bound	they had been bound
Fut.	I shall have been bound	we shall have been bound
Perf.	you will have been bound	you will have been bound
	he (she, it) will have been bound	they will have been bound

IMPERATIVE MOOD
bind

SUBJUNCTIVE MOOD

Pres.	if I be bound	if we be bound
	if you be bound	if you be bound
	if he (she, it) be bound	if they be bound
Past	if I were bound	if we were bound
	if you were bound	if you were bound
	if he (she, it) were bound	if they were bound
Fut.	if I should be bound	if we should be bound
	if you should be bound	if you should be bound
	if he (she, it) should be bound	if they should be bound

151

to bite (active voice) *Principal Parts:* bite, biting, bit, bitten (bit)

Infinitive: to bite *Present Participle:* biting
Perfect Infinitive: to have bitten, bit *Past Participle:* bitten (bit)

INDICATIVE MOOD

Pres.	I bite	we bite
	you bite	you bite
	he (she, it) bites	they bite
Pres.	I am biting	we are biting
Prog.	you are biting	you are biting
	he (she, it) is biting	they are biting
Pres.	I do bite	we do bite
Int.	you do bite	you do bite
	he (she, it) does bite	they do bite
Fut.	I shall bite	we shall bite
	you will bite	you will bite
	he (she, it) will bite	they will bite
Fut.	I will bite *(P)*	we will bite *(P)*
	you shall bite *(C)*	you shall bite *(C)*
	he (she, it) shall bite *(C)*	they shall bite *(C)*
Past	I bit	we bit
	you bit	you bit
	he (she, it) bit	they bit
Past	I was biting	we were biting
Prog.	you were biting	you were biting
	he (she, it) was biting	they were biting
Past	I did bite	we did bite
Int.	you did bite	you did bite
	he (she, it) did bite	they did bite
Pres.	I have bitten, bit	we have bitten, bit
Perf.	you have bitten, bit	you have bitten, bit
	he (she, it) has bitten, bit	they have bitten, bit
Past	I had bitten, bit	we had bitten, bit
Perf.	you had bitten, bit	you had bitten, bit
	he (she, it) had bitten, bit	they had bitten, bit
Fut.	I shall have bitten, bit	we shall have bitten, bit
Perf.	you will have bitten, bit	you will have bitten, bit
	he (she, it) will have bitten, bit	they will have bitten, bit

IMPERATIVE MOOD
bite

SUBJUNCTIVE MOOD

Pres.	if I bite	if we bite
	if you bite	if you bite
	if he (she, it) bite	if they bite
Past	if I bit	if we bit
	if you bit	if you bit
	if he (she, it) bit	if they bit
Fut.	if I should bite	if we should bite
	if you should bite	if you should bite
	if he (she, it) should bite	if they should bite

Infinitive: to be bitten
Perfect Infinitive: to have been bitten (bit)

Present Participle: being bitten (bit)
Past Participle: been bitten (bit)

INDICATIVE MOOD

Pres. I am bitten
you are bitten
he (she, it) is bitten

we are bitten
you are bitten
they are bitten

Pres.
Prog. I am being bitten
you are being bitten
he (she, it) is being bitten

we are being bitten
you are being bitten
they are being bitten

Pres.
Int. I do get bitten
you do get bitten
he (she, it) does get bitten

we do get bitten
you do get bitten
they do get bitten

Fut. I shall be bitten
you will be bitten
he (she, it) will be bitten

we shall be bitten
you will be bitten
they will be bitten

Fut. I will be bitten *(P)*
you shall be bitten *(C)*
he (she, it) shall be bitten *(C)*

we will be bitten *(P)*
you shall be bitten *(C)*
they shall be bitten *(C)*

Past I was bitten
you were bitten
he (she, it) was bitten

we were bitten
you were bitten
they were bitten

Past
Prog. I was being bitten
you were being bitten
he (she, it) was being bitten

we were being bitten
you were being bitten
they were being bitten

Past
Int. I did get bitten
you did get bitten
he (she, it) did get bitten

we did get bitten
you did get bitten
they did get bitten

Pres.
Perf. I have been bitten
you have been bitten
he (she, it) has been bitten

we have been bitten
you have been bitten
they have been bitten

Past
Perf. I had been bitten
you had been bitten
he (she, it) had been bitten

we had been bitten
you had been bitten
they had been bitten

Fut.
Perf. I shall have been bitten
you will have been bitten
he (she, it) will have been bitten

we shall have been bitten
you will have been bitten
they will have been bitten

IMPERATIVE MOOD
be bitten

SUBJUNCTIVE MOOD

Pres. if I be bitten
if you be bitten
if he (she, it) be bitten

if we be bitten
if you be bitten
if they be bitten

Past if I were bitten
if you were bitten
if he (she, it) were bitten

if we were bitten
if you were bitten
if they were bitten

Fut. if I should be bitten
if you should be bitten
if he (she, it) should be bitten

if we should be bitten
if you should be bitten
if they should be bitten

to blow (active voice)　　　*Principal Parts:* blow, blowing, blew, blown

Infinitive: to blow　　　　　　　　　　　*Present Participle:* blowing
Perfect Infinitive: to have blown　　　　　　*Past Participle:* blown

INDICATIVE MOOD

Pres.	I blow	we blow
	you blow	you blow
	he (she, it) blows	they blow

Pres. Prog.	I am blowing	we are blowing
	you are blowing	you are blowing
	he (she, it) is blowing	they are blowing

Pres. Int.	I do blow	we do blow
	you do blow	you do blow
	he (she, it) does blow	they do blow

Fut.	I shall blow	we shall blow
	you will blow	you will blow
	he (she, it) will blow	they will blow

Fut.	I will blow *(P)*	we will blow *(P)*
	you shall blow *(C)*	you shall blow *(C)*
	he (she, it) shall blow *(C)*	they shall blow *(C)*

Past	I blew	we blew
	you blew	you blew
	he (she, it) blew	they blew

Past Prog.	I was blowing	we were blowing
	you were blowing	you were blowing
	he (she, it) was blowing	they were blowing

Past Int.	I did blow	we did blow
	you did blow	you did blow
	he (she, it) did blow	they did blow

Pres. Perf.	I have blown	we have blown
	you have blown	you have blown
	he (she, it) has blown	they have blown

Past Perf.	I had blown	we had blown
	you had blown	you had blown
	he (she, it) had blown	they had blown

Fut. Perf.	I shall have blown	we shall have blown
	you will have blown	you will have blown
	he (she, it) will have blown	they will have blown

IMPERATIVE MOOD
blow

SUBJUNCTIVE MOOD

Pres.	if I blow	if we blow
	if you blow	if you blow
	if he (she, it) blow	if they blow

Past	if I blew	if we blew
	if you blew	if you blew
	if he (she, it) blew	if they blew

Fut.	if I should blow	if we should blow
	if you should blow	if you should blow
	if he (she, it) should blow	if they should blow

Infinitive: to be blown   *Present Participle:* being blown
Perfect Infinitive: to have been blown   *Past Participle:* been blown

INDICATIVE MOOD

Pres.	I am blown	we are blown
	you are blown	you are blown
	he (she, it) is blown	they are blown

Pres.	I am being blown	we are being blown
Prog.	you are being blown	you are being blown
	he (she, it) is being blown	they are being blown

Pres.	I do get blown	we do get blown
Int.	you do get blown	you do get blown
	he (she, it) does get blown	they do get blown

Fut.	I shall be blown	we shall be blown
	you will be blown	you will be blown
	he (she, it) will be blown	they will be blown

Fut.	I will be blown *(P)*	we will be blown *(P)*
	you shall be blown *(C)*	you shall be blown *(C)*
	he (she, it) shall be blown *(C)*	they shall be blown *(C)*

Past	I was blown	we were blown
	you were blown	you were blown
	he (she, it) was blown	they were blown

Past	I was being blown	we were being blown
Prog.	you were being blown	you were being blown
	he (she, it) was being blown	they were being blown

Past	I did get blown	we did get blown
Int.	you did get blown	you did get blown
	he (she, it) did get blown	they did get blown

Pres.	I have been blown	we have been blown
Perf.	you have been blown	you have been blown
	he (she, it) has been blown	they have been blown

Past	I had been blown	we had been blown
Perf.	you had been blown	you had been blown
	he (she, it) had been blown	they had been blown

Fut.	I shall have been blown	we shall have been blown
Perf.	you will have been blown	you will have been blown
	he (she, it) will have been blown	they will have been blown

IMPERATIVE MOOD
be blown

SUBJUNCTIVE MOOD

Pres.	if I be blown	if we be blown
	if you be blown	if you be blown
	if he (she, it) be blown	if they be blown

Past	if I were blown	if we were blown
	if you were blown	if you were blown
	if he (she, it) were blown	if they were blown

Fut.	if I should be blown	if we should be blown
	if you should be blown	if you should be blown
	if he (she, it) should be blown	if they should be blown

to break (active voice)   *Principal Parts:* break, breaking, broke, broken

Infinitive: to break   *Present Participle:* breaking
Perfect Infinitive: to have broken   *Past Participle:* broken

INDICATIVE MOOD

Pres.	I break	we break	
	you break	you break	
	he (she, it) breaks	they break	
Pres. Prog.	I am breaking	we are breaking	
	you are breaking	you are breaking	
	he (she, it) is breaking	they are breaking	
Pres. Int.	I do break	we do break	
	you do break	you do break	
	he (she, it) does break	they do break	
Fut.	I shall break	we shall break	
	you will break	you will break	
	he (she, it) will break	they will break	
Fut.	I will break *(P)*	we will break *(P)*	
	you shall break *(C)*	you shall break *(C)*	
	he (she, it) shall break *(C)*	they shall break *(C)*	
Past	I broke	we broke	
	you broke	you broke	
	he (she, it) broke	they broke	
Past Prog.	I was breaking	we were breaking	
	you were breaking	you were breaking	
	he (she, it) was breaking	they were breaking	
Past Int.	I did break	we did break	
	you did break	you did break	
	he (she, it) did break	they did break	
Pres. Perf.	I have broken	we have broken	
	you have broken	you have broken	
	he (she, it) has broken	they have broken	
Past Perf.	I had broken	we had broken	
	you had broken	you had broken	
	he (she, it) had broken	they had broken	
Fut. Perf.	I shall have broken	we shall have broken	
	you will have broken	you will have broken	
	he (she, it) will have broken	they will have broken	

IMPERATIVE MOOD
break

SUBJUNCTIVE MOOD

Pres.	if I break	if we break
	if you break	if you break
	if he (she, it) break	if they break
Past	if I broke	if we broke
	if you broke	if you broke
	if he (she, it) broke	if they broke
Fut.	if I should break	if we should break
	if you should break	if you should break
	if he (she, it) should break	if they should break

Infinitive: to be broken *Present Participle:* being broken
Perfect Infinitive: to have been broken *Past Participle:* been broken

INDICATIVE MOOD

Pres.	I am broken	we are broken
	you are broken	you are broken
	he (she, it) is broken	they are broken
Pres.	I am being broken	we are being broken
Prog.	you are being broken	you are being broken
	he (she, it) is being broken	they are being broken
Pres.	I do get broken	we do get broken
Int.	you do get broken	you do get broken
	he (she, it) does get broken	they do get broken
Fut.	I shall be broken	we shall be broken
	you will be broken	you will be broken
	he (she, it) will be broken	they will be broken
Fut.	I will be broken *(P)*	we will be broken *(P)*
	you shall be broken *(C)*	you shall be broken *(C)*
	he (she, it) shall be broken *(C)*	they shall be broken *(C)*
Past	I was broken	we were broken
	you were broken	you were broken
	he (she, it) was broken	they were broken
Past	I was being broken	we were being broken
Prog.	you were being broken	you were being broken
	he (she, it) was being broken	they were being broken
Past	I did get broken	we did get broken
Int.	you did get broken	you did get broken
	he (she, it) did get broken	they did get broken
Pres.	I have been broken	we have been broken
Perf.	you have been broken	you have been broken
	he (she, it) has been broken	they have been broken
Past	I had been broken	we had been broken
Perf.	you had been broken	you had been broken
	he (she, it) had been broken	they had been broken
Fut.	I shall have been broken	we shall have been broken
Perf.	you will have been broken	you will have been broken
	he (she, it) will have been broken	they will have been broken

IMPERATIVE MOOD
be broken

SUBJUNCTIVE MOOD

Pres.	if I be broken	if we be broken
	if you be broken	if you be broken
	if he (she, it) be broken	if they be broken
Past	if I were broken	if we were broken
	if you were broken	if you were broken
	if he (she, it) were broken	if they were broken
Fut.	if I should be broken	if we should be broken
	if you should be broken	if you should be broken
	if he (she, it) should be broken	if they should be broken

157

to bring (active voice)

Infinitive: to bring   *Present Participle:* bringing
Perfect Infinitive: to have brought   *Past Participle:* brought

INDICATIVE MOOD

Pres.	I bring	we bring
	you bring	you bring
	he (she, it) brings	they bring

Pres. Prog.	I am bringing	we are bringing
	you are bringing	you are bringing
	he (she, it) is bringing	they are bringing

Pres. Int.	I do bring	we do bring
	you do bring	you do bring
	he (she, it) does bring	they do bring

Fut.	I shall bring	we shall bring
	you will bring	you will bring
	he (she, it) will bring	they will bring

Fut.	I will bring *(P)*	we will bring *(P)*
	you shall bring *(C)*	you shall bring *(C)*
	he (she, it) shall bring *(C)*	they shall bring *(C)*

Past	I brought	we brought
	you brought	you brought
	he (she, it) brought	they brought

Past Prog.	I was bringing	we were bringing
	you were bringing	you were bringing
	he (she, it) was bringing	they were bringing

Past Int.	I did bring	we did bring
	you did bring	you did bring
	he (she, it) did bring	they did bring

Pres. Perf.	I have brought	we have brought
	you have brought	you have brought
	he (she, it) has brought	they have brought

Past Perf.	I had brought	we had brought
	you had brought	you had brought
	he (she, it) had brought	they had brought

Fut. Perf.	I shall have brought	we shall have brought
	you will have brought	you will have brought
	he (she, it) will have brought	they will have brought

IMPERATIVE MOOD
bring

SUBJUNCTIVE MOOD

Pres.	if I bring	if we bring
	if you bring	if you bring
	if he (she, it) bring	if they bring

Past	if I brought	if we brought
	if you brought	if you brought
	if he (she, it) brought	if they brought

Fut.	if I should bring	if we should bring
	if you should bring	if you should bring
	if he (she, it) should bring	if they should bring

Infinitive: to be brought   *Present Participle:* being brought
Perfect Infinitive: to have been brought   *Past Participle:* been brought

INDICATIVE MOOD

Pres.	I am brought	we are brought
	you are brought	you are brought
	he (she, it) is brought	they are brought
Pres.	I am being brought	we are being brought
Prog.	you are being brought	you are being brought
	he (she, it) is being brought	they are being brought
Pres.	I do get brought	we do get brought
Int.	you do get brought	you do get brought
	he (she, it) does get brought	they do get brought
Fut.	I shall be brought	we shall be brought
	you will be brought	you will be brought
	he (she, it) will be brought	they will be brought
Fut.	I will be brought *(P)*	we will be brought *(P)*
	you shall be brought *(C)*	you shall be brought *(C)*
	he (she, it) shall be brought *(C)*	they shall be brought *(C)*
Past	I was brought	we were brought
	you were brought	you were brought
	he (she, it) was brought	they were brought
Past	I was being brought	we were being brought
Prog.	you were being brought	you were being brought
	he (she, it) was being brought	they were being brought
Past	I did get brought	we did get brought
Int.	you did get brought	you did get brought
	he (she, it) did get brought	they did get brought
Pres.	I have been brought	we have been brought
Perf.	you have been brought	you have been brought
	he (she, it) has been brought	they have been brought
Past	I had been brought	we had been brought
Perf.	you had been brought	you had been brought
	he (she, it) had been brought	they had been brought
Fut.	I shall have been brought	we shall have been brought
Perf.	you will have been brought	you will have been brought
	he (she, it) will have been brought	they will have been brought

IMPERATIVE MOOD
be brought

SUBJUNCTIVE MOOD

Pres.	if I be brought	if we be brought
	if you be brought	if you be brought
	if he (she, it) be brought	if they be brought
Past	if I were brought	if we were brought
	if you were brought	if you were brought
	if he (she, it) were brought	if they were brought
Fut.	if I should be brought	if we should be brought
	if you should be brought	if you should be brought
	if he (she, it) should be brought	if they should be brought

to broadcast (active voice)   *Principal Parts:* broadcast, broadcasting,
broadcast (broadcasted)
broadcast (broadcasted)

Infinitive: to broadcast   *Present Participle:* broadcasting
Perfect Infinitive: to have broadcast   *Past Participle:* broadcast

INDICATIVE MOOD

Pres.	I broadcast	we broadcast
	you broadcast	you broadcast
	he (she, it) broadcasts	they broadcast
Pres.	I am broadcasting	we are broadcasting
Prog.	you are broadcasting	you are broadcasting
	he (she, it) is broadcasting	they are broadcasting
Pres.	I do broadcast	we do broadcast
Int.	you do broadcast	you do broadcast
	he (she, it) does broadcast	they do broadcast
Fut.	I shall broadcast	we shall broadcast
	you will broadcast	you will broadcast
	he (she, it) will broadcast	they will broadcast
Fut.	I will broadcast *(P)*	we will broadcast *(P)*
	you shall broadcast *(C)*	you shall broadcast *(C)*
	he (she, it) shall broadcast *(C)*	they shall broadcast *(C)*
Past	I broadcast(ed)	we broadcast(ed)
	you broadcast(ed)	you broadcast(ed)
	he (she, it) broadcast(ed)	they broadcast(ed)
Past	I was broadcasting	we were broadcasting
Prog.	you were broadcasting	you were broadcasting
	he (she, it) was broadcasting	they were broadcasting
Past	I did broadcast	we did broadcast
Int.	you did broadcast	you did broadcast
	he (she, it) did broadcast	they did broadcast
Pres.	I have broadcast(ed)	we have broadcast(ed)
Perf.	you have broadcast(ed)	you have broadcast(ed)
	he (she, it) has broadcast(ed)	they have broadcast(ed)
Past	I had broadcast(ed)	we had broadcast(ed)
Perf.	you had broadcast(ed)	you had broadcast(ed)
	he (she, it) had broadcast(ed)	they had broadcast(ed)
Fut.	I shall have broadcast(ed)	we shall have broadcast(ed)
Perf.	you will have broadcast(ed)	you will have broadcast(ed)
	he (she, it) will have broadcast(ed)	they will have broadcast(ed)

IMPERATIVE MOOD
broadcast

SUBJUNCTIVE MOOD

Pres.	if I broadcast	if we broadcast
	if you broadcast	if you broadcast
	if he (she, it) broadcast	if they broadcast
Past	if I broadcast(ed)	if we broadcast(ed)
	if you broadcast(ed)	if you broadcast(ed)
	if he (she, it) broadcast(ed)	if they broadcast(ed)
Fut.	if I should broadcast	if we should broadcast
	if you should broadcast	if you should broadcast
	if he (she, it) should broadcast	if they should broadcast

(passive voice)

Infinitive: to be broadcast(ed)   *Present Participle:* being broadcast(ed)
Perfect Infinitive: to have been   *Past Participle:* been broadcast(ed)
broadcast(ed)

INDICATIVE MOOD

Pres.	I am broadcast(ed)
	you are broadcast(ed)
	he (she, it) is broadcast(ed)

we are broadcast(ed)
you are broadcast(ed)
they are broadcast(ed)

Pres.
Prog. I am being broadcast(ed)
you are being broadcast(ed)
he (she, it) is being broadcast(ed)

we are being broadcast(ed)
you are being broadcast(ed)
they are being broadcast(ed)

Pres.
Int. I do get broadcast(ed)
you do get broadcast(ed)
he (she, it) does get broadcast(ed)

we do get broadcast(ed)
you do get broadcast(ed)
they do get broadcast(ed)

Fut. I shall be broadcast(ed)
you will be broadcast(ed)
he (she, it) will be broadcast(ed)

we shall be broadcast(ed)
you will be broadcast(ed)
they will be broadcast(ed)

Fut. I will be broadcast(ed) *(P)*
you shall be broadcast(ed) *(C)*
he (she, it) shall be
broadcast(ed) *(C)*

we will be broadcast(ed) *(P)*
you shall be broadcast(ed) *(C)*
they shall be broadcast(ed) *(C)*

Past I was broadcast(ed)
you were broadcast(ed)
he (she, it) was broadcast(ed)

we were broadcast(ed)
you were broadcast(ed)
they were broadcast(ed)

Past
Prog. I was being broadcast(ed)
you were being broadcast(ed)
he (she, it) was being broadcast(ed)

we were being broadcast(ed)
you were being broadcast(ed)
they were being broadcast(ed)

Past
Int. I did get broadcast(ed)
you did get broadcast(ed)
he (she, it) did get broadcast(ed)

we did get broadcast(ed)
you did get broadcast(ed)
they did get broadcast(ed)

Pres.
Perf. I have been broadcast(ed)
you have been broadcast(ed)
he (she, it) has been broadcast(ed)

we have been broadcast(ed)
you have been broadcast(ed)
they have been broadcast(ed)

Past
Perf. I had been broadcast(ed)
you had been broadcast(ed)
he (she, it) had been broadcast(ed)

we had been broadcast(ed)
you had been broadcast(ed)
they had been broadcast(ed)

Fut.
Perf. I shall have been broadcast(ed)
you will have been broadcast(ed)
he (she, it) will have been
broadcast(ed)

we shall have been broadcast(ed)
you will have been broadcast(ed)
they will have been broadcast(ed)

IMPERATIVE MOOD
be broadcast

SUBJUNCTIVE MOOD

Pres. if I be broadcast(ed)
if you be broadcast(ed)
if he (she, it) be broadcast(ed)

if we be broadcast(ed)
if you be broadcast(ed)
if they be broadcast(ed)

Past if I were broadcast(ed)
if you were broadcast(ed)
if he (she, it) were broadcast(ed)

if we were broadcast(ed)
if you were broadcast(ed)
if they were broadcast(ed)

Fut. if I should be broadcast(ed)
if you should be broadcast(ed)
if he (she, it) should be
broadcast(ed)

if we should be broadcast(ed)
if you should be broadcast(ed)
if they should be broadcast(ed)

to build (active voice)   *Principal Parts:* build, building, built, built

Infinitive: to build   *Present Participle:* building
Perfect Infinitive: to have built   *Past Participle:* built

INDICATIVE MOOD

Pres.	I build	we build
	you build	you build
	he (she, it) builds	they build
Pres. Prog.	I am building	we are building
	you are building	you are building
	he (she, it) is building	they are building
Pres. Int.	I do build	we do build
	you do build	you do build
	he (she, it) does build	they do build
Fut.	I shall build	we shall build
	you will build	you will build
	he (she, it) will build	they will build
Fut.	I will build *(P)*	we will build *(P)*
	you shall build *(C)*	you shall build *(C)*
	he (she, it) shall build *(C)*	they shall build *(C)*
Past	I built	we built
	you built	you built
	he (she, it) built	they built
Past Prog.	I was building	we were building
	you were building	you were building
	he (she, it) was building	they were building
Past Int.	I did build	we did build
	you did build	you did build
	he (she, it) did build	they did build
Pres. Perf.	I have built	we have built
	you have built	you have built
	he (she, it) has built	they have built
Past Perf.	I had built	we had built
	you had built	you had built
	he (she, it) had built	they had built
Fut. Perf.	I shall have built	we shall have built
	you will have built	you shall have built
	he (she, it) will have built	they will have built

IMPERATIVE MOOD
build

SUBJUNCTIVE MOOD

Pres.	if I build	if we build
	if you build	if you build
	if he (she, it) build	if they build
Past	if I built	if we built
	if you built	if you built
	if he (she, it) built	if they built
Fut.	if I should build	if we should build
	if you should build	if you should build
	if he (she, it) should build	if they should build

Infinitive: to be built
Perfect Infinitive: to have been built

Present Participle: being built
Past Participle: been built

INDICATIVE MOOD

Pres. I am built
you are built
he (she, it) is built

we are built
you are built
they are built

Pres. I am being built
Prog. you are being built
he (she, it) is being built

we are being built
you are being built
they are being built

Pres. I do get built
Int. you do get built
he (she, it) does get built

we do get built
you do get built
they do get built

Fut. I shall be built
you will be built
he (she, it) will be built

we shall be built
you will be built
they will be built

Fut. I will be built *(P)*
you shall be built *(C)*
he (she, it) shall be built *(C)*

we will be built *(P)*
you shall be built *(C)*
they shall be built *(C)*

Past I was built
you were built
he (she, it) was built

we were built
you were built
they were built

Past I was being built
Prog. you were being built
he (she, it) was being built

we were being built
you were being built
they were being built

Past I did get built
Int. you did get built
he (she, it) did get built

we did get built
you did get built
they did get built

Pres. I have been built
Perf. you have been built
he (she, it) has been built

we have been built
you have been built
they have been built

Past I had been built
Perf. you had been built
he (she, it) had been built

we had been built
you had been built
they had been built

Fut. I shall have been built
Perf. you will have been built
he (she, it) will have been built

we shall have been built
you will have been built
they will have been built

IMPERATIVE MOOD
be built

SUBJUNCTIVE MOOD

Pres. if I be built
if you be built
if he (she, it) be built

if we be built
if you be built
if they be built

Past if I were built
if you were built
if he (she, it) were built

if we were built
if you were built
if they were built

Fut. if I should be built
if you should be built
if he (she, it) should be built

if we should be built
if you should be built
if they should be built

Infinitive: to burst   *Present Participle:* bursting
Perfect Infinitive: to have burst   *Past Participle:* burst

INDICATIVE MOOD

| *Pres.* | I burst
you burst
he (she, it) bursts | we burst
you burst
they burst |

| *Pres.*
Prog. | I am bursting
you are bursting
he (she, it) is bursting | we are bursting
you are bursting
they are bursting |

| *Pres.*
Int. | I do burst
you do burst
he (she, it) does burst | we do burst
you do burst
they do burst |

| *Fut.* | I shall burst
you will burst
he (she, it) will burst | we shall burst
you will burst
they will burst |

| *Fut.* | I will burst *(P)*
you shall burst *(C)*
he (she, it) shall burst *(C)* | we will burst *(P)*
you shall burst *(C)*
they shall burst *(C)* |

| *Past* | I burst
you burst
he (she, it) burst | we burst
you burst
they burst |

| *Past*
Prog. | I was bursting
you were bursting
he (she, it) was bursting | we were bursting
you were bursting
they were bursting |

| *Past*
Int. | I did burst
you did burst
he (she, it) did burst | we did burst
you did burst
they did burst |

| *Pres.*
Perf. | I have burst
you have burst
he (she, it) has burst | we have burst
you have burst
they have burst |

| *Past*
Perf. | I had burst
you had burst
he (she, it) had burst | we had burst
you had burst
they had burst |

| *Fut.*
Perf. | I shall have burst
you will have burst
he (she, it) will have burst | we shall have burst
you will have burst
they will have burst |

IMPERATIVE MOOD
burst

SUBJUNCTIVE MOOD

| *Pres.* | if I burst
if you burst
if he (she, it) burst | if we burst
if you burst
if they burst |

| *Past* | if I burst
if you burst
if he (she, it) burst | if we burst
if you burst
if they burst |

| *Fut.* | if I should burst
if you should burst
if he (she, it) should burst | if we should burst
if you should burst
if they should burst |

Infinitive: to be burst

Perfect Infinitive: to have been burst

Present Participle: being burst

Past Participle: been burst

INDICATIVE MOOD

Pres.	I am burst	we are burst
	you are burst	you are burst
	he (she, it) is burst	they are burst
Pres.	I am being burst	we are being burst
Prog.	you are being burst	you are being burst
	he (she, it) is being burst	they are being burst
Pres.	I do get burst	we do get burst
Int.	you do get burst	you do get burst
	he (she, it) does get burst	they do get burst
Fut.	I shall be burst	we shall be burst
	you will be burst	you will be burst
	he (she, it) will be burst	they will be burst
Fut.	I will be burst *(P)*	we will be burst *(P)*
	you shall be burst *(C)*	you shall be burst *(C)*
	he (she, it) shall be burst *(C)*	they shall be burst *(C)*
Past	I was burst	we were burst
	you were burst	you were burst
	he (she, it) was burst	they were burst
Past	I was being burst	we were being burst
Prog.	you were being burst	you were being burst
	he (she, it) was being burst	they were being burst
Past	I did get burst	we did get burst
Int.	you did get burst	you did get burst
	he (she, it) did get burst	they did get burst
Pres.	I have been burst	we have been burst
Perf.	you have been burst	you have been burst
	he (she, it) has been burst	they have been burst
Past	I had been burst	we had been burst
Perf.	you had been burst	you had been burst
	he (she, it) had been burst	they had been burst
Fut.	I shall have been burst	we shall have been burst
Perf.	you will have been burst	you will have been burst
	he (she, it) will have been burst	they will have been burst

IMPERATIVE MOOD

be burst

SUBJUNCTIVE MOOD

Pres.	if I be burst	if we be burst
	if you be burst	if you be burst
	if he (she, it) be burst	if they be burst
Past	if I were burst	if we were burst
	if you were burst	if you were burst
	if he (she, it) were burst	if they were burst
Fut.	if I should be burst	if we should be burst
	if you should be burst	if you should be burst
	if he (she, it) should be burst	if they should be burst

to buy (active voice)   *Principal Parts:* buy, buying bought, bought

Infinitive: to buy   *Present Participle:* buying
Perfect Infinitive: to have bought   *Past Participle:* bought

INDICATIVE MOOD

Pres.	I buy	we buy
	you buy	you buy
	he (she, it) buys	they buy
Pres. Prog.	I am buying	we are buying
	you are buying	you are buying
	he (she, it) is buying	they are buying
Pres. Int.	I do buy	we do buy
	you do buy	you do buy
	he (she, it) does buy	they do buy
Fut.	I shall buy	we shall buy
	you will buy	you will buy
	he (she, it) will buy	they will buy
Fut.	I will buy *(P)*	we will buy *(P)*
	you shall buy *(C)*	you shall buy *(C)*
	he (she, it) shall buy *(C)*	they shall buy *(C)*
Past	I bought	we bought
	you bought	you bought
	he (she, it) bought	they bought
Past Prog.	I was buying	we were buying
	you were buying	you were buying
	he (she, it) was buying	they were buying
Past Int.	I did buy	we did buy
	you did buy	you did buy
	he (she, it) did buy	they did buy
Pres. Perf.	I have bought	we have bought
	you have bought	you have bought
	he (she, it) has bought	they have bought
Past Perf.	I had bought	we had bought
	you had bought	you had bought
	he (she, it) had bought	they had bought
Fut. Perf.	I shall have bought	we shall have bought
	you will have bought	you will have bought
	he (she, it) will have bought	they will have bought

IMPERATIVE MOOD
buy

SUBJUNCTIVE MOOD

Pres.	if I buy	if we buy
	if you buy	if you buy
	if he (she, it) buy	if they buy
Past	if I bought	if we bought
	if you bought	if you bought
	if he (she, it) bought	if they bought
Fut.	if I should buy	if we should buy
	if you should buy	if you should buy
	if he (she, it) should buy	if they should buy

(passive voice)

Infinitive: to be bought · Perfect Infinitive: to have been bought

Present Participle: being bought · Past Participle: been bought

INDICATIVE MOOD

Pres.	I am bought	we are bought
	you are bought	you are bought
	he (she, it) is bought	they are bought
Prog.	I am being bought	we are being bought
	you are being bought	you are being bought
	he (she, it) is being bought	they are being bought
Int.	I do get bought	we do get bought
	you do get bought	you do get bought
	he (she, it) does get bought	they do get bought
Fut.	I shall be bought	we shall be bought
	you will be bought	you will be bought
	he (she, it) will be bought	they will be bought
Fut.	I will be bought (P)	we will be bought (P)
	you shall be bought (C)	you shall be bought (C)
	he (she, it) shall be bought (C)	they shall be bought (C)
Past	I was bought	we were bought
	you were bought	you were bought
	he (she, it) was bought	they were bought
Prog.	I was being bought	we were being bought
	you were being bought	you were being bought
	he (she, it) was being bought	they were being bought
Past	I did get bought	we did get bought
Int.	you did get bought	you did get bought
	he (she, it) did get bought	they did get bought
Pres.	I have been bought	we have been bought
Perf.	you have been bought	you have been bought
	he (she, it) has been bought	they have been bought
Past	I had been bought	we had been bought
Perf.	you had been bought	you had been bought
	he (she, it) had been bought	they had been bought
Fut.	I shall have been bought	we shall have been bought
Perf.	you will have been bought	you will have been bought
	he (she, it) will have been bought	they will have been bought

IMPERATIVE MOOD

be bought

SUBJUNCTIVE MOOD

Pres.	if I be bought	if we be bought
	if you be bought	if you be bought
	if he (she, it) be bought	if they be bought
Past	if I were bought	if we were bought
	if you were bought	if you were bought
	if he (she, it) were bought	if they were bought
Fut.	if I should be bought	if we should be bought
	if you should be bought	if you should be bought
	if he (she, it) should be bought	if they should be bought

to cast (active voice)

Principal Parts: cast, casting, cast, cast

Infinitive: to cast	*Present Participle:* casting
Perfect Infinitive: to have cast	*Past Participle:* cast

INDICATIVE MOOD

Pres.	I cast	we cast
	you cast	you cast
	he (she, it) casts	they cast

Pres. Prog.	I am casting	we are casting
	you are casting	you are casting
	he (she, it) is casting	they are casting

Pres. Int.	I do cast	we do cast
	you do cast	you do cast
	he (she, it) does cast	they do cast

Fut.	I shall cast	we shall cast
	you will cast	you will cast
	he (she, it) will cast	they will cast

Fut.	I will cast (P)	we will cast (P)
	you shall cast (C)	you shall cast (C)
	he (she, it) shall cast (C)	they shall cast (C)

Past	I cast	we cast
	you cast	you cast
	he (she, it) cast	they cast

Past Prog.	I was casting	we were casting
	you were casting	you were casting
	he (she, it) was casting	they were casting

Past Int.	I did cast	we did cast
	you did cast	you did cast
	he (she, it) did cast	they did cast

Pres. Perf.	I have cast	we have cast
	you have cast	you have cast
	he (she, it) has cast	they have cast

Past Perf.	I had cast	we had cast
	you had cast	you had cast
	he (she, it) had cast	they had cast

Fut. Perf.	I shall have cast	we shall have cast
	you will have cast	you will have cast
	he (she, it) will have cast	they will have cast

IMPERATIVE MOOD

cast

SUBJUNCTIVE MOOD

Pres.	if I cast	if we cast
	if you cast	if you cast
	if he (she, it) cast	if they cast

Past	if I cast	if we cast
	if you cast	if you cast
	if he (she, it) cast	if they cast

Fut.	if I should cast	if we should cast
	if you should cast	if you should cast
	if he (she, it) should cast	if they should cast

Infinitive: to be cast   *Present Participle:* being cast
Perfect Infinitive: to have been cast   *Past Participle:* been cast

INDICATIVE MOOD

Pres.	I am cast	we are cast
	you are cast	you are cast
	he (she, it) is cast	they are cast
Pres.	I am being cast	we are being cast
Prog.	you are being cast	you are being cast
	he (she, it) is being cast	they are being cast
Pres.	I do get cast	we do get cast
Int.	you do get cast	you do get cast
	he (she, it) does get cast	they do get cast
Fut.	I shall be cast	we shall be cast
	you will be cast	you will be cast
	he (she, it) will be cast	they will be cast
Fut.	I will be cast *(P)*	we will be cast *(P)*
	you shall be cast *(C)*	you shall be cast *(C)*
	he (she, it) shall be cast *(C)*	they shall be cast *(C)*
Past	I was cast	we were cast
	you were cast	you were cast
	he (she, it) was cast	they were cast
Past	I was being cast	we were being cast
Prog.	you were being cast	you were being cast
	he (she, it) was being cast	they were being cast
Past	I did get cast	we did get cast
Int.	you did get cast	you did get cast
	he (she, it) did get cast	they did get cast
Pres.	I have been cast	we have been cast
Perf.	you have been cast	you have been cast
	he (she, it) has been cast	they have been cast
Past	I had been cast	we had been cast
Perf.	you had been cast	you had been cast
	he (she, it) had been cast	they had been cast
Fut.	I shall have been cast	we shall have been cast
Perf.	you will have been cast	you will have been cast
	he (she, it) will have been cast	they will have been cast

IMPERATIVE MOOD
be cast

SUBJUNCTIVE MOOD

Pres.	if I be cast	if we be cast
	if you be cast	if you be cast
	if he (she, it) be cast	if they be cast
Past	if I were cast	if we were cast
	if you were cast	if you were cast
	if he (she, it) were cast	if they were cast
Fut.	if I should be cast	if we should be cast
	if you should be cast	if you should be cast
	if he (she, it) should be cast	if they should be cast

to catch (active voice)

Principal Parts: catch, catching, caught, caught

Infinitive: to catch	*Perfect Infinitive:* to have caught
Present Participle: catching	*Past Participle:* caught

INDICATIVE MOOD

Pres.
I catch — we catch
you catch — you catch
he (she, it) catches — they catch

Pres. Prog.
I am catching — we are catching
you are catching — you are catching
he (she, it) is catching — they are catching

Pres. Int.
I do catch — we do catch
you do catch — you do catch
he (she, it) does catch — they do catch

Fut.
I shall catch — we shall catch
you will catch — you will catch
he (she, it) will catch — they will catch

Fut.
I will catch (P) — we will catch (P)
you shall catch (C) — you shall catch (C)
he (she, it) shall catch (C) — they shall catch (C)

Past.
I caught — we caught
you caught — you caught
he (she, it) caught — they caught

Past Prog.
I was catching — we were catching
you were catching — you were catching
he (she, it) was catching — they were catching

Past Int.
I did catch — we did catch
you did catch — you did catch
he (she, it) did catch — they did catch

Pres. Perf.
I have caught — we have caught
you have caught — you have caught
he (she, it) has caught — they have caught

Past Perf.
I had caught — we had caught
you had caught — you had caught
he (she, it) had caught — they had caught

Fut. Perf.
I shall have caught — we shall have caught
you will have caught — you will have caught
he (she, it) will have caught — they will have caught

IMPERATIVE MOOD

catch

SUBJUNCTIVE MOOD

Pres.
if I catch — if we catch
if you catch — if you catch
if he (she, it) catch — if they catch

Past
if I caught — if we caught
if you caught — if you caught
if he (she, it) caught — if they caught

Fut.
if I should catch — if we should catch
if you should catch — if you should catch
if he (she, it) should catch — if they should catch

(passive voice)

Infinitive: to be caught   *Perfect Infinitive:* to have been caught

Present Participle: being caught   *Past Participle:* been caught

INDICATIVE MOOD

Pres.	I am caught	we are caught
	you are caught	you are caught
	he (she, it) is caught	they are caught
Pres.	I am being caught	we are being caught
Prog.	you are being caught	you are being caught
	he (she, it) is being caught	they are being caught
Pres.	I do get caught	we do get caught
Int.	you do get caught	you do get caught
	he (she, it) does get caught	they do get caught
Fut.	I shall be caught	we shall be caught
	you will be caught	you will be caught
	he (she, it) will be caught	they will be caught
Fut.	I will be caught (P)	we will be caught (P)
	he (she, it) shall be caught (C)	you shall be caught (C)
	you shall be caught (C)	they shall be caught (C)
Past	I was caught	we were caught
	you were caught	you were caught
	he (she, it) was caught	they were caught
Past	I was being caught	we were being caught
Prog.	you were being caught	you were being caught
	he (she, it) was being caught	they were being caught
Past	I did get caught	we did get caught
Int.	you did get caught	you did get caught
	he (she, it) did get caught	they did get caught
Pres.	I have been caught	we have been caught
Perf.	you have been caught	you have been caught
	he (she, it) has been caught	they have been caught
Past	I had been caught	we had been caught
Perf.	you had been caught	you had been caught
	he (she, it) had been caught	they had been caught
Fut.	I shall have been caught	we shall have been caught
Perf.	you will have been caught	you will have been caught
	he (she, it) will have been caught	they will have been caught

IMPERATIVE MOOD

be caught

SUBJUNCTIVE MOOD

Pres.	if I be caught	if we be caught
	if you be caught	if you be caught
	if he (she, it) be caught	if they be caught
Past	if I were caught	if we were caught
	if you were caught	if you were caught
	if he (she, it) were caught	if they were caught
Fut.	if I should be caught	if we should be caught
	if you should be caught	if you should be caught
	if he (she, it) should be caught	if they should be caught

to choose (active voice)

Principal Parts: choose, choosing, chose, chosen

Infinitive: to choose	Perfect Infinitive: to have chosen

Present Participle: choosing	Past Participle: chosen

INDICATIVE MOOD

Pres.	I choose	we choose
	you choose	you choose
	he (she, it) chooses	they choose
Pres. Prog.	I am choosing	we are choosing
	you are choosing	you are choosing
	he (she, it) is choosing	they are choosing
Pres. Int.	I do choose	we do choose
	you do choose	you do choose
	he (she, it) does choose	they do choose
Fut.	I shall choose	we shall choose
	you will choose	you will choose
	he (she, it) will choose	they will choose
Fut.	I will choose (P)	we will choose (P)
	you shall choose (C)	you shall choose (C)
	he (she, it) shall choose (C)	they shall choose (C)
Past	I chose	we chose
	you chose	you chose
	he (she, it) chose	they chose
Past Prog.	I was choosing	we were choosing
	you were choosing	you were choosing
	he (she, it) was choosing	they were choosing
Past Int.	I did choose	we did choose
	you did choose	you did choose
	he (she, it) did choose	they did choose
Pres. Perf.	I have chosen	we have chosen
	you have chosen	you have chosen
	he (she, it) has chosen	they have chosen
Past Perf.	I had chosen	we had chosen
	you had chosen	you had chosen
	he (she, it) had chosen	they had chosen
Fut. Perf.	I shall have chosen	we shall have chosen
	you will have chosen	you will have chosen
	he (she, it) will have chosen	they will have chosen

IMPERATIVE MOOD

choose

SUBJUNCTIVE MOOD

Pres.	if I choose	if we choose
	if you choose	if you choose
	if he (she, it) choose	if they choose
Past	if I chose	if we chose
	if you chose	if you chose
	if he (she, it) chose	if they chose
Fut.	if I should choose	if we should choose
	if you should choose	if you should choose
	if he (she, it) should choose	if they should choose

(passive voice)

Infinitive: to be chosen   *Present Participle:* being chosen

Perfect Infinitive: to have been chosen   *Past Participle:* been chosen

INDICATIVE MOOD

Pres.	I am chosen	we are chosen
	you are chosen	you are chosen
	he (she, it) is chosen	they are chosen
Pres.	I am being chosen	we are being chosen
Prog.	you are being chosen	you are being chosen
	he (she, it) is being chosen	they are being chosen
Pres.	I do get chosen	we do get chosen
Int.	you do get chosen	you do get chosen
	he (she, it) does get chosen	they do get chosen
Fut.	I shall be chosen	we shall be chosen
	you will be chosen	you will be chosen
	he (she, it) will be chosen	they will be chosen
Fut.	I will be chosen (P)	we will be chosen (P)
	you shall be chosen (C)	you shall be chosen (C)
	he (she, it) shall be chosen (C)	they shall be chosen (C)
Past	I was chosen	we were chosen
	you were chosen	you were chosen
	he (she, it) was chosen	they were chosen
Past	I was being chosen	we were being chosen
Prog.	you were being chosen	you were being chosen
	he (she, it) was being chosen	they were being chosen
Past	I did get chosen	we did get chosen
Int.	you did get chosen	you did get chosen
	he (she, it) did get chosen	they did get chosen
Pres.	I have been chosen	we have been chosen
Perf.	you have been chosen	you have been chosen
	he (she, it) has been chosen	they have been chosen
Past	I had been chosen	we had been chosen
Perf.	you had been chosen	you had been chosen
	he (she, it) had been chosen	they had been chosen
Fut.	I shall have been chosen	we shall have been chosen
Perf.	you will have been chosen	you will have been chosen
	he (she, it) will have been chosen	they will have been chosen

IMPERATIVE MOOD

be chosen

SUBJUNCTIVE MOOD

Pres.	if I be chosen	if we be chosen
	if you be chosen	if you be chosen
	if he (she, it) be chosen	if they be chosen
Past	if I were chosen	if we were chosen
	if you were chosen	if you were chosen
	if he (she, it) were chosen	if they were chosen
Fut.	if I should be chosen	if we should be chosen
	if you should be chosen	if you should be chosen
	if he (she, it) should be chosen	if they should be chosen

to cling

Principal Parts: cling, clinging, clung, clung

Infinitive: to cling	*Perfect Infinitive:* to have clung
Present Participle: clinging	*Past Participle:* clung

INDICATIVE MOOD

Pres.	I cling	we cling
	you cling	you cling
	he (she, it) clings	they cling
Pres. Prog.	I am clinging	we are clinging
	you are clinging	you are clinging
	he (she, it) is clinging	they are clinging
Pres. Int.	I do cling	we do cling
	you do cling	you do cling
	he (she, it) does cling	they do cling
Fut.	I shall cling	we shall cling
	you will cling	you will cling
	he (she, it) will cling	they will cling
Fut.	I will cling (P)	we will cling (P)
	you shall cling (C)	you shall cling (C)
	he (she, it) shall cling (C)	they shall cling (C)
Past	I clung	we clung
	you clung	you clung
	he (she, it) clung	they clung
Past Prog.	I was clinging	we were clinging
	you were clinging	you were clinging
	he (she, it) was clinging	they were clinging
Past Int.	I did cling	we did cling
	you did cling	you did cling
	he (she, it) did cling	they did cling
Pres. Perf.	I have clung	we have clung
	you have clung	you have clung
	he (she, it) has clung	they have clung
Past Perf.	I had clung	we had clung
	you had clung	you had clung
	he (she, it) had clung	they had clung
Fut. Perf.	I shall have clung	we shall have clung
	you will have clung	you will have clung
	he (she, it) will have clung	they will have clung

IMPERATIVE MOOD

cling

SUBJUNCTIVE MOOD

Pres.	if I cling	if we cling
	if you cling	if you cling
	if he (she, it) cling	if they cling
Past	if I clung	if we clung
	if you clung	if you clung
	if he (she, it) clung	if they clung
Fut.	if I should cling	if we should cling
	if you should cling	if you should cling
	if he (she, it) should cling	if they should cling

Infinitive: to come *Present Participle:* coming
Perfect Infinitive: to have come *Past Participle:* come

INDICATIVE MOOD

Pres.	I come	we come
	you come	you come
	he (she, it) comes	they come
Pres.	I am coming	we are coming
Prog.	you are coming	you are coming
	he (she, it) is coming	they are coming
Pres.	I do come	we do come
Int.	you do come	you do come
	he (she, it) does come	they do come
Fut.	I shall come	we shall come
	you will come	you will come
	he (she, it) will come	they will come
Fut.	I will come *(P)*	we will come *(P)*
	you shall come *(C)*	you shall come *(C)*
	he (she, it) shall come *(C)*	they shall come *(C)*
Past	I came	we came
	you came	you came
	he (she, it) came	they came
Past	I was coming	we were coming
Prog.	you were coming	you were coming
	he (she, it) was coming	they were coming
Past	I did come	we did come
Int.	you did come	you did come
	he (she, it) did come	they did come
Pres.	I have come	we have come
Perf.	you have come	you have come
	he (she, it) has come	they have come
Past	I had come	we had come
Perf.	you had come	you had come
	he (she, it) had come	they had come
Fut.	I shall have come	we shall have come
Perf.	you will have come	you will have come
	he (she, it) will have come	they will have come

IMPERATIVE MOOD
come

SUBJUNCTIVE MOOD

Pres.	if I come	if we come
	if you come	if you come
	if he (she, it) come	if they come
Past	if I came	if we came
	if you came	if you came
	if he (she, it) came	if they came
Fut.	if I should come	if we should come
	if you should come	if you should come
	if he (she, it) should come	if they should come

Infinitive: to creep   *Present Participle:* creeping
Perfect Infinitive: to have crept   *Past Participle:* crept

INDICATIVE MOOD

Pres.	I creep	we creep
	you creep	you creep
	he (she, it) creeps	they creep
Pres.	I am creeping	we are creeping
Prog.	you are creeping	you are creeping
	he (she, it) is creeping	they are creeping
Pres.	I do creep	we do creep
Int.	you do creep	you do creep
	he (she, it) does creep	they do creep
Fut.	I shall creep	we shall creep
	you will creep	you will creep
	he (she, it) will creep	they will creep
Fut.	I will creep *(P)*	we will creep *(P)*
	you shall creep *(C)*	you shall creep *(C)*
	he (she, it) shall creep *(C)*	they shall creep *(C)*
Past	I crept	we crept
	you crept	you crept
	he (she, it) crept	they crept
Past	I was creeping	we were creeping
Prog.	you were creeping	you were creeping
	he (she, it) was creeping	they were creeping
Past	I did creep	we did creep
Int.	you did creep	you did creep
	he (she, it) did creep	they did creep
Pres.	I have crept	we have crept
Perf.	you have crept	you have crept
	he (she, it) has crept	they have crept
Past	I had crept	we had crept
Perf.	you had crept	you had crept
	he (she, it) had crept	they had crept
Fut.	I shall have crept	we shall have crept
Perf.	you will have crept	you will have crept
	he (she, it) will have crept	they will have crept

IMPERATIVE MOOD
creep

SUBJUNCTIVE MOOD

Pres.	if I creep	if we creep
	if you creep	if you creep
	if he (she, it) creep	if they creep
Past	if I crept	if we crept
	if you crept	if you crept
	if he (she, it) crept	if they crept
Fut.	if I should creep	if we should creep
	if you should creep	if you should creep
	if he (she, it) should creep	if they should creep

To creep is an intransitive verb.

It does not take an object.

It describes action, but the action is self-contained.

Like other intransitive verbs, it may be followed by adverbs, adverbial phrases and clauses describing the how, why, when, and where of the action:

HOW: The baby crept *quietly*. (adverb)

WHY: The baby crept *because it could not walk*. (adverbial clause)

WHEN: The baby will creep *soon*. (adverb)

WHERE: The baby crept *around the room*. (adverbial phrase)

Infinitive: to cut　　　　　　　　　　　　*Present Participle:* cutting
Perfect Infinitive: to have cut　　　　　　*Past Participle:* cut

INDICATIVE MOOD

Pres.	I cut	we cut
	you cut	you cut
	he (she, it) cuts	they cut
Pres. Prog.	I am cutting	we are cutting
	you are cutting	you are cutting
	he (she, it) is cutting	they are cutting
Pres. Int.	I do cut	we do cut
	you do cut	you do cut
	he (she, it) does cut	they do cut
Fut.	I shall cut	we shall cut
	you will cut	you will cut
	he (she, it) will cut	they will cut
Fut.	I will cut *(P)*	we will cut *(P)*
	you shall cut *(C)*	you shall cut *(C)*
	he (she, it) shall cut *(C)*	they shall cut *(C)*
Past	I cut	we cut
	you cut	you cut
	he (she, it) cut	they cut
Past Prog.	I was cutting	we were cutting
	you were cutting	you were cutting
	he (she, it) was cutting	they were cutting
Past Int.	I did cut	we did cut
	you did cut	you did cut
	he (she, it) did cut	they did cut
Pres. Perf.	I have cut	we have cut
	you have cut	you have cut
	he (she, it) has cut	they have cut
Past Perf.	I had cut	we had cut
	you had cut	you had cut
	he (she, it) had cut	they had cut
Fut. Perf.	I shall have cut	we shall have cut
	you will have cut	you will have cut
	he (she, it) will have cut	they will have cut

IMPERATIVE MOOD
cut

SUBJUNCTIVE MOOD

Pres.	if I cut	if we cut
	if you cut	if you cut
	if he (she, it) cut	if they cut
Past	if I cut	if we cut
	if you cut	if you cut
	if he (she, it) cut	if they cut
Fut.	if I should cut	if we should cut
	if you should cut	if you should cut
	if he (she, it) should cut	if they should cut

178

Infinitive: to be cut   *Present Participle:* being cut
Perfect Infinitive: to have been cut   *Past Participle:* been cut

INDICATIVE MOOD

Pres.	I am cut	we are cut
	you are cut	you are cut
	he (she, it) is cut	they are cut
Pres. Prog.	I am being cut	we are being cut
	you are being cut	you are being cut
	he (she, it) is being cut	they are being cut
Pres. Int.	I do get cut	we do get cut
	you do get cut	you do get cut
	he (she, it) does get cut	they do get cut
Fut.	I shall be cut	we shall be cut
	you will be cut	you will be cut
	he (she, it) will be cut	they will be cut
Fut.	I will be cut *(P)*	we will be cut *(P)*
	you shall be cut *(C)*	you shall be cut *(C)*
	he (she, it) shall be cut *(C)*	they shall be cut *(C)*
Past	I was cut	we were cut
	you were cut	you were cut
	he (she, it) was cut	they were cut
Past Prog.	I was being cut	we were being cut
	you were being cut	you were being cut
	he (she, it) was being cut	they were being cut
Past Int.	I did get cut	we did get cut
	you did get cut	you did get cut
	he (she, it) did get cut	they did get cut
Pres. Perf.	I have been cut	we have been cut
	you have been cut	you have been cut
	he (she, it) has been cut	they have been cut
Past Perf.	I had been cut	we had been cut
	you had been cut	you had been cut
	he (she, it) had been cut	they had been cut
Fut. Perf.	I shall have been cut	we shall have been cut
	you will have been cut	you will have been cut
	he (she, it) will have been cut	they will have been cut

IMPERATIVE MOOD
be cut

SUBJUNCTIVE MOOD

Pres.	if I be cut	if we be cut
	if you be cut	if you be cut
	if he (she, it) be cut	if they be cut
Past	if I were cut	if we were cut
	if you were cut	if you were cut
	if he (she, it) were cut	if they were cut
Fut.	if I should be cut	if we should be cut
	if you should be cut	if you should be cut
	if he (she, it) should be cut	if they should be cut

to deal (active voice)

Principal Parts: deal, dealing, dealt, dealt

Infinitive: to deal	*Present Participle:* dealing
Perfect Infinitive: to have dealt	*Past Participle:* dealt

INDICATIVE MOOD

Pres.	I deal	we deal
	you deal	you deal
	he (she, it) deals	they deal
Prog. *Pres.*	I am dealing	we are dealing
	you are dealing	you are dealing
	he (she, it) is dealing	they are dealing
Int. *Pres.*	I do deal	we do deal
	you do deal	you do deal
	he (she, it) does deal	they do deal
Fut.	I shall deal	we shall deal
	you will deal	you will deal
	he (she, it) will deal	they will deal
Fut.	I will deal (P)	we will deal (P)
	you shall deal (C)	you shall deal (C)
	he (she, it) shall deal (C)	they shall deal (C)
Past	I dealt	we dealt
	you dealt	you dealt
	he (she, it) dealt	they dealt
Past *Prog.*	I was dealing	we were dealing
	you were dealing	you were dealing
	he (she, it) was dealing	they were dealing
Past *Int.*	I did deal	we did deal
	you did deal	you did deal
	he (she, it) did deal	they did deal
Perf. *Pres.*	I have dealt	we have dealt
	you have dealt	you have dealt
	he (she, it) has dealt	they have dealt
Perf. *Past*	I had dealt	we had dealt
	you had dealt	you had dealt
	he (she, it) had dealt	they had dealt
Perf. *Fut.*	I shall have dealt	we shall have dealt
	you will have dealt	you will have dealt
	he (she, it) will have dealt	they will have dealt

IMPERATIVE MOOD

deal

SUBJUNCTIVE MOOD

Pres.	if I deal	if we deal
	if you deal	if you deal
	if he (she, it) deal	if they deal
Past	if I dealt	if we dealt
	if you dealt	if you dealt
	if he (she, it) dealt	if they dealt
Fut.	if I should deal	if we should deal
	if you should deal	if you should deal
	if he (she, it) should deal	if they should deal

(passive voice)

Infinitive: to be dealt   *Present Participle:* being dealt

Perfect Infinitive: to have been dealt   *Past Participle:* been dealt

INDICATIVE MOOD

Pres.	I am dealt	we are dealt
	he (she, it) is dealt	you are dealt
	you are dealt	they are dealt
Prest Prog.	I am being dealt	we are being dealt
	he (she, it) is being dealt	you are being dealt
	you are being dealt	they are being dealt
Pres. Int.	I do get dealt	we do get dealt
	he (she, it) does get dealt	they do get dealt
	you do get dealt	
Fut.	I shall be dealt	we shall be dealt
	he (she, it) will be dealt	you will be dealt
	you will be dealt	they will be dealt
Fut.	I will be dealt (P)	we will be dealt (P)
	he (she, it) shall be dealt (C)	you shall be dealt (C)
	you shall be dealt (C)	they shall be dealt (C)
Past	I was dealt	we were dealt
	you were dealt	you were dealt
	he (she, it) was dealt	they were dealt
Past Prog.	I was being dealt	we were being dealt
	you were being dealt	they were being dealt
	he (she, it) was being dealt	
Past Int.	I did get dealt	we did get dealt
	you did get dealt	they did get dealt
	he (she, it) did get dealt	
Pres. Perf.	I have been dealt	we have been dealt
	you have been dealt	they have been dealt
	he (she, it) has been dealt	
Past Perf.	I had been dealt	we had been dealt
	you had been dealt	they had been dealt
	he (she, it) had been dealt	
Fut. Perf.	I shall have been dealt	we shall have been dealt
	you will have been dealt	you will have been dealt
	he (she, it) will have been dealt	they will have been dealt

IMPERATIVE MOOD

be dealt

SUBJUNCTIVE MOOD

Pres.	if I be dealt	if we be dealt
	if he (she, it) be dealt	if you be dealt
	if you be dealt	if they be dealt
Past	if I were dealt	if we were dealt
	if he (she, it) were dealt	if you were dealt
	if you were dealt	if they were dealt
Fut.	if I should be dealt	if we should be dealt
	if he (she, it) should be dealt	if you should be dealt
	if you should be dealt	if they should be dealt

Infinitive: to dive   *Present Participle:* diving
Perfect Infinitive: to have dived   *Past Participle:* dived

INDICATIVE MOOD

Pres.	I dive	we dive
	you dive	you dive
	he (she, it) dives	they dive
Pres.	I am diving	we are diving
Prog.	you are diving	you are diving
	he (she, it) is diving	they are diving
Pres.	I do dive	we do dive
Int.	you do dive	you do dive
	he (she, it) does dive	they do dive
Fut.	I shall dive	we shall dive
	you will dive	you will dive
	he (she, it) will dive	they will dive
Fut.	I will dive *(P)*	we will dive *(P)*
	you shall dive *(C)*	you shall dive *(C)*
	he (she, it) shall dive *(C)*	they shall dive *(C)*
Past	I dived, dove	we dived, dove
	you dived, dove	you dived, dove
	he (she, it) dived, dove	they dived, dove
Past	I was diving	we were diving
Prog.	you were diving	you were diving
	he (she, it) was diving	they were diving
Past	I did dive	we did dive
Int.	you did dive	you did dive
	he (she, it) did dive	they did dive
Pres.	I have dived	we have dived
Perf.	you have dived	you have dived
	he (she, it) has dived	they have dived
Past	I had dived	we had dived
Perf.	you had dived	you had dived
	he (she, it) had dived	they had dived
Fut.	I shall have dived	we shall have dived
Perf.	you will have dived	you will have dived
	he (she, it) will have dived	they will have dived

IMPERATIVE MOOD
dive

SUBJUNCTIVE MOOD

Pres.	if I dive	if we dive
	if you dive	if you dive
	if he (she, it) dive	if they dive
Past	if I dived, dove	if we dived, dove
	if you dived, dove	if you dived, dove
	if he (she, it) dived, dove	if they dived, dove
Fut.	if I should dive	if we should dive
	if you should dive	if you should dive
	if he (she, it) should dive	if they should dive

To dive is an intransitive verb.

It does not take an object.

It describes action, but the action is self-contained.

Like other intransitive verbs, it may be followed by adverbs, adverbial phrases and clauses describing the how, why, when, and where of the action:

HOW: She dived *beautifully*. (adverb)

WHY: The submarine dived *because an enemy ship was in sight*. (adverbial clause)

WHEN: The boys dived *until late in the afternoon*. (adverbial phrases)

WHERE: I dived *into the pool*. (adverbial phrase)

to do (active voice)

Principal Parts: do, doing, did, done

Infinitive: to do	*Present Participle:* doing
Perfect Infinitive: to have done	*Past Participle:* done

INDICATIVE MOOD

Pres.
I do — we do
you do — you do
he (she, it) does — they do

Prog. I am doing — we are doing
Pres. you are doing — you are doing
he (she, it) is doing — they are doing

Int. I do — we do
Pres. you do — you do
he (she, it) does — they do

Fut. I shall do — we shall do
you will do — you will do
he (she, it) will do — they will do

Fut. I will do (P) — we will do (P)
you shall do (C) — you shall do (C)
he (she, it) shall do (C) — they shall do (C)

Past I did — we did
you did — you did
he (she, it) did — they did

Past I was doing — we were doing
Prog. you were doing — you were doing
he (she, it) was doing — they were doing

Past I did do — we did do
Int. you did do — you did do
he (she, it) did do — they did do

Pres. I have done — we have done
Perf. you have done — you have done
he (she, it) has done — they have done

Past I had done — we had done
Perf. you had done — you had done
he (she, it) had done — they had done

Fut. I shall have done — we shall have done
Perf. you will have done — you will have done
he (she, it) will have done — they will have done

IMPERATIVE MOOD
do

SUBJUNCTIVE MOOD

Pres. if I do — if we do
if you do — if you do
if he (she, it) do — if they do

Past if I did — if we did
if you did — if you did
if he (she, it) did — if they did

Fut. if I should do — if we should do
if you should do — if you should do
if he (she, it) should do — if they should do

(passive voice)

Infinitive: to be done   *Perfect Infinitive:* to have been done

Present Participle: being done   *Past Participle:* been done

INDICATIVE MOOD

	Singular	Plural
Pres.	I am done	we are done
	you are done	you are done
	he (she, it) is done	they are done
Prog.	I am being done	we are being done
	you are being done	you are being done
	he (she, it) is being done	they are being done
Int.	I do get done	we do get done
	you do get done	you do get done
	he (she, it) does get done	they do get done
Fut.	I shall be done	we shall be done
	you will be done	you will be done
	he (she, it) will be done	they will be done
Fut.	I will be done (P)	we will be done (P)
	you shall be done (C)	you shall be done (C)
	he (she, it) shall be done (C)	they shall be done (C)
Past	I was done	we were done
	you were done	you were done
	he (she, it) was done	they were done
Prog.	I was being done	we were being done
	you were being done	you were being done
	he (she, it) was being done	they were being done
Past	I did get done	we did get done
Int.	you did get done	you did get done
	he (she, it) did get done	they did get done
Pres.	I have been done	we have been done
Perf.	you have been done	you have been done
	he (she, it) has been done	they have been done
Past	I had been done	we had been done
Perf.	you had been done	you had been done
	he (she, it) had been done	they had been done
Fut.	I shall have been done	we shall have been done
Perf.	you will have been done	you will have been done
	he (she, it) will have been done	they will have been done

IMPERATIVE MOOD
be done

SUBJUNCTIVE MOOD

	Singular	Plural
Pres.	if I be done	if we be done
	if you be done	if you be done
	if he (she, it) be done	if they be done
Past	if I were done	if we were done
	if you were done	if you were done
	if he (she, it) were done	if they were done
Fut.	if I should be done	if we should be done
	if you should be done	if you should be done
	if he (she, it) should be done	if they should be done

to draw (active voice)   *Principal Parts:* draw, drawing, drew, drawn

Infinitive: to draw   *Present Participle:* drawing
Perfect Infinitive: to have drawn   *Past Participle:* drawn

INDICATIVE MOOD

Pres.	I draw	we draw
	you draw	you draw
	he (she, it) draws	they draw
Pres. Prog.	I am drawing	we are drawing
	you are drawing	you are drawing
	he (she, it) is drawing	they are drawing
Pres. Int.	I do draw	we do draw
	you do draw	you do draw
	he (she, it) does draw	they do draw
Fut.	I shall draw	we shall draw
	you will draw	you will draw
	he (she, it) will draw	they will draw
Fut.	I will draw *(P)*	we will draw *(P)*
	you shall draw *(C)*	you shall draw *(C)*
	he (she, it) shall draw *(C)*	they shall draw *(C)*
Past	I drew	we drew
	you drew	you drew
	he (she, it) drew	they drew
Past Prog.	I was drawing	we were drawing
	you were drawing	you were drawing
	he (she, it) was drawing	they were drawing
Past Int.	I did draw	we did draw
	you did draw	you did draw
	he (she, it) did draw	they did draw
Pres. Perf.	I have drawn	we have drawn
	you have drawn	you have drawn
	he (she, it) has drawn	they have drawn
Past Perf.	I had drawn	we had drawn
	you had drawn	you had drawn
	he (she, it) had drawn	they had drawn
Fut. Perf.	I shall have drawn	we shall have drawn
	you will have drawn	you will have drawn
	he (she, it) will have drawn	they will have drawn

IMPERATIVE MOOD
draw

SUBJUNCTIVE MOOD

Pres.	if I draw	if we draw
	if you draw	if you draw
	if he (she, it) draw	if they draw
Past	if I drew	if we drew
	if you drew	if you drew
	if he (she, it) drew	if they drew
Fut.	if I should draw	if we should draw
	if you should draw	if you should draw
	if he (she, it) should draw	if they should draw

186

(passive voice)

Infinitive: to be drawn   *Present Participle:* being drawn
Perfect Infinitive: to have been drawn   *Past Participle:* been drawn

INDICATIVE MOOD

Pres.	I am drawn	we are drawn
	you are drawn	you are drawn
	he (she, it) is drawn	they are drawn
Pres.	I am being drawn	we are being drawn
Prog.	you are being drawn	you are being drawn
	he (she, it) is being drawn	they are being drawn
Pres.	I do get drawn	we do get drawn
Int.	you do get drawn	you do get drawn
	he (she, it) does get drawn	they do get drawn
Fut.	I shall be drawn	we shall be drawn
	you will be drawn	you will be drawn
	he (she, it) will be drawn	they will be drawn
Fut.	I will be drawn *(P)*	we will be drawn *(P)*
	you shall be drawn *(C)*	you shall be drawn *(C)*
	he (she, it) shall be drawn *(C)*	they shall be drawn *(C)*
Past	I was drawn	we were drawn
	you were drawn	you were drawn
	he (she, it) was drawn	they were drawn
Past	I was being drawn	we were being drawn
Prog.	you were being drawn	you were being drawn
	he (she, it) was being drawn	they were being drawn
Past	I did get drawn	we did get drawn
Int.	you did get drawn	you did get drawn
	he (she, it) did get drawn	they did get drawn
Pres.	I have been drawn	we have been drawn
Perf.	you have been drawn	you have been drawn
	he (she, it) has been drawn	they have been drawn
Past	I had been drawn	we had been drawn
Perf.	you had been drawn	you had been drawn
	he (she, it) had been drawn	they had been drawn
Fut.	I shall have been drawn	we shall have been drawn
Perf.	you will have been drawn	you will have been drawn
	he (she, it) will have been drawn	they will have been drawn

IMPERATIVE MOOD
be drawn

SUBJUNCTIVE MOOD

Pres.	if I be drawn	if we be drawn
	if you be drawn	if you be drawn
	if he (she, it) be drawn	if they be drawn
Past	if I were drawn	if we were drawn
	if you were drawn	if you were drawn
	if he (she, it) were drawn	if they were drawn
Fut.	if I should be drawn	if we should be drawn
	if you should be drawn	if you should be drawn
	if he (she, it) should be drawn	if they should be drawn

to drink (active voice)

Principal Parts: drink, drinking, drank, drunk

Infinitive: to drink	*Perfect Infinitive:* to have drunk
Present Participle: drinking	*Past Participle:* drunk

INDICATIVE MOOD

Pres.	I drink	we drink
	you drink	you drink
	he (she, it) drinks	they drink
Prog. Pres.	I am drinking	we are drinking
	you are drinking	you are drinking
	he (she, it) is drinking	they are drinking
Int. Pres.	I do drink	we do drink
	you do drink	you do drink
	he (she, it) does drink	they do drink
Fut.	I shall drink	we shall drink
	you will drink	you will drink
	he (she, it) will drink	they will drink
Fut.	I will drink (P)	we will drink (P)
	you shall drink (C)	you shall drink (C)
	he (she, it) shall drink (C)	they shall drink (C)
Past	I drank	we drank
	you drank	you drank
	he (she, it) drank	they drank
Prog. Past	I was drinking	we were drinking
	you were drinking	you were drinking
	he (she, it) was drinking	they were drinking
Int. Past	I did drink	we did drink
	you did drink	you did drink
	he (she, it) did drink	they did drink
Perf. Pres.	I have drunk	we have drunk
	you have drunk	you have drunk
	he (she, it) has drunk	they have drunk
Perf. Past	I had drunk	we had drunk
	you had drunk	you had drunk
	he (she, it) had drunk	they had drunk
Perf. Fut.	I shall have drunk	we shall have drunk
	you will have drunk	you will have drunk
	he (she, it) will have drunk	they will have drunk

IMPERATIVE MOOD

drink

SUBJUNCTIVE MOOD

Pres.	if I drink	if we drink
	if you drink	if you drink
	if he (she, it) drink	if they drink
Past	if I drank	if we drank
	if you drank	if you drank
	if he (she, it) drank	if they drank
Fut.	if I should drink	if we should drink
	if you should drink	if you should drink
	if he (she, it) should drink	if they should drink

(passive voice)

Infinitive: to be drunk

Perfect Infinitive: to have been drunk

Present Participle: being drunk

Past Participle: been drunk

INDICATIVE MOOD

Pres.
I am drunk — we are drunk
you are drunk — you are drunk
he (she, it) is drunk — they are drunk

Prog.
I am being drunk — we are being drunk
you are being drunk — you are being drunk
he (she, it) is being drunk — they are being drunk

Pres.
I do get drunk — we do get drunk
you do get drunk — you do get drunk
he (she, it) does get drunk — they do get drunk

Fut.
I shall be drunk — we shall be drunk
he (she, it) will be drunk — they will be drunk
you will be drunk — you will be drunk

Fut.
I will be drunk (P) — we will be drunk (P)
you shall be drunk (C) — you shall be drunk (C)
he (she, it) shall be drunk (C) — they shall be drunk (C)

Past
I was drunk — we were drunk
you were drunk — you were drunk
he (she, it) was drunk — they were drunk

Prog.
I was being drunk — we were being drunk
you were being drunk — you were being drunk
he (she, it) was being drunk — they were being drunk

Int.
I did get drunk — we did get drunk
you did get drunk — you did get drunk
he (she, it) did get drunk — they did get drunk

Perf.
I have been drunk — we have been drunk
you have been drunk — you have been drunk
he (she, it) has been drunk — they have been drunk

Perf.
I had been drunk — we had been drunk
you had been drunk — you had been drunk
he (she, it) had been drunk — they had been drunk

Perf.
I shall have been drunk — we shall have been drunk
you will have been drunk — you will have been drunk
he (she, it) will have been drunk — they will have been drunk

IMPERATIVE MOOD
be drunk

SUBJUNCTIVE MOOD

Pres.
if I be drunk — if we be drunk
if you be drunk — if you be drunk
if he (she, it) be drunk — if they be drunk

Past
if I were drunk — if we were drunk
if you were drunk — if you were drunk
if he (she, it) were drunk — if they were drunk

Fut.
if I should be drunk — if we should be drunk
if you should be drunk — if you should be drunk
if he (she, it) should be drunk — if they should be drunk

Infinitive: to drive   *Present Participle:* driving
Perfect Infinitive: to have driven   *Past Participle:* driven

INDICATIVE MOOD

Pres.	I drive	we drive
	you drive	you drive
	he (she, it) drives	they drive
Pres. *Prog.*	I am driving	we are driving
	you are driving	you are driving
	he (she, it) is driving	they are driving
Pres. *Int.*	I do drive	we do drive
	you do drive	you do drive
	he (she, it) does drive	they do drive
Fut.	I shall drive	we shall drive
	you will drive	you will drive
	he (she, it) will drive	they will drive
Fut.	I will drive *(P)*	we will drive *(P)*
	you shall drive *(C)*	you shall drive *(C)*
	he (she, it) shall drive *(C)*	they shall drive *(C)*
Past	I drove	we drove
	you drove	you drove
	he (she, it) drove	they drove
Past *Prog.*	I was driving	we were driving
	you were driving	you were driving
	he (she, it) was driving	they were driving
Past *Int.*	I did drive	we did drive
	you did drive	you did drive
	he (she, it) did drive	they did drive
Pres. *Perf.*	I have driven	we have driven
	you have driven	you have driven
	he (she, it) has driven	they have driven
Past *Perf.*	I had driven	we had driven
	you had driven	you had driven
	he (she, it) had driven	they had driven
Fut. *Perf.*	I shall have driven	we shall have driven
	you will have driven	you will have driven
	he (she, it) will have driven	they will have driven

IMPERATIVE MOOD
drive

SUBJUNCTIVE MOOD

Pres.	if I drive	if we drive
	if you drive	if you drive
	if he (she, it) drive	if they drive
Past	if I drove	if we drove
	if you drove	if you drove
	if he (she, it) drove	if they drove
Fut.	if I should drive	if we should drive
	if you should drive	if you should drive
	if he (she, it) should drive	if they should drive

Infinitive: to be driven   *Present Participle:* being driven
Perfect Infinitive: to have been driven   *Past Participle:* been driven

INDICATIVE MOOD

Pres.	I am driven	we are driven
	you are driven	you are driven
	he (she, it) is driven	they are driven
Pres. *Prog.*	I am being driven	we are being driven
	you are being driven	you are being driven
	he (she, it) is being driven	they are being driven
Pres. *Int.*	I do get driven	we do get driven
	you do get driven	you do get driven
	he (she, it) does get driven	they do get driven
Fut.	I shall be driven	we shall be driven
	you will be driven	you will be driven
	he (she, it) will be driven	they will be driven
Fut.	I will be driven *(P)*	we will be driven *(P)*
	you shall be driven *(C)*	you shall be driven *(C)*
	he (she, it) shall be driven *(C)*	they shall be driven *(C)*
Past	I was driven	we were driven
	you were driven	you were driven
	he (she, it) was driven	they were driven
Past *Prog.*	I was being driven	we were being driven
	you were being driven	you were being driven
	he (she, it) was being driven	they were being driven
Past *Int.*	I did get driven	we did get driven
	you did get driven	you did get driven
	he (she, it) did get driven	they did get driven
Pres. *Perf.*	I have been driven	we have been driven
	you have been driven	you have been driven
	he (she, it) has been driven	they have been driven
Past *Perf.*	I had been driven	we had been driven
	you had been driven	you had been driven
	he (she, it) had been driven	they had been driven
Fut. *Perf.*	I shall have been driven	we shall have been driven
	you will have been driven	you will have been driven
	he (she, it) will have been driven	they will have been driven

IMPERATIVE MOOD
be driven

SUBJUNCTIVE MOOD

Pres.	if I be driven	if we be driven
	if you be driven	if you be driven
	if he (she, it) be driven	if they be driven
Past	if I were driven	if we were driven
	if you were driven	if you were driven
	if he (she, it) were driven	if they were driven
Fut.	if I should be driven	if we should be driven
	if you should be driven	if you should be driven
	if he (she, it) should be driven	if they should be driven

to eat (active voice)

Principal Parts: eat, eating, ate, eaten

Infinitive: to eat	Perfect Infinitive: to have eaten
Present Participle: eating	Past Participle: eaten

INDICATIVE MOOD

Pres.	I eat	we eat
	you eat	you eat
	he (she, it) eats	they eat
Prog.	I am eating	we are eating
	you are eating	you are eating
	he (she, it) is eating	they are eating
Int.	I do eat	we do eat
	you do eat	you do eat
	he (she, it) does eat	they do eat
Fut.	I shall eat	we shall eat
	you will eat	you will eat
	he (she, it) will eat	they will eat
Fut.	I will eat (P)	we will eat (P)
	you shall eat (C)	you shall eat (C)
	he (she, it) shall eat (C)	they shall eat (C)
Past	I ate	we ate
	you ate	you ate
	he (she, it) ate	they ate
Past Prog.	I was eating	we were eating
	you were eating	you were eating
	he (she, it) was eating	they were eating
Past Int.	I did eat	we did eat
	you did eat	you did eat
	he (she, it) did eat	they did eat
Pres. Perf.	I have eaten	we have eaten
	you have eaten	you have eaten
	he (she, it) has eaten	they have eaten
Past Perf.	I had eaten	we had eaten
	you had eaten	you had eaten
	he (she, it) had eaten	they had eaten
Fut. Perf.	I shall have eaten	we shall have eaten
	you will have eaten	you will have eaten
	he (she, it) will have eaten	they will have eaten

IMPERATIVE MOOD
eat

SUBJUNCTIVE MOOD

Pres.	if I eat	if we eat
	if you eat	if you eat
	if he (she, it) eat	if they eat
Past	if I ate	if we ate
	if you ate	if you ate
	if he (she, it) ate	if they ate
Fut.	if I should eat	if we should eat
	if you should eat	if you should eat
	if he (she, it) should eat	if they should eat

(passive voice)

Infinitive: to be eaten   Perfect Infinitive: to have been eaten

Present Participle: being eaten   Past Participle: been eaten

INDICATIVE MOOD

Pres.	I am eaten	we are eaten
	you are eaten	you are eaten
	he (she, it) is eaten	they are eaten
Pres.	I am being eaten	we are being eaten
Prog.	you are being eaten	you are being eaten
	he (she, it) is being eaten	they are being eaten
Pres.	I do get eaten	we do get eaten
Int.	you do get eaten	you do get eaten
	he (she, it) does get eaten	they do get eaten
Fut.	I shall be eaten	we shall be eaten
	you will be eaten	you will be eaten
	he (she, it) will be eaten	they will be eaten
Fut.	I will be eaten (P)	we will be eaten (P)
	you shall be eaten (C)	you shall be eaten (C)
	he (she, it) shall be eaten (C)	they shall be eaten (C)
Past	I was eaten	we were eaten
	you were eaten	you were eaten
	he (she, it) was eaten	they were eaten
Prog.	I was being eaten	we were being eaten
Past	you were being eaten	you were being eaten
	he (she, it) was being eaten	they were being eaten
Int.	I did get eaten	we did get eaten
Past	you did get eaten	you did get eaten
	he (she, it) did get eaten	they did get eaten
Pres.	I have been eaten	we have been eaten
Perf.	you have been eaten	you have been eaten
	he (she, it) has been eaten	they have been eaten
Past	I had been eaten	we had been eaten
Perf.	you had been eaten	you had been eaten
	he (she, it) had been eaten	they had been eaten
Fut.	I shall have been eaten	we shall have been eaten
Perf.	you will have been eaten	you will have been eaten
	he (she, it) will have been eaten	they will have been eaten

IMPERATIVE MOOD

be eaten

SUBJUNCTIVE MOOD

Pres.	if I be eaten	if we be eaten
	if you be eaten	if you be eaten
	if he (she, it) be eaten	if they be eaten
Past	if I were eaten	if we were eaten
	if you were eaten	if you were eaten
	if he (she, it) were eaten	if they were eaten
Fut.	if I should be eaten	if we should be eaten
	if you should be eaten	if you should be eaten
	if he (she, it) should be eaten	if they should be eaten

Infinitive: to fall   *Present Participle:* falling
Perfect Infinitive: to have fallen   *Past Participle:* fallen

INDICATIVE MOOD

Pres.	I fall	we fall
	you fall	you fall
	he (she, it) falls	they fall
Pres. *Prog.*	I am falling	we are falling
	you are falling	you are falling
	he (she, it) is falling	they are falling
Pres. *Int.*	I do fall	we do fall
	you do fall	you do fall
	he (she, it) does fall	they do fall
Fut.	I shall fall	we shall fall
	you will fall	you will fall
	he (she, it) will fall	they will fall
Fut.	I will fall *(P)*	we will fall *(P)*
	you shall fall *(C)*	you shall fall *(C)*
	he (she, it) shall fall *(C)*	they shall fall *(C)*
Past	I fell	we fell
	you fell	you fell
	he (she, it) fell	they fell
Past *Prog.*	I was falling	we were falling
	you were falling	you were falling
	he (she, it) was falling	they were falling
Past *Int.*	I did fall	we did fall
	you did fall	you did fall
	he (she, it) did fall	they did fall
Pres. *Perf.*	I have fallen	we have fallen
	you have fallen	you have fallen
	he (she, it) has fallen	they have fallen
Past *Perf.*	I had fallen	we had fallen
	you had fallen	you had fallen
	he (she, it) had fallen	they had fallen
Fut. *Perf.*	I shall have fallen	we shall have fallen
	you will have fallen	you will have fallen
	he (she, it) will have fallen	they will have fallen

IMPERATIVE MOOD
fall

SUBJUNCTIVE MOOD

Pres.	if I fall	if we fall
	if you fall	if you fall
	if he (she, it) fall	if they fall
Past	if I fell	if we fell
	if you fell	if you fell
	if he (she, it) fell	if they fell
Fut.	if I should fall	if we should fall
	if you should fall	if you should fall
	if he (she, it) should fall	if they should fall

To fall is an intransitive verb.

It does not take an object.

It describes action, but the action is self-contained.

Like other intransitive verbs, it may be followed by adverbs, adverbial phrases and clauses describing the how, why, when, and where of the action:

HOW: The rain fell *slowly*. (adverb)

WHY: He fell *because he could not keep his balance*. (adverbial clause)

WHEN: Leaves fall *in the autumn*. (adverbial phrase)

WHERE: He fell *off the ladder*. (adverbial phrase)

to feed (active voice)   *Principal Parts:* feed, feeding, fed, fed

Infinitive: to feed   *Present Participle:* feeding
Perfect Infinitive: to have fed   *Past Participle:* fed

INDICATIVE MOOD

Pres.	I feed	we feed
	you feed	you feed
	he (she, it) feeds	they feed
Pres.	I am feeding	we are feeding
Prog.	you are feeding	you are feeding
	he (she, it) is feeding	they are feeding
Pres.	I do feed	we do feed
Int.	you do feed	you do feed
	he (she, it) does feed	they do feed
Fut.	I shall feed	we shall feed
	you will feed	you will feed
	he (she, it) will feed	they will feed
Fut.	I will feed *(P)*	we will feed *(P)*
	you shall feed *(C)*	you shall feed *(C)*
	he (she, it) shall feed *(C)*	they shall feed *(C)*
Past	I fed	we fed
	you fed	you fed
	he (she, it) fed	they fed
Past	I was feeding	we were feeding
Prog.	you were feeding	you were feeding
	he (she, it) was feeding	they were feeding
Past	I did feed	we did feed
Int.	you did feed	you did feed
	he (she, it) did feed	they did feed
Pres.	I have fed	we have fed
Perf.	you have fed	you have fed
	he (she, it) has fed	they have fed
Past	I had fed	we had fed
Perf.	you had fed	you had fed
	he (she, it) had fed	they had fed
Fut.	I shall have fed	we shall have fed
Perf.	you will have fed	you will have fed
	he (she, it) will have fed	they will have fed

IMPERATIVE MOOD
feed

SUBJUNCTIVE MOOD

Pres.	if I feed	if we feed
	if you feed	if you feed
	if he (she, it) feed	if they feed
Past	if I fed	if we fed
	if you fed	if you fed
	if he (she, it) fed	if they fed
Fut.	if I should feed	if we should feed
	if you should feed	if you should feed
	if he (she, it) should feed	if they should feed

Infinitive: to be fed   *Present Participle:* being fed
Perfect Infinitive: to have been fed   *Past Participle:* been fed

INDICATIVE MOOD

Pres.	I am fed	we are fed
	you are fed	you are fed
	he (she, it) is fed	they are fed
Pres.	I am being fed	we are being fed
Prog.	you are being fed	you are being fed
	he (she, it) is being fed	they are being fed
Pres.	I do get fed	we do get fed
Int.	you do get fed	you do get fed
	he (she, it) does get fed	they do get fed
Fut.	I shall be fed	we shall be fed
	you will be fed	you will be fed
	he (she, it) will be fed	they will be fed
Fut.	I will be fed *(P)*	we will be fed *(P)*
	you shall be fed *(C)*	you shall be fed *(C)*
	he (she, it) shall be fed *(C)*	they shall be fed *(C)*
Past	I was fed	we were fed
	you were fed	you were fed
	he (she, it) was fed	they were fed
Past	I was being fed	we were being fed
Prog.	you were being fed	you were being fed
	he (she, it) was being fed	they were being fed
Past	I did get fed	we did get fed
Int.	you did get fed	you did get fed
	he (she, it) did get fed	they did get fed
Pres.	I have been fed	we have been fed
Perf.	you have been fed	you have been fed
	he (she, it) has been fed	they have been fed
Past	I had been fed	we had been fed
Perf.	you had been fed	you had been fed
	he (she, it) had been fed	they had been fed
Fut.	I shall have been fed	we shall have been fed
Perf.	you will have been fed	you will have been fed
	he (she, it) will have been fed	they will have been fed

IMPERATIVE MOOD
be fed

SUBJUNCTIVE MOOD

Pres.	if I be fed	if we be fed
	if you be fed	if you be fed
	if he (she, it) be fed	if they be fed
Past	if I were fed	if we were fed
	if you were fed	if you were fed
	if he (she, it) were fed	if they were fed
Fut.	if I should be fed	if we should be fed
	if you should be fed	if you should be fed
	if he (she, it) should be fed	if they should be fed

to fight (active voice)

Principal Parts: fight, fighting, fought, fought

Infinitive: to fight	*Present Participle:* fighting
Perfect Infinitive: to have fought	*Past Participle:* fought

INDICATIVE MOOD

Pres.	I fight	we fight
	you fight	you fight
	he (she, it) fights	they fight
Prog.	I am fighting	we are fighting
Pres.	you are fighting	you are fighting
	he (she, it) is fighting	they are fighting
Pres.	I do fight	we do fight
Int.	you do fight	you do fight
	he (she, it) does fight	they do fight
Fut.	I shall fight	we shall fight
	you will fight	you will fight
	he (she, it) will fight	they will fight
Fut.	I will fight (P)	we will fight (P)
	you shall fight (C)	you shall fight (C)
	he (she, it) shall fight (C)	they shall fight (C)
Past	I fought	we fought
	you fought	you fought
	he (she, it) fought	they fought
Past	I was fighting	we were fighting
Prog.	you were fighting	you were fighting
	he (she, it) was fighting	they were fighting
Past	I did fight	we did fight
Int.	you did fight	you did fight
	he (she, it) did fight	they did fight
Perf.	I have fought	we have fought
Pres.	you have fought	you have fought
	he (she, it) has fought	they have fought
Past	I had fought	we had fought
Perf.	you had fought	you had fought
	he (she, it) had fought	they had fought
Fut.	I shall have fought	we shall have fought
Perf.	you will have fought	you will have fought
	he (she, it) will have fought	they will have fought

IMPERATIVE MOOD
fight

SUBJUNCTIVE MOOD

Pres.	if I fight	if we fight
	if you fight	if you fight
	if he (she, it) fight	if they fight
Past	if I fought	if we fought
	if you fought	if you fought
	if he (she, it) fought	if they fought
Fut.	if I should fight	if we should fight
	if you should fight	if you should fight
	if he (she, it) should fight	if they should fight

Infinitive: to be fought   *Present Participle:* being fought
Perfect Infinitive: to have been fought   *Past Participle:* been fought

INDICATIVE MOOD

Pres.	I am fought	we are fought
	you are fought	you are fought
	he (she, it) is fought	they are fought
Pres.	I am being fought	we are being fought
Prog.	you are being fought	you are being fought
	he (she, it) is being fought	they are being fought
Pres.	I do get fought	we do get fought
Int.	you do get fought	you do get fought
	he (she, it) does get fought	they do get fought
Fut.	I shall be fought	we shall be fought
	you will be fought	you will be fought
	he (she, it) will be fought	they will be fought
Fut.	I will be fought *(P)*	we will be fought *(P)*
	you shall be fought *(C)*	you shall be fought *(C)*
	he (she, it) shall be fought *(C)*	they shall be fought *(C)*
Past	I was fought	we were fought
	you were fought	you were fought
	he (she, it) was fought	they were fought
Past	I was being fought	we were being fought
Prog.	you were being fought	you were being fought
	he (she, it) was being fought	they were being fought
Past	I did get fought	we did get fought
Int.	you did get fought	you did get fought
	he (she, it) did get fought	they did get fought
Pres.	I have been fought	we have been fought
Perf.	you have been fought	you have been fought
	he (she, it) has been fought	they have been fought
Past	I had been fought	we had been fought
Perf.	you had been fought	you had been fought
	he (she, it) had been fought	they had been fought
Fut.	I shall have been fought	we shall have been fought
Perf.	you will have been fought	you will have been fought
	he (she, it) will have been fought	they will have been fought

IMPERATIVE MOOD
be fought

SUBJUNCTIVE MOOD

Pres.	if I be fought	if we be fought
	if you be fought	if you be fought
	if he (she, it) be fought	if they be fought
Past	if I were fought	if we were fought
	if you were fought	if you were fought
	if he (she, it) were fought	if they were fought
Fut.	if I should be fought	if we should be fought
	if you should be fought	if you should be fought
	if he (she, it) should be fought	if they should be fought

to find (active voice)

Principal Parts: find, finding, found, found

Infinitive: to find	Present Participle: finding
Perfect Infinitive: to have found	Past Participle: found

INDICATIVE MOOD

Pres.
I find / we find
you find / you find
he (she, it) finds / they find

Prog. Pres.
I am finding / we are finding
you are finding / you are finding
he (she, it) is finding / they are finding

Int. Pres.
I do find / we do find
you do find / you do find
he (she, it) does find / they do find

Fut.
I shall find / we shall find
you will find / you will find
he (she, it) will find / they will find

Fut.
I will find (P) / we will find (P)
you shall find (C) / you shall find (C)
he (she, it) shall find (C) / they shall find (C)

Past
I found / we found
you found / you found
he (she, it) found / they found

Past Prog.
I was finding / we were finding
you were finding / you were finding
he (she, it) was finding / they were finding

Int. Past
I did find / we did find
you did find / you did find
he (she, it) did find / they did find

Perf. Pres.
I have found / we have found
you have found / you have found
he (she, it) has found / they have found

Perf. Past
I had found / we had found
you had found / you had found
he (she, it) had found / they had found

Perf. Fut.
I shall have found / we shall have found
you will have found / you will have found
he (she, it) will have found / they will have found

IMPERATIVE MOOD

find

SUBJUNCTIVE MOOD

Pres.
if I find / if we find
if you find / if you find
if he (she, it) find / if they find

Past
if I found / if we found
if you found / if you found
if he (she, it) found / if they found

Fut.
if I should find / if we should find
if you should find / if you should find
if he (she, it) should find / if they should find

(Passive voice)

Infinitive: to be found *Present Participle:* being found
Perfect Infinitive: to have been found *Past Participle:* been found

INDICATIVE MOOD

Pres.	I am found	we are found
	you are found	you are found
	he (she, it) is found	they are found
Pres. Prog.	I am being found	we are being found
	you are being found	you are being found
	he (she, it) is being found	they are being found
Pres. Int.	I do get found	we do get found
	you do get found	you do get found
	he (she, it) does get found	they do get found
Fut.	I shall be found	we shall be found
	you will be found	you will be found
	he (she, it) will be found	they will be found
Fut.	I will be found (P)	we will be found (P)
	you shall be found (C)	you shall be found (C)
	he (she, it) shall be found (C)	they shall be found (C)
Past	I was found	we were found
	you were found	you were found
	he (she, it) was found	they were found
Past Prog.	I was being found	we were being found
	you were being found	you were being found
	he (she, it) was being found	they were being found
Past Int.	I did get found	we did get found
	you did get found	you did get found
	he (she, it) did get found	they did get found
Pres. Perf.	I have been found	we have been found
	you have been found	you have been found
	he (she, it) has been found	they have been found
Past Perf.	I had been found	we had been found
	you had been found	you had been found
	he (she, it) had been found	they had been found
Fut. Perf.	I shall have been found	we shall have been found
	you will have been found	you will have been found
	he (she, it) will have been found	they will have been found

IMPERATIVE MOOD
be found

SUBJUNCTIVE MOOD

Pres.	if I be found	if we be found
	if you be found	if you be found
	if he (she, it) be found	if they be found
Past	if I were found	if we were found
	if you were found	if you were found
	if he (she, it) were found	if they were found
Fut.	if I should be found	if we should be found
	if you should be found	if you should be found
	if he (she, it) should be found	if they should be found

Infinitive: to flee   *Present Participle:* fleeing
Perfect Infinitive: to have fled   *Past Participle:* fled

INDICATIVE MOOD

Pres.	I flee	we flee
	you flee	you flee
	he (she, it) flees	they flee
Pres.	I am fleeing	we are fleeing
Prog.	You are fleeing	you are fleeing
	he (she, it) is fleeing	they are fleeing
Pres.	I do flee	we do flee
Int.	you do flee	you do flee
	he (she, it) does flee	they do flee
Fut.	I shall flee	we shall flee
	you will flee	you will flee
	he (she, it) will flee	they will flee
Fut.	I will flee *(P)*	we will flee *(P)*
	you shall flee *(C)*	you shall flee *(C)*
	he (she, it) shall flee *(C)*	they shall flee *(C)*
Past	I fled	we fled
	you fled	you fled
	he (she, it) fled	they fled
Past	I was fleeing	we were fleeing
Prog.	you were fleeing	you were fleeing
	he (she, it) was fleeing	they were fleeing
Past	I did flee	we did flee
Int.	you did flee	you did flee
	he (she, it) did flee	they did flee
Pres.	I have fled	we have fled
Perf.	you have fled	you have fled
	he (she, it) has fled	they have fled
Past	I had fled	we had fled
Perf.	you had fled	you had fled
	he (she, it) had fled	they had fled
Fut.	I shall have fled	we shall have fled
Perf.	you will have fled	you will have fled
	he (she, it) will have fled	they will have fled

IMPERATIVE MOOD
flee

SUBJUNCTIVE MOOD

Pres.	if I flee	if we flee
	if you flee	if you flee
	if he (she, it) flee	if they flee
Past	if I fled	if we fled
	if you fled	if you fled
	if he (she, it) fled	if they fled
Fut.	if I should flee	if we should flee
	if you should flee	if you should flee
	if he (she, it) should flee	if they should flee

To flee is an intransitive verb.

It does not take an object.

It describes action, but the action is self-contained.

Like other intransitive verbs, it may be followed by adverbs, adverbial phrases and clauses describing the how, why, when, and where of the action:

HOW: The thieves fled *quickly*. (adverb)

WHY: He fled *because he was wanted for murder*. (adverbial clause)

WHEN: The army will flee *when it meets the enemy*. (adverbial clause)

WHERE: He fled *into the forest*. (adverbial phrase)

Infinitive: to fling   *Present Participle:* flinging
Perfect Infinitive: to have flung   *Past Participle:* flung

INDICATIVE MOOD

Pres.	I fling	we fling
	you fling	you fling
	he (she, it) flings	they fling
Pres.	I am flinging	we are flinging
Prog.	you are flinging	you are flinging
	he (she, it) is flinging	they are flinging
Pres.	I do fling	we do fling
Int.	you do fling	you do fling
	he (she, it) does fling	they do fling
Fut.	I shall fling	we shall fling
	you will fling	you will fling
	he (she, it) will fling	they will fling
Fut.	I will fling *(P)*	we will fling *(P)*
	you shall fling *(C)*	you shall fling *(C)*
	he (she, it) shall fling *(C)*	they shall fling *(C)*
Past	I flung	we flung
	you flung	you flung
	he (she, it) flung	they flung
Past	I was flinging	we were flinging
Prog.	you were flinging	you were flinging
	he (she, it) was flinging	they were flinging
Past	I did fling	we did fling
Int.	you did fling	you did fling
	he (she, it) did fling	they did fling
Pres.	I have flung	we have flung
Perf.	you have flung	you have flung
	he (she, it) has flung	they have flung
Past	I had flung	we had flung
Perf.	you had flung	you had flung
	he (she, it) had flung	they had flung
Fut.	I shall have flung	we shall have flung
Perf.	you will have flung	you will have flung
	he (she, it) will have flung	they will have flung

IMPERATIVE MOOD
fling

SUBJUNCTIVE MOOD

Pres.	if I fling	if we fling
	if you fling	if you fling
	if he (she, it) fling	if they fling
Past	if I flung	if we flung
	if you flung	if you flung
	if he (she, it) flung	if they flung
Fut.	if I should fling	if we should fling
	if you should fling	if you should fling
	if he (she, it) should fling	if they should fling

Infinitive: to be flung   *Present Participle:* being flung
Perfect Infinitive: to have been flung   *Past Participle:* been flung

INDICATIVE MOOD

Pres.	I am flung	we are flung
	you are flung	you are flung
	he (she, it) is flung	they are flung
Pres.	I am being flung	we are being flung
Prog.	you are being flung	you are being flung
	he (she, it) is being flung	they are being flung
Pres.	I do get flung	we do get flung
Int.	you do get flung	you do get flung
	he (she, it) does get flung	they do get flung
Fut.	I shall be flung	we shall be flung
	you will be flung	you will be flung
	he (she, it) will be flung	they will be flung
Fut.	I will be flung *(P)*	we will be flung *(P)*
	you shall be flung *(C)*	you shall be flung *(C)*
	he (she, it) shall be flung *(C)*	they shall be flung *(C)*
Past	I was flung	we were flung
	you were flung	you were flung
	he (she, it) was flung	they were flung
Past	I was being flung	we were being flung
Prog.	you were being flung	you were being flung
	he (she, it) was being flung	they were being flung
Past	I did get flung	we did get flung
Int.	you did get flung	you did get flung
	he (she, it) did get flung	they did get flung
Pres.	I have been flung	we have been flung
Perf.	you have been flung	you have been flung
	he (she, it) has been flung	they have been flung
Past	I had been flung	we had been flung
Perf.	you had been flung	you had been flung
	he (she, it) had been flung	they had been flung
Fut.	I shall have been flung	we shall have been flung
Perf.	you will have been flung	you will have been flung
	he (she, it) will have been flung	they will have been flung

IMPERATIVE MOOD
be flung

SUBJUNCTIVE MOOD

Pres.	if I be flung	if we be flung
	if you be flung	if you be flung
	if he (she, it) be flung	if they be flung
Past	if I were flung	if we were flung
	if you were flung	if you were flung
	if he (she, it) were flung	if they were flung
Fut.	if I should be flung	if we should be flung
	if you should be flung	if you should be flung
	if he (she, it) should be flung	if they should be flung

Principal Parts: fly, flying, flew, flown

Infinitive: to fly   *Present Participle:* flying
Perfect Infinitive: to have flown   *Past Participle:* flown

INDICATIVE MOOD

Pres.	I fly	we fly
	you fly	you fly
	he (she, it) flies	they fly
Pres.	I am flying	we are flying
Prog.	you are flying	you are flying
	he (she, it) is flying	they are flying
Pres.	I do fly	we do fly
Int.	you do fly	you do fly
	he (she, it) does fly	they do fly
Fut.	I shall fly	we shall fly
	you will fly	you will fly
	he (she, it) will fly	they will fly
Fut.	I will fly *(P)*	we will fly *(P)*
	you shall fly *(C)*	you shall fly *(C)*
	he (she, it) shall fly *(C)*	they shall fly *(C)*
Past	I flew	we flew
	you flew	you flew
	he (she, it) flew	they flew
Past	I was flying	we were flying
Prog.	you were flying	you were flying
	he (she, it) was flying	they were flying
Past	I did fly	we did fly
Int.	you did fly	you did fly
	he (she, it) did fly	they did fly
Pres.	I have flown	we have flown
Perf.	you have flown	you have flown
	he (she, it) has flown	they have flown
Past	I had flown	we had flown
Perf.	you had flown	you had flown
	he (she, it) had flown	they had flown
Fut.	I shall have flown	we shall have flown
Perf.	you will have flown	you will have flown
	he (she, it) will have flown	they will have flown

IMPERATIVE MOOD
fly

SUBJUNCTIVE MOOD

Pres.	if I fly	if we fly
	if you fly	if you fly
	if he (she, it) fly	if they fly
Past	if I flew	if we flew
	if you flew	if you flew
	if he (she, it) flew	if they flew
Fut.	if I should fly	if we should fly
	if you should fly	if you should fly
	if he (she, it) should fly	if they should fly

Infinitive: to be flown   *Present Participle:* being flown
Perfect Infinitive: to have been flown   *Past Participle:* been flown

INDICATIVE MOOD

Pres.	I am flown	we are flown
	you are flown	you are flown
	he (she, it) is flown	they are flown
Pres.	I am being flown	we are being flown
Prog.	you are being flown	you are being flown
	he (she, it) is being flown	they are being flown
Pres.	I do get flown	we do get flown
Int.	you do get flown	you do get flown
	he (she, it) does get flown	they do get flown
Fut.	I shall be flown	we shall be flown
	you will be flown	you will be flown
	he (she, it) will be flown	they will be flown
Fut.	I will be flown *(P)*	we will be flown *(P)*
	you shall be flown *(C)*	you shall be flown *(C)*
	he (she, it) shall be flown *(C)*	they shall be flown *(C)*
Past	I was flown	we were flown
	you were flown	you were flown
	he (she, it) was flown	they were flown
Past	I was being flown	we were being flown
Prog.	you were being flown	you were being flown
	he (she, it) was being flown	they were being flown
Past	I did get flown	we did get flown
Int.	you did get flown	you did get flown
	he (she, it) did get flown	they did get flown
Pres.	I have been flown	we have been flown
Perf.	you have been flown	you have been flown
	he (she, it) has been flown	they have been flown
Past	I had been flown	we had been flown
Perf.	you had been flown	you had been flown
	he (she, it) had been flown	they had been flown
Fut.	I shall have been flown	we shall have been flown
Perf.	you will have been flown	you will have been flown
	he (she, it) will have been flown	they will have been flown

IMPERATIVE MOOD
be flown

SUBJUNCTIVE MOOD

Pres.	if I be flown	if we be flown
	if you be flown	if you be flown
	if he (she, it) be flown	if they be flown
Past	if I were flown	if we were flown
	if you were flown	if you were flown
	if he (she, it) were flown	if they were flown
Fut.	if I should be flown	if we should be flown
	if you should be flown	if you should be flown
	if he (she, it) should be flown	if they should be flown

to forbid (active voice)   *Principal Parts:* forbid, forbidding, forbade
(forbad), forbidden

Infinitive: to forbid	*Present Participle:* forbidding
Perfect Infinitive: to have forbidden	*Past Participle:* forbidden

INDICATIVE MOOD

Pres.	I forbid	we forbid
	you forbid	you forbid
	he (she, it) forbids	they forbid
Pres.	I am forbidding	we are forbidding
Prog.	you are forbidding	you are forbidding
	he (she, it) is forbidding	they are forbidding
Pres.	I do forbid	we do forbid
Int.	you do forbid	you do forbid
	he (she, it) does forbid	they do forbid
Fut.	I shall forbid	we shall forbid
	you will forbid	you will forbid
	he (she, it) will forbid	they will forbid
Fut.	I will forbid *(P)*	we will forbid *(P)*
	you shall forbid *(C)*	you shall forbid *(C)*
	he (she, it) shall forbid *(C)*	they shall forbid *(C)*
Past	I forbade, forbad	we forbade, forbad
	you forbade, forbad	you forbade, forbad
	he (she, it) forbade, forbad	they forbade, forbad
Past	I was forbidding	we were forbidding
Prog.	you were forbidding	you were forbidding
	he (she, it) was forbidding	they were forbidding
Past	I did forbid	we did forbid
Int.	you did forbid	you did forbid
	he (she, it) did forbid	they did forbid
Pres.	I have forbidden	we have forbidden
Perf.	you have forbidden	you have forbidden
	he (she, it) has forbidden	they have forbidden
Past	I had forbidden	we had forbidden
Perf.	you had forbidden	you had forbidden
	he (she, it) had forbidden	they had forbidden
Fut.	I shall have forbidden	we shall have forbidden
Perf.	you will have forbidden	you will have forbidden
	he (she, it) will have forbidden	they will have forbidden

IMPERATIVE MOOD
forbid

SUBJUNCTIVE MOOD

Pres.	if I forbid	if we forbid
	if you forbid	if you forbid
	if he (she, it) forbid	if they forbid
Past	if I forbade, forbad	if we forbade, forbad
	if you forbade, forbad	if you forbade, forbad
	if he (she, it) forbade, forbad	if they forbade, forbad
Fut.	if I should forbid	if we should forbid
	if you should forbid	if you should forbid
	if he (she, it) should forbid	if they should forbid

Infinitive: to be forbidden   *Present Participle:* being forbidden
Perfect Infinitive: to have been forbidden   *Past Participle:* been forbidden

INDICATIVE MOOD

Pres.	I am forbidden	we are forbidden
	you are forbidden	you are forbidden
	he (she, it) is forbidden	they are forbidden
Pres.	I am being forbidden	we are being forbidden
Prog.	you are being forbidden	you are being forbidden
	he (she, it) is being forbidden	they are being forbidden
Pres.	I do get forbidden	we do get forbidden
Int.	you do get forbidden	you do get forbidden
	he (she, it) does get forbidden	they do get forbidden
Fut.	I shall be forbidden	we shall be forbidden
	you will be forbidden	you will be forbidden
	he (she, it) will be forbidden	they will be forbidden
Fut.	I will be forbidden *(P)*	we will be forbidden *(P)*
	you shall be forbidden *(C)*	you shall be forbidden *(C)*
	he (she, it) shall be forbidden *(C)*	they shall be forbidden *(C)*
Past	I was forbidden	we were forbidden
	you were forbidden	you were forbidden
	he (she, it) was forbidden	they were forbidden
Past	I was being forbidden	we were being forbidden
Prog.	you were being forbidden	you were being forbidden
	he (she, it) was being forbidden	they were being forbidden
Past	I did get forbidden	we did get forbidden
Int.	you did get forbidden	you did get forbidden
	he (she, it) did get forbidden	they did get forbidden
Pres.	I have been forbidden	we have been forbidden
Perf.	you have been forbidden	you have been forbidden
	he (she, it) has been forbidden	they have been forbidden
Past	I had been forbidden	we had been forbidden
Perf.	you had been forbidden	you had been forbidden
	he (she, it) had been forbidden	they had been forbidden
Fut.	I shall have been forbidden	we shall have been forbidden
Perf.	you will have been forbidden	you will have been forbidden
	he (she, it) will have been forbidden	they will have been forbidden

IMPERATIVE MOOD
be forbidden

SUBJUNCTIVE MOOD

Pres.	if I be forbidden	if we be forbidden
	if you be forbidden	if you be forbidden
	if he (she, it) be forbidden	if they be forbidden
Past	if I were forbidden	if we were forbidden
	if you were forbidden	if you were forbidden
	if he (she, it) were forbidden	if they were forbidden
Fut.	if I should be forbidden	if we should be forbidden
	if you should be forbidden	if you should be forbidden
	if he (she, it) should be forbidden	if they should be forbidden

to forget (active voice)　　　*Principal Parts:* forget, forgetting, forgot, forgotten (forgot)

Infinitive: to forget　　　　　　　　*Present Participle:* forgetting
Perfect Infinitive: to have forgotten　　*Past Participle:* forgotten, forgot

INDICATIVE MOOD

Pres.	I forget	we forget
	you forget	you forget
	he (she, it) forgets	they forget
Pres.	I am forgetting	we are forgetting
Prog.	you are forgetting	you are forgetting
	he (she, it) is forgetting	they are forgetting
Pres.	I do forget	we do forget
Int.	you do forget	you do forget
	he (she, it) does forget	they do forget
Fut.	I shall forget	we shall forget
	you will forget	you will forget
	he (she, it) will forget	they will forget
Fut.	I will forget *(P)*	we will forget *(P)*
	you shall forget *(C)*	you shall forget *(C)*
	he (she, it) shall forget *(C)*	they shall forget *(C)*
Past	I forgot	we forgot
	you forgot	you forgot
	he (she, it) forgot	they forgot
Past	I was forgetting	we were forgetting
Prog.	you were forgetting	you were forgetting
	he (she, it) was forgetting	they were forgetting
Past	I did forget	we did forget
Int.	you did forget	you did forget
	he (she, it) did forget	they did forget
Pres.	I have forgotten, forgot	we have forgotten, forgot
Perf.	you have forgotten, forgot	you have forgotten, forgot
	he (she, it) has forgotten, forgot	they have forgotten, forgot
Past	I had forgotten, forgot	we had forgotten, forgot
Perf.	you had forgotten, forgot	you had forgotten, forgot
	he (she, it) had forgotten, forgot	they had forgotten, forgot
Fut.	I shall have forgotten, forgot	we shall have forgotten, forgot
Perf.	you will have forgotten, forgot	you will have forgotten, forgot
	he (she, it) will have forgotten, forgot	they will have forgotten, forgot

IMPERATIVE MOOD
forget

SUBJUNCTIVE MOOD

Pres.	if I forget	if we forget
	if you forget	if you forget
	if he (she, it) forget	if they forget
Past	if I forgot	if we forgot
	if you forgot	if you forgot
	if he (she, it) forgot	if they forgot
Fut.	if I should forget	if we should forget
	if you should forget	if you should forget
	if he (she, it) should forget	if they should forget

(passive voice)

Infinitive: to be forgotten
Perfect Infinitive: to have been forgotten
Present Participle: being forgotten
Past Participle: been forgotten

INDICATIVE MOOD

Pres.	I am forgotten, forgot you are forgotten, forgot he (she, it) is forgotten, forgot	we are forgotten, forgot you are forgotten, forgot they are forgotten, forgot
Pres. *Prog.*	I am being forgotten, forgot you are being forgotten, forgot he (she, it) is being forgotten, forgot	we are being forgotten, forgot you are being forgotten, forgot they are being forgotten, forgot
Pres. *Int.*	I do get forgotten, forgot you do get forgotten, forgot he (she, it) does get forgotten, forgot	we do get forgotten, forgot you do get forgotten, forgot they do get forgotten, forgot
Fut.	I shall be forgotten, forgot you will be forgotten, forgot he (she, it) will be forgotten, forgot	we shall be forgotten, forgot you will be forgotten, forgot they will be forgotten, forgot
Fut.	I will be forgotten, forgot *(P)* you shall be forgotten, forgot *(C)* he (she, it) shall be forgotten, forgot *(C)*	we will be forgotten, forgot *(P)* you shall be forgotten, forgot *(C)* they shall be forgotten, forgot *(C)*
Past	I was forgotten, forgot you were forgotten, forgot he (she, it) was forgotten, forgot	we were forgotten, forgot you were forgotten, forgot they were forgotten, forgot
Past *Prog.*	I was being forgotten, forgot you were being forgotten, forgot he (she, it) was being forgotten, forgot	we were being forgotten, forgot you were being forgotten, forgot they were being forgotten, forgot
Past *Int.*	I did get forgotten, forgot you did get forgotten, forgot he (she, it) did get forgotten, forgot	we did get forgotten, forgot you did get forgotten, forgot they did get forgotten, forgot
Pres. *Perf.*	I have been forgotten, forgot you have been forgotten, forgot he (she, it) has been forgotten, forgot	we have been forgotten, forgot you have been forgotten, forgot they have been forgotten, forgot
Past *Perf.*	I had been forgotten, forgot you had been forgotten, forgot he (she, it) had been forgotten, forgot	we had been forgotten, forgot you had been forgotten, forgot they have been forgotten, forgot
Fut. *Perf.*	I shall have been forgotten, forgot you will have been forgotten, forgot he (she, it) will have been forgotten, forgot	we shall have been forgotten, forgot you will have been forgotten, forgot they will have been forgotten, forgot

IMPERATIVE MOOD
be forgotten

SUBJUNCTIVE MOOD

Pres. if I be forgotten, forgot
if you be forgotten, forgot
if he (she, it) be forgotten, forgot

if we be forgotten, forgot
if you be forgotten, forgot
if they be forgotten, forgot

Past if I were forgotten, forgot
if you were forgotten, forgot
if he (she, it) were forgotten, forgot

if we were forgotten, forgot
if you were forgotten, forgot
if they were forgotten, forgot

Fut. if I should be forgotten, forgot
if you should be forgotten, forgot
if he (she, it) should be forgotten,
forgot

if we should be forgotten, forgot
if you should be forgotten, forgot
if they should be forgotten,
forgot

Typical Verb Usages

The verb *to forget* offers convenient illustrations of the many shades of meaning made possible by the different voices, moods, and tenses of English verbs.

Active Voice

Present: I *forget* nearly everything I learn.

Present Progressive: She *is* always *forgetting* to bring her notebook.

Present Intensive: You certainly *do forget* a great deal.

Future: You *will* probably *forget* me before long.

Future (Promise): I *will* never *forget* you.

Future (Command): The observers of this crime *shall forget* what they have seen or they will live to regret it.

Past: John *forgot* to lock the door.

Past Progressive: The children *were* always *forgetting* to drink their milk.

Past Intensive: They really *did forget* to drink their milk.

Present Perfect: The old man *has forgotten* his childhood.

Past Perfect: I *had forgotten* that I promised to meet you.

Future Perfect: When winter comes, I *shall have forgotten* our summer vacation.

SUBJUNCTIVE MOOD

Present: *If* I *forget* to meet you, go without me.

Past: *If* they *forgot* their tickets, they weren't able to hear the concert.

Future: *If* I *should forget* to leave a key, go to my neighbor's house.

Passive voice

Present: Telephone numbers *are* easily *forgotten*.

Present Progressive: I *am being forgotten* by all my friends.

Present Intensive: Your directions really *do get forgotten* easily.

Future: The words of the song *will be forgotten* very quickly.

Future (Promise): I will so live that I *will* not *be forgotten*.

Future (Command): Your bad habits *shall be forgotten*!

Past: The novel *was forgotten* by most people.

Past Progressive: The lessons *were being forgotten* almost as quickly as they were learned.

Past Intensive: You *did* not *get forgotten* after all.

Past Perfect: All the old times *have been forgotten*.

Future Perfect: When you have reached my age, your youth *will have been forgotten*.

SUBJUNCTIVE MOOD

Present: *If* his words *be forgotten*, he will have spoken in vain.

Past: *If* you *were forgotten*, it was through no fault of mine.

Future: *If* the lesson *should be forgotten*, it can be easily learned again.

to forgive (active voice)   *Principal Parts:* forgive, forgiving, forgave, forgiven

Infinitive: to forgive   *Present Participle:* forgiving
Perfect Infinitive: to have forgiven   *Past Participle:* forgiven

INDICATIVE MOOD

Pres.	I forgive	we forgive
	you forgive	you forgive
	he (she, it) forgives	they forgive
Pres.	I am forgiving	we are forgiving
Prog.	you are forgiving	you are forgiving
	he (she, it) is forgiving	they are forgiving
Pres.	I do forgive	we do forgive
Int.	you do forgive	you do forgive
	he (she, it) does forgive	they do forgive
Fut.	I shall forgive	we shall forgive
	you will forgive	you will forgive
	he (she, it) will forgive	they will forgive
Fut.	I will forgive *(P)*	we will forgive *(P)*
	you shall forgive *(C)*	you shall forgive *(C)*
	he (she, it) shall forgive *(C)*	they shall forgive *(C)*
Past	I forgave	we forgave
	you forgave	you forgave
	he (she, it) forgave	they forgave
Past	I was forgiving	we were forgiving
Prog.	you were forgiving	you were forgiving
	he (she, it) was forgiving	they were forgiving
Past	I did forgive	we did forgive
Int.	you did forgive	you did forgive
	he (she, it) did forgive	they did forgive
Pres.	I have forgiven	we have forgiven
Perf.	you have forgiven	you have forgiven
	he (she, it) has forgiven	they have forgiven
Past	I had forgiven	we had forgiven
Perf.	you had forgiven	you had forgiven
	he (she, it) had forgiven	they have forgiven
Fut.	I shall have forgiven	we shall have forgiven
Perf.	you will have forgiven	you will have forgiven
	he (she, it) will have forgiven	they will have forgiven

IMPERATIVE MOOD
forgive

SUBJUNCTIVE MOOD

Pres.	if I forgive	if we forgive
	if you forgive	if you forgive
	if he (she, it) forgive	if they forgive
Past	if I forgave	if we forgave
	if you forgave	if you forgave
	if he (she, it) forgave	if they forgave
Fut.	if I should forgive	if we should forgive
	if you should forgive	if you should forgive
	if he (she, it) should forgive	if they should forgive

Infinitive: to be forgiven   *Present Participle:* being forgiven
Perfect Infinitive: to have been forgiven   *Past Participle:* been forgiven

INDICATIVE MOOD

Pres.	I am forgiven	we are forgiven
	you are forgiven	you are forgiven
	he (she, it) is forgiven	they are forgiven
Pres.	I am being forgiven	we are being forgiven
Prog.	you are being forgiven	you are being forgiven
	he (she, it) is being forgiven	they are being forgiven
Pres.	I do get forgiven	we do get forgiven
Int.	you do get forgiven	you do get forgiven
	he (she, it) does get forgiven	they do get forgiven
Fut.	I shall be forgiven	we shall be forgiven
	you will be forgiven	you will be forgiven
	he (she, it) will be forgiven	they will be forgiven
Fut.	I will be forgiven *(P)*	we will be forgiven *(P)*
	you shall be forgiven *(C)*	you shall be forgiven *(C)*
	he (she, it) shall be forgiven *(C)*	they shall be forgiven *(C)*
Past	I was forgiven	we were forgiven
	you were forgiven	you were forgiven
	he (she, it) was forgiven	they were forgiven
Past	I was being forgiven	we were being forgiven
Prog.	you were being forgiven	you were being forgiven
	he (she, it) was being forgiven	they were being forgiven
Past	I did get forgiven	we did get forgiven
Int.	you did get forgiven	you did get forgiven
	he (she, it) did get forgiven	they did get forgiven
Pres.	I have been forgiven	we have been forgiven
Perf.	you have been forgiven	you have been forgiven
	he (she, it) has been forgiven	they have been forgiven
Past	I had been forgiven	we had been forgiven
Perf.	you had been forgiven	you had been forgiven
	he (she, it) had been forgiven	they had been forgiven
Fut.	I shall have been forgiven	we shall have been forgiven
Perf.	you will have been forgiven	you will have been forgiven
	he (she, it) will have been forgiven	they will have been forgiven

IMPERATIVE MOOD
be forgiven

SUBJUNCTIVE MOOD

Pres.	if I be forgiven	if we be forgiven
	if you be forgiven	if you be forgiven
	if he (she, it) be forgiven	if they be forgiven
Past	if I were forgiven	if we were forgiven
	if you were forgiven	if you were forgiven
	if he (she, it) were forgiven	if they were forgiven
Fut.	if I should be forgiven	if we should be forgiven
	if you should be forgiven	if you should be forgiven
	if he (she, it) should be forgiven	if they should be forgiven

215

to forsake (active voice)

Infinitive: to forsake	*Present Participle:* forsaking
Perfect Infinitive: to have forsaken	*Past Participle:* forsaken

INDICATIVE MOOD

Pres.	I forsake	we forsake
	you forsake	you forsake
	he (she, it) forsakes	they forsake
Pres.	I am forsaking	we are forsaking
Prog.	you are forsaking	you are forsaking
	he (she, it) is forsaking	they are forsaking
Pres.	I do forsake	we do forsake
Int.	you do forsake	you do forsake
	he (she, it) does forsake	they do forsake
Fut.	I shall forsake	we shall forsake
	you will forsake	you will forsake
	he (she, it) will forsake	they will forsake
Fut.	I will forsake *(P)*	we will forsake *(P)*
	you shall forsake *(C)*	you shall forsake *(C)*
	he (she, it) shall forsake *(C)*	they shall forsake *(C)*
Past	I forsook	we forsook
	you forsook	you forsook
	he (she, it) forsook	they forsook
Past	I was forsaking	we were forsaking
Prog.	you were forsaking	you were forsaking
	he (she, it) was forsaking	they were forsaking
Past	I did forsake	we did forsake
Int.	you did forsake	you did forsake
	he (she, it) did forsake	they did forsake
Pres.	I have forsaken	we have forsaken
Perf.	you have forsaken	you have forsaken
	he (she, it) has forsaken	they have forsaken
Past	I had forsaken	we had forsaken
Perf.	you had forsaken	you had forsaken
	he (she, it) had forsaken	they had forsaken
Fut.	I shall have forsaken	we shall have forsaken
Perf.	you will have forsaken	you will have forsaken
	he (she, it) will have forsaken	they will have forsaken

IMPERATIVE MOOD
forsake

SUBJUNCTIVE MOOD

Pres.	if I forsake	if we forsake
	if you forsake	if you forsake
	if he (she, it) forsake	if they forsake
Past	if I forsook	if we forsook
	if you forsook	if you forsook
	if he (she, it) forsook	if they forsook
Fut.	if I should forsake	if we should forsake
	if you should forsake	if you should forsake
	if he (she, it) should forsake	if they should forsake

Infinitive: to be forsaken   *Present Participle:* being forsaken
Perfect Infinitive: to have been forsaken   *Past Participle:* been forsaken

INDICATIVE MOOD

Pres.	I am forsaken	we are forsaken
	You are forsaken	you are forsaken
	he (she, it) is forsaken	they are forsaken
Pres.	I am being forsaken	we are being forsaken
Prog.	You are being forsaken	you are being forsaken
	he (she, it) is being forsaken	they are being forsaken
Pres.	I do get forsaken	we do get forsaken
Int.	you do get forsaken	you do get forsaken
	he (she, it) does get forsaken	they do get forsaken
Fut.	I shall be forsaken	we shall be forsaken
	you will be forsaken	you will be forsaken
	he (she, it) will be forsaken	they will be forsaken
Fut.	I will be forsaken *(P)*	we will be forsaken *(P)*
	you shall be forsaken *(C)*	you shall be forsaken *(C)*
	he (she, it) shall be forsaken *(C)*	they shall be forsaken *(C)*
Past	I was forsaken	we were forsaken
	you were forsaken	you were forsaken
	he (she, it) was forsaken	they were forsaken
Past	I was being forsaken	we were being forsaken
Prog.	you were being forsaken	you were being forsaken
	he (she, it) was being forsaken	they were being forsaken
Past	I did get forsaken	we did get forsaken
Int.	you did get forsaken	you did get forsaken
	he (she, it) did get forsaken	they did get forsaken
Pres.	I have been forsaken	we have been forsaken
Perf.	you have been forsaken	you have been forsaken
	he (she, it) has been forsaken	they have been forsaken
Past	I had been forsaken	we had been forsaken
Perf.	you have been forsaken	you had been forsaken
	he (she, it) had been forsaken	they had been forsaken
Fut.	I shall have been forsaken	we shall have been forsaken
Perf.	you will have been forsaken	you will have been forsaken
	he (she, it) will have been forsaken	they will have been forsaken

IMPERATIVE MOOD
be forsaken

SUBJUNCTIVE MOOD

Pres.	if I be forsaken	if we be forsaken
	if you be forsaken	if you be forsaken
	if you were forsaken	if they be forsaken
Past	if I were forsaken	if we were forsaken
	if you were forsaken	if you were forsaken
	if he (she, it) were forsaken	if they were forsaken
Fut.	if I should be forsaken	if we should be forsaken
	if you should be forsaken	if you should be forsaken
	if he (she, it) should be forsaken	if they should be forsaken

217

Infinitive: to freeze   *Present Participle:* freezing
Perfect Infinitive: to have frozen   *Past Participle:* frozen

INDICATIVE MOOD

Pres.	I freeze	we freeze
	you freeze	you freeze
	he (she, it) freezes	they freeze
Pres. *Prog.*	I am freezing	we are freezing
	you are freezing	you are freezing
	he (she, it) is freezing	they are freezing
Pres. *Int.*	I do freeze	we do freeze
	you do freeze	you do freeze
	he (she, it) does freeze	they do freeze
Fut.	I shall freeze	we shall freeze
	you will freeze	you will freeze
	he (she, it) will freeze	they will freeze
Fut.	I will freeze *(P)*	we will freeze *(P)*
	you shall freeze *(C)*	you shall freeze *(C)*
	he (she, it) shall freeze *(C)*	they shall freeze *(C)*
Past	I froze	we froze
	you froze	you froze
	he (she, it) froze	they froze
Past *Prog.*	I was freezing	we were freezing
	you were freezing	you were freezing
	he (she, it) was freezing	they were freezing
Past *Int.*	I did freeze	we did freeze
	you did freeze	you did freeze
	he (she, it) did freeze	they did freeze
Pres. *Perf.*	I have frozen	we have frozen
	you have frozen	you have frozen
	he (she, it) has frozen	they have frozen
Past *Perf.*	I had frozen	we had frozen
	you had frozen	you had frozen
	he (she, it) had frozen	they had frozen
Fut. *Perf.*	I shall have frozen	we shall have frozen
	you will have frozen	you will have frozen
	he (she, it) will have frozen	they will have frozen

IMPERATIVE MOOD
freeze

SUBJUNCTIVE MOOD

Pres.	if I freeze	if we freeze
	if you freeze	if you freeze
	if he (she, it) freeze	if they freeze
Past	if I froze	if we froze
	if you froze	if you froze
	if he (she, it) froze	if they froze
Fut.	if I should freeze	if we should freeze
	if you should freeze	if you should freeze
	if he (she, it) should freeze	if they should freeze

(passive voice)

Infinitive: to be frozen   *Present Participle:* being frozen
Perfect Infinitive: to have been frozen   *Past Participle:* been frozen

INDICATIVE MOOD

Pres.	I am frozen	we are frozen
	you are frozen	you are frozen
	he (she, it) is frozen	they are frozen
Pres.	I am being frozen	we are being frozen
Prog.	you are being frozen	you are being frozen
	he (she, it) is being frozen	they are being frozen
Pres.	I do get frozen	we do get frozen
Int.	you do get frozen	you do get frozen
	he (she, it) does get frozen	they do get frozen
Fut.	I shall be frozen	we shall be frozen
	you will be frozen	you will be frozen
	he (she, it) will be frozen	they will be frozen
Fut.	I will be frozen *(P)*	we will be frozen *(P)*
	you shall be frozen *(C)*	you shall be frozen *(C)*
	he (she, it) shall be frozen *(C)*	they shall be frozen *(C)*
Past	I was frozen	we were frozen
	you were frozen	you were frozen
	he (she, it) was frozen	they were frozen
Past	I was being frozen	we were being frozen
Prog.	you were being frozen	you were being frozen
	he (she, it) was being frozen	they were being frozen
Past	I did get frozen	we did get frozen
Int.	you did get frozen	you did get frozen
	he (she, it) did get frozen	they did get frozen
Pres.	I have been frozen	we have been frozen
Perf.	you have been frozen	you have been frozen
	he (she, it) has been frozen	they have been frozen
Past	I had been frozen	we had been frozen
Perf.	you had been frozen	you had been frozen
	he (she, it) had been frozen	they had been frozen
Fut.	I shall have been frozen	we shall have been frozen
Perf.	you will have been frozen	you will have been frozen
	he (she, it) will have been frozen	they will have been frozen

IMPERATIVE MOOD
be frozen

SUBJUNCTIVE MOOD

Pres.	if I be frozen	if we be frozen
	if you be frozen	if you be frozen
	if he (she, it) be frozen	if they be frozen
Past	if I were frozen	if we were frozen
	if you were frozen	if you were frozen
	if he (she, it) were frozen	if they were frozen
Fut.	if I should be frozen	if we should be frozen
	if you should be frozen	if you should be frozen
	if he (she, it) should be frozen	if they should be frozen

to get (active voice)

Principal Parts: get, getting, got (gotten)

Infinitive: to get	*Present Participle:* getting
Perfect Infinitive: to have got, gotten	*Past Participle:* got, gotten

INDICATIVE MOOD

Pres.	I get	we get
	you get	you get
	he (she, it) gets	they get
Prog. Pres.	I am getting	we are getting
	you are getting	you are getting
	he (she, it) is getting	they are getting
Pres. Int.	I do get	we do get
	you do get	you do get
	he (she, it) does get	they do get
Fut.	I shall get	we shall get
	you will get	you will get
	he (she, it) will get	they will get
Fut.	I will get (P)	we will get (P)
	you shall get (C)	you shall get (C)
	he (she, it) shall get (C)	they shall get (C)
Past	I got	we got
	you got	you got
	he (she, it) got	they got
Past Prog.	I was getting	we were getting
	you were getting	you were getting
	he (she, it) was getting	they were getting
Past Int.	I did get	we did get
	you did get	you did get
	he (she, it) did get	they did get
Perf. Pres.	I have got, gotten	we have got, gotten
	you have got, gotten	you have got, gotten
	he (she, it) has got, gotten	they have got, gotten
Perf. Past	I had got, gotten	we had got, gotten
	you had got, gotten	you had got, gotten
	he (she, it) had got, gotten	they had got, gotten
Perf. Fut.	I shall have got, gotten	we shall have got, gotten
	you will have got, gotten	you will have got, gotten
	he (she, it) will have got, gotten	they will have got, gotten

IMPERATIVE MOOD

get

SUBJUNCTIVE MOOD

Pres.	if I get	if we get
	if you get	if you get
	if he (she, it) get	if they get
Past	if I got	if we got
	if you got	if you got
	if he (she, it) got	if they got
Fut.	if I should get	if we should get
	if you should get	if you should get
	if he (she, it) should get	if they should get

Infinitive: to be gotten
Perfect Infinitive: to have been gotten

Present Participle: being gotten
Past Participle: been gotten

INDICATIVE MOOD

Pres.	I am gotten	we are gotten
	you are gotten	you are gotten
	he (she, it) is gotten	they are gotten
Pres.	I am being gotten	we are being gotten
Prog.	you are being gotten	you are being gotten
	he (she, it) is being gotten	they are being gotten
Pres.	I do get gotten	we do get gotten
Int.	you do get gotten	you do get gotten
	he (she, it) does get gotten	they do get gotten
Fut.	I shall be gotten	we shall be gotten
	you will be gotten	you will be gotten
	he (she, it) will be gotten	they will be gotten
Fut.	I will be gotten *(P)*	we will be gotten *(P)*
	you shall be gotten *(C)*	you shall be gotten *(C)*
	he (she, it) shall be gotten *(C)*	they shall be gotten *(C)*
Past	I was gotten	we were gotten
	you were gotten	you were gotten
	he (she, it) was gotten	they were gotten
Past	I was being gotten	we were being gotten
Prog.	you were being gotten	you were being gotten
	he (she, it) was being gotten	they were being gotten
Past	I did get gotten	we did get gotten
Int.	you did get gotten	you did get gotten
	he (she, it) did get gotten	they did get gotten
Pres.	I have been gotten	we have been gotten
Perf.	you have been gotten	you have been gotten
	he (she, it) has been gotten	they have been gotten
Past	I had been gotten	we had been gotten
Perf.	you had been gotten	you had been gotten
	he (she, it) had been gotten	they had been gotten
Fut.	I shall have been gotten	we shall have been gotten
Perf.	you will have been gotten	you will have been gotten
	he (she, it) will have been gotten	they will have been gotten

IMPERATIVE MOOD
be gotten

SUBJUNCTIVE MOOD

Pres.	if I be gotten	if we be gotten
	if you be gotten	if you be gotten
	if he (she, it) be gotten	if they be gotten
Past	if I were gotten	if we were gotten
	if you were gotten	if you were gotten
	if he (she, it) were gotten	if they were gotten
Fut.	if I should be gotten	if we should be gotten
	if you should be gotten	if you should be gotten
	if he (she, it) should be gotten	if they should be gotten

221

Principal Parts: give, giving, gave, given

Infinitive: to give

Present Participle: giving

Perfect Infinitive: to have given

Past Participle: given

INDICATIVE MOOD

Pres.	I give	we give
	you give	you give
	he (she, it) gives	they give
Pres.	I am giving	we are giving
Prog.	you are giving	you are giving
	he (she, it) is giving	they are giving
Pres.	I do give	we do give
Int.	you do give	you do give
	he (she, it) does give	they do give
Fut.	I shall give	we shall give
	you will give	you will give
	he (she, it) will give	they will give
Fut.	I will give *(P)*	we will give *(P)*
	you shall give *(C)*	you shall give *(C)*
	he (she, it) shall give *(C)*	they shall give *(C)*
Past	I gave	we gave
	you gave	you gave
	he (she, it) gave	they gave
Past	I was giving	we were giving
Prog.	you were giving	you were giving
	he (she, it) was giving	they were giving
Past	I did give	we did give
Int.	you did give	you did give
	he (she, it) did give	they did give
Pres.	I have given	we have given
Perf.	you have given	you have given
	he (she, it) has given	they have given
Past	I had given	we had given
Perf.	you had given	you had given
	he (she, it) had given	they had given
Fut.	I shall have given	we shall have given
Perf.	you will have given	you will have given
	he (she, it) will have given	they will have given

IMPERATIVE MOOD

give

SUBJUNCTIVE MOOD

Pres.	if I give	if we give
	if you give	if you give
	if he (she, it) give	if they give
Past	if I gave	if we gave
	if you gave	if you gave
	if he (she, it) gave	if they gave
Fut.	if I should give	if we should give
	if you should give	if you should give
	if he (she, it) should give	if they should give

Infinitive: to be given   *Present Participle:* being given
Perfect Infinitive: to have been given   *Past Participle:* been given

INDICATIVE MOOD

Pres.	I am given	we are given
	you are given	you are given
	he (she, it) is given	they are given
Pres.	I am being given	we are being given
Prog.	you are being given	you are being given
	he (she, it) is being given	they are being given
Pres.	I do get given	we do get given
Int.	you do get given	you do get given
	he (she, it) does get given	they do get given
Fut.	I shall be given	we shall be given
	you will be given	you will be given
	he (she, it) will be given	they will be given
Fut.	I will be given *(P)*	we will be given *(P)*
	you shall be given *(C)*	you shall be given *(C)*
	he (she, it) shall be given *(C)*	they shall be given *(C)*
Past	I was given	we were given
	you were given	you were given
	he (she, it) was given	they were given
Past	I was being given	we were being given
Prog.	you were being given	you were being given
	he (she, it) was being given	they were being given
Past	I did get given	we did get given
Int.	you did get given	you did get given
	he (she, it) did get given	they did get given
Pres.	I have been given	we have been given
Perf.	you have been given	you have been given
	he (she, it) has been given	they have been given
Past	I had been given	we had been given
Perf.	you had been given	you had been given
	he (she, it) had been given	they had been given
Fut.	I shall have been given	we shall have been given
Perf.	you will have been given	you will have been given
	he (she, it) will have been given	they will have been given

IMPERATIVE MOOD
be given

SUBJUNCTIVE MOOD

Pres.	if I be given	if we be given
	if you be given	if you be given
	if he (she, it) be given	if they be given
Past	if I were given	if we were given
	if you were given	if you were given
	if he (she, it) were given	if they were given
Fut.	if I should be given	if we should be given
	if you should be given	if you should be given
	if he (she, it) should be given	if they should be given

223

Infinitive: to go   *Present Participle:* going
Perfect Infinitive: to have gone   *Past Participle:* gone

INDICATIVE MOOD

Pres.	I go	we go
	you go	you go
	he (she, it) goes	they go
Pres. Prog.	I am going	we are going
	you are going	you are going
	he (she, it) is going	they are going
Pres. Int.	I do go	we do go
	you do go	you do go
	he (she, it) does go	they do go
Fut.	I shall go	we shall go
	you will go	you will go
	he (she, it) will go	they will go
Fut.	I will go *(P)*	we will go *(P)*
	you shall go *(C)*	you shall go *(C)*
	he (she, it) shall go *(C)*	they shall go *(C)*
Past	I went	we went
	you went	you went
	he (she, it) went	they went
Past Prog.	I was going	we were going
	you were going	you were going
	he (she, it) was going	they were going
Past Int.	I did go	we did go
	you did go	you did go
	he (she, it) did go	they did go
Pres. Perf.	I have gone	we have gone
	you have gone	you have gone
	he (she, it) has gone	they have gone
Past Perf.	I had gone	we had gone
	you had gone	you had gone
	he (she, it) had gone	they had gone
Fut. Perf.	I shall have gone	we shall have gone
	you will have gone	you will have gone
	he (she, it) will have gone	they will have gone

IMPERATIVE MOOD
go

SUBJUNCTIVE MOOD

Pres.	if I go	if we go
	if you go	if you go
	if he (she, it) go	if they go
Past	if I went	if we went
	if you went	if you went
	if he (she, it) went	if they went
Fut.	if I should go	if we should go
	if you should go	if you should go
	if he (she, it) should go	if they should go

To go is an intransitive verb.

It does not take an object.

It describes action, but the action is self-contained.

Like other intransitive verbs, it may be followed by adverbs, adverbial phrases and clauses describing the how, why, when, and where of the action:

HOW: They will go *slowly.* (adverb)

WHY: Mary went *to meet her mother.* (adverbial phrase)

WHEN: All the birds will have gone *when winter comes.* (adverbial clause)

WHERE: The evening sun goes *down.* (adverb)

to grow (active voice)   *Principal Parts:* grow, growing, grew, grown

Infinitive: to grow   *Present Participle:* growing
Perfect Infinitive: to have grown   *Past Participle:* grown

INDICATIVE MOOD

Pres.	I grow	we grow
	you grow	you grow
	he (she, it) grows	they grow
Pres.	I am growing	we are growing
Prog.	you are growing	you are growing
	he (she, it) is growing	they are growing
Pres.	I do grow	we do grow
Int.	you do grow	you do grow
	he (she, it) does grow	they do grow
Fut.	I shall grow	we shall grow
	you will grow	you will grow
	he (she, it) will grow	they will grow
Fut.	I will grow *(P)*	we will grow *(P)*
	you shall grow *(C)*	you shall grow *(C)*
	he (she, it) shall grow *(C)*	they shall grow *(C)*
Past	I grew	we grew
	you grew	you grew
	he (she, it) grew	they grew
Past	I was growing	we were growing
Prog.	you were growing	you were growing
	he (she, it) was growing	they were growing
Past	I did grow	we did grow
Int.	you did grow	you did grow
	he (she, it) did grow	they did grow
Pres.	I have grown	we have grown
Perf.	you have grown	you have grown
	he (she, it) has grown	they have grown
Past	I had grown	we had grown
Perf.	you had grown	you had grown
	he (she, it) had grown	they had grown
Fut.	I shall have grown	we shall have grown
Perf.	you will have grown	you will have grown
	he (she, it) will have grown	they will have grown

IMPERATIVE MOOD
grow

SUBJUNCTIVE MOOD

Pres.	if I grow	if we grow
	if you grow	if you grow
	if he (she, it) grow	if they grow
Past	if I grew	if we grew
	if you grew	if you grew
	if he (she, it) grew	if they grew
Fut.	if I should grow	if we should grow
	if you should grow	if you should grow
	if he (she, it) should grow	if they should grow

Infinitive: to be grown   *Present Participle:* being grown
Perfect Infinitive: to have been grown   *Past Participle:* been grown

INDICATIVE MOOD

Pres.   I am grown   we are grown
you are grown   you are grown
he (she, it) is grown   they are grown

Pres.   I am being grown   we are being grown
Prog.   you are being grown   you are being grown
he (she, it) is being grown   they are being grown

Pres.   I do get grown   we do get grown
Int.   you do get grown   you do get grown
he (she, it) does get grown   they do get grown

Fut.   I shall be grown   we shall be grown
you will be grown   you will be grown
he (she, it) will be grown   they will be grown

Fut.   I will be grown *(P)*   we will be grown *(P)*
you shall be grown *(C)*   you shall be grown *(C)*
he (she, it) shall be grown *(C)*   they shall be grown *(C)*

Past   I was grown   we were grown
you were grown   you were grown
he (she, it) was grown   they were grown

Past   I was being grown   we were being grown
Prog.   you were being grown   you were being grown
he (she, it) was being grown   they were being grown

Past   I did get grown   we did get grown
Int.   you did get grown   you did get grown
he (she, it) did get grown   they did get grown

Pres.   I have been grown   we have been grown
Perf.   you have been grown   you have been grown
he (she, it) has been grown   they have been grown

Past   I had been grown   we had been grown
Perf.   you had been grown   you had been grown
he (she, it) had been grown   they had been grown

Fut.   I shall have been grown   we shall have been grown
Perf.   you will have been grown   you will have been grown
he (she, it) will have been grown   they will have been grown

IMPERATIVE MOOD
be grown

SUBJUNCTIVE MOOD

Pres.   if I be grown   if we be grown
if you be grown   if you be grown
if he (she, it) be grown   if they be grown

Past   if I were grown   if we were grown
if you were grown   if you were grown
if he (she, it) were grown   if they were grown

Fut.   if I should be grown   if we should be grown
if you should be grown   if you should be grown
if he (she, it) should be grown   if they should be grown

to hang (active voice)

Principal Parts: hang, hanging, hung, hung

(to fasten to an elevated point)

Infinitive: to hang	*Perfect Infinitive:* to have hung
Present Participle: hanging	*Past Participle:* hung

INDICATIVE MOOD

Pres.	I hang	we hang
	you hang	you hang
	he (she, it) hangs	they hang
Pres.	I am hanging	we are hanging
Prog.	you are hanging	you are hanging
	he (she, it) is hanging	they are hanging
Pres.	I do hang	we do hang
Int.	you do hang	you do hang
	he (she, it) does hang	they do hang
Fut.	I shall hang	we shall hang
	you will hang	you will hang
	he (she, it) will hang	they will hang
Fut.	I will hang (P)	we will hang (P)
	you shall hang (C)	you shall hang (C)
	he (she, it) shall hang (C)	they shall hang (C)
Past	I hung	we hung
	you hung	you hung
	he (she, it) hung	they hung
Past	I was hanging	we were hanging
Prog.	you were hanging	you were hanging
	he (she, it) was hanging	they were hanging
Past	I did hang	we did hang
Int.	you did hang	you did hang
	he (she, it) did hang	they did hang
Pres.	I have hung	we have hung
Perf.	you have hung	you have hung
	he (she, it) has hung	they have hung
Past	I had hung	we had hung
Perf.	you had hung	you had hung
	he (she, it) had hung	they had hung
Fut.	I shall have hung	we shall have hung
Perf.	you will have hung	you will have hung
	he (she, it) will have hung	they will have hung

IMPERATIVE MOOD

hang

SUBJUNCTIVE MOOD

Pres.	if I hang	if we hang
	if you hang	if you hang
	if he (she, it) hang	if they hang
Past	if I hung	if we hung
	if you hung	if you hung
	if he (she, it) hung	if they hung
Fut.	if I should hang	if we should hang
	if you should hang	if you should hang
	if he (she, it) should hang	if they should hang

(passive voice)

Infinitive: to be hung *Perfect Infinitive:* to have been hung

Present Participle: to be hung *Past Participle:* been hung

INDICATIVE MOOD

Pres. I am hung	we are hung
you are hung	you are hung
he (she, it) is hung	they are hung
Prog. I am being hung	we are being hung
Pres. you are being hung	you are being hung
he (she, it) is being hung	they are being hung
Pres. I do get hung	we do get hung
Int. you do get hung	you do get hung
he (she, it) does get hung	they do get hung
Fut. I shall be hung	we shall be hung
you will be hung	you will be hung
he (she, it) will be hung	they will be hung
Fut. I will be hung (P)	we will be hung (P)
you shall be hung (C)	you shall be hung (C)
he (she, it) shall be hung (C)	they shall be hung (C)
Past I was hung	we were hung
you were hung	you were hung
he (she, it) was hung	they were hung
Prog. I was being hung	we were being hung
Past you were being hung	you were being hung
he (she, it) was being hung	they were being hung
Past I did get hung	we did get hung
Int. you did get hung	you did get hung
he (she, it) did get hung	they did get hung
Perf. I have been hung	we have been hung
Pres. you have been hung	you have been hung
he (she, it) has been hung	they have been hung
Perf. I had been hung	we had been hung
Past you had been hung	you had been hung
he (she, it) had been hung	they had been hung
Perf. I shall have been hung	we shall have been hung
Fut. you will have been hung	you will have been hung
he (she, it) will have been hung	they will have been hung

IMPERATIVE MOOD
be hung

SUBJUNCTIVE MOOD

Pres. if I be hung	if we be hung
if you be hung	if you be hung
if he (she, it) be hung	if they be hung
Past if I were hung	if we were hung
if you were hung	if you were hung
if he (she, it) were hung	if they were hung
Fut. if I should be hung	if we should be hung
if you should be hung	if you should be hung
if he (she, it) should be hung	if they should be hung

to hang (active voice)

Principal Parts: hang, hanging, hanged,
hanged (executed)

Infinitive: to hang	*Present Participle:* hanging	*Past Participle:* hanged
Perfect Infinitive: to have hanged		

INDICATIVE MOOD

Pres.	I hang	we hang
	you hang	you hang
	he (she, it) hangs	they hang
Prog. *Pres.*	I am hanging	we are hanging
	you are hanging	you are hanging
	he (she, it) is hanging	they are hanging
Pres. *Int.*	I do hang	we do hang
	you do hang	you do hang
	he (she, it) does hang	they do hang
Fut.	I shall hang	we shall hang
	you will hang	you will hang
	he (she, it) will hang	they will hang
Fut.	I will hang (P)	we will hang (P)
	you shall hang (C)	you shall hang (C)
	he (she, it) shall hang (C)	they shall hang (C)
Past	I hanged	we hanged
	you hanged	you hanged
	he (she, it) hanged	they hanged
Past *Prog.*	I was hanging	we were hanging
	you were hanging	you were hanging
	he (she, it) was hanging	they were hanging
Past *Int.*	I did hang	we did hang
	you did hang	you did hang
	he (she, it) did hang	they did hang
Pres. *Perf.*	I have hanged	we have hanged
	you have hanged	you have hanged
	he (she, it) has hanged	they have hanged
Past *Perf.*	I had hanged	we had hanged
	you had hanged	you had hanged
	he (she, it) had hanged	they had hanged
Fut. *Perf.*	I shall have hanged	we shall have hanged
	you will have hanged	you will have hanged
	he (she, it) will have hanged	they will have hanged

IMPERATIVE MOOD

hang

SUBJUNCTIVE MOOD

Pres.	if I hang	if we hang
	if you hang	if you hang
	if he (she, it) hang	if they hang
Past	if I hanged	if we hanged
	if you hanged	if you hanged
	if he (she, it) hanged	if they hanged
Fut.	if I should hang	if we should hang
	if you should hang	if you should hang
	if he (she, it) should hang	if they should hang

(passive voice)

Infinitive: to be hanged

Perfect Infinitive: to have been hanged

Present Participle: being hanged

Past Participle: been hanged

INDICATIVE MOOD

Pres. I am hanged	we are hanged
you are hanged	you are hanged
he (she, it) is hanged	they are hanged
Prog. I am being hanged	we are being hanged
you are being hanged	you are being hanged
he (she, it) is being hanged	they are being hanged
Pres. I do get hanged	we do get hanged
Int. you do get hanged	you do get hanged
he (she, it) does get hanged	they do get hanged
Fut. I shall be hanged	we shall be hanged
you will be hanged	you will be hanged
he (she, it) will be hanged	they will be hanged
Fut. I will be hanged (P)	we will be hanged (P)
you shall be hanged (C)	you shall be hanged (C)
he (she, it) shall be hanged (C)	they shall be hanged (C)
Past I was hanged	we were hanged
you were hanged	you were hanged
he (she, it) was hanged	they were hanged
Prog. I was being hanged	we were being hanged
Past you wore being hanged	you were being hanged
he (she, it) was being hanged	they were being hanged
Past I did get hanged	we did get hanged
Int. you did get hanged	you did get hanged
he (she, it) did get hanged	they did get hanged
Pres. I have been hanged	we have been hanged
Perf. you have been hanged	you have been hanged
he (she, it) has been hanged	they have been hanged
Past I had been hanged	we had been hanged
Perf. you had been hanged	you had been hanged
he (she, it) had been hanged	they had been hanged
Fut. I shall have been hanged	we shall have been hanged
Perf. you will have been hanged	you will have been hanged
he (she, it) will have been hanged	they will have been hanged

IMPERATIVE MOOD

be hanged

SUBJUNCTIVE MOOD

Pres. if I be hanged	if we be hanged
if you be hanged	if you be hanged
if he (she, it) be hanged	if they be hanged
Past if I were hanged	if we were hanged
if you were hanged	if you were hanged
if he (she, it) were hanged	if they were hanged
Fut. if I should be hanged	if we should be hanged
if you should be hanged	if you should be hanged
if he (she, it) should be hanged	if they should be hanged

Infinitive: to have   *Present Participle:* having
Perfect Infinitive: to have had   *Past Participle:* had

INDICATIVE MOOD

Pres.	I have	we have
	you have	you have
	he (she, it) has	they have
Pres.	I am having	we are having
Prog.	you are having	you are having
	he (she, it) is having	they are having
Pres.	I do have	we do have
Int.	you do have	you do have
	he (she, it) does have	they do have
Fut.	I shall have	we shall have
	you will have	you will have
	he (she, it) will have	they will have
Fut.	I will have *(P)*	we will have *(P)*
	you shall have *(C)*	you shall have *(C)*
	he (she, it) shall have *(C)*	they shall have *(C)*
Past	I had	we had
	you had	you had
	he (she, it) had	they had
Past	I was having	we were having
Prog.	you were having	you were having
	he (she, it) was having	they were having
Past	I did have	we did have
Int.	you did have	you did have
	he (she, it) did have	they did have
Pres.	I have had	we have had
Perf.	you have had	you have had
	he (she, it) has had	they have had
Past	I had had	we had had
Perf.	you had had	you had had
	he (she, it) had had	they had had
Fut.	I shall have had	you shall have had
Perf.	you will have had	you will have had
	he (she, it) will have had	they will have had

IMPERATIVE MOOD
have

SUBJUNCTIVE MOOD

Pres.	if I have	if we have
	if you have	if you have
	if he (she, it) have	if they have
Past	if I had	if we had
	if you had	if you had
	if he (she, it) had	if they had
Fut.	if I should have	if we should have
	if you should have	if you should have
	if he (she, it) should have	if they would have

Infinitive: to be had   *Present Participle:* being had
Perfect Infinitive: to have been had   *Past Participle:* been had

INDICATIVE MOOD

Pres.	I am had	we are had
	you are had	you are had
	he (she, it) is had	they are had
Pres.	I am being had	we are being had
Prog.	you are being had	you are being had
	he (she, it) is being had	they are being had
Pres.	I do get had	we do get had
Int.	you do get had	you do get had
	he (she, it) does get had	they do get had
Fut.	I shall be had	we shall be had
	you will be had	you will be had
	he (she, it) will be had	they will be had
Fut.	I will be had *(P)*	we will be had *(P)*
	you shall be had *(C)*	you shall be had *(C)*
	he (she, it) shall be had *(C)*	they shall be had *(C)*
Past	I was had	we were had
	you were had	you were had
	he (she, it) was had	they were had
Past	I was being had	we were being had
Prog.	you were being had	you were being had
	he (she, it) was being had	they were being had
Past	I did get had	we did get had
Int.	you did get had	you did get had
	he (she, it) did get had	they did get had
Pres.	I have been had	we have been had
Perf.	you have been had	you have been had
	he (she, it) has been had	they had been had
Past.	I had been had	we had been had
Perf.	you had been had	you had been had
	he (she, it) had been had	they had been had
Fut.	I shall have been had	we shall have been had
Perf.	you will have been had	you will have been had
	he (she, it) will have been had	they will have been had

IMPERATIVE MOOD
be had

SUBJUNCTIVE MOOD

Pres.	if I be had	if we be had
	if you be had	if you be had
	if he (she, it) be had	if they be had
Past	if I were had	if we were had
	if you were had	if you were had
	if he (she, it) were had	if they were had
Fut.	if I should be had	if we should be had
	if you should be had	if you should be had
	if he (she, it) should be had	if they should be had

to hear (active voice)

Principal Parts: hear, hearing, heard, heard

Infinitive: to hear
Perfect Infinitive: to have heard
Present Participle: hearing
Past Participle: heard

INDICATIVE MOOD

Pres.	I hear	we hear
	you hear	you hear
	he (she, it) hears	they hear
Pres. *Prog.*	I am hearing	we are hearing
	you are hearing	you are hearing
	he (she, it) is hearing	they are hearing
Pres. *Int.*	I do hear	we do hear
	you do hear	you do hear
	he (she, it) does hear	they do hear
Fut.	I shall hear	we shall hear
	you will hear	you will hear
	he (she, it) will hear	they will hear
Fut.	I will hear (P)	we will hear (P)
	you shall hear (C)	you shall hear (C)
	he (she, it) shall hear (C)	they shall hear (C)
Past	I heard	we heard
	you heard	you heard
	he (she, it) heard	they heard
Past *Prog.*	I was hearing	we were hearing
	you were hearing	you were hearing
	he (she, it) was hearing	they were hearing
Past *Int.*	I did hear	we did hear
	you did hear	you did hear
	he (she, it) did hear	they did hear
Pres. *Perf.*	I have heard	we have heard
	you have heard	you have heard
	he (she, it) has heard	they have heard
Past *Perf.*	I had heard	we had heard
	you had heard	you had heard
	he (she, it) had heard	they had heard
Fut. *Perf.*	I shall have heard	we shall have heard
	you will have heard	you will have heard
	he (she, it) will have heard	they will have heard

IMPERATIVE MOOD

hear

SUBJUNCTIVE MOOD

Pres.	if I hear	if we hear
	if you hear	if you hear
	if he (she, it) hear	if they hear
Past	if I heard	if we heard
	if you heard	if you heard
	if he (she, it) heard	if they heard
Fut.	if I should hear	if we should hear
	if you should hear	if you should hear
	if he (she, it) should hear	if they should hear

(passive voice)

Infinitive: to be heard   *Perfect Infinitive:* to have been heard

Present Participle: being heard   *Past Participle:* been heard

INDICATIVE MOOD

Pres.	I am heard	we are heard	
	you are heard		
	he (she, it) is heard	they are heard	
Prog. *Pres.*	I am being heard	we are being heard	
	you are being heard		
	he (she, it) is being heard	they are being heard	
Pres. *Int.*	I do get heard	we do get heard	
	you do get heard		
	he (she, it) does get heard	they do get heard	
Fut.	I shall be heard	we shall be heard	
	you will be heard		
	he (she, it) will be heard	they will be heard	
Fut.	I will be heard (P)	we will be heard (P)	
	you shall be heard (C)		
	he (she, it) shall be heard (C)	they shall be heard (C)	
Past	I was heard	we were heard	
	you were heard		
	he (she, it) was heard	they were heard	
Past *Prog.*	I was being heard	we were being heard	
	you were being heard		
	he (she, it) was being heard	they were being heard	
Past *Int.*	I did get heard	we did get heard	
	you did get heard		
	he (she, it) did get heard	they did get heard	
Pres. *Perf.*	I have been heard	we have been heard	
	you have been heard		
	he (she, it) has been heard	they have been heard	
Past *Perf.*	I had been heard	we had been heard	
	you had been heard		
	he (she, it) had been heard	they had been heard	
Fut. *Perf.*	I shall have been heard	we shall have been heard	
	you will have been heard		
	he (she, it) will have been heard	they will have been heard	

IMPERATIVE MOOD

be heard

SUBJUNCTIVE MOOD

Pres.	if I be heard	if we be heard	
	if you be heard	if you be heard	
	if he (she, it) be heard	if they be heard	
Past	if I were heard	if we were heard	
	if you were heard	if you were heard	
	if he (she, it) were heard	if they were heard	
Fut.	if I should be heard	if we should be heard	
	if you should be heard	if you should be heard	
	if he (she, it) should be heard	if they should be heard	

to hit (active voice)

Principal Parts: hit, hitting, hit, hit		
Infinitive: to hit	Present Participle: hitting	
Perfect Infinitive: to have hit	Past Participle: hit	

INDICATIVE MOOD

Pres.	I hit	we hit
	you hit	you hit
	he (she, it) hits	they hit
Pres. Prog.	I am hitting	we are hitting
	you are hitting	you are hitting
	he (she, it) is hitting	they are hitting
Pres. Int.	I do hit	we do hit
	you do hit	you do hit
	he (she, it) does hit	they do hit
Fut.	I shall hit	we shall hit
	you will hit	you will hit
	he (she, it) will hit	they will hit
Fut.	I will hit (P)	we will hit (P)
	you shall hit (C)	you shall hit (C)
	he (she, it) shall hit (C)	they shall hit (C)
Past	I hit	we hit
	you hit	you hit
	he (she, it) hit	they hit
Past Prog.	I was hitting	we were hitting
	you were hitting	you were hitting
	he (she, it) was hitting	they were hitting
Past Int.	I did hit	we did hit
	you did hit	you did hit
	he (she, it) did hit	they did hit
Pres. Perf.	I have hit	we have hit
	you have hit	you have hit
	he (she, it) has hit	they have hit
Past Perf.	I had hit	we had hit
	you had hit	you had hit
	he (she, it) had hit	they had hit
Fut. Perf.	I shall have hit	we shall have hit
	you will have hit	you will have hit
	he (she, it) will have hit	they will have hit

IMPERATIVE MOOD

hit

SUBJUNCTIVE MOOD

Pres.	if I hit	if we hit
	if you hit	if you hit
	if he (she, it) hit	if they hit
Past	if I hit	if we hit
	if you hit	if you hit
	if he (she, it) hit	if they hit
Fut.	if I should hit	if we should hit
	if you should hit	if you should hit
	if he (she, it) should hit	if they should hit

Infinitive: to be hit   *Present Participle:* being hit
Perfect Infinitive: to have been hit   *Past Participle:* been hit

INDICATIVE MOOD

Pres.	I am hit	we are hit
	you are hit	you are hit
	he (she, it) is hit	they are hit

Pres.	I am being hit	we are being hit
Prog.	you are being hit	you are being hit
	he (she, it) is being hit	they are being hit

Pres.	I do get hit	we do get hit
Int.	you do get hit	you do get hit
	he (she, it) does get hit	they do get hit

Fut.	I shall be hit	we shall be hit
	you will be hit	you will be hit
	he (she, it) will be hit	they will be hit

Fut.	I will be hit *(P)*	we will be hit *(P)*
	you shall be hit *(C)*	you shall be hit *(C)*
	he (she, it) shall be hit *(C)*	they shall be hit *(C)*

Past	I was hit	we were hit
	you were hit	you were hit
	he (she, it) was hit	they were hit

Past	I was being hit	we were being hit
Prog.	you were being hit	you were being hit
	he (she, it) was being hit	they were being hit

Past	I did get hit	we did get hit
Int.	you did get hit	you did get hit
	he (she, it) did get hit	they did get hit

Pres.	I have been hit	we have been hit
Perf.	you have been hit	you have been hit
	he (she, it) have been hit	they have been hit

Past	I had been hit	we had been hit
Perf.	you had been hit	you had been hit
	he (she, it) had been hit	they had been hit

Fut.	I shall have been hit	we shall have been hit
Perf.	you will have been hit	you will have been hit
	he (she, it) will have been hit	they will have been hit

IMPERATIVE MOOD
be hit

SUBJUNCTIVE MOOD

Pres.	if I be hit	if we be hit
	if you be hit	if you be hit
	if he (she, it) be hit	if they be hit

Past	if I were hit	if we were hit
	if you were hit	if you were hit
	if he (she, it) were hit	if they were hit

Fut.	if I should be hit	if we should be hit
	if you should be hit	if you should be hit
	if he (she, it) should be hit	if they should be hit

to hold (active voice)

Principal Parts: hold, holding, held, held

Infinitive: to hold	*Present Participle:* holding
Perfect Infinitive: to have held	*Past Participle:* held

INDICATIVE MOOD

Pres.	I hold	we hold
	you hold	you hold
	he (she, it) holds	they hold
Prog. Pres.	I am holding	we are holding
	you are holding	you are holding
	he (she, it) is holding	they are holding
Int. Pres.	I do hold	we do hold
	you do hold	you do hold
	he (she, it) does hold	they do hold
Fut.	I shall hold	we shall hold
	you will hold	you will hold
	he (she, it) will hold	they will hold
Fut.	I will hold (P)	we will hold (P)
	you shall hold (C)	you shall hold (C)
	he (she, it) shall hold (C)	they shall hold (C)
Past	I held	we held
	you held	you held
	he (she, it) held	they held
Prog. Past	I was holding	we were holding
	you were holding	you were holding
	he (she, it) was holding	they were holding
Int. Past	I did hold	we did hold
	you did hold	you did hold
	he (she, it) did hold	they did hold
Perf. Pres.	I have held	we have held
	you have held	you have held
	he (she, it) has held	they have held
Past Perf.	I had held	we had held
	you had held	you had held
	he (she, it) had held	they had held
Fut. Perf.	I shall have held	we shall have held
	you will have held	you will have held
	he (she, it) will have held	they will have held

IMPERATIVE MOOD

hold

SUBJUNCTIVE MOOD

Pres.	if I hold	if we hold
	if you hold	if you hold
	if he (she, it) hold	if they hold
Past	if I held	if we held
	if you held	if you held
	if he (she, it) held	if they held
Fut.	if I should hold	if we should hold
	if you should hold	if you should hold
	if he (she, it) should hold	if they should hold

(passive voice)

Infinitive: to be held	*Perfect Infinitive:* to have been held
Present Participle: being held	*Past Participle:* been held

INDICATIVE MOOD

Pres.	I am held	we are held
	you are held	you are held
	he (she, it) is held	they are held
Pres. *Prog.*	I am being held	we are being held
	you are being held	you are being held
	he (she, it) is being held	they are being held
Pres. *Int.*	I do get held	we do get held
	you do get held	you do get held
	he (she, it) does get held	they do get held
Fut.	I shall be held	we shall be held
	you will be held	you will be held
	he (she, it) will be held	
Fut.	I will be held (P)	we will be held (C)
	you shall be held (C)	you shall be held (P)
	he (she, it) shall be held (C)	they shall be held (C)
Past	I was held	we were held
	you were held	you were held
	he (she, it) was held	they were held
Past *Prog.*	I was being held	we were being held
	you were being held	you were being held
	he (she, it) was being held	they were being held
Past *Int.*	I did get held	we did get held
	you did get held	you did get held
	he (she, it) did get held	they did get held
Pres. *Perf.*	I have been held	we have been held
	you have been held	you have been held
	he (she, it) has been held	they have been held
Past *Perf.*	I had been held	we had been held
	you had been held	you had been held
	he (she, it) had been held	they had been held
Fut. *Perf.*	I shall have been held	we shall have been held
	you will have been held	you will have been held
	he (she, it) will have been held	they will have been held

IMPERATIVE MOOD
be held

SUBJUNCTIVE MOOD

Pres.	if I be held	if we be held
	if you be held	if you be held
	if he (she, it) be held	if they be held
Past	if I were held	if we were held
	if you were held	if you were held
	if he (she, it) were held	if they were held
Fut.	if I should be held	if we should be held
	if you should be held	if you should be held
	if he (she, it) should be held	if they should be held

to hurt (active voice)

Principal Parts: hurt, hurting, hurt, hurt

Infinitive: to hurt   *Present Participle:* hurting   *Past Participle:* hurt

Perfect Infinitive: to have hurt

INDICATIVE MOOD

Pres.	I hurt	we hurt	
	you hurt		
	he (she, it) hurts	you hurt	
Prog.	I am hurting	we are hurting	
Pres.	you are hurting		
	he (she, it) is hurting	they are hurting	
Pres.	I do hurt	we do hurt	
Int.	you do hurt		
	he (she, it) does hurt	they do hurt	
Fut.	I shall hurt	we shall hurt	
	you will hurt		
	he (she, it) will hurt	they will hurt	
Fut.	I will hurt (P)	we will hurt (P)	
	you shall hurt (C)		
	he (she, it) shall hurt (C)	they shall hurt (C)	
Past	I hurt	we hurt	
	you hurt		
	he (she, it) hurt	they hurt	
Past	I was hurting	we were hurting	
Prog.	you were hurting		
	he (she, it) was hurting	they were hurting	
Past	I did hurt	we did hurt	
Int.	you did hurt		
	he (she, it) did hurt	they did hurt	
Pres.	I have hurt	we have hurt	
Perf.	you have hurt		
	he (she, it) has hurt	they have hurt	
Past.	I had hurt	we had hurt	
Perf.	you had hurt		
	he (she, it) has hurt	they had hurt	
Fut.	I shall have hurt	we shall have hurt	
Perf.	you will have hurt		
	he (she, it) will have hurt	they will have hurt	

IMPERATIVE MOOD

hurt

SUBJUNCTIVE MOOD

Pres.	if I hurt	if we hurt	
	if you hurt		
	if he (she, it) hurt	if they hurt	
Past	if I hurt	if we hurt	
	if you hurt		
	if he (she, it) hurt	if they hurt	
Fut.	if I should hurt	if we should hurt	
	if you should hurt		
	if he (she, it) should hurt	if they should hurt	

(passive voice)

Infinitive: to be hurt *Perfect Infinitive:* to have been hurt
Present Participle: being hurt *Past Participle:* been hurt

INDICATIVE MOOD

Pres.	I am hurt	we are hurt
	you are hurt	you are hurt
	he (she, it) is hurt	they are hurt
Prog. Pres.	I am being hurt	we are being hurt
	you are being hurt	you are being hurt
	he (she, it) is being hurt	they are being hurt
Pres. Int.	I do get hurt	we do get hurt
	you do get hurt	you do get hurt
	he (she, it) does get hurt	they do get hurt
Fut.	I shall be hurt	we shall be hurt
	you will be hurt	you will be hurt
	he (she, it) will be hurt	they will be hurt
Fut.	I will be hurt (P)	we will be hurt (P)
	you shall be hurt (C)	you shall be hurt (C)
	he (she, it) shall be hurt (C)	they shall be hurt (C)
Past	I was hurt	we were hurt
	you were hurt	you were hurt
	he (she, it) was hurt	they were hurt
Prog. Past	I was being hurt	we were being hurt
	you were being hurt	you were being hurt
	he (she, it) was being hurt	they were being hurt
Past Int.	I did get hurt	we did get hurt
	you did get hurt	you did get hurt
	he (she, it) did get hurt	they did get hurt
Perf. Pres.	I have been hurt	we have been hurt
	you have been hurt	you have been hurt
	he (she, it) has been hurt	they have been hurt
Perf. Past	I had been hurt	we had been hurt
	you had been hurt	you had been hurt
	he (she, it) had been hurt	they had been hurt
Perf. Fut.	I shall have been hurt	we shall have been hurt
	you will have been hurt	you will have been hurt
	he (she, it) will have been hurt	they will have been hurt

IMPERATIVE MOOD
be hurt

SUBJUNCTIVE MOOD

Pres.	if I be hurt	if we be hurt
	if you be hurt	if you be hurt
	if he (she, it) be hurt	if they be hurt
Past	if I were hurt	if we were hurt
	if you were hurt	if you were hurt
	if he (she, it) were hurt	if they were hurt
Fut.	if I should be hurt	if we should be hurt
	if you should be hurt	if you should be hurt
	if he (she, it) should be hurt	if they should be hurt

to kneel

Principal Parts: kneel, kneeling, knelt (kneeled), knelt

Infinitive: to kneel

Perfect Infinitive: to have knelt

Present Participle: kneeling

Past Participle: knelt

INDICATIVE MOOD

Pres. I kneel	we kneel
he (she, it) kneels	you kneel
	they kneel
Pres. I am kneeling	we are kneeling
Prog. you are kneeling	
he (she, it) is kneeling	they are kneeling
Pres. I do kneel	we do kneel
Int. you do kneel	
he (she, it) does kneel	they do kneel
Fut. I shall kneel	we shall kneel
you will kneel	
he (she, it) will kneel	they will kneel
Fut. I will kneel (P)	we will kneel (P)
you shall kneel (C)	
he (she, it) shall kneel (C)	they shall kneel (C)
Past I knelt, kneeled	we knelt, kneeled
you knelt, kneeled	
he (she, it) knelt, kneeled	they knelt, kneeled
Past I was kneeling	we were kneeling
Prog. you were kneeling	
he (she, it) was kneeling	they were kneeling
Past I did kneel	we did kneel
Int. you did kneel	
he (she, it) did kneel	they did kneel
Pres. I have knelt	we have knelt
Perf. you have knelt	
he (she, it) has knelt	they have knelt
Past I had knelt	we had knelt
Perf. you had knelt	
he (she, it) had knelt	they had knelt
Fut. I shall have knelt	we shall have knelt
Perf. you will have knelt	
he (she, it) will have knelt	they will have knelt

IMPERATIVE MOOD

kneel

SUBJUNCTIVE MOOD

Pres. if I kneel	if we kneel
if you kneel	
if he (she, it) kneel	if they kneel
Past if I knelt	if we knelt
if you knelt	
if he (she, it) knelt	if they knelt
Fut. if I should kneel	if we should kneel
if you should kneel	
if he (she, it) should kneel	if they should kneel

To kneel is an intransitive verb.

It does not take an object.

It describes action, but the action is self-contained.

Like other intransitive verbs, it may be followed by adverbs, adverbial phrases and clauses describing the how, why, when, and where of the action:

HOW: The congregation knelt *slowly*. (adverb)

WHY: The people will kneel *to pray*. (adverbial phrase)

WHEN: I *always* kneel *when I say my prayers*. (adverb and adverbial clause)

WHERE: The page knelt *in front of the king*. (adverbial phrase)

to know (active voice)

Principal Parts: know, knowing, knew, known

Infinitive: to know   *Present Participle:* knowing
Perfect Infinitive: to have known   *Past Participle:* known

INDICATIVE MOOD

Pres.	I know	we know
	you know	you know
	he (she, it) knows	they know
Pres. Int.	I do know	we do know
	you do know	you do know
	he (she, it) does know	they do know
Fut.	I shall know	we shall know
	you will know	you will know
	he (she, it) will know	they will know
Fut.	I will know *(P)*	we will know *(P)*
	you shall know *(C)*	you shall know *(C)*
	he (she, it) shall know *(C)*	they shall know *(C)*
Past	I knew	we knew
	you knew	you knew
	he (she, it) knew	they knew
Past Int.	I did know	we did know
	you did know	you did know
	he (she, it) did know	they did know
Pres. Perf.	I have known	we have known
	you have known	you have known
	he (she, it) has known	they have known
Past Perf.	I had known	we had known
	you had known	you had known
	he (she, it) had known	they had known
Fut. Perf.	I shall have known	we shall have known
	you will have known	you will have known
	he (she, it) will have known	they will have known

IMPERATIVE MOOD
know

SUBJUNCTIVE MOOD

Pres.	if I know	if we know
	if you know	if you know
	if he (she, it) know	if they know
Past	if I knew	if we knew
	if you knew	if you knew
	if he (she, it) knew	if they knew
Fut.	if I should know	if we should know
	if you should know	if you should know
	if he (she, it) should know	if they should know

Infinitive: to be known   *Present Participle:* being known
Perfect Infinitive: to have been known   *Past Participle:* been known

INDICATIVE MOOD

Pres.	I am known	we are known
	you are known	you are known
	he (she, it) is known	they are known
Pres.	I am being known	we are being known
	you are being known	you are being known
	he (she, it) is being known	they are being known
Pres.	I do get known	we do get known
Int.	you do get known	you do get known
	he (she, it) does get known	they do get known
Fut.	I shall be known	we shall be known
	you will be known	you will be known
	he (she, it) will be known	they will be known
Fut.	I will be known *(P)*	we will be known *(P)*
	you shall be known *(C)*	you shall be known *(C)*
	he (she, it) shall be known *(C)*	they shall be known *(C)*
Past	I was known	we were known
	you were known	you were known
	he (she, it) was known	they were known
Past	I was being known	we were being known
Prog.	you were being known	you were being known
	he (she, it) was being known	they were being known
Past	I did get known	we did get known
Int.	you did get known	you did get known
	he (she, it) did get known	they did get known
Pres.	I have been known	we have been known
Perf.	you have been known	you have been known
	he (she, it) has been known	they have been known
Past	I had been known	we had been known
Perf.	you had been known	you had been known
	he (she, it) had been known	they had been known
Fut.	I shall have been known	we shall have been known
Perf.	you will have been known	you will have been known
	he (she, it) will have been known	they will have been known

IMPERATIVE MOOD
be known

SUBJUNCTIVE MOOD

Pres.	if I be known	if we be known
	if you be known	if you be known
	if he (she, it) be known	if they be known
Past	if I were known	if we were known
	if you were known	if you were known
	if he (she, it) were known	if they were known
Fut.	if I should be known	if we should be known
	if you should be known	if you should be known
	if he (she, it) should be known	if they should be known

to lay (active voice)

Principal Parts: lay, laying, laid, laid

Infinitive: to lay	*Perfect Infinitive:* to have laid
Present Participle: laying	*Past Participle:* laid

INDICATIVE MOOD

Pres.
I lay — we lay
you lay — you lay
he (she, it) lays — they lay

Pres. Prog.
I am laying — we are laying
you are laying — you are laying
he (she, it) is laying — they are laying

Int.
I do lay — we do lay
you do lay — you do lay
he (she, it) does lay — they do lay

Fut.
I shall lay — we shall lay
you will lay — you will lay
he (she, it) will lay — they will lay

Fut.
I will lay (P) — we will lay (P)
you shall lay (C) — you shall lay (C)
he (she, it) shall lay (C) — they shall lay (C)

Past
I laid — we laid
you laid — you laid
he (she, it) laid — they laid

Past Prog.
I was laying — we were laying
you were laying — you were laying
he (she, it) was laying — they were laying

Past Int.
I did lay — we did lay
you did lay — you did lay
he (she, it) did lay — they did lay

Pres. Perf.
I have laid — we have laid
you have laid — you have laid
he (she, it) has laid — they have laid

Past Perf.
I had laid — we had laid
you had laid — you had laid
he (she, it) had laid — they had laid

Fut. Perf.
I shall have laid — we shall have laid
you will have laid — you will have laid
he (she, it) will have laid — they will have laid

IMPERATIVE MOOD

lay

SUBJUNCTIVE MOOD

Pres.
if I lay — if we lay
if you lay — if you lay
if he (she, it) lay — if they lay

Past
if I laid — if we laid
if you laid — if you laid
if he (she, it) laid — if they laid

Fut.
if I should lay — if we should lay
if you should lay — if you should lay
if he (she, it) should lay — if they should lay

Infinitive: to be laid

Past Participle: been laid

Perfect Infinitive: to have been laid

Present Participle: being laid

INDICATIVE MOOD

Pres. I am laid	we are laid
you are laid	you are laid
he (she, it) is laid	they are laid

Pres. I am being laid	we are being laid
Prog. you are being laid	you are being laid
he (she, it) is being laid	they are being laid

Pres. I do get laid	we do get laid
Int. you do get laid	you do get laid
he (she, it) does get laid	they do get laid

Fut. I shall be laid	we shall be laid
you will be laid	you will be laid
he (she, it) will be laid	they will be laid

Fut. I will be laid *(P)*	we will be laid *(P)*
you shall be laid *(C)*	you shall be laid *(C)*
he (she, it) shall be laid *(C)*	they shall be laid *(C)*

Past I was laid	we were laid
you were laid	you were laid
he (she, it) was laid	they were laid

Past I was being laid	we were being laid
Prog. you were being laid	you were being laid
he (she, it) was being laid	they were being laid

Past I did get laid	we did get laid
Int. you did get laid	you did get laid
he (she, it) did get laid	they did get laid

Pres. I have been laid	we have been laid
Perf. you have been laid	you have been laid
he (she, it) has been laid	they have been laid

Past I had been laid	we had been laid
Perf. you had been laid	you had been laid
he (she, it) had been laid	they had been laid

Fut. I shall have been laid	we shall have been laid
Perf. you will have been laid	you will have been laid
he (she, it) will have been laid	they will have been laid

IMPERATIVE MOOD

be laid

SUBJUNCTIVE MOOD

Pres. if I be laid	if we be laid
if you be laid	if you be laid
if he (she, it) be laid	if they be laid

Past if I were laid	if we were laid
if you were laid	if you were laid
if he (she, it) were laid	if they were laid

Fut. if I should be laid	if we should be laid
if you should be laid	if you should be laid
if he (she, it) should be laid	if they should be laid

Infinitive: to lead   *Present Participle:* leading
Perfect Infinitive: to have led   *Past Participle:* led

INDICATIVE MOOD

Pres.	I lead	we lead
	you lead	you lead
	he (she, it) leads	they lead
Pres. Prog.	I am leading	we are leading
	you are leading	you are leading
	he (she, it) is leading	they are leading
Pres. Int.	I do lead	we do lead
	you do lead	you do lead
	he (she, it) does lead	they do lead
Fut.	I shall lead	we shall lead
	you will lead	you will lead
	he (she, it) will lead	they will lead
Fut.	I will lead *(P)*	we will lead *(P)*
	you shall lead *(C)*	you shall lead *(C)*
	he (she, it) shall lead *(C)*	they shall lead *(C)*
Past	I led	we led
	you led	you led
	he (she, it) led	they led
Past Prog.	I was leading	we were leading
	you were leading	you were leading
	he (she, it) was leading	they were leading
Past Int.	I did lead	we did lead
	you did lead	you did lead
	he (she, it) did lead	they did lead
Pres. Perf.	I have led	we have led
	you have led	you have led
	he (she, it) has led	they have led
Past Perf.	I had led	we had led
	you had led	you had led
	he (she, it) had led	they had led
Fut. Perf.	I shall have led	we shall have led
	you will have led	you will have led
	he (she, it) will have led	they will have led

IMPERATIVE MOOD
lead

SUBJUNCTIVE MOOD

Pres.	if I lead	if we lead
	if you lead	if you lead
	if he (she, it) lead	if they lead
Past	if I led	if we led
	if you led	if you led
	if he (she, it) led	if they led
Fut.	if I should lead	if we should lead
	if you should lead	if you should lead
	if he (she, it) should lead	if they should lead

Infinitive: to be led   *Present Participle:* being led
Perfect Infinitive: to have been led   *Past Participle:* been led

INDICATIVE MOOD

Pres.	I am led	we are led
	you are led	you are led
	he (she, it) is led	they are led
Pres. Prog.	I am being led	we are being led
	you are being led	you are being led
	he (she, it) is being led	they are being led
Pres. Int.	I do get led	we do get led
	you do get led	you do get led
	he (she, it) does get led	they do get led
Fut.	I shall be led	we shall be led
	you will be led	you will be led
	he (she, it) will be led	they will be led
Fut.	I will be led *(P)*	we will be led *(P)*
	you shall be led *(C)*	you shall be led *(C)*
	he (she, it) shall be led *(C)*	they shall be led *(C)*
Past	I was led	we were led
	you were led	you were led
	he (she, it) was led	they were led
Past Prog.	I was being led	we were being led
	you were being led	you were being led
	he (she, it) was being led	they were being led
Past Int.	I did get led	we did get led
	you did get led	you did get led
	he (she, it) did get led	they did get led
Pres. Perf.	I have been led	we have been led
	you have been led	you have been led
	he (she, it) has been led	they have been led
Past Perf.	I had been led	we had been led
	you had been led	you had been led
	he (she, it) had been led	they had been led
Fut. Perf.	I shall have been led	we shall have been led
	you will have been led	you will have been led
	he (she, it) will have been led	they will have been led

IMPERATIVE MOOD
be led

SUBJUNCTIVE MOOD

Pres.	if I be led	if we be led
	if you be led	if you be led
	if he (she, it) be led	if they be led
Past	if I were led	if we were led
	if you were led	if you were led
	if he (she, it) were led	if they were led
Fut.	if I should be led	if we should be led
	if you should be led	if you should be led
	if he (she, it) should be led	if they should be led

Infinitive: to leap   *Present Participle:* leaping
Perfect Infinitive: to have leaped (leapt)   *Past Participle:* leaped (leapt)

INDICATIVE MOOD

Pres.	I leap	we leap
	you leap	you leap
	he (she, it) leaps	they leap
Pres. *Prog.*	I am leaping	we are leaping
	you are leaping	you are leaping
	he (she, it) is leaping	they are leaping
Pres. *Int.*	I do leap	we do leap
	you do leap	you do leap
	he (she, it) do leap	they do leap
Fut.	I shall leap	we shall leap
	you will leap	you will leap
	he (she, it) will leap	they will leap
Fut.	I will leap *(P)*	we will leap *(P)*
	you shall leap *(C)*	you shall leap *(C)*
	he (she, it) shall leap *(C)*	they shall leap *(C)*
Past	I leaped, leapt	we leaped, leapt
	you leaped, leapt	you leaped, leapt
	he (she, it) leaped, leapt	they leaped, leapt
Past *Prog.*	I was leaping	we were leaping
	you were leaping	you were leaping
	he (she, it) was leaping	they were leaping
Past *Int.*	I did leap	we did leap
	you did leap	you did leap
	he (she, it) did leap	they did leap
Pres. *Perf.*	I have leaped, leapt	we have leaped, leapt
	you have leaped, leapt	you have leaped, leapt
	he (she, it) has leaped, leapt	they have leaped, leapt
Past *Perf.*	I had leaped, leapt	we had leaped, leapt
	you had leaped, leapt	you had leaped, leapt
	he (she, it) had leaped, leapt	they had leaped, leapt
Fut. *Perf.*	I shall have leaped, leapt	we shall have leaped, leapt
	you will have leaped, leapt	you will have leaped, leapt
	he (she, it) will have leaped, leapt	they will have leaped, leapt

IMPERATIVE MOOD
leap

SUBJUNCTIVE MOOD

Pres.	if I leap	if we leap
	if you leap	if you leap
	if he (she, it) leap	if they leap
Past	if I leaped, leapt	if we leaped, leapt
	if you leaped, leapt	if you leaped, leapt
	if he (she, it) leaped, leapt	if they leaped, leapt
Fut.	if I should leap	if we should leap
	if you should leap	if you should leap
	if he (she, it) should leap	if they should leap

To leap is an intransitive verb.

It does not take an object.
It describes action, but the action is self-contained.
Like other intransitive verbs, it may be followed by adverbs, adverbial phrases and clauses describing the how, when, and where of the action:

HOW: The dancers leapt *vigorously*. (adverb)
WHY: They leapt *for joy*. (adverbial phrase)
WHEN: The fish will be leaping *as soon as the ice leaves the lake*. (adverbial clause)
WHERE: I shall leap *into my bed*. (adverbial phrase)

Infinitive: to leave   *Present Participle:* leaving
Perfect Infinitive: to have left   *Past Participle:* left

INDICATIVE MOOD

Pres.	I leave	we leave
	you leave	you leave
	he (she, it) leaves	they leave
Pres.	I am leaving	we are leaving
Prog.	you are leaving	you are leaving
	he (she, it) is leaving	they are leaving
Pres.	I do leave	we do leave
Int.	you do leave	you do leave
	he (she, it) does leave	they do leave
Fut.	I shall leave	we shall leave
	you will leave	you will leave
	he (she, it) will leave	they will leave
Fut.	I will leave *(P)*	we will leave *(P)*
	you shall leave *(C)*	you shall leave *(C)*
	he (she, it) shall leave *(C)*	they shall leave *(C)*
Past	I left	we left
	you left	you left
	he (she, it) left	they left
Past	I was leaving	we were leaving
Prog.	you were leaving	you were leaving
	he (she, it) was leaving	they were leaving
Past	I did leave	we did leave
Int.	you did leave	you did leave
	he (she, it) did leave	they did leave
Pres.	I have left	we have left
Perf.	you have left	you have left
	he (she, it) has left	they have left
Past	I had left	we had left
Perf.	you had left	you had left
	he (she, it) had left	they had left
Fut.	I shall have left	we shall have left
	you will have left	you will have left
	he (she, it) will have left	they will have left

IMPERATIVE MOOD
leave

SUBJUNCTIVE MOOD

Pres.	if I leave	if we leave
	if you leave	if you leave
	if he (she, it) leave	if they leave
Past	if I left	if we left
	if you left	if you left
	if he (she, it) left	if they left
Fut.	if I should leave	if we should leave
	if you should leave	if you should leave
	if he (she, it) should leave	if they should leave

Infinitive: to be left · *Present Participle:* being left
Perfect Infinitive: to have been left · · · · · · · · · · · · *Past Participle:* been left

INDICATIVE MOOD

Pres.	I am left	we are left
	you are left	you are left
	he (she, it) is left	they are left

Pres.	I am being left	we are being left
Prog.	you are being left	you are being left
	he (she, it) is being left	they are being left

Pres.	I do get left	we do get left
Int.	you do get left	you do get left
	he (she, it) does get left	they do get left

Fut.	I shall be left	we shall be left
	you will be left	you will be left
	he (she, it) will be left	they will be left

Fut.	I will be left *(P)*	we will be left *(P)*
	you shall be left *(C)*	you shall be left *(C)*
	he (she, it) shall be left *(C)*	they shall be left *(C)*

Past	I was left	we were left
	you were left	you were left
	he (she, it) was left	they were left

Past	I was being left	we were being left
Prog.	you were being left	you were being left
	he (she, it) was being left	they were being left

Past	I did get left	we did get left
Int.	you did get left	you did get left
	he (she, it) did get left	they did get left

Pres.	I have been left	we have been left
Perf.	you have been left	you have been left
	he (she, it) has been left	they have been left

Past	I had been left	we had been left
Perf.	you had been left	you had been left
	he (she, it) had been left	they had been left

Fut.	I shall have been left	we shall have been left
Perf.	you will have been left	you will have been left
	he (she, it) will have been left	they will have been left

IMPERATIVE MOOD
be left

SUBJUNCTIVE MOOD

Pres.	if I be left	if we be left
	if you be left	if you be left
	if he (she, it) be left	if they be left

Past	if I were left	if we were left
	if you were left	if you were left
	if he (she, it) were left	if they were left

Fut.	if I should be left	if we should be left
	if you should be left	if you should be left
	if he (she, it) should be left	if they should be left

Infinitive: to lend   *Present Participle:* lending
Perfect Infinitive: to have lent   *Past Participle:* been lent

INDICATIVE MOOD

Pres.	I lend	we lend
	you lend	you lend
	he (she, it) lends	they lend

Pres. Prog.	I am lending	we are lending
	you are lending	you are lending
	he (she, it) is lending	they are lending

Pres. Int.	I do lend	we do lend
	you do lend	you do lend
	he (she, it) does lend	they do lend

Fut.	I shall lend	we shall lend
	you will lend	you will lend
	he (she, it) will lend	they will lend

Fut.	I will lend *(P)*	we will lend *(P)*
	you shall lend *(C)*	you shall lend *(C)*
	he (she, it) shall lend *(C)*	they shall lend *(C)*

Past	I lent	we lent
	you lent	you lent
	he (she, it) lent	they lent

Past Prog.	I was lending	we were lending
	you were lending	you were lending
	he (she, it) was lending	they were lending

Past Int.	I did lend	we did lend
	you did lend	you did lend
	he (she, it) did lend	they did lend

Pres. Perf.	I have lent	we have lent
	you have lent	you have lent
	he (she, it) has lent	they have lent

Past Perf.	I had lent	we had lent
	you had lent	you had lent
	he (she, it) had lent	they had lent

Fut. Perf.	I shall have lent	we shall have lent
	you will have lent	you will have lent
	he (she, it) will have lent	they will have lent

IMPERATIVE MOOD
lend

SUBJUNCTIVE MOOD

Pres.	if I lend	if we lend
	if you lend	if you lend
	if he (she, it) lend	if they lend

Past	if I lent	if we lent
	if you lent	if you lent
	if he (she, it) lent	if they lent

Fut.	if I should lend	if we should lend
	if you should lend	if you should lend
	if he (she, it) should lend	if they should lend

Infinitive: to be lent   *Present Participle:* being lent
Perfect Infinitive: to have been lent   *Past Participle:* been lent

INDICATIVE MOOD

Pres.	I am lent	we are lent
	you are lent	you are lent
	he (she, it) is lent	they are lent
Pres.	I am being lent	we are being lent
Prog.	you are being lent	you are being lent
	he (she, it) is being lent	they are being lent
Pres.	I do get lent	we do get lent
Int.	you do get lent	you do get lent
	he (she, it) does get lent	they do get lent
Fut.	I shall be lent	we shall be lent
	you will be lent	you will be lent
	he (she, it) will be lent	they will be lent
Fut.	I will be lent *(P)*	we will be lent *(P)*
	you shall be lent *(C)*	you shall be lent *(C)*
	he (she, it) shall be lent *(C)*	they shall be lent *(C)*
Past	I was lent	we were lent
	you were lent	you were lent
	he (she, it) was lent	they were lent
Past	I was being lent	we were being lent
Prog.	you were being lent	you were being lent
	he (she, it) was being lent	they were being lent
Past	I did get lent	we did get lent
Int.	you did get lent	you did get lent
	he (she, it) did get lent	they did get lent
Pres.	I have been lent	we have been lent
Perf.	you have been lent	you have been lent
	he (she, it) has been lent	they have been lent
Past	I had been lent	we had been lent
Perf.	you had been lent	you had been lent
	he (she, it) had been lent	they had been lent
Fut.	I shall have been lent	we shall have been lent
Perf.	you will have been lent	you will have been lent
	he (she, it) will have been lent	they will have been lent

IMPERATIVE MOOD
be lent

SUBJUNCTIVE MOOD

Pres.	if I be lent	if we be lent
	if you be lent	if you be lent
	if he (she, it) be lent	if they be lent
Past	if I were lent	if we were lent
	if you were lent	if you were lent
	if he (she, it) were lent	if they were lent
Fut.	if I should be lent	if we should be lent
	if you should be lent	if you should be lent
	if he (she, it) should be lent	if they should be lent

to let (active voice) *Principal Parts:* let, letting, let, let

Infinitive: to let *Present Participle:* letting
Perfect Infinitive: to have let *Past Participle:* let

INDICATIVE MOOD

Pres.	I let	we let
	you let	you let
	he (she, it) lets	they let
Pres.	I am letting	we are letting
Prog.	you are letting	you are letting
	he (she, it) is letting	they are letting
Pres.	I do let	we do let
Int.	you do let	you do let
	he (she, it) does let	they do let
Fut.	I shall let	we shall let
	you will let	you will let
	he (she, it) will let	they will let
Fut.	I will let *(P)*	we will let *(P)*
	you shall let *(C)*	you shall let *(C)*
	he (she, it) shall let *(C)*	they shall let *(C)*
Past	I let	we let
	you let	you let
	he (she, it) lets	they let
Past	I was letting	we were letting
Prog.	you were letting	you were letting
	he (she, it) was letting	they were letting
Past	I did let	we did let
Int.	you did let	you did let
	he (she, it) did let	they did let
Pres.	I have let	we have let
Perf.	you have let	you have let
	he (she, it) has let	they have let
Past	I had let	we had let
Perf.	you had let	you had let
	he (she, it) had let	they had let
Fut.	I shall have let	we shall have let
Perf.	you will have let	you will have let
	he (she, it) will have let	they will have let

IMPERATIVE MOOD
let

SUBJUNCTIVE MOOD

Pres.	if I let	if we let
	if you let	if you let
	if he (she, it) let	if they let
Past	if I let	if we let
	if you let	if you let
	if he (she, it) let	if they let
Fut.	if I should let	if we should let
	if you should let	if you should let
	if he (she, it) should let	if they should let

Infinitive: to be let   *Present Participle:* being let
Perfect Infinitive: to have been let   *Past Participle:* been let

INDICATIVE MOOD

Pres.	I am let	we are let
	you are let	you are let
	he (she, it) is let	they are let
Pres.	I am being let	we are being let
Prog.	you are being let	you are being let
	he (she, it) is being let	they are being let
Pres.	I do get let	we do get let
Int.	you do get let	you do get let
	he (she, it) does get let	they do get let
Fut.	I shall be let	we shall be let
	you will be let	you will be let
	he (she, it) will be let	they will be let
Fut.	I will be let *(P)*	we will be let *(P)*
	you shall be let *(C)*	you shall be let *(C)*
	he (she, it) shall be let *(C)*	they shall be let *(C)*
Past	I was let	we were let
	you were let	you were let
	he (she, it) was let	they were let
Past	I was being let	we were being let
Prog.	you were being let	you were being let
	he (she, it) was being let	they were being let
Past	I did get let	we did get let
Int.	you did get let	you did get let
	he (she, it) did get let	they did get let
Pres.	I have been let	we have been let
Perf.	you have been let	you have been let
	he (she, it) has been let	they have been let
Past	I had been let	we had been let
Perf.	you had been let	you had been let
	he (she, it) had been let	they had been let
Fut.	I shall have been let	we shall have been let
Perf.	you will have been let	you will have been let
	he (she, it) will have been let	they will have been let

IMPERATIVE MOOD
be let

SUBJUNCTIVE MOOD

Pres.	if I be let	if we be let
	if you be let	if you be let
	if he (she, it) be let	if they be let
Past	if I were let	if we were let
	if you were let	if you were let
	if he (she, it) were let	if they were let
Fut.	if I should be let	if we should be let
	if you should be let	if you should be let
	if he (she, it) should be let	if they should be let

Infinitive: to lie   *Present Participle:* lying
Perfect Infinitive: to have lain   *Past Participle:* lain

INDICATIVE MOOD

Pres.	I lie	we lie
	you lie	you lie
	he (she, it) lies	they lie

Pres.	I am lying	we are lying
Prog.	you are lying	you are lying
	he (she, it) is lying	they are lying

Pres.	I do lie	we do lie
Int.	you do lie	you do lie
	he (she, it) does lie	they do lie

Fut.	I shall lie	we shall lie
	you will lie	you will lie
	he (she, it) will lie	they will lie

Fut.	I will lie *(P)*	we will lie *(P)*
	you shall lie *(C)*	you shall lie *(C)*
	he (she, it) shall lie *(C)*	they shall lie *(C)*

Past	I lay	we lay
	you lay	you lay
	he (she, it) lay	they lay

Past	I was lying	we were lying
Prog.	you were lying	you were lying
	he (she, it) was lying	they were lying

Past	I did lay	we did lay
Int.	you did lay	you did lay
	he (she, it) did lay	they did lay

Pres.	I have lain	we have lain
Perf.	you have lain	you have lain
	he (she, it) has lain	they have lain

Past	I had lain	we had lain
Perf.	you had lain	you had lain
	he (she, it) had lain	they had lain

Fut.	I shall have lain	we shall have lain
Perf.	you will have lain	you will have lain
	he (she, it) will have lain	they will have lain

IMPERATIVE MOOD
lay

SUBJUNCTIVE MOOD

Pres.	if I lie	if we lie
	if you lie	if you lie
	if he (she, it) lie	if they lie

Past	if I lay	if we lay
	if you lay	if you lay
	if he (she, it) lay	if they lay

Fut.	if I should lie	if we should lie
	if you should lie	if you should lie
	if he (she, it) should lie	if they should lie

To lie is an intransitive verb.

It does not take an object.
It describes action, but the action is self-contained.
Like other intransitive verbs, it may be followed by adverbs, adverbial phrases and clauses describing the how, why, when, and where of the action:

HOW: The body lay *in a strange position.* (adverbial phrase)
WHY: She will lie down *to take a nap.* (adverbial phrase)
WHEN: The books have lain untouched *ever since I bought them.* (adverbial clause)
WHERE: It seemed best to lie *low.* (adverb)

to lose (active voice)

Principal Parts: lose, losing, lost, lost

Infinitive: to lose	*Perfect Infinitive:* to have lost
Present Participle: losing	*Past Participle:* lost

INDICATIVE MOOD

Pres.	I lose	we lose
	you lose	you lose
	he (she, it) loses	they lose
Prog.	I am losing	we are losing
	you are losing	you are losing
	he (she, it) is losing	they are losing
Int.	I do lose	we do lose
	you do lose	you do lose
	he (she, it) does lose	they do lose
Fut.	I shall lose	we shall lose
	you will lose	you will lose
	he (she, it) will lose	they will lose
Fut.	I will lose (P)	we will lose (P)
	you shall lose (C)	you shall lose (C)
	he (she, it) shall lose (C)	they shall lose (C)
Past	I lost	we lost
	you lost	you lost
	he (she, it) lost	they lost
Prog.	I was losing	we were losing
	you were losing	you were losing
	he (she, it) was losing	they were losing
Past	I did lose	we did lose
Int.	you did lose	you did lose
	he (she, it) did lose	they did lose
Pres.	I have lost	we have lost
Perf.	you have lost	you have lost
	he (she, it) has lost	they have lost
Past	I had lost	we had lost
Perf.	you had lost	you had lost
	he (she, it) had lost	they had lost
Fut.	I shall have lost	we shall have lost
Perf.	you will have lost	you will have lost
	he (she, it) will have lost	they will have lost

IMPERATIVE MOOD

lose

SUBJUNCTIVE MOOD

Pres.	if I lose	if we lose
	if you lose	if you lose
	if he (she, it) lose	if they lose
Past	if I lost	if we lost
	if you lost	if you lost
	if he (she, it) lost	if they lost
Fut.	if I should lose	if we should lose
	if you should lose	if you should lose
	if he (she, it) should lose	if they should lose

(passive voice)

Infinitive: to be lost   *Perfect Infinitive:* to have been lost

Present Participle: being lost   *Past Participle:* been lost

INDICATIVE MOOD

Pres.	I am lost	we are lost	
	you are lost	you are lost	
	he (she, it) is lost	they are lost	
Prog.	I am being lost	we are being lost	
	you are being lost	you are being lost	
	he (she, it) is being lost	they are being lost	
Pres.	I do get lost	we do get lost	
	you do get lost	you do get lost	
	he (she, it) does get lost	they do get lost	
Fut.	I shall be lost	we shall be lost	
	you will be lost	you will be lost	
	he (she, it) will be lost	they will be lost	
Fut.	I will be lost (P)	we will be lost (P)	
	you shall be lost (C)	you shall be lost (C)	
	he (she, it) shall be lost (C)	they shall be lost (C)	
Past	I was lost	we were lost	
	you were lost	you were lost	
	he (she, it) was lost	they were lost	
Prog.	I was being lost	we were being lost	
	you were being lost	you were being lost	
	he (she, it) was being lost	they were being lost	
Past	I did get lost	we did get lost	
	you did get lost	you did get lost	
	he (she, it) did get lost	they did get lost	
Pres.	I have been lost	we have been lost	
	you have been lost	you have been lost	
	he (she, it) has been lost	they have been lost	
Past	I had been lost	we had been lost	
	you had been lost	you had been lost	
	he (she, it) had been lost	they had been lost	
Fut.	I shall have been lost	we shall have been lost	
	you will have been lost	you will have been lost	
	he (she, it) will have been lost	they will have been lost	

IMPERATIVE MOOD

be lost

SUBJUNCTIVE MOOD

Pres.	if I be lost	if we be lost	
	if you be lost	if you be lost	
	if he (she, it) be lost	if they be lost	
Past	if I were lost	if we were lost	
	if you were lost	if you were lost	
	if he (she, it) were lost	if they were lost	
Fut.	if I should be lost	if we should be lost	
	if you should be lost	if you should be lost	
	if he (she, it) should be lost	if they should be lost	

Infinitive: to make   *Present Participle:* making
Perfect Infinitive: to have made   *Past Participle:* made

INDICATIVE MOOD

Pres.	I make	we make
	you make	you make
	he (she, it) makes	they make

Pres.	I am making	we are making
Prog.	you are making	you are making
	he (she, it) is making	they are making

Pres.	I do make	we do make
Int.	you do make	you do make
	he (she, it) does make	they do make

Fut.	I shall make	we shall make
	you will make	you will make
	he (she, it) will make	they will make

Fut.	I will make *(P)*	we will make *(P)*
	you shall make *(C)*	you shall make *(C)*
	he (she, it) shall make *(C)*	they shall make *(C)*

Past	I made	we made
	you made	you made
	he (she, it) made	they made

Past	I was making	we were making
Prog.	you were making	you were making
	he (she, it) was making	they were making

Past	I did make	we did make
Int.	you did make	you did make
	he (she, it) did make	they did make

Pres.	I have made	we have made
Perf.	you have made	you have made
	he (she, it) has made	they have made

Past	I had made	we had made
Perf.	you had made	you had made
	he (she, it) had made	they had made

Fut.	I shall have made	we shall have made
Perf.	you will have made	you will have made
	he (she, it) will have made	they will have made

IMPERATIVE MOOD
make

SUBJUNCTIVE MOOD

Pres.	if I make	if we make
	if you make	if you make
	if he (she, it) make	if they make

Past	if I made	if we made
	if you made	if you made
	if he (she, it) made	if they made

Fut.	if I should make	if we should make
	if you should make	if you should make
	if he (she, it) should make	if they should make

Infinitive: to be made   *Present Participle:* being made
Perfect Infinitive: to have been made   *Past Participle:* been made

INDICATIVE MOOD

Pres. I am made	we are made
you are made	you are made
he (she, it) is made	they are made

Pres. I am being made	we are being made
Prog. you are being made	you are being made
he (she, it) is being made	they are being made

Pres. I do get made	we do get made
Int. you do get made	you do get made
he (she, it) does get made	they do get made

Fut. I shall be made	we shall be made
you will be made	you will be made
he (she, it) will be made	they will be made

Fut. I will be made *(P)*	we will be made *(P)*
you shall be made *(C)*	you shall be made *(C)*
he (she, it) shall be made *(C)*	they shall be made *(C)*

Past I was made	we were made
you were made	you were made
he (she, it) was made	they were made

Past I was being made	we were being made
Prog. you were being made	you were being made
he (she, it) was being made	they were being made

Past I did get made	we did get made
Int. you did get made	you did get made
he (she, it) did get made	they did get made

Pres. I have been made	we have been made
Perf. you have been made	you have been made
he (she, it) has been made	they have been made

Past I had been made	we had been made
Perf. you had been made	you had been made
he (she, it) had been made	they had been made

Fut. I shall have been made	we shall have been made
Perf. you will have been made	you will have been made
he (she, it) will have been made	they will have been made

IMPERATIVE MOOD
be made

SUBJUNCTIVE MOOD

Pres. if I be made	if we be made
if you be made	if you be made
if he (she, it) be made	if they be made

Past if I were made	if we were made
if you were made	if you were made
if he (she, it) were made	if they were made

Fut. if I should be made	if we should be made
if you should be made	if you should be made
if he (she, it) should be made	if they should be made

Infinitive: to meet   *Present Participle:* meeting
Perfect Infinitive: to have met   *Past Participle:* met

INDICATIVE MOOD

Pres.	I meet	we meet
	you meet	you meet
	he (she, it) meets	they meet
Pres.	I am meeting	we are meeting
Prog.	you are meeting	you are meeting
	he (she, it) is meeting	they are meeting
Pres.	I do meet	we do meet
Int.	you do meet	you do meet
	he (she, it) does meet	they do meet
Fut.	I shall meet	we shall meet
	you will meet	you will meet
	he (she, it) will meet	they will meet
Fut.	I will meet *(P)*	we will meet *(P)*
	you shall meet *(C)*	you shall meet *(C)*
	he (she, it) shall meet *(C)*	they shall meet *(C)*
Past	I met	we met
	you met	you met
	he (she, it) met	they met
Past	I was meeting	we were meeting
Prog.	you were meeting	you were meeting
	he (she, it) was meeting	they were meeting
Past	I did meet	we did meet
Int.	you did meet	you did meet
	he (she, it) did meet	they did meet
Pres.	I have met	we have met
Perf.	you have met	you have met
	he (she, it) has met	they have met
Past	I had met	we had met
Perf.	you had met	you had met
	he (she, it) had met	they had met
Fut.	I shall have met	we shall have met
Perf.	you will have met	you will have met
	he (she, it) will have met	they will have met

IMPERATIVE MOOD
meet

SUBJUNCTIVE MOOD

Pres.	if I meet	if we meet
	if you meet	if you meet
	if he (she, it) meet	if they meet
Past	if I met	if we met
	if you met	if you met
	if he (she, it) met	if they met
Fut.	if I should meet	if we should meet
	if you should meet	if you should meet
	if he (she, it) should meet	if they should meet

Infinitive: to be met   *Present Participle:* being met
Perfect Infinitive: to have been met   *Past Participle:* been met

INDICATIVE MOOD

Pres.	I am met	we are met
	you are met	you are met
	he (she, it) is met	they are met

Pres.	I am being met	we are being met
Prog.	you are being met	you are being met
	he (she, it) is being met	they are being met

Pres.	I do get met	we do get met
Int.	you do get met	you do get met
	he (she, it) does get met	they do get met

Fut.	I shall be met	we shall be met
	you will be met	you will be met
	he (she, it) will be met	they will be met

Fut.	I will be met *(P)*	we will be met *(P)*
	you shall be met *(C)*	you shall be met *(C)*
	he (she, it) shall be met *(C)*	they shall be met *(C)*

Past	I was met	we were met
	you were met	you were met
	he (she, it) was met	they were met

Past	I was being met	we were being met
Prog.	you were being met	you were being met
	he (she, it) was being met	they were being met

Past	I did get met	we did get met
Int.	you did get met	you did get met
	he (she, it) did get met	they did get met

Pres.	I have been met	we have been met
Perf.	you have been met	you have been met
	he (she, it) had been met	they have been met

Past	I had been met	we had been met
Perf.	you had been met	you had been met
	he (she, it) had been met	they had been met

Fut.	I shall have been met	we shall have been met
Perf.	you will have been met	you will have been met
	he (she, it) will have been met	they will have been met

IMPERATIVE MOOD
be met

SUBJUNCTIVE MOOD

Pres.	if I be met	if we be met
	if you be met	if you be met
	if he (she, it) be met	if they be met

Past	if I were met	if we were met
	if you were met	if you were met
	if he (she, it) were met	if they were met

Fut.	if I should be met	if we should be met
	if you should be met	if you should be met
	if he (she, it) should be met	if they should be met

to pay (active voice)

Principal Parts: pay, paying, paid, paid

Infinitive: to pay	*Present Participle:* paying
Perfect Infinitive: to have paid	*Past Participle:* paid

INDICATIVE MOOD

Pres.	I pay	we pay
	you pay	you pay
	he (she, it) pays	they pay
Pres. Prog.	I am paying	we are paying
	you are paying	you are paying
	he (she, it) is paying	they are paying
Pres. Int.	I do pay	we do pay
	you do pay	you do pay
	he (she, it) does pay	they do pay
Fut.	I shall pay	we shall pay
	you will pay	you will pay
	he (she, it) will pay	they will pay
Fut.	I will pay (P)	we will pay (P)
	you shall pay (C)	you shall pay (C)
	he (she, it) shall pay (C)	they shall pay (C)
Past	I paid	we paid
	you paid	you paid
	he (she, it) paid	they paid
Past Prog.	I was paying	we were paying
	you were paying	you were paying
	he (she, it) was paying	they were paying
Past Int.	I did pay	we did pay
	you did pay	you did pay
	he (she, it) did pay	they did pay
Pres. Perf.	I have paid	we have paid
	you have paid	you have paid
	he (she, it) has paid	they have paid
Past Perf.	I had paid	we had paid
	you had paid	you had paid
	he (she, it) had paid	they had paid
Fut. Perf.	I shall have paid	we shall have paid
	you will have paid	you will have paid
	he (she, it) will have paid	they will have paid

IMPERATIVE MOOD

pay

SUBJUNCTIVE MOOD

Pres.	if I pay	if we pay
	if you pay	if you pay
	if he (she, it) pay	if they pay
Past	if I paid	if we paid
	if you paid	if you paid
	if he (she, it) paid	if they paid
Fut.	if I should pay	if we should pay
	if you should pay	if you should pay
	if he (she, it) should pay	if they should pay

(passive voice)

Infinitive: to be paid *Perfect Infinitive:* to have been paid

Present Participle: being paid *Past Participle:* been paid

INDICATIVE MOOD

Pres.
I am paid we are paid
you are paid
he (she, it) is paid they are paid

Pres. Prog.
I am being paid we are being paid
you are being paid
he (she, it) is being paid they are being paid

Pres. Int.
I do get paid we do get paid
you do get paid
he (she, it) does get paid they do get paid

Fut.
I shall be paid we shall be paid
you will be paid
he (she, it) will be paid they will be paid

Fut.
I will be paid (P) we will be paid (P)
you shall be paid (C)
he (she, it) shall be paid (C) they shall be paid (C)

Past
I was paid we were paid
you were paid
he (she, it) was paid they were paid

Past Prog.
I was being paid we were being paid
you were being paid
he (she, it) was being paid they were being paid

Past Int.
I did get paid we did get paid
you did get paid
he (she, it) did get paid they did get paid

Pres. Perf.
I have been paid we have been paid
you have been paid
he (she, it) has been paid they have been paid

Past Perf.
I had been paid we had been paid
you had been paid
he (she, it) had been paid they had been paid

Fut. Perf.
I shall have been paid we shall have been paid
you will have been paid
he (she, it) will have been paid they will have been paid

IMPERATIVE MOOD

be paid

SUBJUNCTIVE MOOD

Pres.
if I be paid if we be paid
if you be paid
if he (she, it) be paid if they be paid

Past
if I were paid if we were paid
if you were paid
if he (she, it) were paid if they were paid

Fut.
if I should be paid if we should be paid
if you should be paid
if he (she, it) should be paid if they should be paid

to put (active voice)   *Principal Parts:* put, putting, put, put

Infinitive: to put   *Present Participle:* putting
Perfect Infinitive: to have put   *Past Participle:* put

INDICATIVE MOOD

Pres.	I put	we put
	you put	you put
	he (she, it) puts	they put
Pres. Prog.	I am putting	we are putting
	you are putting	you are putting
	he (she, it) is putting	they are putting
Pres. Int.	I do put	we do put
	you do put	you do put
	he (she, it) does put	they do put
Fut.	I shall put	we shall put
	you will put	you will put
	he (she, it) will put	they will put
Fut.	I will put *(P)*	we will put *(P)*
	you shall put *(C)*	you shall put *(C)*
	he (she, it) shall put *(C)*	they shall put *(C)*
Past	I put	we put
	you put	you put
	he (she, it) put	they put
Past Prog.	I was putting	we were putting
	you were putting	you were putting
	he (she, it) was putting	they were putting
Past Int.	I did put	we did put
	you did put	you did put
	he (she, it) did put	they did put
Pres. Perf.	I have put	we have put
	you have put	you have put
	he (she, it) has put	they have put
Past Perf.	I had put	we had put
	you had put	you had put
	he (she, it) had put	they had put
Fut. Perf.	I shall have put	we shall have put
	you will have put	you will have put
	he (she, it) will have put	they will have put

IMPERATIVE MOOD
put

SUBJUNCTIVE MOOD

Pres.	if I put	if we put
	if you put	if you put
	if he (she, it) put	if they put
Past	if I put	if we put
	if you put	if you put
	if he (she, it) put	if they put
Fut.	if I should put	if we should put
	if you should put	if you should put
	if he (she, it) should put	if they should put

Infinitive: to be put   *Present Participle:* being put
Perfect Infinitive: to have been put   *Past Participle:* been put

INDICATIVE MOOD

Pres.	I am put	we are put
	you are put	you are put
	he (she, it) is put	they are put
Pres.	I am being put	we are being put
Prog.	you are being put	you are being put
	he (she, it) is being put	they are being put
Pres.	I do get put	we do get put
Int.	you do get put	you do get put
	he (she, it) does get put	they do get put
Fut.	I shall be put	we shall be put
	you will be put	you will be put
	he (she, it) will be put	they will be put
Fut.	I will be put *(P)*	we will be put be put *(P)*
	you shall be put *(C)*	you shall be put *(C)*
	he (she, it) shall be put *(C)*	they shall be put *(C)*
Past	I was put	we were put
	you were put	you were put
	he (she, it) was put	they were put
Past	I was being put	we were being put
Prog.	you were being put	you were being put
	he (she, it) was being put	they were being put
Past	I did get put	we did get put
Int.	you did get put	you did get put
	he (she, it) did get put	they did get put
Pres.	I have been put	we have been put
Perf.	you have been put	you have been put
	he (she, it) has been put	they have been put
Past	I had been put	we had been put
Perf.	you had been put	you had been put
	he (she, it) had been put	they had been put
Fut.	I shall have been put	we shall have been put
Perf.	you will have been put	you will have been put
	he (she, it) will have been put	they will have been put

IMPERATIVE MOOD
be put

SUBJUNCTIVE MOOD

Pres.	if I be put	if we be put
	if you be put	if you be put
	if he (she, it) be put	if they be put
Past	if I were put	if we were put
	if you were put	if you were put
	if he (she, it) were put	if they were put
Fut.	if I should be put	if we should be put
	if you should be put	if you should be put
	if he (she, it) should be put	if they should be put

Infinitive: to read   *Present Participle:* reading
Perfect Infinitive: to have read   *Past Participle:* read

INDICATIVE MOOD

Pres.	I read	we read
	you read	you read
	he (she, it) reads	they read
Pres.	I am reading	we are reading
Prog.	you are reading	you are reading
	he (she, it) is reading	they are reading
Pres.	I do read	we do read
Int.	you do read	you do read
	he (she, it) does read	they do read
Fut.	I shall read	we shall read
	you will read	you will read
	he (she, it) will read	they will read
Fut.	I will read *(P)*	we will read *(P)*
	you shall read *(C)*	you shall read *(C)*
	he (she, it) shall read *(C)*	they shall read *(C)*
Past	I read	we read
	you read	you read
	he (she, it) read	they read
Past	I was reading	we were reading
Prog.	you were reading	you were reading
	he (she, it) was reading	they were reading
Past	I did read	we did read
Int.	you did read	you did read
	he (she, it) did read	they did read
Pres.	I have read	we have read
Perf.	you have read	you have read
	he (she, it) has read	they have read
Past	I had read	we had read
Perf.	you had read	you had read
	he (she, it) had read	they had read
Fut.	I shall have read	we shall have read
Perf.	you will have read	you will have read
	he (she, it) will have read	they will have read

IMPERATIVE MOOD
read

SUBJUNCTIVE MOOD

Pres.	if I read	if we read
	if you read	if you read
	if he (she, it) read	if they read
Past	if I read	if we read
	if you read	if you read
	if he (she, it) read	if they read
Fut.	if I should read	if we should read
	if you should read	if you should read
	if he (she, it) should read	if they should read

(passive voice)

Infinitive: to be read   *Present Participle:* being read

Perfect Infinitive: to have been read   *Past Participle:* been read

INDICATIVE MOOD

Pres.	I am read	we are read
	you are read	you are read
	he (she, it) is read	they are read
Pres. Prog.	I am being read	we are being read
	you are being read	you are being read
	he (she, it) is being read	they are being read
Pres. Int.	I do get read	we do get read
	you do get read	you do get read
	he (she, it) does get read	they do get read
Fut.	I shall be read	we shall be read
	you will be read	you will be read
	he (she, it) will be read	they will be read
Fut.	I will be read (P)	we will be read (P)
	you shall be read (C)	you shall be read (C)
	he (she, it) shall be read (C)	they shall be read (C)
Past	I was read	we were read
	you were read	you were read
	he (she, it) was read	they were read
Past Prog.	I was being read	we were being read
	you were being read	you were being read
	he (she, it) was being read	they were being read
Past Int.	I did get read	we did get read
	you did get read	you did get read
	he (she, it) did get read	they did get read
Pres. Perf.	I have been read	we have been read
	you have been read	you have been read
	he (she, it) has been read	they have been read
Past Perf.	I had been read	we had been read
	you had been read	you had been read
	he (she, it) had been read	they had been read
Fut. Perf.	I shall have been read	we shall have been read
	you will have been read	you will have been read
	he (she, it) will have been read	they will have been read

IMPERATIVE MOOD

be read

SUBJUNCTIVE MOOD

Pres.	if I be read	if we be read
	if you be read	if you be read
	if he (she, it) be read	if they be read
Past	if I were read	if we were read
	if you were read	if you were read
	if he (she, it) were read	if they were read
Fut.	if I should be read	if we should be read
	if you should be read	if you should be read
	if he (she, it) should be read	if they should be read

to ride (active voice)

Principal Parts: ride, riding, rode, ridden

Infinitive: to ride	*Present Participle:* riding
Perfect Infinitive: to have ridden	*Past Participle:* ridden

INDICATIVE MOOD

Pres.	I ride	we ride
	you ride	you ride
	he (she, it) rides	they ride

Prog. *Pres.*	I am riding	we are riding
	you are riding	you are riding
	he (she, it) is riding	they are riding

Pres. *Int.*	I do ride	we do ride
	you do ride	you do ride
	he (she, it) does ride	they do ride

Fut.	I shall ride	we shall ride
	you will ride	you will ride
	he (she, it) will ride	they will ride

Fut.	I will ride (P)	we will ride (P)
	you shall ride (C)	you shall ride (C)
	he (she, it) shall ride (C)	they shall ride (C)

Past	I rode	we rode
	you rode	you rode
	he (she, it) rode	they rode

Prog. *Past*	I was riding	we were riding
	you were riding	you were riding
	he (she, it) was riding	they were riding

Int. *Past*	I did ride	we did ride
	you did ride	you did ride
	he (she, it) did ride	they did ride

Pres. *Perf.*	I have ridden	we have ridden
	you have ridden	you have ridden
	he (she, it) has ridden	they have ridden

Past *Perf.*	I had ridden	we had ridden
	you had ridden	you had ridden
	he (she, it) had ridden	they had ridden

Fut. *Perf.*	I shall have ridden	we shall have ridden
	you will have ridden	you will have ridden
	he (she, it) will have ridden	they will have ridden

IMPERATIVE MOOD

ride

SUBJUNCTIVE MOOD

Pres.	if I ride	if we ride
	if you ride	if you ride
	if he (she, it) ride	if they ride

Past	if I rode	if we rode
	if you rode	if you rode
	if he (she, it) rode	if they rode

Fut.	if I should ride	if we should ride
	if you should ride	if you should ride
	if he (she, it) should ride	if they should ride

Infinitive: to be ridden   Perfect Infinitive: to have been ridden
Present Participle: being ridden   Past Participle: been ridden

(passive voice)

INDICATIVE MOOD

	Singular	Plural
Pres.	I am ridden	we are ridden
	you are ridden	you are ridden
	he (she, it) is ridden	they are ridden
Prog. Pres.	I am being ridden	we are being ridden
	you are being ridden	you are being ridden
	he (she, it) is being ridden	they are being ridden
Pres. Int.	I do get ridden	we do get ridden
	you do get ridden	you do get ridden
	he (she, it) does get ridden	they do get ridden
Fut.	I shall be ridden	we shall be ridden
	you will be ridden	you will be ridden
	he (she, it) will be ridden	they will be ridden
Fut.	I will be ridden (P)	we will be ridden (P)
	you shall be ridden (C)	you shall be ridden (C)
	he (she, it) shall be ridden (C)	they shall be ridden (C)
Past	I was ridden	we were ridden
	you were ridden	you were ridden
	he (she, it) was ridden	they were ridden
Past Prog.	I was being ridden	we were being ridden
	you were being ridden	you were being ridden
	he (she, it) was being ridden	they were being ridden
Past Int.	I did get ridden	we did get ridden
	you did get ridden	you did get ridden
	he (she, it) did get ridden	they did get ridden
Perf. Pres.	I have been ridden	we have been ridden
	you have been ridden	you have been ridden
	he (she, it) has been ridden	they have been ridden
Past Perf.	I had been ridden	we had been ridden
	you had been ridden	you had been ridden
	he (she, it) had been ridden	they had been ridden
Fut. Perf.	I shall have been ridden	we shall have been ridden
	you will have been ridden	you will have been ridden
	he (she, it) will have been ridden	they will have been ridden

IMPERATIVE MOOD
be ridden

SUBJUNCTIVE MOOD

	Singular	Plural
Pres.	if I be ridden	if we be ridden
	if you be ridden	if you be ridden
	if he (she, it) be ridden	if they be ridden
Past	if I were ridden	if we were ridden
	if you were ridden	if you were ridden
	if he (she, it) were ridden	if they were ridden
Fut.	if I should be ridden	if we should be ridden
	if you should be ridden	if you should be ridden
	if he (she, it) should be ridden	if they should be ridden

to ring (active voice)　　　*Principal Parts:* ring, ringing, rang, rung

Infinitive: to ring　　　　　　　　　　　*Present Participle:* ringing
Perfect Infinitive: to have rung　　　　　*Past Participle:* rung

INDICATIVE MOOD

Pres.	I ring	we ring
	you ring	you ring
	he (she, it) rings	they ring
Pres.	I am ringing	we are ringing
Prog.	you are ringing	you are ringing
	he (she, it) is ringing	they are ringing
Pres.	I do ring	we do ring
Int.	you do ring	you do ring
	he (she, it) does ring	they do ring
Fut.	I shall ring	we shall ring
	you will ring	you will ring
	he (she, it) will ring	they will ring
Fut.	I will ring *(P)*	we will ring *(P)*
	you shall ring *(C)*	you shall ring *(C)*
	he (she, it) shall ring *(C)*	they shall ring *(C)*
Past	I rang	we rang
	you rang	you rang
	he (she, it) rang	they rang
Past	I was ringing	we were ringing
Prog.	you were ringing	you were ringing
	he (she, it) was ringing	they were ringing
Past	I did ring	we did ring
Int.	you did ring	you did ring
	he (she, it) did ring	they did ring
Pres.	I have rung	we have rung
Perf.	you have rung	you have rung
	he (she, it) has rung	they have rung
Past	I had rung	we had rung
Perf.	you had rung	you had rung
	he (she, it) had rung	they had rung
Fut.	I shall have rung	we shall have rung
Perf.	you will have rung	you will have rung
	he (she, it) will have rung	they will have rung

IMPERATIVE MOOD
ring

SUBJUNCTIVE MOOD

Pres.	if I ring	if we ring
	if you ring	if you ring
	if he (she, it) ring	if they ring
Past	if I rang	if we rang
	if you rang	if you rang
	if he (she, it) rang	if they rang
Fut.	if I should ring	if we should ring
	if you should ring	if you should ring
	if he (she, it) should ring	if they should ring

(Passive Voice)

Infinitive: to be rung *Present Participle:* being rung
Perfect Infinitive: to have been rung *Past Participle:* been rung

INDICATIVE MOOD

Pres.	I am rung	we are rung
	you are rung	you are rung
	he (she, it) is rung	they are rung
Prog. *Pres.*	I am being rung	we are being rung
	you are being rung	you are being rung
	he (she, it) is being rung	they are being rung
Int. *Pres.*	I do get rung	we do get rung
	you do get rung	you do get rung
	he (she, it) does get rung	they do get rung
Fut.	I shall be rung	we shall be rung
	you will be rung	you will be rung
	he (she, it) will be rung	they will be rung
Fut.	I will be rung (P)	we will be rung (P)
	you shall be rung (C)	you shall be rung (C)
	he (she, it) shall be rung (C)	they shall be rung (C)
Past	I was rung	we were rung
	you were rung	you were rung
	he (she, it) was rung	they were rung
Prog. *Past*	I was being rung	we were being rung
	you were being rung	you were being rung
	he (she, it) was being rung	they were being rung
Int. *Past*	I did get rung	we did get rung
	you did get rung	you did get rung
	he (she, it) did get rung	they did get rung
Perf. *Pres.*	I have been rung	we have been rung
	you have been rung	you have been rung
	he (she, it) has been rung	they have been rung
Perf. *Past*	I had been rung	we had been rung
	you had been rung	you had been rung
	he (she, it) had been rung	they had been rung
Perf. *Fut.*	I shall have been rung	we shall have been rung
	you will have been rung	you will have been rung
	he (she, it) will have been rung	they will have been rung

IMPERATIVE MOOD

be rung

SUBJUNCTIVE MOOD

Pres.	if I be rung	if we be rung
	if you be rung	if you be rung
	if he (she, it) be rung	if they be rung
Past	if I were rung	if we were rung
	if you were rung	if you were rung
	if he (she, it) were rung	if they were rung
Fut.	if I should be rung	if we should be rung
	if you should be rung	if you should be rung
	if he (she, it) should be rung	if they should be rung

Infinitive: to rise   *Present Participle:* rising
Perfect Infinitive: to have risen   *Past Participle:* risen

INDICATIVE MOOD

Pres.	I rise	we rise
	you rise	you rise
	he (she, it) rises	they rise
Pres.	I am rising	we are rising
Prog.	you are rising	you are rising
	he (she, it) is rising	they are rising
Pres.	I do rise	we do rise
Int.	you do rise	you do rise
	he (she, it) does rise	they do rise
Fut.	I shall rise	we shall rise
	you will rise	you will rise
	he (she, it) will rise	they will rise
Fut.	I will rise *(P)*	we will rise *(P)*
	you shall rise *(C)*	you shall rise *(C)*
	he (she, it) shall rise *(C)*	they shall rise *(C)*
Past	I rose	we rose
	you rose	you rose
	he (she, it) rose	they rose
Past	I was rising	we were rising
Prog.	you were rising	you were rising
	he (she, it) was rising	they were rising
Past	I did rise	we did rise
Int.	you did rise	you did rise
	he (she, it) did rise	they did rise
Pres.	I have risen	we have risen
Perf.	you have risen	you have risen
	he (she, it) has risen	they have risen
Past	I had risen	we had risen
Perf.	you had risen	you had risen
	he (she, it) had risen	they had risen
Fut.	I shall have risen	we shall have risen
Perf.	you will have risen	you will have risen
	he (she, it) will have risen	they will have risen

IMPERATIVE MOOD
rise

SUBJUNCTIVE MOOD

Pres.	if I rise	if we rise
	if you rise	if you rise
	if he (she, it) rise	if they rise
Past	if I rose	if we rose
	if you rose	if you rose
	if he (she, it) rose	if they rose
Fut.	if I should rise	if we should rise
	if you should rise	if you should rise
	if he (she, it) should rise	if they should rise

To rise is an intransitive verb.

It does not take an object.
It describes action, but the action is self-contained.
Like other intransitive verbs, it may be followed by adverbs, adverbial phrases and clauses describing the how, why, when, and where of the action.

HOW: The sun rose *brilliantly*. (adverb)
WHY: He rose *to address the audience*. (adverbial phrase)
WHEN: I always rise *when the alarm rings*. (adverbial clause)
WHERE: The moon has risen *above the horizon*. (adverbial phrase)

Infinitive: to run   *Present Participle:* running
Perfect Infinitive: to have run   *Past Participle:* run

INDICATIVE MOOD

Pres.	I run	we run
	you run	you run
	he (she, it) runs	they run
Pres.	I am running	we are running
Prog.	you are running	you are running
	he (she, it) is running	they are running
Pres.	I do run	we do run
Int.	you do run	you do run
	he (she, it) does run	they do run
Fut.	I shall run	we shall run
	you will run	you will run
	he (she, it) will run	they will run
Fut.	I will run *(P)*	we will run *(P)*
	you shall run *(C)*	you shall run *(C)*
	he (she, it) shall run *(C)*	they shall run *(C)*
Past	I ran	we ran
	you ran	you ran
	he (she, it) ran	they ran
Past	I was running	we were running
Prog.	you were running	you were running
	he (she, it) was running	they were running
Past	I did run	we did run
Int.	you did run	you did run
	he (she, it) did run	they did run
Pres.	I have run	we have run
Perf.	you have run	you have run
	he (she, it) has run	they have run
Past	I had run	we had run
Perf.	you had run	you had run
	he (she, it) had run	they had run
Fut.	I shall have run	we shall have run
Perf.	you will have run	you will have run
	he (she, it) will have run	they will have run

IMPERATIVE MOOD
run

SUBJUNCTIVE MOOD

Pres.	if I run	if we run
	if you run	if you run
	if he (she, it) run	if they run
Past	if I ran	if we ran
	if you ran	if you ran
	if he (she, it) ran	if they ran
Fut.	if I should run	if we should run
	if you should run	if you should run
	if he (she, it) should run	if they should run

(passive voice)

Infinitive: to be run   *Present Participle:* being run
Perfect Infinitive: to have been run   *Past Participle:* been run

INDICATIVE MOOD

Pres.	I am run	we are run
	you are run	you are run
	he (she, it) is run	they are run
Pres.	I am being run	we are being run
Prog.	you are being run	you are being run
	he (she, it) is being run	they are being run
Pres.	I do get run	we do get run
Int.	you do get run	you do get run
	he (she, it) does get run	they do get run
Fut.	I shall be run	we shall be run
	you will be run	you will be run
	he (she, it) will be run	they will be run
Fut.	I will be run *(P)*	we will be run *(P)*
	you shall be run *(C)*	you shall be run *(C)*
	he (she, it) shall be run *(C)*	they shall be run *(C)*
Past	I was run	we were run
	you were run	you were run
	he (she, it) was run	they were run
Past	I was being run	we were being run
Prog.	you were being run	you were being run
	he (she, it) was being run	they were being run
Past	I did get run	we did get run
Int.	you did get run	you did get run
	he (she, it) did get run	they did get run
Pres.	I have been run	we have been run
Perf.	you have been run	you have been run
	he (she, it) has been run	they have been run
Past	I had been run	we had been run
Perf.	you had been run	you had been run
	he (she, it) had been run	they had been run
Fut.	I shall have been run	we shall have been run
Perf.	you will have been run	you will have been run
	he (she, it) will have been run	they will have been run

IMPERATIVE MOOD
be run

SUBJUNCTIVE MOOD

Pres.	if I be run	if we be run
	if you be run	if you be run
	if he (she, it) be run	if they be run
Past	if I were run	if we were run
	if you were run	if you were run
	if he (she, it) were run	if they were run
Fut.	if I should be run	if we should be run
	if you should be run	if you should be run
	if he (she, it) should be run	if they should be run

to say (active voice)

Principal Parts: say, saying, said, said

Infinitive: to say	*Present Participle:* saying
Perfect Infinitive: to have said	*Past Participle:* said

INDICATIVE MOOD

Pres.
I say — we say
you say — you say
he (she, it) says — they say

Prog.
I am saying — we are saying
you are saying — you are saying
he (she, it) is saying — they are saying

Pres. Int.
I do say — we do say
you do say — you do say
he (she, it) does say — they do say

Fut.
I shall say — we shall say
you will say — you will say
he (she, it) will say — they will say

Fut.
I will say (P) — we will say (P)
you shall say (C) — you shall say (C)
he (she, it) shall say (C) — they shall say (C)

Past
I said — we said
you said — you said
he (she, it) said — they said

Past Prog.
I was saying — we were saying
you were saying — you were saying
he (she, it) was saying — they were saying

Past Int.
I did say — we did say
you did say — you did say
he (she, it) did say — they did say

Pres. Perf.
I have said — we have said
you have said — you have said
he (she, it) has said — they have said

Past Perf.
I had said — we had said
you had said — you had said
he (she, it) had said — they had said

Fut. Perf.
I shall have said — we shall have said
you will have said — you will have said
he (she, it) will have said — they will have said

IMPERATIVE MOOD

say

SUBJUNCTIVE MOOD

Pres.
if I say — if we say
if you say — if you say
if he (she, it) say — if they say

Past
if I said — if we said
if you said — if you said
if he (she, it) said — if they said

Fut.
if I should say — if we should say
if you should say — if you should say
if he (she, it) should say — if they should say

(passive voice)

Infinitive: to be said		*Perfect Infinitive:* to have been said
Present Participle: being said		*Past Participle:* been said

INDICATIVE MOOD

Pres.	I am said	we are said
	you are said	you are said
	he (she, it) is said	they are said
Pres. Prog.	I am being said	we are being said
	you are being said	you are being said
	he (she, it) is being said	they are being said
Pres. Int.	I do get said	we do get said
	you do get said	you do get said
	he (she, it) does get said	they do get said
Fut.	I shall be said	we shall be said
	you will be said	you will be said
	he (she, it) will be said	they will be said
Fut.	I will be said (P)	we will be said (P)
	you shall be said (C)	you shall be said (C)
	he (she, it) shall be said (C)	they shall be said (C)
Past	I was said	we were said
	you were said	you were said
	he (she, it) was said	they were said
Past Prog.	I was being said	we were being said
	you were being said	you were being said
	he (she, it) was being said	they were being said
Past Int.	I did get said	we did get said
	you did get said	you did get said
	he (she, it) did get said	they did get said
Pres. Perf.	I have been said	we have been said
	you have been said	you have been said
	he (she, it) has been said	they have been said
Past Perf.	I had been said	we had been said
	you had been said	you had been said
	he (she, it) had been said	they had been said
Fut. Perf.	I shall have been said	we shall have been said
	you will have been said	you will have been said
	he (she, it) will have been said	they will have been said

IMPERATIVE MOOD
be said

SUBJUNCTIVE MOOD

Pres.	if I be said	if we be said
	if you be said	if you be said
	if he (she, it) be said	if they be said
Past	if I were said	if we were said
	if you were said	if you were said
	if he (she, it) were said	if they were said
Fut.	if I should be said	if we should be said
	if you should be said	if you should be said
	if he (she, it) should be said	if they should be said

Principal Parts: see, seeing, saw, seen

Infinitive: to see   *Present Participle:* seeing
Perfect Infinitive: to have seen   *Past Participle:* seen

INDICATIVE MOOD

Pres.	I see	we see
	you see	you see
	he (she, it) sees	they see
Pres.	I am seeing	we are seeing
Prog.	you are seeing	you are seeing
	he (she, it) is seeing	they are seeing
Pres.	I do see	we do see
Int.	you do see	you do see
	he (she, it) does see	they do see
Fut.	I shall see	we shall see
	you will see	you will see
	he (she, it) will see	they will see
Fut.	I will see *(P)*	we will see *(P)*
	you shall see *(C)*	you shall see *(C)*
	he (she, it) shall see *(C)*	they shall see *(C)*
Past	I saw	we saw
	you saw	you saw
	he (she, it) saw	they saw
Past	I was seeing	we were seeing
Prog.	you were seeing	you were seeing
	he (she, it) was seeing	they were seeing
Past	I did see	we did see
Int.	you did see	you did see
	he (she, it) did see	they did see
Pres.	I have seen	we have seen
Perf.	you have seen	you have seen
	he (she, it) has seen	they have seen
Past	I had seen	we had seen
Perf.	you had seen	you had seen
	he (she, it) had seen	they had seen
Fut.	I shall have seen	we shall have seen
Perf.	you will have seen	you will have seen
	he (she, it) will have seen	they will have seen

IMPERATIVE MOOD
see

SUBJUNCTIVE MOOD

Pres.	if I see	if we see
	if you see	if you see
	if he (she, it) see	if they see
Past	if I saw	if we saw
	if you saw	if you saw
	if he (she, it) saw	if they saw
Fut.	if I should see	if we should see
	if you should see	if you should see
	if he (she, it) should see	if they should see

Infinitive: to be seen   *Present Participle:* being seen
Perfect Infinitive: to have been seen   *Past Participle:* been seen

INDICATIVE MOOD

Pres.	I am seen	we are seen
	you are seen	you are seen
	he (she, it) is seen	they are seen
Pres. Prog.	I am being seen	we are being seen
	you are being seen	you are being seen
	he (she, it) is being seen	they are being seen
Pres. Int.	I do get seen	we do get seen
	you do get seen	you do get seen
	he (she, it) does get seen	they do get seen
Fut.	I shall be seen	we shall be seen
	you will be seen	you will be seen
	he (she, it) will be seen	they will be seen
Fut.	I will be seen *(P)*	we will be seen *(P)*
	you shall be seen *(C)*	you shall be seen *(C)*
	he (she, it) shall be seen *(C)*	they shall be seen *(C)*
Past	I was seen	we were seen
	you were seen	you were seen
	he (she, it) was seen	they were seen
Past Prog.	I was being seen	we were being seen
	you were being seen	you were being seen
	he (she, it) was being seen	they were being seen
Past Int.	I did get seen	we did get seen
	you did get seen	you did get seen
	he (she, it) did get seen	they did get seen
Pres. Perf.	I have been seen	we have been seen
	you have been seen	you have been seen
	he (she, it) has been seen	they have been seen
Past Perf.	I had been seen	we had been seen
	you had been seen	you had been seen
	he (she, it) had been seen	they had been seen
Fut. Perf.	I shall have been seen	we shall have been seen
	you will have been seen	you will have been seen
	he (she, it) will have been seen	they will have been seen

IMPERATIVE MOOD
be seen

SUBJUNCTIVE MOOD

Pres.	if I be seen	if we be seen
	if you be seen	if you be seen
	if he (she, it) be seen	if they be seen
Past	if I were seen	if we were seen
	if you were seen	if you were seen
	if he (she, it) were seen	if they were seen
Fut.	if I should be seen	if we should be seen
	if you should be seen	if you should be seen
	if he (she, it) should be seen	if they should be seen

to seek (active voice)

Principal Parts: seek, seeking, sought

Infinitive: to seek	*Present Participle:* seeking
Perfect Infinitive: to have sought	*Past Participle:* sought

INDICATIVE MOOD

Pres.	I seek	we seek
	you seek	you seek
	he (she, it) seeks	they seek
Pres. Prog.	I am seeking	we are seeking
	you are seeking	you are seeking
	he (she, it) is seeking	they are seeking
Pres. Int.	I do seek	we do seek
	you do seek	you do seek
	he (she, it) does seek	they do seek
Fut.	I shall seek	we shall seek
	you will seek	you will seek
	he (she, it) will seek	they will seek
Fut.	I will seek (P)	we will seek (P)
	you shall seek (C)	you shall seek (C)
	he (she, it) shall seek (C)	they shall seek (C)
Past	I sought	we sought
	you sought	you sought
	he (she, it) sought	they sought
Past Prog.	I was seeking	we were seeking
	you were seeking	you were seeking
	he (she, it) was seeking	they were seeking
Past Int.	I did seek	we did seek
	you did seek	you did seek
	he (she, it) did seek	they did seek
Pres. Perf.	I have sought	we have sought
	you have sought	you have sought
	he (she, it) has sought	they have sought
Past Perf.	I had sought	we had sought
	you had sought	you had sought
	he (she, it) had sought	they had sought
Fut. Perf.	I shall have sought	we shall have sought
	you will have sought	you will have sought
	he (she, it) will have sought	they will have sought

IMPERATIVE MOOD

seek

SUBJUNCTIVE MOOD

Pres.	if I seek	if we seek
	if you seek	if you seek
	if he (she, it) seek	if they seek
Past	if I sought	if we sought
	if you sought	if you sought
	if he (she, it) sought	if they sought
Fut.	if I should seek	if we should seek
	if you should seek	if you should seek
	if he (she, it) should seek	if they should seek

Infinitive: to be sought   *Present Participle:* being sought
Perfect Infinitive: to have been sought   *Past Participle:* been sought

INDICATIVE MOOD

Pres.	I am sought	we are sought
	you are sought	you are sought
	he (she, it) is sought	they are sought
Pres.	I am being sought	we are being sought
Prog.	you are being sought	you are being sought
	he (she, it) is being sought	they are being sought
Pres.	I do get sought	we do get sought
Int.	you do get sought	you do get sought
	he (she, it) does get sought	they do get sought
Fut.	I shall be sought	we shall be sought
	you will be sought	you will be sought
	he (she, it) will be sought	they will be sought
Fut.	I will be sought *(P)*	we will be sought *(P)*
	you shall be sought *(C)*	you shall be sought *(C)*
	he (she, it) shall be sought *(C)*	they shall be sought *(C)*
Past	I was sought	we were sought
	you were sought	you were sought
	he (she, it) was sought	they were sought
Past	I was being sought	we were being sought
Prog.	you were being sought	you were being sought
	he (she, it) was being sought	they were being sought
Past	I did get sought	we did get sought
Int.	you did get sought	you did get sought
	he (she, it) did get sought	they did get sought
Pres.	I have been sought	we have been sought
Perf.	you have been sought	you have been sought
	he (she, it) has been sought	they have been sought
Past	I had been sought	we had been sought
Perf.	you had been sought	you had been sought
	he (she, it) had been sought	they had been sought
Fut.	I shall have been sought	we shall have been sought
Perf.	you will have been sought	you shall have been sought
	he (she, it) will have been sought	they will have been sought

IMPERATIVE MOOD
be sought

SUBJUNCTIVE MOOD

Pres.	if I be sought	if we be sought
	if you be sought	if you be sought
	if he (she, it) be sought	if they be sought
Past	if I were sought	if we were sought
	if you were sought	if you were sought
	if he (she, it) were sought	if they were sought
Fut.	if I should be sought	if we should be sought
	if you should be sought	if you should be sought
	if he (she, it) should be sought	if they should be sought

to sell (active voice)

Principal Parts: sell, selling, sold, sold

Infinitive: to sell *Perfect Infinitive:* to have sold
Present Participle: selling *Past Participle:* sold

INDICATIVE MOOD

Pres.	I sell	we sell
	you sell	you sell
	he (she, it) sells	they sell
Pres. Prog.	I am selling	we are selling
	you are selling	you are selling
	he (she, it) is selling	they are selling
Pres. Int.	I do sell	we do sell
	you do sell	you do sell
	he (she, it) does sell	they do sell
Fut.	I shall sell	we shall sell
	you will sell	you will sell
	he (she, it) will sell	they will sell
Fut.	I will sell (P)	we will sell (P)
	you shall sell (C)	you shall sell (C)
	he (she, it) shall sell (C)	they shall sell (C)
Past	I sold	we sold
	you sold	you sold
	he (she, it) sold	they sold
Past Prog.	I was selling	we were selling
	you were selling	you were selling
	he (she, it) was selling	they were selling
Past Int.	I did sell	we did sell
	you did sell	you did sell
	he (she, it) did sell	they did sell
Pres. Perf.	I have sold	we have sold
	you have sold	you have sold
	he (she, it) has sold	they have sold
Past Perf.	I had sold	we had sold
	you had sold	you had sold
	he (she, it) had sold	they had sold
Fut. Perf.	I shall have sold	we shall have sold
	you will have sold	you will have sold
	he (she, it) will have sold	they will have sold

IMPERATIVE MOOD

sell

SUBJUNCTIVE MOOD

Pres.	if I sell	if we sell
	if you sell	if you sell
	if he (she, it) sell	if they sell
Past	if I sold	if we sold
	if you sold	if you sold
	if he (she, it) sold	if they sold
Fut.	if I should sell	if we should sell
	if you should sell	if you should sell
	if he (she, it) should sell	if they should sell

(passive voice)

Infinitive: to be sold   *Present Participle:* being sold
Perfect Infinitive: to have been sold   *Past Participle:* been sold

INDICATIVE MOOD

Pres.	I am sold	we are sold
	you are sold	you are sold
	he (she, it) is sold	they are sold
Pres.	I am being sold	we are being sold
Prog.	you are being sold	you are being sold
	he (she, it) is being sold	they are being sold
Pres.	I do get sold	we do get sold
Int.	you do get sold	you do get sold
	he (she, it) does get sold	they do get sold
Fut.	I shall be sold	we shall be sold
	you will be sold	you will be sold
	he (she, it) will be sold	they will be sold
Fut.	I will be sold *(P)*	we will be sold *(P)*
	you shall be sold *(C)*	you shall be sold *(C)*
	he (she, it) shall be sold *(C)*	they shall be sold *(C)*
Past	I was sold	we were sold
	you were sold	you were sold
	he (she, it) was sold	they were sold
Past	I was being sold	we were being sold
Prog.	you were being sold	you were being sold
	he (she, it) was being sold	they were being sold
Past	I did get sold	we did get sold
Int.	you did get sold	you did get sold
	he (she, it) did get sold	they did get sold
Pres.	I have been sold	we have been sold
Perf.	you have been sold	you have been sold
	he (she, it) has been sold	they have been sold
Past	I had been sold	we had been sold
Perf.	you had been sold	you had been sold
	he (she, it) had been sold	they had been sold
Fut.	I shall have been sold	we shall have been sold
Perf.	you will have been sold	you will have been sold
	he (she, it) will have been sold	they will have been sold

IMPERATIVE MOOD
be sold

SUBJUNCTIVE MOOD

Pres.	if I be sold	if we be sold
	if you be sold	if you be sold
	if he (she, it) be sold	if they be sold
Past	if I were sold	if we were sold
	if you were sold	if you were sold
	if he (she, it) were sold	if they were sold
Fut.	if I should be sold	if we should be sold
	if you should be sold	if you should be sold
	if he (she, it) should be sold	if they should be sold

to send (active voice)

Principal Parts: send, sending, sent, sent

Infinitive: to send	*Perfect Infinitive:* to have sent
Present Participle: sending	*Past Participle:* sent

INDICATIVE MOOD

Pres.	I send	we send
	you send	you send
	he (she, it) sends	they send

Pres.	I am sending	we are sending
Prog.	you are sending	you are sending
	he (she, it) is sending	they are sending

Pres.	I do send	we do send
Int.	you do send	you do send
	he (she, it) does send	they do send

Fut.	I shall send	we shall send
	you will send	you will send
	he (she, it) will send	they will send

Fut.	I will send (P)	we will send (P)
	he (she, it) will send	they will send
	you shall send (C)	you shall send (C)

Past	I sent	we sent
	you sent	you sent
	he (she, it) sent	they sent

Past	I was sending	we were sending
Prog.	you were sending	you were sending
	he (she, it) was sending	they were sending

Past	I did send	we did send
Int.	you did send	you did send
	he (she, it) did send	they did send

Perf.	I have sent	we have sent
	you have sent	you have sent
	he (she, it) has sent	they have sent

Past	I had sent	we had sent
Perf.	you had sent	you had sent
	he (she, it) had sent	they had sent

Fut.	I shall have sent	we shall have sent
Perf.	you will have sent	you will have sent
	he (she, it) will have sent	they will have sent

IMPERATIVE MOOD

send

SUBJUNCTIVE MOOD

Pres.	if I send	if we send
	if you send	if you send
	if he (she, it) send	if they send

Past	if I sent	if we sent
	if you sent	if you sent
	if he (she, it) sent	if they sent

Fut.	if I should send	if we should send
	if you should send	if you should send
	if he (she, it) should send	if they should send

Infinitive: to be sent   *Present Participle:* being sent
Perfect Infinitive: to have been sent   *Past Participle:* been sent

INDICATIVE MOOD

Pres.   I am sent   we are sent
         you are sent   you are sent
         he (she, it) is sent   they are sent

Pres.   I am being sent   we are being sent
Prog.   you are being sent   you are being sent
         he (she, it) is being sent   they are being sent

Pres.   I do get sent   we do get sent
Int.   you do get sent   you do get sent
         he (she, it) does get sent   they do get sent

Fut.   I shall be sent   we shall be sent
         you will be sent   you will be sent
         he (she, it) will be sent   they will be sent

Fut.   I will be sent *(P)*   we will be sent *(P)*
         you shall be sent *(C)*   you shall be sent *(C)*
         he (she, it) shall be sent *(C)*   they shall be sent *(C)*

Past   I was sent   we were sent
         you were sent   you were sent
         he (she, it) was sent   they were sent

Past   I was being sent   we were being sent
Prog.   you were being sent   you were being sent
         he (she, it) was being sent   they were being sent

Past   I did get sent   we did get sent
Int.   you did get sent   you did get sent
         he (she, it) did get sent   they did get sent

Pres.   I have been sent   we have been sent
Perf.   you have been sent   you have been sent
         he (she, it) has been sent   they have been sent

Past   I had been sent   we had been sent
Perf.   you had been sent   you had been sent
         he (she, it) had been sent   they had been sent

Fut.   I shall have been sent   we shall have been sent
Perf.   you will have been sent   you will have been sent
         he (she, it) will have been sent   they will have been sent

IMPERATIVE MOOD
be sent

SUBJUNCTIVE MOOD

Pres.   if I be sent   if we be sent
         if you be sent   if you be sent
         if he (she, it) be sent   if they be sent

Past   if I were sent   if we were sent
         if you were sent   if you were sent
         if he (she, it) were sent   if they were sent

Fut.   if I should be sent   if we should be sent
         if you should be sent   if you should be sent
         if he (she, it) should be sent   if they should be sent

Infinitive: to set　　　　　　　　　*Present Participle:* setting
Perfect Infinitive: to have set　　　　*Past Participle:* set

INDICATIVE MOOD

Pres.	I set	we set
	you set	you set
	he (she, it) sets	they set
Pres.	I am setting	we are setting
Prog.	you are setting	you are setting
	he (she, it) is setting	they are setting
Pres.	I do set	we do set
Int.	you do set	you do set
	he (she, it) does set	they do set
Fut.	I shall set	we shall set
	you will set	you will set
	he (she, it) will set	they will set
Fut.	I will set *(P)*	we will set *(P)*
	you shall set *(C)*	you shall set *(C)*
	he (she, it) shall set *(C)*	they shall set *(C)*
Past	I set	we set
	you set	you set
	he (she, it) set	they set
Past	I was setting	we were setting
Prog.	you were setting	you were setting
	he (she, it) was setting	they were setting
Past	I did set	we did set
Int.	you did set	you did set
	he (she, it) did set	they did set
Pres.	I have set	we have set
Perf.	you have set	you have set
	he (she, it) has set	they have set
Past	I had set	we had set
Perf.	you had set	you had set
	he (she, it) had set	they had set
Fut.	I shall have set	we shall have set
Perf.	you will have set	you will have set
	he (she, it) will have set	they will have set

IMPERATIVE MOOD
set

SUBJUNCTIVE MOOD

Pres.	if I set	if we set
	if you set	if you set
	if he (she, it) set	if they set
Past	if I set	if we set
	if you set	if you set
	if he (she, it) set	if they set
Fut.	if I should set	if we should set
	if you should set	if you should set
	if he (she, it) should set	if they should set

(passive voice)

Infinitive: to be set   *Perfect Infinitive:* to have been set
Present Participle: being set   *Past Participle:* been set

INDICATIVE MOOD

Pres.	I am set	we are set
	you are set	you are set
	he (she, it) is set	they are set
Prog. *Pres.*	I am being set	we are being set
	you are being set	you are being set
	he (she, it) is being set	they are being set
Pres.	I do get set	we do get set
	you do get set	you do get set
	he (she, it) does get set	they do get set
Fut.	I shall be set	we shall be set
	you will be set	you will be set
	he (she, it) will be set	they will be set
Fut.	I will be set (P)	we will be set (P)
	you shall be set (C)	you shall be set (C)
	he (she, it) shall be set (C)	they shall be set (C)
Past	I was set	we were set
	you were set	you were set
	he (she, it) was set	they were set
Prog. *Past*	I was being set	we were being set
	you were being set	you were being set
	he (she, it) was being set	they were being set
Past *Int.*	I did get set	we did get set
	you did get set	you did get set
	he (she, it) did get set	they did get set
Perf. *Pres.*	I have been set	we have been set
	you have been set	you have been set
	he (she, it) has been set	they have been set
Perf. *Past*	I had been set	we had been set
	you had been set	you had been set
	he (she, it) had been set	they had been set
Perf. *Fut.*	I shall have been set	we shall have been set
	you will have been set	you will have been set
	he (she, it) will have been set	they will have been set

IMPERATIVE MOOD

be set

SUBJUNCTIVE MOOD

Pres.	if I be set	if we be set
	if you be set	if you be set
	if he (she, it) be set	if they be set
Past	if I were set	if we were set
	if you were set	if you were set
	if he (she, it) were set	if they were set
Fut.	if I should be set	if we should be set
	if you should be set	if you should be set
	if he (she, it) should be set	if they should be set

to shake (active voice)

Principal Parts: shake, shaking, shook, shaken

Infinitive: to shake	*Present Participle:* shaking	
Perfect Infinitive: to have shaken	*Past Participle:* shaken	

INDICATIVE MOOD

Pres.	I shake		we shake
	you shake		you shake
	he (she, it) shakes		they shake
Prog	I am shaking		we are shaking
	you are shaking		you are shaking
	he (she, it) is shaking		they are shaking
Int.	I do shake		we do shake
	you do shake		you do shake
	he (she, it) does shake		they do shake
Fut.	I shall shake		we shall shake
	you will shake		you will shake
	he (she, it) will shake		they will shake
Fut.	I will shake (P)		we will shake (P)
	you shall shake (C)		you shall shake (C)
	he (she, it) shall shake (C)		they shall shake (C)
Past	I shook		we shook
	you shook		you shook
	he (she, it) shook		they shook
Past Prog	I was shaking		we were shaking
	you were shaking		you were shaking
	he (she, it) was shaking		they were shaking
Past Int.	I did shake		we did shake
	you did shake		you did shake
	he (she, it) did shake		they did shake
Pres Perf	I have shaken		we have shaken
	you have shaken		you have shaken
	he (she, it) has shaken		they have shaken
Past Perf	I had shaken		we had shaken
	you had shaken		you had shaken
	he (she, it) had shaken		they had shaken
Fut Perf	I shall have shaken		we shall have shaken
	you will have shaken		you will have shaken
	he (she, it) will have shaken		they will have shaken

IMPERATIVE MOOD

shake

SUBJUNCTIVE MOOD

Pres.	if I shake		if we shake
	if you shake		if you shake
	if he (she, it) shake		if they shake
Past	if I shook		if we shook
	if you shook		if you shook
	if he (she, it) shook		if they shook
Fut.	if I should shake		if we should shake
	if you should shake		if you should shake
	if he (she, it) should shake		if they should shake

(passive voice)

INDICATIVE MOOD

Infinitive: to be shaken	*Present Participle:* being shaken
Perfect Infinitive: to have been shaken	*Past Participle:* been shaken

Pres. I am shaken
    he (she, it) is shaken

Pres. we are shaken
    you are shaken
    they are shaken

Prog. I am being shaken
    he (she, it) is being shaken

Pres. Prog. we are being shaken
    you are being shaken
    they are being shaken

Int. I do get shaken
    you do get shaken
    he (she, it) does get shaken

    we do get shaken
    you do get shaken
    they do get shaken

Fut. I shall be shaken
    you will be shaken
    he (she, it) will be shaken

    we shall be shaken
    they will be shaken

Fut. I will be shaken (P)
    you shall be shaken (C)
    he (she, it) shall be shaken (C)

    we will be shaken (P)
    you shall be shaken (C)
    they shall be shaken (C)

Past I was shaken
    you were shaken
    he (she, it) was shaken

    we were shaken
    they were shaken

Prog. I was being shaken
    you were being shaken
    he (she, it) was being shaken

    we were being shaken
    you were being shaken
    they were being shaken

Int. I did get shaken
    you did get shaken
    he (she, it) did get shaken

    we did get shaken
    you did get shaken
    they did get shaken

Perf. I have been shaken
    you have been shaken
    he (she, it) has been shaken

    we have been shaken
    you have been shaken
    they have been shaken

Perf. I had been shaken
    you had been shaken
    he (she, it) had been shaken

    we had been shaken
    you had been shaken
    they had been shaken

Perf. I shall have been shaken
    you will have been shaken
    he (she, it) will have been shaken

    we shall have been shaken
    you will have been shaken
    they will have been shaken

IMPERATIVE MOOD
be shaken

SUBJUNCTIVE MOOD

Pres. if I be shaken
    if you be shaken
    if he (she, it) be shaken

    if we be shaken
    if you be shaken
    if they be shaken

Past if I were shaken
    if you were shaken
    if he (she, it) were shaken

    if we were shaken
    if you were shaken
    if they were shaken

Fut. if I should be shaken
    if you should be shaken
    if he (she, it) should be shaken

    if we should be shaken
    if you should be shaken
    if they should be shaken

to shine (active voice)   *Principal Parts:* shine, shining, shone (shined),
shone (shined)

Infinitive: to shine   *Present Participle:* shining
Perfect Infinitive: to have shone, shined   *Past Participle:* shone, shined

INDICATIVE MOOD

Pres.	I shine	we shine
	you shine	you shine
	he (she, it) shines	they shine
Pres.	I am shining	we are shining
Prog.	you are shining	you are shining
	he (she, it) is shining	they are shining
Pres.	I do shine	we do shine
Int.	you do shine	you do shine
	he (she, it) does shine	they do shine
Fut.	I shall shine	we shall shine
	you will shine	you will shine
	he (she, it) will shine	they will shine
Fut.	I will shine *(P)*	we will shine *(P)*
	you shall shine *(C)*	you shall shine *(C)*
	he (she, it) shall shine *(C)*	they shall shine *(C)*
Past	I shone, shined	we shone, shined
	you shone, shined	you shone, shined
	he (she, it) shone, shined	they shone, shined
Past	I was shining	we were shining
Prog.	you were shining	you were shining
	he (she, it) was shining	they were shining
Past	I did shine	we did shine
Int.	you did shine	you did shine
	he (she, it) did shine	they did shine
Pres.	I have shone, shined	we have shone, shined
Perf.	you have shone, shined	you have shone, shined
	he (she, it) has shone, shined	they have shone, shined
Past	I had shone, shined	we had shone, shined
Perf.	you had shone, shined	you had shone, shined
	he (she, it) had shone, shined	they had shone, shined
Fut.	I shall have shone, shined	we shall have shone, shined
Perf.	you will have shone, shined	you will have shone, shined
	he (she, it) will have shone, shined	they will have shone, shined

IMPERATIVE MOOD
shine

SUBJUNCTIVE MOOD

Pres.	if I shine	if we shine
	if you shine	if you shine
	if he (she, it) shine	if they shine
Past	if I shone, shined	if we shone, shined
	if you shone, shined	if you shone, shined
	if he (she, it) shone, shined	if they shone, shined
Fut.	if I should shine	if we should shine
	if you should shine	if you should shine
	if he (she, it) should shine	if they should shine

(passive voice)

Infinitive: to be shone, shined
Perfect Infinitive: to have been shone, shined

Present Participle: being shone, shined
Past Participle: been shone, shined

INDICATIVE MOOD

Pres. I am shone, shined — we are shone, shined
you are shone, shined — you are shone, shined
he (she, it) is shone, shined — they are shone, shined

Prog. I am being shone, shined — we are being shone, shined
Pres. you are being shone, shined — you are being shone, shined
he (she, it) is being shone, shined — they are being shone, shined

Int. I do get shone, shined — we do get shone, shined
Pres. you do get shone, shined — you do get shone, shined
he (she, it) does get shone, shined — they do get shone, shined

Fut. I shall be shone, shined — we shall be shone, shined
you will be shone, shined — you will be shone, shined
he (she, it) will be shone, shined — they will be shone, shined

Fut. I will be shone, shined (P) — we will be shone, shined (P)
you shall be shone, shined (C) — you shall be shone, shined (C)
he (she, it) shall be shone, shined (C) — they shall be shone, shined (C)

Past I was shone, shined — we were shone, shined
you were shone, shined — you were shone, shined
he (she, it) was shone, shined — they were shone, shined

Past I was being shone, shined — we were being shone, shined
Prog. you were being shone, shined — you were being shone, shined
he (she, it) was being shone, shined — they were being shone, shined

Past I did get shone, shined — we did get shone, shined
Int. you did get shone, shined — you did get shone, shined
he (she, it) did get shone, shined — they did get shone, shined

Pres. I have been shone, shined — we have been shone, shined
Perf. you have been shone, shined — you have been shone, shined
he (she, it) has been shone, shined — they have been shone, shined

Past I had been shone, shined — we had been shone, shined
Perf. you had been shone, shined — you had been shone, shined
he (she, it) had been shone, shined — they had been shone, shined

Fut. I shall have been shone, shined — we shall have been shone, shined
Perf. you will have been shone, shined — you will have been shone, shined
he (she, it) will have been shone, shined — they will have been shone, shined

IMPERATIVE MOOD
be shone, shined

SUBJUNCTIVE MOOD

Pres. if I be shone, shined — if we be shone, shined
if you be shone, shined — if you be shone, shined
if he (she, it) be shone, shined — if they be shone, shined

Past if I were shone, shined — if we were shone, shined
if you were shone, shined — if you were shone, shined
if he (she, it) were shone, shined — if they were shone, shined

Fut. if I should be shone, shined — if we should be shone, shined
if you should be shone, shined — if you should be shone, shined
if he (she, it) should be shone, shined — if they should be shone, shined

to shoot (active voice)

Infinitive: to shoot   *Present Participle:* shooting

Perfect Infinitive: to have shot   *Past Participle:* shot

INDICATIVE MOOD

Pres.   I shoot | we shoot
you shoot | you shoot
he (she, it) shoots | they shoot

Prog. *Pres.*   I am shooting | we are shooting
you are shooting | you are shooting
he (she, it) is shooting | they are shooting

Int. *Pres.*   I do shoot | we do shoot
you do shoot | you do shoot
he (she, it) does shoot | they do shoot

Fut.   I shall shoot | we shall shoot
you will shoot | you will shoot
he (she, it) will shoot | they will shoot

Fut.   I will shoot (P) | we will shoot (P)
you shall shoot (C) | you shall shoot (C)
he (she, it) shall shoot (C) | they shall shoot (C)

Past   I shot | we shot
you shot | you shot
he (she, it) shot | they shot

Past Prog.   I was shooting | we were shooting
you were shooting | you were shooting
he (she, it) was shooting | they were shooting

Past Int.   I did shoot | we did shoot
you did shoot | you did shoot
he (she, it) did shoot | they did shoot

Pres. Perf.   I have shot | we have shot
you have shot | you have shot
he (she, it) has shot | they have shot

Past Perf.   I had shot | we had shot
you had shot | you had shot
he (she, it) had shot | they had shot

Fut. Perf.   I shall have shot | we shall have shot
you will have shot | you will have shot
he (she, it) will have shot | they will have shot

IMPERATIVE MOOD
shoot

SUBJUNCTIVE MOOD

Pres.   if I shoot | if we shoot
if you shoot | if you shoot
if he (she, it) shoot | if they shoot

Past   if I shot | if we shot
if you shot | if you shot
if he (she, it) shot | if they shot

Fut.   if I should shoot | if we should shoot
if you should shoot | if you should shoot
if he (she, it) should shoot | if they should shoot

Infinitive: to be shot   *Present Participle:* being shot
Perfect Infinitive: to have been shot   *Past Participle:* been shot

INDICATIVE MOOD

Pres.	I am shot	we are shot
	you are shot	you are shot
	he (she, it) is shot	they are shot

Pres.	I am being shot	we are being shot
Prog.	you are being shot	you are being shot
	he (she, it) is being shot	they are being shot

Pres.	I do get shot	we do get shot
Int.	you do get shot	you do get shot
	he (she, it) does get shot	they do get shot

Fut.	I shall be shot	we shall be shot
	you will be shot	you will be shot
	he (she, it) will be shot	they will be shot

Fut.	I will be shot *(P)*	we will be shot *(P)*
	you shall be shot *(C)*	you shall be shot *(C)*
	he (she, it) shall be shot *(C)*	they shall be shot *(C)*

Past	I was shot	we were shot
	you were shot	you were shot
	he (she, it) was shot	they were shot

Past	I was being shot	we were being shot
Prog.	you were being shot	you were being shot
	he (she, it) was being shot	they were being shot

Past	I did get shot	we did get shot
Int.	you did get shot	you did get shot
	he (she, it) did get shot	they did get shot

Pres.	I have been shot	we have been shot
Perf.	you have been shot	you have been shot
	he (she, it) has been shot	they have been shot

Past	I had been shot	we had been shot
Perf.	you had been shot	you had been shot
	he (she, it) had been shot	they had been shot

Fut.	I shall have been shot	we shall have been shot
Perf.	you will have been shot	you will have been shot
	he (she, it) will have been shot	they will have been shot

IMPERATIVE MOOD
be shot

SUBJUNCTIVE MOOD

Pres.	if I be shot	if we be shot
	if you be shot	if you be shot
	if he (she, it) be shot	if they be shot

Past	if I were shot	if we were shot
	if you were shot	if you were shot
	if he (she, it) were shot	if they were shot

Fut.	if I should be shot	if we should be shot
	if you should be shot	if you should be shot
	if (she, it) should be shot	if they should be shot

to shrink (active voice)

Principal Parts: shrink, shrinking, shrank
(shrunk), shrunk (shrunken)

Infinitive: to shrink

Perfect Infinitive: to have shrunk (shrunken)

Present Participle: shrinking

Past Participle: shrunk, shrunken

INDICATIVE MOOD

Pres.	I shrink	we shrink
	you shrink	you shrink
	he (she, it) shrinks	they shrink
Pres.	I am shrinking	we are shrinking
Prog.	you are shrinking	you are shrinking
	he (she, it) is shrinking	they are shrinking
Pres.	I do shrink	we do shrink
Int.	you do shrink	you do shrink
	he (she, it) does shrink	they do shrink
Fut.	I shall shrink	we shall shrink
	you will shrink	you will shrink
	he (she, it) will shrink	they will shrink
Fut.	I will shrink *(P)*	we will shrink *(P)*
	you shall shrink *(C)*	you shall shrink *(C)*
	he (she, it) shall shrink *(C)*	they shall shrink *(C)*
Past	I shrank, shrunk	we shrank, shrunk
	you shrank, shrunk	you shrank, shrunk
	he (she, it) shrank, shrunk	they shrank, shrunk
Past	I was shrinking	we were shrinking
Prog.	you were shrinking	you were shrinking
	he (she, it) was shrinking	they were shrinking
Past	I did shrink	we did shrink
Int.	you did shrink	you did shrink
	he (she, it) did shrink	they did shrink
Pres.	I have shrunk, shrunken	we have shrunk, shrunken
Perf.	you have shrunk, shrunken	you have shrunk, shrunken
	he (she, it) has shrunk, shrunken	they have shrunk, shrunken
Past	I had shrunk, shrunken	we had shrunk, shrunken
Perf.	you had shrunk, shrunken	you had shrunk, shrunken
	he (she, it) had shrunk, shrunken	they had shrunk, shrunken
Fut.	I shall have shrunk, shrunken	we shall have shrunk, shrunken
Perf.	you will have shrunk, shrunken	you will have shrunk, shrunken
	he (she, it) will have shrunk, shrunken	they will have shrunk, shrunken

IMPERATIVE MOOD
shrink

SUBJUNCTIVE MOOD

Pres.	if I shrink	if we shrink
	if you shrink	if you shrink
	if he (she, it) shrink	if they shrink
Past	if I shrank	if we shrank
	if you shrank	if you shrank
	if he (she, it) shrank	if they shrank
Fut.	if I should shrink	if we should shrink
	if you should shrink	if you should shrink
	if he (she, it) should shrink	if they should shrink

Infinitive: to be shrunk, shrunken
Perfect Infinitive: to have been shrunk, shrunken
Present Participle: being shrunk, shrunken
Past Participle: been shrunk, shrunken

INDICATIVE MOOD

Pres.	I am shrunk, shrunken	we are shrunk, shrunken
	you are shrunk, shrunken	you are shrunk, shrunken
	he (she, it) is shrunk, shrunken	they are shrunk, shrunken
Pres.	I am being shrunk, shrunken	we are being shrunk, shrunken
Prog.	you are being shrunk, shrunken	you are being shrunk, shrunken
	he (she, it) is being shrunk, shrunken	they are being shrunk, shrunken
Pres.	I do get shrunk, shrunken	we do get shrunk, shrunken
Int.	you do get shrunk, shrunken	you do get shrunk, shrunken
	he (she, it) does get shrunk, shrunken	they do get shrunk, shrunken
Fut.	I shall be shrunk, shrunken	we shall be shrunk, shrunken
	you will be shrunk, shrunken	you will be shrunk, shrunken
	he (she, it) will be shrunk, shrunken	they will be shrunk, shrunken
Fut.	I will be shrunk, shrunken *(P)*	we will be shrunk, shrunken *(P)*
	you shall be shrunk, shrunken *(C)*	you shall be shrunk, shrunken *(C)*
	he (she, it) shall be shrunk, shrunken *(C)*	they shall be shrunk, shrunken *(C)*
Past	I was shrunk, shrunken	we were shrunk, shrunken
	you were shrunk, shrunken	you were shrunk, shrunken
	he (she, it) was shrunk, shrunken	they were shrunk, shrunken
Past	I was being shrunk	we were being shrunk
Prog.	you were being shrunk	you were being shrunk
	he (she, it) was being shrunk	they were being shrunk
Past	I did get shrunk, shrunken	we did get shrunk, shrunken
Int.	you did get shrunk, shrunken	you did get shrunk, shrunken
	he (she, it) did get shrunk, shrunken	they did get shrunk, shrunken
Pres.	I have been shrunk, shrunken	we have been shrunk, shrunken
Perf.	you have been shrunk, shrunken	you have been shrunk, shrunken
	he (she, it) has been shrunk, shrunken	they have been shrunk, shrunken
Past	I had been shrunk, shrunken	we had been shrunk, shrunken
Perf.	you had been shrunk, shrunken	you had been shrunk, shrunken
	he (she, it) had been shrunk, shrunken	they had been shrunk, shrunken
Fut.	I shall have been shrunk, shrunken	we shall have been shrunk, shrunken
Perf.	you will have been shrunk, shrunken	you will have been shrunk, shrunken
	he (she, it) will have been shrunk, shrunken	they will have been shrunk, shrunken

IMPERATIVE MOOD
be shrunk

SUBJUNCTIVE MOOD

Pres.
if I be shrunk, shrunken
if you be shrunk, shrunken
if he (she, it) be shrunk, shrunken

if we be shrunk, shrunken
if you be shrunk, shrunken
if they be shrunk, shrunken

Past
if I were shrunk, shrunken
if you were shrunk, shrunken
if he (she, it) were shrunk, shrunken

if we were shrunk, shrunken
if you were shrunk, shrunken
if they were shrunk, shrunken

Fut.
if I should be shrunk, shrunken
if you should be shrunk, shrunken
if he (she, it) should be shrunk,
shrunken

if we should be shrunk, shrunken
if you should be shrunk, shrunken
if they should be shrunk,
shrunken

To shrink is a transitive and intransitive verb.

The verb *to shrink*, meaning to diminish in size, like a woolen sweater after being washed in hot water, is both a transitive and intransitive verb. As a transitive verb it describes the action of someone causing something to shrink: a person *shrinks* a sweater by putting it into hot water. As a result (passive voice) the sweater is shrunken by the person.

But *to shrink* is also an intransitive verb in the sense that the shrinking can be thought of as a self-contained action: "The sweater *is shrinking* in the hot water" or "My capital *is shrinking* every day because stock market prices are falling."

The verb also has a figurative meaning *to draw back*, implying *becoming smaller* or *attempting to become inconspicuous* as in the face of danger or embarrassment: "He *shrank* from a confrontation with his angry father."

Principal Parts: sing, singing, sang, sung

Infinitive: to sing

Perfect Infinitive: to have sung

Present Participle: singing

Past Participle: sung

INDICATIVE MOOD

Pres.	I sing	we sing
	you sing	you sing
	he (she, it) sings	they sing

Pres.	I am singing	we are singing
Prog.	you are singing	you are singing
	he (she, it) is singing	they are singing

Pres.	I do sing	we do sing
Int.	you do sing	you do sing
	he (she, it) does sing	they do sing

Fut.	I shall sing	we shall sing
	you will sing	you will sing
	he (she, it) will sing	they will sing

Fut.	I will sing *(P)*	we will sing *(P)*
	you shall sing *(C)*	you shall sing *(C)*
	he (she, it) shall sing *(C)*	they shall sing *(C)*

Past	I sang	we sang
	you sang	you sang
	he (she, it) sang	they sang

Past	I was singing	we were singing
Prog.	you were singing	you were singing
	he (she, it) was singing	they were singing

Past	I did sing	we did sing
Int.	you did sing	you did sing
	he (she, it) did sing	they did sing

Pres.	I have sung	we have sung
Perf.	you have sung	you have sung
	he (she, it) has sung	they have sung

Past	I had sung	we had sung
Perf.	you had sung	you had sung
	he (she, it) had sung	they had sung

Fut.	I shall have sung	we shall have sung
Perf.	you will have sung	you will have sung
	he (she, it) will have sung	they will have sung

IMPERATIVE MOOD

sing

SUBJUNCTIVE MOOD

Pres.	if I sing	if we sing
	if you sing	if you sing
	if he (she, it) sing	if they sing

Past	if I sang	if we sang
	if you sang	if you sang
	if he (she, it) sang	if they sang

Fut.	if I should sing	if we should sing
	if you should sing	if you should sing
	if he (she, it) should sing	if they should sing

Infinitive: to be sung
Perfect Infinitive: to have been sung

Present Participle: being sung
Past Participle: been sung

INDICATIVE MOOD

Pres.	I am sung	we are sung
	you are sung	you are sung
	he (she, it) is sung	they are sung

Pres.	I am being sung	we are being sung
Prog.	you are being sung	you are being sung
	he (she, it) is being sung	they are being sung

Pres.	I do get sung	we do get sung
Int.	you do get sung	you do get sung
	he (she, it) does get sung	they do get sung

Fut.	I shall be sung	we shall be sung
	you will be sung	you will be sung
	he (she, it) will be sung	they will be sung

Fut.	I will be sung *(P)*	we will be sung *(P)*
	you shall be sung *(C)*	you shall be sung *(C)*
	he (she, it) shall be sung *(C)*	they shall be sung *(C)*

Past	I was sung	we were sung
	you were sung	you were sung
	he (she, it) was sung	they were sung

Past	I was being sung	we were being sung
Prog.	you were being sung	you were being sung
	he (she, it) was being sung	they were being sung

Past	I did get sung	we did get sung
Int.	you did get sung	you did get sung
	he (she, it) did get sung	they did get sung

Pres.	I have been sung	we have been sung
Perf.	you have been sung	you have been sung
	he (she, it) has been sung	they have been sung

Past	I had been sung	we had been sung
Perf.	you had been sung	you had been sung
	he (she, it) had been sung	they had been sung

Fut.	I shall have been sung	we shall have been sung
Perf.	you will have been sung	you will have been sung
	he (she, it) will have been sung	they will have been sung

IMPERATIVE MOOD
be sung

SUBJUNCTIVE MOOD

Pres.	if I be sung	if we be sung
	if you be sung	if you be sung
	if he (she, it) be sung	if they be sung

Past	if I were sung	if we were sung
	if you were sung	if you were sung
	if he (she, it) were sung	if they were sung

Fut.	if I should be sung	if we should be sung
	if you should be sung	if you should be sung
	if he (she, it) should be sung	if they should be sung

to sink (active voice)

Principal Parts: sink, sinking, sank, sunk

Infinitive: to sink   *Present Participle:* sinking

Perfect Infinitive: to have sunk   *Past Participle:* sunk

INDICATIVE MOOD

Pres.	I sink	we sink
	you sink	you sink
	he (she, it) sinks	they sink
Pres. Prog.	I am sinking	we are sinking
	you are sinking	you are sinking
	he (she, it) is sinking	they are sinking
Pres. Int.	I do sink	we do sink
	you do sink	you do sink
	he (she, it) does sink	they do sink
Fut.	I shall sink	we shall sink
	you will sink	you will sink
	he (she, it) will sink	they will sink
Fut.	I will sink (P)	we will sink (P)
	you shall sink (C)	you shall sink (C)
	he (she, it) shall sink (C)	they shall sink (C)
Past	I sank	we sank
	you sank	you sank
	he (she, it) sank	they sank
Past Prog.	I was sinking	we were sinking
	you were sinking	you were sinking
	he (she, it) was sinking	they were sinking
Past Int.	I did sink	we did sink
	you did sink	you did sink
	he (she, it) did sink	they did sink
Pres. Perf.	I have sunk	we have sunk
	you have sunk	you have sunk
	he (she, it) has sunk	they have sunk
Past Perf.	I had sunk	we had sunk
	you had sunk	you had sunk
	he (she, it) had sunk	they had sunk
Fut. Perf.	I shall have sunk	we shall have sunk
	you will have sunk	you will have sunk
	he (she, it) will have sunk	they will have sunk

IMPERATIVE MOOD

sink

SUBJUNCTIVE MOOD

Pres.	if I sink	if we sink
	if you sink	if you sink
	if he (she, it) sink	if they sink
Past	if I sank	if we sank
	if you sank	if you sank
	if he (she, it) sank	if they sank
Fut.	if I should sink	if we should sink
	if you should sink	if you should sink
	if he (she, it) should sink	if they should sink

Infinitive: to be sunk *Present Participle:* being sunk
Perfect Infinitive: to have been sunk *Past Participle:* been sunk

INDICATIVE MOOD

Pres.	I am sunk	we are sunk
	you are sunk	you are sunk
	he (she, it) is sunk	they are sunk
Pres.	I am being sunk	we are being sunk
Prog.	you are being sunk	you are being sunk
	he (she, it) is being sunk	they are being sunk
Pres.	I do get sunk	we do get sunk
Int.	you do get sunk	you do get sunk
	he (she, it) does get sunk	they do get sunk
Fut.	I shall be sunk	we shall be sunk
	you will be sunk	you will be sunk
	he (she, it) will be sunk	they will be sunk
Fut.	I will be sunk *(P)*	we will be sunk *(P)*
	you shall be sunk *(C)*	you shall be sunk *(C)*
	he (she, it) shall be sunk *(C)*	they shall be sunk *(C)*
Past	I was sunk	we were sunk
	you were sunk	you were sunk
	he (she, it) was sunk	they were sunk
Past	I was being sunk	we were being sunk
Prog.	you were being sunk	you were being sunk
	he (she, it) was being sunk	they were being sunk
Past	I did get sunk	we did get sunk
Int.	you did get sunk	you did get sunk
	he (she, it) did get sunk	they did get sunk
Pres.	I have been sunk	we have been sunk
Perf.	you have been sunk	you have been sunk
	he (she, it) has been sunk	they have been sunk
Past	I had been sunk	we had been sunk
Perf.	you had been sunk	you had been sunk
	he (she, it) had been sunk	they had been sunk
Fut.	I shall have been sunk	we shall have been sunk
Perf.	you will have been sunk	you will have been sunk
	he (she, it) will have been sunk	they will have been sunk

IMPERATIVE MOOD
be sunk

SUBJUNCTIVE MOOD

Pres.	if I be sunk	if we be sunk
	if you be sunk	if you be sunk
	if he (she, it) be sunk	if they be sunk
Past	if I were sunk	if we were sunk
	if you were sunk	if you were sunk
	if he (she, it) were sunk	if they were sunk
Fut.	if I should be sunk	if we should be sunk
	if you should be sunk	if you should be sunk
	if he (she, it) should be sunk	if they should be sunk

Infinitive: to sit   *Present Participle:* sitting
Perfect Infinitive: to have sat   *Past Participle:* sat

INDICATIVE MOOD

Pres.	I sit	we sit
	you sit	you sit
	he (she, it) sits	they sit
Pres.	I am sitting	we are sitting
Prog.	you are sitting	you are sitting
	he (she, it) is sitting	they are sitting
Pres.	I do sit	we do sit
Int.	you do sit	you do sit
	he (she, it) does sit	they do sit
Fut.	I shall sit	we shall sit
	you will sit	you will sit
	he (she, it) will sit	they will sit
Fut.	I will sit *(P)*	we will sit *(P)*
	you shall sit *(C)*	you shall sit *(C)*
	he (she, it) shall sit *(C)*	they shall sit *(C)*
Past	I sat	we sat
	you sat	you sat
	he (she, it) sat	they sat
Past	I was sitting	we were sitting
Prog.	you were sitting	you were sitting
	he (she, it) was sitting	they were sitting
Past	I did sit	we did sit
Int.	you did sit	you did sit
	he (she, it) did sit	they did sit
Pres.	I have sat	we have sat
Perf.	you have sat	you have sat
	he (she, it) has sat	they have sat
Past	I had sat	we had sat
Perf.	you had sat	you had sat
	he (she, it) had sat	they had sat
Fut.	I shall have sat	we shall have sat
Perf.	you will have sat	you will have sat
	he (she, it) will have sat	they will have sat

IMPERATIVE MOOD
sit

SUBJUNCTIVE MOOD

Pres.	if I sit	if we sit
	if you sit	if you sit
	if he (she, it) sit	if they sit
Past	if I sat	if we sat
	if you sat	if you sat
	if he (she, it) sat	if they sat
Fut.	if I should sit	if we should sit
	if you should sit	if you should sit
	if he (she, it) should sit	if they should sit

To sit is an intransitive verb.

It does not take an object.

It describes action, but the action is self-contained.

Like other intransitive verbs, it may be followed by adverbs, adverbial phrases and clauses describing the how, why, when, and where of the action:

HOW: John, sit *straight!* (adverb)

WHY: They were sitting *because they were tired.* (adverbial clause)

WHEN: I expect to be sitting *all day.* (adverbial phrase)

WHERE: The baby sat *on a high chair.* (adverbial phrase)

Infinitive: to slay   *Present Participle:* slaying
Perfect Infinitive: to have slain   *Past Participle:* slain

INDICATIVE MOOD

Pres.	I slay	we slay
	you slay	you slay
	he (she, it) slays	they slay
Pres.	I am slaying	we are slaying
Prog.	you are slaying	you are slaying
	he (she, it) is slaying	they are slaying
Pres.	I do slay	we do slay
Int.	you do slay	you do slay
	he (she, it) does slay	they do slay
Fut.	I shall slay	we shall slay
	you will slay	you will slay
	he (she, it) will slay	they will slay
Fut.	I will slay *(P)*	we will slay *(P)*
	you shall slay *(C)*	you shall slay *(C)*
	he (she, it) shall slay *(C)*	they shall slay *(C)*
Past	I slew	we slew
	you slew	you slew
	he (she, it) slew	they slew
Past	I was slaying	we were slaying
Prog.	you were slaying	you were slaying
	he (she, it) was slaying	they were slaying
Past	I did slay	we did slay
Int.	you did slay	you did slay
	he (she, it) did slay	they did slay
Pres.	I have slain	we have slain
Perf.	you have slain	you have slain
	he (she, it) has slain	they have slain
Past	I had slain	we had slain
Perf.	you had slain	you had slain
	he (she, it) had slain	they had slain
Fut.	I shall have slain	we shall have slain
Perf.	you will have slain	you will have slain
	he (she, it) will have slain	they will have slain

IMPERATIVE MOOD
slay

SUBJUNCTIVE MOOD

Pres.	if I slay	if we slay
	if you slay	if you slay
	if he (she, it) slay	if they slay
Past	if I slew	if we slew
	if you slew	if you slew
	if he (she, it) slew	if they slew
Fut.	if I should slay	if we should slay
	if you should slay	if you should slay
	if he (she, it) should slay	if they should slay

(passive voice)

Infinitive: to be slain   Perfect Infinitive: to have been slain

Present Participle: being slain   Past Participle: been slain

INDICATIVE MOOD

Pres.	I am slain	we are slain
	you are slain	you are slain
	he (she, it) is slain	they are slain
Prog. *Pres.*	I am being slain	we are being slain
	you are being slain	you are being slain
	he (she, it) is being slain	they are being slain
Pres. *Int.*	I do get slain	we do get slain
	you do get slain	you do get slain
	he (she, it) does get slain	they do get slain
Fut.	I shall be slain	we shall be slain
	you will be slain	you will be slain
	he (she, it) will be slain	they will be slain
Fut.	I will be slain (P)	we will be slain (P)
	you shall be slain (C)	you shall be slain (C)
	he (she, it) shall be slain (C)	they shall be slain (C)
Past	I was slain	we were slain
	you were slain	you were slain
	he (she, it) was slain	they were slain
Past *Prog.*	I was being slain	we were being slain
	you were being slain	you were being slain
	he (she, it) was being slain	they were being slain
Past *Int.*	I did get slain	we did get slain
	you did get slain	you did get slain
	he (she, it) did get slain	they did get slain
Pres. *Perf.*	I have been slain	we have been slain
	you have been slain	you have been slain
	he (she, it) has been slain	they have been slain
Past *Perf.*	I had been slain	we had been slain
	you had been slain	you had been slain
	he (she, it) had been slain	they had been slain
Fut. *Perf.*	I shall have been slain	we shall have been slain
	you will have been slain	you will have been slain
	he (she, it) will have been slain	they will have been slain

IMPERATIVE MOOD
be slain

SUBJUNCTIVE MOOD

Pres.	if I be slain	if we be slain
	if you be slain	if you be slain
	if he (she, it) be slain	if they be slain
Past	if I were slain	if we were slain
	if you were slain	if you were slain
	if he (she, it) were slain	if they were slain
Fut.	if I should be slain	if we should be slain
	if you should be slain	if you should be slain
	if he (she, it) should be slain	if they should be slain

Infinitive: to sleep — *Present Participle:* sleeping
Perfect Infinitive: to have slept — *Past Participle:* slept

INDICATIVE MOOD

Pres.	I sleep	we sleep
	you sleep	you sleep
	he (she, it) sleeps	they sleep
Pres.	I am sleeping	we are sleeping
Prog.	you are sleeping	you are sleeping
	he (she, it) is sleeping	they are sleeping
Pres.	I do sleep	we do sleep
Int.	you do sleep	you do sleep
	he (she, it) does sleep	they do sleep
Fut.	I shall sleep	we shall sleep
	you will sleep	you will sleep
	he (she, it) will sleep	they will sleep
Fut.	I will sleep *(P)*	we will sleep *(P)*
	you shall sheep *(C)*	you shall sleep *(C)*
	he (she, it) shall sleep *(C)*	they shall sleep *(C)*
Past	I slept	we slept
	you slept	you slept
	he (she, it) slept	they slept
Past	I was sleeping	we were sleeping
Prog.	you were sleeping	you were sleeping
	he (she, it) was sleeping	they were sleeping
Past	I did sleep	we did sleep
Int.	you did sleep	you did sleep
	he (she, it) did sleep	they did sleep
Pres.	I have slept	we have slept
Perf.	you have slept	you have slept
	he (she, it) has slept	they have slept
Past	I had slept	we had slept
Perf.	you had slept	you had slept
	he (she, it) had slept	they had slept
Fut.	I shall have slept	we shall have slept
Perf.	you will have slept	you will have slept
	he (she, it) will have slept	they will have slept

IMPERATIVE MOOD
sleep

SUBJUNCTIVE MOOD

Pres.	if I sleep	if we sleep
	if you sleep	if you sleep
	if he (she, it) sleep	if they sleep
Past	if I slept	if we slept
	if you slept	if you slept
	if he (she, it) slept	if they slept
Fut.	if I should sleep	if we should sleep
	if you should sleep	if you should sleep
	if he (she, it) should sleep	if they should sleep

To sleep is an intransitive verb.

It does not take an object.

It describes action, but the action is self-contained.

Like other intransitive verbs, it may be followed by adverbs, adverbial phrases and clauses describing the how, why, when, and where of the action:

HOW: Sleep *well*. (adverb)

WHY: She was sleeping *because she was tired*. (adverbial clause)

WHEN: Most people sleep *at night*. (adverbial phrase)

WHERE: I always sleep *when I ride on a train*. (adverbial clause)

to slide (active voice)

Principal Parts: slide, sliding, slid

Infinitive: to slide	*Present Participle:* sliding
Perfect Infinitive: to have slid	*Past Participle:* slid

INDICATIVE MOOD

Pres.
I slide — we slide
you slide
he (she, it) slides — they slide

Pres. Prog.
I am sliding — we are sliding
you are sliding
he (she, it) is sliding — they are sliding

Pres. Int.
I do slide — we do slide
you do slide
he (she, it) does slide — they do slide

Fut.
I shall slide — we shall slide
you will slide — you will slide
he (she, it) will slide — they will slide

Fut.
I will slide (P) — we will slide (P)
you shall slide (C) — you shall slide (C)
he (she, it) shall slide (C) — they shall slide (C)

Past
I slid — we slid
you slid — you slid
he (she, it) slid — they slid

Past Prog.
I was sliding — we were sliding
you were sliding — you were sliding
he (she, it) was sliding — they were sliding

Past Int.
I did slide — we did slide
you did slide — you did slide
he (she, it) did slide — they did slide

Pres. Perf.
I have slid — we have slid
you have slid — you have slid
he (she, it) has slid — they have slid

Past Perf.
I had slid — we had slid
you had slid — you had slid
he (she, it) had slid — they had slid

Fut. Perf.
I shall have slid — we shall have slid
you will have slid — you will have slid
he (she, it) will have slid — they will have slid

IMPERATIVE MOOD
slide

SUBJUNCTIVE MOOD

Pres.
if I slide — if we slide
if you slide — if you slide
if he (she, it) slide — if they slide

Past
if I slid — if we slid
if you slid — if you slid
if he (she, it) slid — if they slid

Fut.
if I should slide — if we should slide
if you should slide — if you should slide
if he (she, it) should slide — if they should slide

Infinitive: to be slid
Present Participle: being slid
Perfect Infinitive: to have been slid
Past Participle: been slid

INDICATIVE MOOD

Pres.	I am slid you are slid he (she, it) is slid	we are slid you are slid they are slid
Pres. *Prog.*	I am being slid you are being slid he (she, it) is being slid	we are being slid you are being slid they are being slid
Pres. *Int.*	I do get slid you do get slid he (she, it) does get slid	we do get slid you do get slid they do get slid
Fut.	I shall be slid you will be slid he (she, it) will be slid	we shall be slid you will be slid they will be slid
Fut.	I will be slid *(P)* you shall be slid *(C)* he (she, it) shall be slid *(C)*	we will be slid *(P)* you shall be slid *(C)* they shall be slid *(C)*
Past	I was slid you were slid he (she, it) was slid	we were slid you were slid they were slid
Past *Prog.*	I was being slid you were being slid he (she, it) was being slid	we were being slid you were being slid they were being slid
Past *Int.*	I did get slid you did get slid he (she, it) did get slid	we did get slid you did get slid they did get slid
Pres. *Perf.*	I have been slid you have been slid he (she, it) has been slid	we have been slid you have been slid they have been slid
Past *Perf.*	I had been slid you had been slid he (she, it) had been slid	we had been slid you had been slid they had been slid
Fut. *Perf.*	I shall have been slid you will have been slid he (she, it) will have been slid	we shall have been slid you will have been slid they will have been slid

IMPERATIVE MOOD
be slid

SUBJUNCTIVE MOOD

Pres.	if I be slid if you be slid if he (she, it) be slid	if we be slid if you be slid if they be slid
Past	if I were slid if you were slid if he (she, it) were slid	if we were slid if you were slid if they were slid
Fut.	if I should be slid if you should be slid if he (she, it) should be slid	if we should be slid if you should be slid if they should be slid

to speak (active voice)

Principal Parts: speak, speaking,
speak, spoken

Infinitive: to speak   *Present Participle:* speaking
Perfect Infinitive: to have spoken   *Past Participle:* spoken

INDICATIVE MOOD

Pres.	I speak	we speak

Pres.   I speak   we speak
        you speak   you speak
        he (she, it) speaks   they speak

Pres.   I am speaking   we are speaking
Prog.   you are speaking   you are speaking
        he (she, it) is speaking   they are speaking

Pres.   I do speak   we do speak
Int.   you do speak   you do speak
        he (she, it) does speak   they do speak

Fut.   I shall speak   we shall speak
        you will speak   you will speak
        he (she, it) will speak   they will speak

Fut.   I will speak *(P)*   we will speak *(P)*
        you shall speak *(C)*   you shall speak *(C)*
        he (she, it) shall speak *(C)*   they shall speak *(C)*

Past   I spoke   we spoke
        you spoke   you spoke
        he (she, it) spoke   they spoke

Past   I was speaking   we were speaking
Prog.   you were speaking   you were speaking
        he (she, it) was speaking   they were speaking

Past   I did speak   we did speak
Int.   you did speak   you did speak
        he (she, it) did speak   they did speak

Pres.   I have spoken   we have spoken
Perf.   you have spoken   you have spoken
        he (she, it) has spoken   they have spoken

Past   I had spoken   we had spoken
Perf.   you had spoken   you had spoken
        he (she, it) had spoken   they had spoken

Fut.   I shall have spoken   we shall have spoken
Perf.   you will have spoken   you will have spoken
        he (she, it) will have spoken   they will have spoken

IMPERATIVE MOOD
speak

SUBJUNCTIVE MOOD

Pres.   if I speak   if we speak
        if you speak   if you speak
        if he (she, it) speak   if they speak

Past   if I spoke   if we spoke
        if you spoke   if you spoke
        if he (she, it) spoke   if they spoke

Fut.   if I should speak   if we should speak
        if you should speak   if you should speak
        if he (she, it) should speak   if they should speak

(passive voice)

Infinitive: to be spoken

Perfect Infinitive: to have been spoken

Present Participle: being spoken

Past Participle: been spoken

INDICATIVE MOOD

Pres.	I am spoken	we are spoken
	you are spoken	you are spoken
	he (she, it) is spoken	they are spoken
Pres.	I am being spoken	we are being spoken
Prog.	you are being spoken	you are being spoken
	he (she, it) is being spoken	they are being spoken
Pres.	I do get spoken	we do get spoken
Int.	you do get spoken	you do get spoken
	he (she, it) does get spoken	they do get spoken
Fut.	I shall be spoken	we shall be spoken
	you will be spoken	you will be spoken
	he (she, it) will be spoken	they will be spoken
Fut.	I will be spoken (P)	we will be spoken (P)
	you shall be spoken (C)	you shall be spoken (C)
	he (she, it) shall be spoken (C)	they shall be spoken (C)
Past	I was spoken	we were spoken
	you were spoken	you were spoken
	he (she, it) was spoken	they were spoken
Past	I was being spoken	we were being spoken
Prog.	you were being spoken	you were being spoken
	he (she, it) was being spoken	they were being spoken
Past	I did get spoken	we did get spoken
Int.	you did get spoken	you did get spoken
	he (she, it) did get spoken	they did get spoken
Pres.	I have been spoken	we have been spoken
Perf.	you have been spoken	you have been spoken
	he (she, it) has been spoken	they have been spoken
Past	I had been spoken	we had been spoken
Perf.	you had been spoken	you had been spoken
	he (she, it) had been spoken	they had been spoken
Fut.	I shall have been spoken	we shall have been spoken
Perf.	you will have been spoken	you will have been spoken
	he (she, it) will have been spoken	they will have been spoken

IMPERATIVE MOOD

be spoken

SUBJUNCTIVE MOOD

Pres.	if I be spoken	if we be spoken
	if you be spoken	if you be spoken
	if he (she, it) be spoken	if they be spoken
Past	if I were spoken	if we were spoken
	if you were spoken	if you were spoken
	if he (she, it) were spoken	if they were spoken
Fut.	if I should be spoken	if we should be spoken
	if you should be spoken	if you should be spoken
	if he (she, it) should be spoken	if they should be spoken

to spend (active voice)

Infinitive: to spend	*Perfect Infinitive:* having spent
Present Participle: spending	*Past Participle:* spent

Principal Parts: spend, spending, spent, spent

INDICATIVE MOOD

Pres. I spend   we spend
you spend   you spend
he (she, it) spends   they spend

Pres. I am spending   we are spending
Prog. you are spending   you are spending
he (she, it) is spending   they are spending

Pres. I do spend   we do spend
Int. you do spend   you do spend
he (she, it) does spend   they do spend

Fut. I shall spend   we shall spend
you will spend   you will spend
he (she, it) will spend   they will spend

Fut. I will spend (P)   we will spend (P)
you shall spend (C)   you shall spend (C)
he (she, it) shall spend (C)   they shall spend (C)

Past I spent   we spent
you spent   you spent
he (she, it) spent   they spent

Past I was spending   we were spending
Prog. you were spending   you were spending
he (she, it) was spending   they were spending

Past I did spend   we did spend
Int. you did spend   you did spend
he (she, it) did spend   they did spend

Pres. I have spent   we have spent
Perf. you have spent   you have spent
he (she, it) has spent   they have spent

Past I had spent   we had spent
Perf. you had spent   you had spent
he (she, it) had spent   they had spent

Fut. I shall have spent   we shall have spent
Perf. you will have spent   you will have spent
he (she, it) will have spent   they will have spent

IMPERATIVE MOOD

spend

SUBJUNCTIVE MOOD

Pres. if I spend   if we spend
if you spend   if you spend
if he (she, it) spend   if they spend

Past if I spent   if we spent
if you spent   if you spent
if he (she, it) spent   if they spent

Fut. if I should spend   if we should spend
if you should spend   if you should spend
if he (she, it) should spend   if they should spend

Infinitive: to be spent   *Present Participle:* being spent
Perfect Infinitive: to have been spent   *Past Participle:* been spent

INDICATIVE MOOD

Pres.	I am spent	we are spent
	you are spent	you are spent
	he (she, it) is spent	they are spent
Pres.	I am being spent	we are being spent
Prog.	you are being spent	you are being spent
	he (she, it) is being spent	they are being spent
Pres.	I do get spent	we do get spent
Int.	you do get spent	you do get spent
	he (she, it) does get spent	they do get spent
Fut.	I shall be spent	we shall be spent
	you will be spent	you will be spent
	he (she, it) will be spent	they will be spent
Fut.	I will be spent *(P)*	we will be spent *(P)*
	you shall be spent *(C)*	you shall be spent *(C)*
	he (she, it) shall be spent *(C)*	they shall be spent *(C)*
Past	I was spent	we were spent
	you were spent	you were spent
	he (she, it) was spent	they were spent
Past	I was being spent	we were being spent
Prog.	you were being spent	you were being spent
	he (she, it) was being spent	they were being spent
Past	I did get spent	we did get spent
Int.	you did get spent	you did get spent
	he (she, it) did get spent	they did get spent
Pres.	I have been spent	we have been spent
Perf.	you have been spent	you have been spent
	he (she, it) has been spent	they have been spent
Past	I had been spent	we had been spent
Perf.	you had been spent	you had been spent
	he (she, it) had been spent	they had been spent
Fut.	I shall have been spent	we shall have been spent
Perf.	you will have been spent	you will have been spent
	he (she, it) will have been spent	they will have been spent

IMPERATIVE MOOD
be spent

SUBJUNCTIVE MOOD

Pres.	if I be spent	if we be spent
	if you be spent	if you be spent
	if he (she, it) be spent	if they be spent
Past	if I were spent	if we were spent
	if you were spent	if you were spent
	if he (she, it) were spent	if they were spent
Fut.	if I should be spent	if we should be spent
	if you should be spent	if you should be spent
	if he (she, it) should be spent	if they should be spent

to spin (active voice)   *Principal Parts:* spin, spinning, spun, spun

Infinitive: to spin   *Present Participle:* spinning
Perfect Infinitive: to have spun   *Past Participle:* spun

INDICATIVE MOOD

Pres.	I spin	we spin
	you spin	you spin
	he (she, it) spins	they spin
Pres.	I am spinning	we are spinning
Prog.	you are spinning	you are spinning
	he (she, it) is spinning	they are spinning
Pres.	I do spin	we do spin
Int.	you do spin	you do spin
	he (she, it) does spin	they do spin
Fut.	I shall spin	we shall spin
	you will spin	you will spin
	he (she, it) will spin	they will spin
Fut.	I will spin *(P)*	we will spin *(P)*
	you shall spin *(C)*	you shall spin *(C)*
	he (she, it) shall spin *(C)*	they shall spin *(C)*
Past	I spun	we spun
	you spun	you spun
	he (she, it) spun	they spun
Past	I was spinning	we were spinning
Prog.	you were spinning	you were spinning
	he (she, it) was spinning	they were spinning
Past	I did spin	we did spin
Int.	you did spin	you did spin
	he (she, it) did spin	they did spin
Pres.	I have spun	we have spun
Perf.	you have spun	you have spun
	he (she, it) has spun	they have spun
Past	I had spun	we had spun
Perf.	you had spun	you had spun
	he (she, it) had spun	they had spun
Fut.	I shall have spun	we shall have spun
Perf.	you will have spun	you will have spun
	he (she, it) will have spun	they will have spun

IMPERATIVE MOOD
spin

SUBJUNCTIVE MOOD

Pres.	if I spin	if we spin
	if you spin	if you spin
	if he (she, it) spin	if they spin
Past	if I spin	if we spin
	if you spin	if you spin
	if he (she, it) spin	if they spin
Fut.	if I should spin	if we should spin
	if you should spin	if you should spin
	if he (she, it) should spin	if they should spin

318

Infinitive: to be spun   *Present Participle:* being spun
Perfect Infinitive: to have been spun   *Past Participle:* been spun

INDICATIVE MOOD

Pres.	I am spun	we are spun
	you are spun	you are spun
	he (she, it) is spun	they are spun
Pres.	I am being spun	we are being spun
Prog.	you are being spun	you are being spun
	he (she, it) is being spun	they are being spun
Pres.	I do get spun	we do get spun
Int.	you do get spun	you do get spun
	he (she, it) does get spun	they do get spun
Fut.	I shall be spun	we shall be spun
	you will be spun	you will be spun
	he (she, it) will be spun	they will be spun
Fut.	I will be spun *(P)*	we will be spun *(P)*
	you shall be spun *(C)*	you shall be spun *(C)*
	he (she, it) shall be spun *(C)*	they shall be spun *(C)*
Past	I was spun	we were spun
	you were spun	you were spun
	he (she, it) was spun	they were spun
Past	I was being spun	we were being spun
Prog.	you were being spun	you were being spun
	he (she, it) was being spun	they were being spun
Past	I did get spun	we did get spun
Int.	you did get spun	you did get spun
	he (she, it) did get spun	they did get spun
Pres.	I have been spun	we have been spun
Perf.	you have been spun	you have been spun
	he (she, it) has been spun	they have been spun
Past	I had been spun	we had been spun
Perf.	you had been spun	you had been spun
	he (she, it) had been spun	they had been spun
Fut.	I shall have been spun	we shall have been spun
Perf.	you will have been spun	you will have been spun
	he (she, it) will have been spun	they will have been spun

IMPERATIVE MOOD
be spun

SUBJUNCTIVE MOOD

Pres.	if I be spun	if we be spun
	if you be spun	if you be spun
	if he (she, it) be spun	if they be spun
Past	if I were spun	if we were spun
	if you were spun	if you were spun
	if he (she, it) were spun	if they were spun
Fut.	if I should be spun	if we should be spun
	if you should be spun	if you should be spun
	if he (she, it) should be spun	if they should be spun

to spring (active voice)   *Principal Parts:* spring, springing, sprang
(sprung), sprung

Infinitive: to spring   *Present Participle:* springing
Perfect Infinitive: to have sprung   *Past Participle:* sprung

INDICATIVE MOOD

Pres.	I spring	we spring
	you spring	you spring
	he (she, it) springs	they spring
Pres.	I am springing	we are springing
Prog.	you are springing	you are springing
	he (she, it) is springing	they are springing
Pres.	I do spring	we do spring
Int.	you do spring	you do spring
	he (she, it) does spring	they do spring
Fut.	I shall spring	we shall spring
	you will spring	you will spring
	he (she, it) will spring	they will spring
Fut.	I will spring *(P)*	we will spring *(P)*
	you shall spring *(C)*	you shall spring *(C)*
	he (she, it) shall spring *(C)*	they shall spring *(C)*
Past	I sprang, sprung	we sprang, sprung
	you sprang, sprung	you sprang, sprung
	he (she, it) sprang, sprung	they sprang, sprung
Past	I was springing	we were springing
Prog.	you were springing	you were springing
	he (she, it) was springing	they were springing
Past	I did spring	we did spring
Int.	you did spring	you did spring
	he (she, it) did spring	they did spring
Pres.	I have sprung	we have sprung
Perf.	you have sprung	you have sprung
	he (she, it) has sprung	they have sprung
Past	I had sprung	we had sprung
Perf.	you had sprung	you had sprung
	he (she, it) had sprung	they had sprung
Fut.	I shall have sprung	we shall have sprung
Perf.	you will have sprung	you will have sprung
	he (she, it) will have sprung	they will have sprung

IMPERATIVE MOOD
spring

SUBJUNCTIVE MOOD

Pres.	if I spring	if we spring
	if you spring	if you spring
	if he (she, it) spring	if they spring
Past	if I sprang, sprung	if we sprang, sprung
	if you sprang, sprung	if you sprang, sprung
	if he (she, it) sprang, sprung	if they sprang, sprung
Fut.	if I should spring	if we should spring
	if you should spring	if you should spring
	if he (she, it) should spring	if they should spring

Infinitive: to be sprung   *Present Participle:* being sprung
Perfect Infinitive: to have been sprung   *Past Participle:* been sprung

INDICATIVE MOOD

Pres.	I am sprung you are sprung he (she, it) is sprung	we are sprung you are sprung they are sprung
Pres. *Prog.*	I am being sprung you are being sprung he (she, it) is being sprung	we are being sprung you are being sprung they are being sprung
Pres. *Int.*	I do get sprung you do sprung he (she, it) does get sprung	we do get sprung you do get sprung they do get sprung
Fut.	I shall be sprung you will be sprung he (she, it) will be sprung	we shall be sprung you will be sprung they will be sprung
Fut.	I will be sprung *(P)* you shall be sprung *(C)* he (she, it) shall be sprung *(C)*	we will be sprung *(P)* you shall be sprung *(C)* they shall be sprung *(C)*
Past	I was sprung you were sprung he (she, it) was sprung	we were sprung you were sprung they were sprung
Past *Prog.*	I was being sprung you were being sprung he (she, it) was being sprung	we were being sprung you were being sprung they were being sprung
Past *Int.*	I did get sprung you did get sprung he (she, it) did get sprung	we did get sprung you did get sprung they did get sprung
Pres. *Perf.*	I have been sprung you have been sprung he (she, it) has been sprung	we have been sprung you have been sprung they have been sprung
Past *Perf.*	I had been sprung you had been sprung he (she, it) had been sprung	we had been sprung you had been sprung they had been sprung
Fut. *Perf.*	I shall have been sprung you will have been sprung he (she, it) will have been sprung	we shall have been sprung you will have been sprung they will have been sprung

IMPERATIVE MOOD
be sprung

SUBJUNCTIVE MOOD

Pres.	if I be sprung if you be sprung if he (she, it) be sprung	if we be sprung if you be sprung if they be sprung
Past	if I were sprung if you were sprung if he (she, it) were sprung	if we were sprung if you were sprung if they were sprung
Fut.	if I should be sprung if you should be sprung if he (she, it) should be sprung	if we should be sprung if you should be sprung if they should be sprung

to steal (active voice)   *Principal Parts:* steal, stealing, stole, stolen

Infinitive: to steal   *Present Participle:* stealing
Perfect Infinitive: to have stolen   *Past Participle:* stolen

INDICATIVE MOOD

Pres.	I steal	we steal
	you steal	you steal
	he (she, it) steals	they steal
Pres.	I am stealing	we are stealing
Prog.	you are stealing	you are stealing
	he (she, it) is stealing	they are stealing
Pres.	I do steal	we do steal
Int.	you do steal	you do steal
	he (she, it) does steal	they do steal
Fut.	I shall steal	we shall steal
	you will steal	you will steal
	he (she, it) will steal	they will steal
Fut.	I will steal *(P)*	we will steal *(P)*
	you shall steal *(C)*	you shall steal *(C)*
	he (she, it) shall steal *(C)*	they shall steal *(C)*
Past	I stole	we stole
	you stole	you stole
	he (she, it) stole	they stole
Past	I was stealing	we were stealing
Prog.	you were stealing	you were stealing
	he (she, it) was stealing	they were stealing
Past	I did steal	we did steal
Int.	you did steal	you did steal
	he (she, it) did steal	they did steal
Pres.	I have stolen	we have stolen
Perf.	you have stolen	you have stolen
	he (she, it) has stolen	they have stolen
Past	I had stolen	we had stolen
Perf.	you had stolen	you had stolen
	he (she, it) had stolen	they had stolen
Fut.	I shall have stolen	we shall have stolen
Perf.	you will have stolen	you will have stolen
	he (she, it) will have stolen	they will have stolen

IMPERATIVE MOOD
steal

SUBJUNCTIVE MOOD

Pres.	if I steal	if we steal
	if you steal	if you steal
	if he (she, it) steal	if they steal
Past	if I stole	if we stole
	if you stole	if you stole
	if he (she, it) stole	if they stole
Fut.	if I should steal	if we should steal
	if you should steal	if you should steal
	if he (she, it) should steal	if they should steal

Infinitive: to be stolen   *Present Participle:* being stolen
Perfect Infinitive: to have been stolen   *Past Participle:* been stolen

INDICATIVE MOOD

Pres.	I am stolen	we are stolen
	you are stolen	you are stolen
	he (she, it) is stolen	they are stolen
Pres.	I am being stolen	we are being stolen
Prog.	you are being stolen	you are being stolen
	he (she, it) is being stolen	they are being stolen
Pres.	I do get stolen	we do get stolen
Int.	you do get stolen	you do get stolen
	he (she, it) does get stolen	they do get stolen
Fut.	I shall be stolen	we shall be stolen
	you will be stolen	you will be stolen
	he (she, it) will be stolen	they will be stolen
Fut.	I will be stolen *(P)*	we will be stolen *(P)*
	you shall be stolen *(C)*	you shall be stolen *(C)*
	he (she, it) shall be stolen *(C)*	they shall be stolen *(C)*
Past	I was stolen	we were stolen
	you were stolen	you were stolen
	he (she, it) was stolen	they were stolen
Past	I was being stolen	we were being stolen
Prog.	you were being stolen	you were being stolen
	he (she, it) was being stolen	they were being stolen
Past	I did get stolen	we did get stolen
Int.	you did get stolen	you did get stolen
	he (she, it) did get stolen	they did get stolen
Pres.	I have been stolen	we have been stolen
Perf.	you have been stolen	you have been stolen
	he (she, it) has been stolen	they have been stolen
Past	I had been stolen	we had been stolen
Perf.	you had been stolen	you had been stolen
	he (she, it) had been stolen	they had been stolen
Fut.	I shall have been stolen	we shall have been stolen
Perf.	you will have been stolen	you will have been stolen
	he (she, it) will have been stolen	they will have been stolen

IMPERATIVE MOOD
be stolen

SUBJUNCTIVE MOOD

Pres.	if I be stolen	if we be stolen
	if you be stolen	if you be stolen
	if he (she, it) be stolen	if they be stolen
Past	if I were stolen	if we were stolen
	if you were stolen	if you were stolen
	if he (she, it) were stolen	if they were stolen
Fut.	if I should be stolen	if we should be stolen
	if you should be stolen	if you should be stolen
	if he (she, it) should be stolen	if they should be stolen

Infinitive: to stick   *Present Participle:* sticking
Perfect Infinitive: to have stuck   *Past Participle:* stuck

INDICATIVE MOOD

Pres.	I stick	we stick
	you stick	you stick
	he (she, it) sticks	they stick

Pres. Prog.	I am sticking	we are sticking
	you are sticking	you are sticking
	he (she, it) is sticking	they are sticking

Pres. Int.	I do stick	we do stick
	you do stick	you do stick
	he (she, it) does stick	they do stick

Fut.	I shall stick	we shall stick
	you will stick	you will stick
	he (she, it) will stick	they will stick

Fut.	I will stick *(P)*	we will stick *(P)*
	you shall stick *(C)*	you shall stick *(C)*
	he (she, it) shall stick *(C)*	they shall stick *(C)*

Past	I stuck	we stuck
	you stuck	you stuck
	he (she, it) stuck	they stuck

Past Prog.	I was sticking	we were sticking
	you were sticking	you were sticking
	he (she, it) was sticking	they were sticking

Past Int.	I did stick	we did stick
	you did stick	you did stick
	he (she, it) did stick	they did stick

Pres. Perf.	I have stuck	we have stuck
	you have stuck	you have stuck
	he (she, it) has stuck	they have stuck

Past Perf.	I had stuck	we had stuck
	you had stuck	you had stuck
	he (she, it) had stuck	they had stuck

Fut. Perf.	I shall have stuck	we shall have stuck
	you will have stuck	you will have stuck
	he (she, it) will have stuck	they will have stuck

IMPERATIVE MOOD
stick

SUBJUNCTIVE MOOD

Pres.	if I stick	if we stick
	if you stick	if you stick
	if he (she, it) stick	if they stick

Past	if I stuck	if we stuck
	if you stuck	if you stuck
	if he (she, it) stuck	if they stuck

Fut.	if I should stick	if we should stick
	if you should stick	if you should stick
	if he (she, it) should stick	if they should stick

Infinitive: to be stuck　　　　　　　　　　*Present Participle:* being stuck
Perfect Infinitive: to have been stuck　　　　*Past Participle:* been stuck

INDICATIVE MOOD

Pres.	I am stuck	we are stuck
	you are stuck	you are stuck
	he (she, it) is stuck	they are stuck
Pres. *Prog.*	I am being stuck	we are being stuck
	you are being stuck	you are being stuck
	he (she, it) is being stuck	they are being stuck
Pres. *Int.*	I do get stuck	we do get stuck
	you do get stuck	you do get stuck
	he (she, it) does get stuck	they do get stuck
Fut.	I shall be stuck	we shall be stuck
	you will be stuck	you will be stuck
	he (she, it) will be stuck	they will be stuck
Fut.	I will be stuck *(P)*	we will be stuck *(P)*
	you shall be stuck *(C)*	you shall be stuck *(C)*
	he (she, it) shall be stuck *(C)*	they shall be stuck *(C)*
Past	I was stuck	we were stuck
	you were stuck	you were stuck
	he (she, it) was stuck	they were stuck
Past *Prog.*	I was being stuck	we were being stuck
	you were being stuck	you were being stuck
	he (she, it) was being stuck	they were being stuck
Past *Int.*	I did get stuck	we did get stuck
	you did get stuck	you did get stuck
	he (she, it) did get stuck	they did get stuck
Pres. *Perf.*	I have been stuck	we have been stuck
	you have been stuck	you have been stuck
	he (she, it) has been stuck	they have been stuck
Past *Perf.*	I had been stuck	we had been stuck
	you had been stuck	you had been stuck
	he (she, it) had been stuck	they had been stuck
Fut. *Perf.*	I shall have been stuck	we shall have been stuck
	you will have been stuck	you will have been stuck
	he (she, it) will have been stuck	they will have been stuck

IMPERATIVE MOOD
be stuck

SUBJUNCTIVE MOOD

Pres.	if I be stuck	if we be stuck
	if you be stuck	if you be stuck
	if he (she, it) be stuck	if they be stuck
Past	if I were stuck	if we were stuck
	if you were stuck	if you were stuck
	if he (she, it) were stuck	if they were stuck
Fut.	if I should be stuck	if we should be stuck
	if you should be stuck	if you should be stuck
	if he (she, it) should be stuck	if they should be stuck

to sting (active voice)

Principal Parts: sting, stung, stinging, stung

Infinitive: to sting *Perfect Infinitive:* to have stung

Present Participle: stinging *Past Participle:* stung

INDICATIVE MOOD

Pres.	I sting	we sting
	you sting	you sting
	he (she, it) stings	they sting
Pres. Prog.	I am stinging	we are stinging
	you are stinging	you are stinging
	he (she, it) is stinging	they are stinging
Pres. Int.	I do sting	we do sting
	you do sting	you do sting
	he (she, it) does sting	they do sting
Fut.	I shall sting	we shall sting
	you will sting	you will sting
	he (she, it) will sting	they will sting
Fut.	I will sting (P)	we will sting (P)
	you shall sting (C)	you shall sting (C)
	he (she, it) shall sting (C)	they shall sting (C)
Past	I stung	we stung
	you stung	you stung
	he (she, it) stung	they stung
Past Prog.	I was stinging	we were stinging
	you were stinging	you were stinging
	he (she, it) was stinging	they were stinging
Past Int.	I did sting	we did sting
	you did sting	you did sting
	he (she, it) did sting	they did sting
Pres. Perf.	I have stung	we have stung
	you have stung	you have stung
	he (she, it) has stung	they have stung
Past Perf.	I had stung	we had stung
	you had stung	you had stung
	he (she, it) had stung	they had stung
Fut. Perf.	I shall have stung	we shall have stung
	you will have stung	you will have stung
	he (she, it) will have stung	they will have stung

IMPERATIVE MOOD

sting

SUBJUNCTIVE MOOD

Pres.	if I sting	if we sting
	if you sting	if you sting
	if he (she, it) sting	if they sting
Past	if I stung	if we stung
	if you stung	if you stung
	if he (she, it) stung	if they stung
Fut.	if I should sting	if we should sting
	if you should sting	if you should sting
	if he (she, it) should sting	if they should sting

Infinitive: to be stung   *Present Participle:* being stung
Perfect Infinitive: to have been stung   *Past Participle:* been stung

INDICATIVE MOOD

Pres.	I am stung	we are stung
	you are stung	you are stung
	he (she, it) is stung	they are stung
Pres.	I am being stung	we are being stung
Prog.	you are being stung	you are being stung
	he (she, it) is being stung	they are being stung
Pres.	I do get stung	we do get stung
Int.	you do get stung	you do get stung
	he (she, it) does get stung	they do get stung
Fut.	I shall be stung	we shall be stung
	you will be stung	you will be stung
	he (she, it) will be stung	they will be stung
Fut.	I will be stung *(P)*	we will be stung *(P)*
	you shall be stung *(C)*	you shall be stung *(C)*
	he (she, it) shall be stung *(C)*	they shall be stung *(C)*
Past	I was stung	we were stung
	you were stung	you were stung
	he (she, it) was stung	they were stung
Past	I was being stung	we were being stung
Prog.	you were being stung	you were being stung
	he (she, it) was being stung	they were being stung
Past	I did get stung	we did get stung
Int.	you did get stung	you did get stung
	he (she, it) did get stung	they did get stung
Pres.	I have been stung	we have been stung
Perf.	you have been stung	you have been stung
	he (she, it) has been stung	they have been stung
Past	I had been stung	we had been stung
Perf.	you had been stung	you had been stung
	he (she, it) had been stung	they had been stung
Fut.	I shall have been stung	we shall have been stung
Perf.	you will have been stung	you will have been stung
	he (she, it) will have been stung	they will have been stung

IMPERATIVE MOOD
be stung

SUBJUNCTIVE MOOD

Pres.	if I be stung	if we be stung
	if you be stung	if you be stung
	if he (she, it) be stung	if they be stung
Past	if I were stung	if we were stung
	if you were stung	if you were stung
	if he (she, it) were stung	if they were stung
Fut.	if I should be stung	if we should be stung
	if you should be stung	if you should be stung
	if he (she, it) should be stung	if they should be stung

to stride

Principal Parts: stride, striding, strode, stridden

Infinitive: to stride
Perfect Infinitive: to have stridden

Present Participle: striding
Past Participle: stridden

INDICATIVE MOOD

Pres.	I stride	we stride
	you stride	you stride
	he (she, it) strides	they stride
Pres. Prog.	I am striding	we are striding
	you are striding	you are striding
	he (she, it) is striding	they are striding
Pres. Int.	I do stride	we do stride
	you do stride	you do stride
	he (she, it) does stride	they do stride
Fut.	I shall stride	we shall stride
	you will stride	you will stride
	he (she, it) will stride	they will stride
Fut.	I will stride *(P)*	we will stride *(P)*
	you shall stride *(C)*	you shall stride *(C)*
	he (she, it) shall stride *(C)*	they shall stride *(C)*
Past	I strode	we strode
	you strode	you strode
	he (she, it) strode	they strode
Past Prog.	I was striding	we were striding
	you were striding	you were striding
	he (she, it) was striding	they were striding
Past Int.	I did stride	we did stride
	you did stride	you did stride
	he (she, it) did stride	they did stride
Pres. Perf.	I have stridden	we have stridden
	you have stridden	you have stridden
	he (she, it) has stridden	they have stridden
Past Perf.	I had stridden	we had stridden
	you had stridden	you had stridden
	he (she, it) had stridden	they had stridden
Fut. Perf.	I shall have stridden	we shall have stridden
	you will have stridden	you will have stridden
	he (she, it) will have stridden	they will have stridden

IMPERATIVE MOOD
stride

SUBJUNCTIVE MOOD

Pres.	if I stride	if we stride
	if you stride	if you stride
	if he (she, it) stride	if they stride
Past	if I strode	if we strode
	if you strode	if you strode
	if he (she, it) strode	if they strode
Fut.	if I should stride	if we should stride
	if you should stride	if you should stride
	if he (she, it) should stride	if they should stride

To stride is an intransitive verb.

It does not take an object.

It describes action, but the action is self-contained.

Like other intransitive verbs, it may be followed by adverbs, adverbial phrases and clauses describing the how, why, when, and where of the action:

HOW: The giant strode *mightily*. (adverb)

WHY: He was striding *to impress people with his vitality*. (adverbial phrase)

WHEN: Mephistopheles strode *when he left Arcadia to return to German soil*. (adverbial clause)

WHERE: I shall stride *into the room*. (adverbial phrase)

to strike (active voice)

Infinitive: to strike   *Present Participle:* striking
Perfect Infinitive: to have struck, stricken   *Past Participle:* struck, stricken

INDICATIVE MOOD

Pres. I strike	we strike
you strike	you strike
he (she, it) strikes	they strike
Pres. I am striking	we are striking
Prog. you are striking	you are striking
he (she, it) is striking	they are striking
Pres. I do strike	we do strike
Int. you do strike	you do strike
he (she, it) does strike	they do strike
Fut. I shall strike	we shall strike
you will strike	you will strike
he (she, it) will strike	they will strike
Fut. I will strike *(P)*	we will strike *(P)*
you shall strike *(C)*	you shall strike *(C)*
he (she, it) shall strike *(C)*	they shall strike *(C)*
Past I struck	we struck
you struck	you struck
he (she, it) struck	they struck
Past I was striking	we were striking
Prog. you were striking	you were striking
he (she, it) was striking	they were striking
Past I did strike	we did strike
Int. you did strike	you did strike
he (she, it) did strike	they did strike
Pres. I have struck, stricken	we have struck, stricken
Perf. you have struck, stricken	you have struck, stricken
he (she, it) has struck, stricken	they have struck, stricken
Past I had struck, stricken	we had struck, stricken
Perf. you had struck, stricken	you had struck, stricken
he (she, it) had struck, stricken	they had struck, stricken
Fut. I shall have struck, stricken	we shall have struck, stricken
Perf. you will have struck, stricken	you will have struck, stricken
he (she, it) will have struck, stricken	they will have struck, stricken

IMPERATIVE MOOD
strike

SUBJUNCTIVE MOOD

Pres. if I strike	if we strike
if you strike	if you strike
if he (she, it) strike	if they strike
Past if I struck	if we struck
if you struck	if you struck
if he (she, it) struck	if they struck
Fut. if I should strike	if we should strike
if you should strike	if you should strike
if he (she, it) should strike	if they should strike

Infinitive: to be struck, stricken
Perfect Infinitive: to have been struck, stricken
Present Participle: being struck, stricken
Past Participle: struck, stricken

INDICATIVE MOOD

Pres.	I am struck, stricken	we are struck, stricken
	you are struck, stricken	you are struck, stricken
	he (she, it) is struck, stricken	they are struck, stricken
Pres.	I am being struck, stricken	we are being struck, stricken
Prog.	you are being struck, stricken	you are being struck, stricken
	he (she, it) is being struck, stricken	they are being struck, stricken
Pres.	I do get struck, stricken	we do get struck, stricken
Int.	you do get struck, stricken	you do get struck, stricken
	he (she, it) does get struck, stricken	they do get struck, stricken
Fut.	I shall be struck, stricken	we shall be struck, stricken
	you will be struck, stricken	you will be struck, stricken
	he (she, it) will be struck, stricken	they will be struck, stricken
Fut.	I will be struck, stricken *(P)*	we will be struck, stricken *(P)*
	you shall be struck, stricken *(C)*	you shall be struck, stricken *(C)*
	he (she, it) shall be struck, stricken *(C)*	they shall be struck, stricken *(C)*
Past	I was struck, stricken	we were struck, stricken
	you were struck, stricken	you were struck, stricken
	he (she, it) was struck, stricken	they were struck, stricken
Past	I was being struck, stricken	we were being struck, stricken
Prog.	you were being struck, stricken	you were being struck, stricken
	he (she, it) was being struck, stricken	they were being struck, stricken
Past	I did get struck, stricken	we did get struck, stricken
Int.	you did get struck, stricken	you did get struck, stricken
	he (she, it) did get struck, stricken	they did get struck, stricken
Pres.	I have been struck, stricken	we have been struck, stricken
Perf.	you have been struck, stricken	you have been struck, stricken
	he (she, it) has been struck, stricken	they have been struck, stricken
Past	I had been struck, stricken	we had been struck, stricken
Perf.	you had been struck, stricken	you had been struck, stricken
	he (she, it) had been struck, stricken	they had been struck, stricken
Fut.	I shall have been struck, stricken	we shall have been struck, stricken
Perf.	you will have been struck, stricken	you will have been struck, stricken
	he (she, it) will have been struck, stricken	they will have been struck, stricken

IMPERATIVE MOOD
be struck

SUBJUNCTIVE MOOD

Pres. if I be struck, stricken   if we be struck, stricken
if you be struck, stricken   if you be struck, stricken
if he (she, it) be struck, stricken   if they be struck, stricken

Past if I were struck, stricken   if we were struck, stricken
if you were struck, stricken   if you were struck, stricken
if he (she, it) were struck, stricken   if they were struck, stricken

Fut. if I should be struck, stricken   if we should be struck, stricken
if you should be struck, stricken   if you should be struck, stricken
if he (she, it) should be struck,   if they should be struck, stricken
stricken

Infinitive: to strive   *Present Participle:* striving
Perfect Infinitive: to have striven   *Past Participle:* striven

INDICATIVE MOOD

Pres.	I strive	we strive
	you strive	you strive
	he (she, it) strives	they strive
Pres.	I am striving	we are striving
Prog.	you are striving	you are striving
	he (she, it) is striving	they are striving
Pres.	I do strive	we do strive
Int.	you do strive	you do strive
	he (she, it) does strive	they do strive
Fut.	I shall strive	we shall strive
	you will strive	you will strive
	he (she, it) will strive	they will strive
Fut.	I will strive *(P)*	we will strive *(P)*
	you shall strive *(C)*	you shall strive *(C)*
	he (she, it) shall strive *(C)*	they shall strive *(C)*
Past	I strove	we strove
	you strove	you strove
	he (she, it) strove	they strove
Past	I was striving	we were striving
Prog.	you were striving	you were striving
	he (she, it) was striving	they were striving
Past	I did strive	we did strive
Int.	you did strive	you did strive
	he (she, it) did strive	they did strive
Pres.	I have striven	we have striven
Perf.	you have striven	you have striven
	he (she, it) has striven	they have striven
Past	I had striven	we had striven
Perf.	you had striven	you had striven
	he (she, it) had striven	they had striven
Fut.	I shall have striven	we shall have striven
Perf.	you will have striven	you will have striven
	he (she, it) will have striven	they will have striven

IMPERATIVE MOOD
strive

SUBJUNCTIVE MOOD

Pres.	if I strive	if we strive
	if you strive	if you strive
	if he (she, it) strive	if they strive
Past	if I strove	if we strove
	if you strove	if you strove
	if he (she, it) strove	if they strove
Fut.	if I should strive	if we should strive
	if you should strive	if you should strive
	if he (she, it) should strive	if they should strive

to swear (active voice)   *Principal Parts:* swear, swearing, swore, sworn

Infinitive: to swear   *Present Participle:* swearing
Perfect Infinitive: to have sworn   *Past Participle:* sworn

INDICATIVE MOOD

Pres.	I swear	we swear
	you swear	you swear
	he (she, it) swears	they swear

Pres. Prog.	I am swearing	we are swearing
	you are swearing	you are swearing
	he (she, it) is swearing	they are swearing

Pres. Int.	I do swear	we do swear
	you do swear	you do swear
	he (she, it) does swear	they do swear

Fut.	I shall swear	we shall swear
	you will swear	you will swear
	he (she, it) will swear	they will swear

Fut.	I will swear *(P)*	we will swear *(P)*
	you shall swear *(C)*	you shall swear *(C)*
	he (she, it) shall swear *(C)*	they shall swear *(C)*

Past	I swore	we swore
	you swore	you swore
	he (she, it) swore	they swore

Past Prog.	I was swearing	we were swearing
	you were swearing	you were swearing
	he (she, it) was swearing	they were swearing

Past Int.	I did swear	we did swear
	you did swear	you did swear
	he (she, it) did swear	they did swear

Pres. Perf.	I have sworn	we have sworn
	you have sworn	you have sworn
	he (she, it) has sworn	they have sworn

Past Perf.	I had sworn	we had sworn
	you had sworn	you had sworn
	he (she, it) had sworn	they had sworn

Fut. Perf.	I shall have sworn	we shall have sworn
	you will have sworn	you will have sworn
	he (she, it) will have sworn	they will have sworn

IMPERATIVE MOOD
swear

SUBJUNCTIVE MOOD

Pres.	if I swear	if we swear
	if you swear	if you swear
	if he (she, it) swear	if they swear

Past	if I swore	if we swore
	if you swore	if you swore
	if he (she, it) swore	if they swore

Fut.	if I should swear	if we should swear
	if you should swear	if you should swear
	if he (she, it) should swear	if they should swear

Infinitive: to be sworn   *Present Participle:* being sworn
Perfect Infinitive: to have been sworn   *Past Participle:* been sworn

INDICATIVE MOOD

Pres. I am sworn	we are sworn
you are sworn	you are sworn
he (she, it) is sworn	they are sworn
Pres. I am being sworn	we are being sworn
Prog. you are being sworn	you are being sworn
he (she, it) is being sworn	they are being sworn
Pres. I do get sworn	we do get sworn
Int. you do get sworn	you do get sworn
he (she, it) does get sworn	they do get sworn
Fut. I shall be sworn	we shall be sworn
you will be sworn	you will be sworn
he (she, it) will be sworn	they will be sworn
Fut. I will be sworn *(P)*	we will be sworn *(P)*
you shall be sworn *(C)*	you shall be sworn *(C)*
he (she, it) shall be sworn *(C)*	they shall be sworn *(C)*
Past I was sworn	we were sworn
you were sworn	you were sworn
he (she, it) was sworn	they were sworn
Past I was being sworn	we were being sworn
Prog. you were being sworn	you were being sworn
he (she, it) was being sworn	they were being sworn
Past I did get sworn	we did get sworn
Int. you did get sworn	you did get sworn
he (she, it) did get sworn	they did get sworn
Pres. I have been sworn	we have been sworn
Perf. you have been sworn	you have been sworn
he (she, it) has been sworn	they have been sworn
Past I had been sworn	we had been sworn
Perf. you had been sworn	you had been sworn
he (she, it) had been sworn	they had been sworn
Fut. I shall have been sworn	we shall have been sworn
Perf. you will have been sworn	you will have been sworn
he (she, it) will have been sworn	they will have been sworn

IMPERATIVE MOOD
be sworn

SUBJUNCTIVE MOOD

Pres. if I be sworn	if we be sworn
if you be sworn	if you be sworn
if he (she, it) be sworn	if they be sworn
Past if I were sworn	if we were sworn
if you were sworn	if you were sworn
if he (she, it) were sworn	if they were sworn
Fut if I should be sworn	if we should be sworn
if you should be sworn	if you should be sworn
if he (she, it) should be sworn	if they should be sworn

to sweat (active voice)   *Principal Parts:* sweat, sweating, sweat
                                      (sweated), sweated

Infinitive: to sweat   *Present Participle:* sweating
Perfect Infinitive: to have sweated   *Past Participle:* sweated

INDICATIVE MOOD

Pres.	I sweat	we sweat
	you sweat	you sweat
	he (she, it) sweats	they sweat
Pres. Prog.	I am sweating	we are sweating
	you are sweating	you are sweating
	he (she, it) is sweating	they are sweating
Pres. Int.	I do sweat	we do sweat
	you do sweat	you do sweat
	he (she, it) does sweat	they do sweat
Fut.	I shall sweat	we shall sweat
	you will sweat	you will sweat
	he (she, it) will sweat	they will sweat
Fut.	I will sweat *(P)*	we will sweat *(P)*
	you shall sweat *(C)*	you shall sweat *(C)*
	he (she, it) shall sweat *(C)*	they shall sweat *(C)*
Past	I sweat, sweated	we sweat, sweated
	you sweat, sweated	you sweat, sweated
	he (she, it) sweat, sweated	they sweat, sweated
Past Prog.	I was sweating	we were sweating
	you were sweating	you were sweating
	he (she, it) was sweating	they were sweating
Past Int.	I did sweat	we did sweat
	you did sweat	you did sweat
	he (she, it) did sweat	they did sweat
Pres. Perf.	I have sweated	we have sweated
	you have sweated	you have sweated
	he (she, it) has sweated	they have sweated
Past Perf.	I had sweated	we had sweated
	you had sweated	you had sweated
	he (she, it) had	they had sweated
Fut. Perf.	I shall have sweated	we shall have sweated
	you will have sweated	you will have sweated
	he (she, it) will have sweated	they will have sweated

IMPERATIVE MOOD
sweat

SUBJUNCTIVE MOOD

Pres.	if I sweat	if we sweat
	if you sweat	if you sweat
	if he (she, it) sweat	if they sweat
Past	if I sweat, sweated	if we sweat, sweated
	if you sweat, sweated	if you sweat, sweated
	if he (she, it) sweat, sweated	if they sweat, sweated
Fut.	if I should sweat	if we should sweat
	if you should sweat	if you should sweat
	if he (she, it) should sweat	if they should sweat

(passive voice)

Infinitive: to be sweated *Present Participle:* being sweated
Perfect Infinitive: to have been sweated *Past Participle:* been sweated

INDICATIVE MOOD

Pres.	I am sweated	we are sweated
	you are sweated	you are sweated
	he (she, it) is sweated	they are sweated
Pres.	I am being sweated	we are being sweated
Prog.	you are being sweated	you are being sweated
	he (she, it) is being sweated	they are being sweated
Pres.	I do get sweated	we do get sweated
Int.	you do get sweated	you do get sweated
	he (she, it) does get sweated	they do get sweated
Fut.	I shall be sweated	we shall be sweated
	you will be sweated	you will be sweated
	he (she, it) will be sweated	they will be sweated
Fut.	I will be sweated *(P)*	we will be sweated *(P)*
	you shall be sweated *(C)*	you shall be sweated *(C)*
	he (she, it) shall be sweated *(C)*	they shall be sweated *(C)*
Past	I was sweated	we were sweated
	you were sweated	you were sweated
	he (she, it) was sweated	they were sweated
Past	I was being sweated	we were being sweated
Prog.	you were being sweated	you were being sweated
	he (she, it) was being sweated	they were being sweated
Past	I did get sweated	we did get sweated
Int.	you did get sweated	you did get sweated
	he (she, it) did get sweated	they did get sweated
Pres.	I have been sweated	we have been sweated
Perf.	you have been sweated	you have been sweated
	he (she, it) has been sweated	they have been sweated
Past	I had been sweated	we had been sweated
Perf.	you had been sweated	you had been sweated
	he (she, it) had been sweated	they had been sweated
Fut.	I shall have been sweated	we shall have been sweated
Perf.	you will have been sweated	you will have been sweated
	he (she, it) will have been sweated	they will have been sweated

IMPERATIVE MOOD
be sweated

SUBJUNCTIVE MOOD

Pres.	if I be sweated	if we be sweated
	if you be sweated	if you be sweated
	if he (she, it) be sweated	if they be sweated
Past	if I were sweated	if we were sweated
	if you were sweated	if you were sweated
	if he (she, it) were sweated	if they were sweated
Fut.	if I should be sweated	if we should be sweated
	if you should be sweated	if you should be sweated
	if he (she, it) should be sweated	if they should be sweated

to sweep (active voice) *Principal Parts:* sweep, sweeping, swept, swept

---

Infinitive: to sweep *Present Participle:* sweeping
Perfect Infinitive: to have swept *Past Participle:* swept

INDICATIVE MOOD

Pres.	I sweep	we sweep
	you sweep	you sweep
	he (she, it) sweeps	they sweep
Pres.	I am sweeping	we are sweeping
Prog.	you are sweeping	you are sweeping
	he (she, it) is sweeping	they are sweeping
Pres.	I do sweep	we do sweep
Int.	you do sweep	you do sweep
	he (she, it) does sweep	they do sweep
Fut.	I shall sweep	we shall sweep
	you will sweep	you will sweep
	he (she, it) will sweep	they will sweep
Fut.	I will sweep *(P)*	we will sweep *(P)*
	you shall sweep *(C)*	you shall sweep *(C)*
	he (she, it) shall sweep *(C)*	they shall sweep *(C)*
Past	I swept	we swept
	you swept	you swept
	he (she, it) swept	they swept
Past	I was sweeping	we were sweeping
Prog.	you were sweeping	you were sweeping
	he (she, it) was sweeping	they were sweeping
Past	I did sweep	we did sweep
Int.	you did sweep	you did sweep
	he (she, it) did sweep	they did sweep
Pres.	I have swept	we have swept
Perf.	you have swept	you have swept
	he (she, it) has swept	they have swept
Past	I had swept	we had swept
Perf.	you had swept	you had swept
	he (she, it) had swept	they had swept
Fut.	I shall have swept	we shall have swept
Perf.	you will have swept	you will have swept
	he (she, it) will have swept	they will have swept

IMPERATIVE MOOD
sweep

SUBJUNCTIVE MOOD

Pres.	if I sweep	if we sweep
	if you sweep	if you sweep
	if he (she, it) sweep	if they sweep
Past	if I swept	if we swept
	if you swept	if you swept
	if he (she, it) swept	if they swept
Fut.	if I should sweep	if we should sweep
	if you should sweep	if you should sweep
	if he (she, it) should sweep	if they should sweep

(passive voice)

Infinitive: to be swept   *Present Participle:* being swept
Perfect Infinitive: to have been swept   *Past Participle:* been swept

INDICATIVE MOOD

Pres.	I am swept	we are swept
	you are swept	you are swept
	he (she, it) is swept	they are swept
Pres. Prog.	I am being swept	we are being swept
	you are being swept	you are being swept
	he (she, it) is being swept	they are being swept
Pres. Int.	I do get swept	we do get swept
	you do get swept	you do get swept
	he (she, it) does get swept	they do get swept
Fut.	I shall be swept	we shall be swept
	you will be swept	you will be swept
	he (she, it) will be swept	they will be swept
Fut.	I will be swept *(P)*	we will be swept *(P)*
	you shall be swept *(C)*	you shall be swept *(C)*
	he (she, it) shall be swept *(C)*	they shall be swept *(C)*
Past	I was swept	we were swept
	you were swept	you were swept
	he (she, it) was swept	they were swept
Past Prog.	I was being swept	we were being swept
	you were being swept	you were being swept
	he (she, it) was being swept	they were being swept
Past Int.	I did get swept	we did get swept
	you did get swept	you did get swept
	he (she, it) did get swept	they did get swept
Pres. Perf.	I have been swept	we have been swept
	you have been swept	you have been swept
	he (she, it) has been swept	they have been swept
Past Perf.	I had been swept	we had been swept
	you had been swept	you had been swept
	he (she, it) had been swept	they had been swept
Fut. Perf.	I shall have been swept	we shall have been swept
	you will have been swept	you will have been swept
	he (she, it) will have been swept	they will have been swept

IMPERATIVE MOOD
be swept

SUBJUNCTIVE MOOD

Pres.	if I be swept	if we be swept
	if you be swept	if you be swept
	if he (she, it) be swept	if they be swept
Past	if I were swept	if we were swept
	if you were swept	if you were swept
	if he (she, it) were swept	if they were swept
Fut.	if I should be swept	if we should be swept
	if you should be swept	if you should be swept
	if he (she, it) should be swept	if they should be swept

to swim (active voice)　　　*Principal Parts:* swim, swimming, swam,
　　　　　　　　　　　　　　　　　　　　　　　swum

Infinitive: to swim　　　　　　　　　　*Present Participle:* swimming
Perfect Infinitive: to have swum　　　　　*Past Participle:* swum

INDICATIVE MOOD

Pres.	I swim	we swim
	you swim	you swim
	he (she, it) swims	they swim
Pres.	I am swimming	we are swimming
Prog.	you are swimming	you are swimming
	he (she, it) is swimming	they are swimming
Pres.	I do swim	we do swim
Int.	you do swim	you do swim
	he (she, it) does swim	they do swim
Fut.	I shall swim	we shall swim
	you will swim	you will swim
	he (she, it) will swim	they will swim
Fut.	I will swim *(P)*	we will swim *(P)*
	you shall swim *(C)*	you shall swim *(C)*
	he (she, it) shall swim *(C)*	they shall swim *(C)*
Past	I swam	we swam
	you swam	you swam
	he (she, it) swam	they swam
Past	I was swimming	we were swimming
Prog.	you were swimming	you were swimming
	he (she, it) was swimming	they were swimming
Past	I have swum	we have swum
Int.	you have swum	you have swum
	he (she, it) has swum	they have swum
Pres.	I have swum	we have swum
Perf.	you have swum	you have swum
	he (she, it) has swum	they have swum
Past	I had swum	we had swum
Perf.	you had swum	you had swum
	he (she, it) had swum	they had swum
Fut.	I shall have swum	we shall have swum
Perf.	you will have swum	you will have swum
	he (she, it) will have swum	they will have swum

IMPERATIVE MOOD
swim

SUBJUNCTIVE MOOD

Pres.	if I swim	if we swim
	if you swim	if you swim
	if he (she, it) swim	if they swim
Past	if I swam	if we swam
	if you swam	if you swam
	if he (she, it) swam	if they swam
Fut.	if I should swim	if we should swim
	if you should swim	if you should swim
	if he (she, it) should swim	if they should swim

Infinitive: to be swum*   *Present Participle:* being swum
Perfect Infinitive: to have been swum   *Past Participle:* been swum

INDICATIVE MOOD

Pres.	I am swum	we are swum
	you are swum	you are swum
	he (she, it) is swum	they are swum
Pres.	I am being swum	we are being swum
Prog.	you are being swum	you are being swum
	he (she, it) is being swum	they are being swum
Pres.	I do get swum	we do get swum
Int.	you do get swum	you do get swum
	he (she, it) does get swum	they do get swum
Fut.	I shall be swum	we shall be swum
	you will be swum	you will be swum
	he (she, it) will be swum	they will be swum
Fut.	I will be swum *(P)*	we will be swum *(C)*
	you shall be swum *(C)*	you shall be swum *(C)*
	he (she, it) shall be swum *(C)*	they shall be swum *(C)*
Past	I was swum	we were swum
	you were swum	you were swum
	he (she, it) was swum	they were swum
Past	I was being swum	we were being swum
Prog.	you were being swum	you were being swum
	he (she, it) was being swum	they were being swum
Past	I did get swum	we did get swum
Int.	you did get swum	you did get swum
	he (she, it) did get swum	they did get swum
Pres.	I have been swum	we have been swum
Perf.	you have been swum	you have been swum
	he (she, it) has been swum	they have been swum
Past	I had been swum	we had been swum
Perf.	you had been swum	you had been swum
	he (she, it) had been swum	they had been swum
Fut.	I shall have been swum	we shall have been swum
Perf.	you will have been swum	you will have been swum
	he (she, it) will have been swum	they will have been swum

IMPERATIVE MOOD
be swum

SUBJUNCTIVE MOOD

Pres.	if I be swum	if we be swum
	if you be swum	if you be swum
	if he (she, it) be swum	if they be swum
Past	if I were swum	if we were swum
	if you were swum	if you were swum
	if he (she, it) were swum	if they were swum
Fut.	if I should be swum	if we should be swum
	if you should be swum	if you should be swum
	if he (she, it) should be swum	if they should be swum

* Although grammatically correct, this form is rarely used.

to swing (active voice)

Principal Parts: swing, swinging, swung.

Infinitive: to swing	Perfect Infinitive: to have swung
Present Participle: swinging	Past Participle: swung

INDICATIVE MOOD

Pres.	I swing	we swing
	you swing	you swing
	he (she, it) swings	they swing
Prog. Pres.	I am swinging	we are swinging
	you are swinging	you are swinging
	he (she, it) is swinging	they are swinging
Int. Pres.	I do swing	we do swing
	you do swing	you do swing
	he (she, it) does swing	they do swing
Fut.	I shall swing	we shall swing
	you will swing	you will swing
	he (she, it) will swing	they will swing
Fut.	I will swing (P)	we will swing (P)
	you shall swing (C)	you shall swing (C)
	he (she, it) shall swing (C)	they shall swing (C)
Past	I swung	we swung
	you swung	you swung
	he (she, it) swung	they swung
Prog. Past	I was swinging	we were swinging
	you were swinging	you were swinging
	he (she, it) was swinging	they were swinging
Int. Past	I did swing	we did swing
	you did swing	you did swing
	he (she, it) did swing	they did swing
Perf. Pres.	I have swung	we have swung
	you have swung	you have swung
	he (she, it) has swung	they have swung
Perf. Past	I had swung	we had swung
	you had swung	you had swung
	he (she, it) had swung	they had swung
Perf. Fut.	I shall have swung	we shall have swung
	you will have swung	you will have swung
	he (she, it) will have swung	they will have swung

IMPERATIVE MOOD

swing

SUBJUNCTIVE MOOD

Pres.	if I swing	if we swing
	if you swing	if you swing
	if he (she, it) swing	if they swing
Past	if I swung	if we swung
	if you swung	if you swung
	if he (she, it) swung	if they swung
Fut.	if I should swing	if we should swing
	if you should swing	if you should swing
	if he (she, it) should swing	if they should swing

Infinitive: to be swung

Present Participle: being swung

Perfect Infinitive: to have been swung

Past Participle: been swung

INDICATIVE MOOD

Pres. I am swung
you are swung
he (she, it) is swung

we are swung
you are swung
they are swung

Pres.
Prog. I am being swung
you are being swung
he (she, it) is being swung

we are being swung
you are being swung
they are being swung

Pres.
Int. I do get swung
you do get swung
he (she, it) does get swung

we do get swung
you do get swung
they do get swung

Fut. I shall be swung
you will be swung
he (she, it) will be swung

we shall be swung
you will be swung
they will be swung

Fut. I will be swung *(P)*
you shall be swung *(C)*
he (she, it) shall be swung *(C)*

we will be swung *(P)*
you shall be swung *(C)*
they shall be swung *(C)*

Past I was swung
you were swung
he (she, it) was swung

we were swung
you were swung
they were swung

Past
Prog. I was being swung
you were being swung
he (she, it) was being swung

we were being swung
you were being swung
they were being swung

Past
Int. I did get swung
you did get swung
he (she, it) did get swung

we did get swung
you did get swung
they did get swung

Pres.
Perf. I have been swung
you have been swung
he (she, it) has been swung

we have been swung
you have been swung
they have been swung

Past
Perf. I had been swung
you had been swung
he (she, it) had been swung

we had been swung
you had been swung
they had been swung

Fut.
Perf. I shall have been swung
you will have been swung
he (she, it) will have been swung

we should have been swung
you will have been swung
they will have been swung

IMPERATIVE MOOD
be swung

SUBJUNCTIVE MOOD

Pres. if I be swung
if you be swung
if he (she, it) be swung

if we be swung
if you be swung
if they be swung

Past if I were swung
if you were swung
if he (she, it) were swung

if we were swung
if you were swung
if they were swung

Fut. if I should be swung
if you should be swung
if he (she, it) should be swung

if we should be swung
if you should be swung
if they should be swung

Infinitive: to take *Present Participle:* taking
Perfect Infinitive: to have taken *Past Participle:* taken

INDICATIVE MOOD

Pres.	I take	we take
	you take	you take
	he (she, it) takes	they take
Pres.	I am taking	we are taking
Prog.	you are taking	you are taking
	he (she, it) is taking	they are taking
Pres.	I do take	we do take
Int.	you do take	you do take
	he (she, it) does take	they do take
Fut.	I shall take	we shall take
	you will take	you will take
	he (she, it) will take	they will take
Fut.	I will take *(P)*	we will take *(P)*
	you shall take *(C)*	you shall take *(C)*
	he (she, it) shall take *(C)*	they shall take *(C)*
Past	I took	we took
	you took	you took
	he (she, it) took	they took
Past	I was taking	we were taking
Prog.	you were taking	you were taking
	he (she, it) was taking	they were taking
Past	I did take	we did take
Int.	you did take	you did take
	he (she, it) did take	they did take
Pres.	I have taken	we have taken
Perf.	you have taken	you have taken
	he (she, it) has taken	they have taken
Past	I had taken	we had taken
Perf.	you had taken	you had taken
	he (she, it) had taken	they had taken
Fut.	I shall have taken	we shall have taken
Perf.	you will have taken	you will have taken
	he (she, it) will have taken	they will have taken

IMPERATIVE MOOD
take

SUBJUNCTIVE MOOD

Pres.	if I take	if we take
	if you take	if you take
	if he (she, it) take	if they take
Past	if I took	if we took
	if you took	if you took
	if he (she, it) took	if they took
Fut.	if I should take	if we should take
	if you should take	if you should take
	if he (she, it) should take	if they should take

(passive voice)

Infinitive: to be taken   *Present Participle:* being taken
Perfect Infinitive: to have been taken   *Past Participle:* been taken

INDICATIVE MOOD

Pres.	I am taken	we are taken
	you are taken	you are taken
	he (she, it) is taken	they are taken
Pres.	I am being taken	we are being taken
Prog.	you are being taken	you are being taken
	he (she, it) is being taken	they are being taken
Pres.	I do get taken	we do get taken
Int.	you do get taken	you do get taken
	he (she, it) does get taken	they do get taken
Fut.	I shall be taken	we shall be taken
	you will be taken	you will be taken
	he (she, it) will be taken	they will be taken
Fut.	I will be taken *(P)*	we will be taken *(P)*
	you shall be taken *(C)*	you shall be taken *(C)*
	he (she, it) shall be taken *(C)*	they shall be taken *(C)*
Past	I was taken	we were taken
	you were taken	you were taken
	he (she, it) was taken	they were taken
Past	I was being taken	we were being taken
Prog.	you were being taken	you were being taken
	he (she, it) was being taken	they were being taken
Past	I did get taken	we did get taken
Int.	you did get taken	you did get taken
	he (she, it) did get taken	they did get taken
Pres.	I have been taken	we have been taken
Perf.	you have been taken	you have been taken
	he (she, it) has been taken	they have been taken
Past	I had been taken	we had been taken
Perf.	you had been taken	you had been taken
	he (she, it) had been taken	they had been taken
Fut.	I shall have been taken	we shall have been taken
Perf.	you will have been taken	you will have been taken
	he (she, it) will have been taken	they will have been taken

IMPERATIVE MOOD
be taken

SUBJUNCTIVE MOOD

Pres.	if I be taken	if we be taken
	if you be taken	if you be taken
	if he (she, it) be taken	if they be taken
Past	if I were taken	if we were taken
	if you were taken	if you were taken
	if he (she, it) were taken	if they were taken
Fut.	if I should be taken	if we should be taken
	if you should be taken	if you should be taken
	if he (she, it) should be taken	if they should be taken

to teach (active voice)

Principal Parts: teach, teaching, taught, taught

| *Infinitive:* to teach | *Present Participle:* teaching |
| *Perfect Infinitive:* to have taught | *Past Participle:* taught |

INDICATIVE MOOD

Pres.	I teach	we teach
	you teach	you teach
	he (she, it) teaches	they teach
Pres.	I am teaching	we are teaching
Prog.	you are teaching	you are teaching
	he (she, it) is teaching	they are teaching
Pres.	I do teach	we do teach
Int.	you do teach	you do teach
	he (she, it) does teach	they do teach
Fut.	I shall teach	we shall teach
	you will teach	you will teach
	he (she, it) will teach	they will teach
Fut.	I will teach (P)	we will teach (P)
	you will teach	you will teach
	he (she, it) shall teach (C)	they shall teach (C)
Past	I taught	we taught
	you taught	you taught
	he (she, it) taught	they taught
Past	I was teaching	we were teaching
Prog.	you were teaching	you were teaching
	he (she, it) was teaching	they were teaching
Past	I did teach	we did teach
Int.	you did teach	you did teach
	he (she, it) did teach	they did teach
Pres.	I have taught	we have taught
Perf.	you have taught	you have taught
	he (she, it) has taught	they have taught
Past	I had taught	we had taught
Perf.	you had taught	you had taught
	he (she, it) had taught	they had taught
Fut.	I shall have taught	we shall have taught
Perf.	you will have taught	you will have taught
	he (she, it) will have taught	they will have taught

IMPERATIVE MOOD

teach
teach

SUBJUNCTIVE MOOD

Pres.	if I teach	if we teach
	if you teach	if you teach
	if he (she, it) teach	if they teach
Past	if I taught	if we taught
	if you taught	if you taught
	if he (she, it) taught	if they taught
Fut.	if I should teach	if we should teach
	if you should teach	if you should teach
	if he (she, it) should teach	if they should teach

(passive voice)

Infinitive: to be taught   *Perfect Infinitive:* to have been taught

Present Participle: being taught   *Past Participle:* been taught

INDICATIVE MOOD

	Singular	Plural
Pres.	I am taught	we are taught
	you are taught	you are taught
	he (she, it) is taught	they are taught
Prog.	I am being taught	we are being taught
	you are being taught	you are being taught
	he (she, it) is being taught	they are being taught
Pres. Int.	I do get taught	we do get taught
	you do get taught	you do get taught
	he (she, it) does get taught	they do get taught
Fut.	I shall be taught	we shall be taught
	you will be taught	you will be taught
	he (she, it) will be taught	they will be taught
Fut.	I will be taught (P)	we will be taught (P)
	you shall be taught (C)	you shall be taught (C)
	he (she, it) shall be taught (C)	they shall be taught (C)
Past	I was taught	we were taught
	you were taught	you were taught
	he (she, it) was taught	they were taught
Prog.	I was being taught	we were being taught
	you were being taught	you were being taught
	he (she, it) was being taught	they were being taught
Past Int.	I did get taught	we did get taught
	you did get taught	you did get taught
	he (she, it) did get taught	they did get taught
Perf.	I have been taught	we have been taught
	you have been taught	you have been taught
	he (she, it) has been taught	they have been taught
Past Perf.	I had been taught	we had been taught
	you had been taught	you had been taught
	he (she, it) had been taught	they had been taught
Fut. Perf.	I shall have been taught	we shall have been taught
	you will have been taught	you will have been taught
	he (she, it) will have been taught	they will have been taught

IMPERATIVE MOOD

be taught

SUBJUNCTIVE MOOD

	Singular	Plural
Pres.	if I be taught	if we be taught
	if you be taught	if you be taught
	if he (she, it) be taught	if they be taught
Past	if I were taught	if we were taught
	if you were taught	if you were taught
	if he (she, it) were taught	if they were taught
Fut.	if I should be taught	if we should be taught
	if you should be taught	if you should be taught
	if he (she, it) should be taught	if they should be taught

Infinitive: to tear *Present Participle:* tearing
Perfect Infinitive: to have torn *Past Participle:* torn

INDICATIVE MOOD

Pres.	I tear	we tear
	you tear	you tear
	he (she, it) tears	they tear
Pres. Prog.	I am tearing	we are tearing
	you are tearing	you are tearing
	he (she, it) is tearing	they are tearing
Pres. Int.	I do tear	we do tear
	you do tear	you do tear
	he (she, it) does tear	they do tear
Fut.	I shall tear	we shall tear
	you will tear	you will tear
	he (she, it) will tear	they will tear
Fut.	I will tear *(P)*	we will tear *(P)*
	you shall tear *(C)*	you shall tear *(C)*
	he (she, it) shall tear *(C)*	they shall tear *(C)*
Past	I tore	we tore
	you tore	you tore
	he (she, it) tore	they tore
Past Prog.	I was tearing	we were tearing
	you were tearing	you were tearing
	he (she, it) was tearing	they were tearing
Past Int.	I did tear	we did tear
	you did tear	you did tear
	he (she, it) did tear	they did tear
Pres. Perf.	I have torn	we have torn
	you have torn	you have torn
	he (she, it) has torn	they have torn
Past Perf.	I had torn	we had torn
	you had torn	you had torn
	he (she, it) had torn	they had torn
Fut. Perf.	I shall have torn	we shall have torn
	you will have torn	you will have torn
	he (she, it) will have torn	they will have torn

IMPERATIVE MOOD
tear

SUBJUNCTIVE MOOD

Pres.	if I tear	if we tear
	if you tear	if you tear
	if he (she, it) tear	if they tear
Past	if I tore	if we tore
	if you tore	if you tore
	if he (she, it) tore	if they tore
Fut.	if I should tear	if we should tear
	if you should tear	if you should tear
	if he (she, it) should tear	if they should tear

348

Infinitive: to be torn   *Present Participle:* being torn
Perfect Infinitive: to have been torn   *Past Participle:* been torn

INDICATIVE MOOD

Pres.	I am torn	we are torn
	you are torn	you are torn
	he (she, it) is torn	they are torn
Pres.	I am being torn	we are being torn
Prog.	you are being torn	you are being torn
	he (she, it) is being torn	they are being torn
Pres.	I do get torn	we do get torn
Int.	you do get torn	you do get torn
	he (she, it) does get torn	they do get torn
Fut.	I shall be torn	we shall be torn
	you will be torn	you will be torn
	he (she, it) will be torn	they will be torn
Fut.	I will be torn *(P)*	we will be torn *(P)*
	you shall be torn *(C)*	you shall be torn *(C)*
	he (she, it) shall be torn *(C)*	they shall be torn *(C)*
Past	I was torn	we were torn
	you were torn	you were torn
	he (she, it) was torn	they were torn
Past	I was being torn	we were being torn
Prog.	you were being torn	you were being torn
	he (she, it) was being torn	they were being torn
Past	I did get torn	we did get torn
Int.	you did get torn	you did get torn
	he (she, it) did get torn	they did get torn
Pres.	I have been torn	we have been torn
Perf.	you have been torn	you have been torn
	he (she, it) has been torn	they have been torn
Past	I had been torn	we had been torn
Perf.	you had been torn	you had been torn
	he (she, it) had been torn	they had been torn
Fut.	I shall have been torn	we shall have been torn
Perf.	you will have been torn	you will have been torn
	he (she, it) will have been torn	they will have been torn

IMPERATIVE MOOD
be torn

SUBJUNCTIVE MOOD

Pres.	if I be torn	if we be torn
	if you be torn	if you be torn
	if he (she, it) be torn	if they be torn
Past	if I were torn	if we were torn
	if you were torn	if you were torn
	if he (she, it) were torn	if they were torn
Fut.	if I should be torn	if we should be torn
	if you should be torn	if you should be torn
	if he (she, it) should be torn	if they should be torn

349

to tell (active voice)

Principal Parts: tell, telling, told, told

Infinitive: to tell
Perfect Infinitive: to have told

Present Participle: telling
Past Participle: told

INDICATIVE MOOD

Pres.	I tell	we tell
	you tell	you tell
	he (she, it) tells	they tell
Prog.	I am telling	we are telling
	you are telling	you are telling
	he (she, it) is telling	they are telling
Int.	I do tell	we do tell
	you do tell	you do tell
	he (she, it) does tell	they do tell
Fut.	I shall tell	we shall tell
	you will tell	you will tell
	he (she, it) will tell	they will tell
	I will tell (P)	we will tell (P)
	you shall tell (C)	you shall tell (C)
	he (she, it) shall tell (C)	they shall tell (C)
Past	I told	we told
	you told	you told
	he (she, it) told	they told
Past Prog.	I was telling	we were telling
	you were telling	you were telling
	he (she, it) was telling	they were telling
Past Int.	I did tell	we did tell
	you did tell	you did tell
	he (she, it) did tell	they did tell
Pres. Perf.	I have told	we have told
	you have told	you have told
	he (she, it) has told	they have told
Past Perf.	I had told	we had told
	you had told	you had told
	he (she, it) had told	they had told
Fut. Perf.	I shall have told	we shall have told
	you will have told	you will have told
	he (she, it) will have told	they will have told

IMPERATIVE MOOD

tell

SUBJUNCTIVE MOOD

Pres.	if I tell	if we tell
	if you tell	if you tell
	if he (she, it) tell	if they tell
Past	if I told	if we told
	if you told	if you told
	if he (she, it) told	if they told
Fut.	if I should tell	if we should tell
	if you should tell	if you should tell
	if he (she, it) should tell	if they should tell

Infinitive: to be told   *Present Participle:* being told
Perfect Infinitive: to have been told   *Past Participle:* been told

INDICATIVE MOOD

Pres.	I am told	we are told
	you are told	you are told
	he (she, it) is told	they are told
Pres.	I am being told	we are being told
Prog.	you are being told	you are being told
	he (she, it) is being told	they are being told
Pres.	I do get told	we do get told
Int.	you do get told	you do get told
	he (she, it) does get told	they do get told
Fut.	I shall be told	we shall be told
	you will be told	you will be told
	he (she, it) will be told	they will be told
Fut.	I will be told *(P)*	we will be told *(P)*
	you shall be told *(C)*	you shall be told *(C)*
	he (she, it) shall be told *(C)*	they shall be told *(C)*
Past	I was told	we were told
	you were told	you were told
	he (she, it) was told	they were told
Past	I was being told	we were being told
Prog.	you were being told	you were being told
	he (she, it) was being told	they were being told
Past	I did get told	we did get told
Int.	you did get told	you did get told
	he (she, it) did get told	they did get told
Pres.	I have been told	we have been told
Perf.	you have been told	you have been told
	he (she, it) has been told	they have been told
Past	I had been told	we had been told
Perf.	you had been told	you had been told
	he (she, it) had been told	they had been told
Fut.	I shall have been told	we shall have been told
Perf.	you will have been told	you will have been told
	he (she, it) will have been told	they will have been told

IMPERATIVE MOOD
be told

SUBJUNCTIVE MOOD

Pres.	if I be told	if we be told
	if you bo told	if you be told
	if he (she, it) be told	if they be told
Past	if I were told	if we were told
	if you were told	if you were told
	if he (she, it) were told	if they were told
Fut.	if I should be told	if we should be told
	if you should be told	if you should be told
	if he (she, it) should be told	if they should be told

to think (active voice)

Principal Parts: think, thinking, thought, thought

Infinitive: to think	*Perfect Infinitive:* to have thought
Present Participle: thinking	*Past Participle:* thought

INDICATIVE MOOD

Pres.	I think	we think
	you think	you think
	he (she, it) thinks	they think
Pres. Prog.	I am thinking	we are thinking
	you are thinking	you are thinking
	he (she, it) is thinking	they are thinking
Pres. Int.	I do think	we do think
	you do think	you do think
	he (she, it) does think	they do think
Fut.	I shall think	we shall think
	you will think	you will think
	he (she, it) will think	they will think
Fut.	I will think (P)	we will think (P)
	you shall think (C)	you shall think (C)
	he (she, it) shall think (C)	they shall think (C)
Past	I thought	we thought
	you thought	you thought
	he (she, it) thought	they thought
Past Prog.	I was thinking	we were thinking
	you were thinking	you were thinking
	he (she, it) was thinking	they were thinking
Past Int.	I did think	we did think
	you did think	you did think
	he (she, it) did think	they did think
Pres. Perf.	I have thought	we have thought
	you have thought	you have thought
	he (she, it) has thought	they have thought
Past Perf.	I had thought	we had thought
	you had thought	you had thought
	he (she, it) had thought	they had thought
Fut. Perf.	I shall have thought	we shall have thought
	you will have thought	you will have thought
	he (she, it) will have thought	they will have thought

IMPERATIVE MOOD

think
think

SUBJUNCTIVE MOOD

Pres.	if I think	if we think
	if you think	if you think
	if he (she, it) think	if they think
Past	if I thought	if we thought
	if you thought	if you thought
	if he (she, it) thought	if they thought
Fut.	if I should think	if we should think
	if you should think	if you should think
	if he (she, it) should think	if they should think

(passive voice)

Infinitive: to be thought	*Perfect Infinitive:* to have been thought
Present Participle: being thought	*Past Participle:* been thought

INDICATIVE MOOD

Pres.	I am thought	we are thought
	he (she, it) is thought	you are thought
		they are thought
Pres. Prog.	I am being thought	we are being thought
	you are being thought	you are being thought
	he (she, it) is being thought	they are being thought
Pres.	I do get thought	we do get thought
Int.	you do get thought	you do get thought
	he (she, it) does get thought	they do get thought
Fut.	I shall be thought	we shall be thought
	you will be thought	you will be thought
	he (she, it) will be thought	they will be thought
Fut.	I will be thought (P)	we will be thought (P)
	you shall be thought (C)	you shall be thought (C)
	he (she, it) shall be thought (C)	they shall be thought (C)
Past	I was thought	we were thought
	you were thought	you were thought
	he (she, it) was thought	they were thought
Past Prog.	I was being thought	we were being thought
	you were being thought	you were being thought
	he (she, it) was being thought	they were being thought
Past Int.	I did get thought	we did get thought
	you did get thought	you did get thought
	he (she, it) did get thought	they did get thought
Pres. Perf.	I have been thought	we have been thought
	you have been thought	you have been thought
	he (she, it) has been thought	they have been thought
Past Perf.	I had been thought	we had been thought
	you had been thought	you had been thought
	he (she, it) had been thought	they had been thought
Fut. Perf.	I shall have been thought	we shall have been thought
	you will have been thought	you will have been thought
	he (she, it) will have been thought	they will have been thought

IMPERATIVE MOOD

be thought

SUBJUNCTIVE MOOD

Pres.	if I be thought	if we be thought
	if you be thought	if you be thought
	if he (she, it) be thought	if they be thought
Past	if I were thought	if we were thought
	if you were thought	if you were thought
	if he (she, it) were thought	if they were thought
Fut.	if I should be thought	if we should be thought
	if you should be thought	if you should be thought
	if he (she, it) should be thought	if they should be thought

to thrive

Principal Parts: thrive, thriving, throve (thrived), thriven (thrived)

Infinitive: to thrive *Perfect Infinitive:* to have thrived, thriven

Present Participle: thriving *Past Participle:* thrived, thriven

INDICATIVE MOOD

Pres.	I thrive	we thrive
	you thrive	you thrive
	he (she, it) thrives	they thrive
Pres. Prog.	I am thriving	we are thriving
	you are thriving	you are thriving
	he (she, it) is thriving	they are thriving
Pres. Int.	I do thrive	we do thrive
	you do thrive	you do thrive
	he (she, it) does thrive	they do thrive
Fut.	I shall thrive	we shall thrive
	you will thrive	you will thrive
	he (she, it) will thrive	they will thrive
Fut.	I will thrive (P)	we will thrive (P)
	you shall thrive (C)	you shall thrive (C)
	he (she, it) shall thrive (C)	they shall thrive (C)
Past	I throve, thrived	we throve, thrived
	you throve, thrived	you throve, thrived
	he (she, it) throve, thrived	they throve, thrived
Past Prog.	I was thriving	we were thriving
	you were thriving	you were thriving
	he (she, it) was thriving	they were thriving
Past Int.	I did thrive	we did thrive
	you did thrive	you did thrive
	he (she, it) did thrive	they did thrive
Pres. Perf.	I have thrived, thriven	we have thrived, thriven
	you have thrived, thriven	you have thrived, thriven
	he (she, it) has thrived, thriven	they have thrived, thriven
Past Perf.	I had thrived, thriven	we had thrived, thriven
	you had thrived, thriven	you had thrived, thriven
	he (she, it) had thrived, thriven	they had thrived, thriven
Fut. Perf.	I shall have thrived, thriven	we shall have thrived, thriven
	you will have thrived, thriven	you will have thrived, thriven
	he (she, it) will have thrived, thriven	they will have thrived, thriven

IMPERATIVE MOOD

thrive

SUBJUNCTIVE MOOD

Pres.	if I thrive	if we thrive
	if you thrive	if you thrive
	if he (she, it) thrive	if they thrive
Past	if I throve, thrived	if we throve, thrived
	if you throve, thrived	if you throve, thrived
	if he (she, it) throve, thrived	if they throve, thrived
Fut.	if I should thrive	if we should thrive
	if you should thrive	if you should thrive
	if he (she, it) should thrive	if they should thrive

To thrive is an intransitive verb.

It does not take an object.

It describes action, but the action is self-contained.

Like other intransitive verbs, it may be followed by adverbs, adverbial phrases and clauses describing the how, why, when, and where of the action:

HOW: The family has thriven *wonderfully*. (adverb)

WHY: The crops are thriving *because of the unusually warm weather*. (adverbial phrase)

WHEN: The animals will be thriving *when spring comes*. (adverbial clause)

WHERE: He was thriving *in his job at the bank*. (adverbial phrase)

to throw (active voice)

Principal Parts: throw, throwing, threw, thrown

Infinitive: to throw	*Perfect Infinitive:* to have thrown
Present Participle: throwing	*Past Participle:* thrown

INDICATIVE MOOD

Pres.	I throw	we throw
	you throw	you throw
	he (she, it) throw	they throw
Prog.	I am throwing	we are throwing
Pres.	you are throwing	you are throwing
	he (she, it) is throwing	they are throwing
Int.	I do throw	we do throw
Pres.	you do throw	you do throw
	he (she, it) does throw	they do throw
Fut.	I shall throw	we shall throw
	you will throw	you will throw
	he (she, it) will throw	they will throw
Fut.	I will throw (P)	we will throw (P)
	you shall throw (C)	you shall throw (C)
	he (she, it) shall throw (C)	they shall throw (C)
Past	I threw	we threw
	you threw	you threw
	he (she, it) threw	they threw
Prog.	I was throwing	we were throwing
Past	you were throwing	you were throwing
	he (she, it) was throwing	they were throwing
Int.	I did throw	we did throw
Past	you did throw	you did throw
	he (she, it) did throw	they did throw
Pres.	I have thrown	we have thrown
Perf.	you have thrown	you have thrown
	he (she, it) has thrown	they have thrown
Past	I had thrown	we had thrown
Perf.	you had thrown	you had thrown
	he (she, it) had thrown	they had thrown
Fut.	I shall have thrown	we shall have thrown
Perf.	you will have thrown	you will have thrown
	he (she, it) will have thrown	they will have thrown

IMPERATIVE MOOD

throw

SUBJUNCTIVE MOOD

Pres.	if I throw	if we throw
	if you throw	if you throw
	if he (she, it) throw	if they throw
Past	if I threw	if we threw
	if you threw	if you threw
	if he (she, it) threw	if they threw
Fut.	if I should throw	if we should throw
	if you should throw	if you should throw
	if he (she, it) should throw	if they should throw

Infinitive: to be thrown   *Present Participle:* being thrown
Perfect Infinitive: to have been thrown   *Past Participle:* been thrown

INDICATIVE MOOD

Pres.	I am thrown	we are thrown
	you are thrown	you are thrown
	he (she, it) is thrown	they are thrown
Pres. Prog.	I am being thrown	we are being thrown
	you are being thrown	you are being thrown
	he (she, it) is being thrown	they are being thrown
Pres. Int.	I do get thrown	we do get thrown
	you do get thrown	you do get thrown
	he (she, it) does get thrown	they do get thrown
Fut.	I shall be thrown	we shall be thrown
	you will be thrown	you will be thrown
	he (she, it) will be thrown	they will be thrown
Fut.	I will be thrown *(P)*	we will be thrown *(P)*
	you shall be thrown *(C)*	you shall be thrown *(C)*
	he (she, it) shall be thrown *(C)*	they shall be thrown *(C)*
Past	I was thrown	we were thrown
	you were thrown	you were thrown
	he (she, it) was thrown	they were thrown
Past Prog.	I was being thrown	we were being thrown
	you were being thrown	you were being thrown
	he (she, it) was being thrown	they were being thrown
Past Int.	I did get thrown	we did get thrown
	you did get thrown	you did get thrown
	he (she, it) did get thrown	they did get thrown
Pres. Perf.	I have been thrown	we have been thrown
	you have been thrown	you have been thrown
	he (she, it) has been thrown	they have been thrown
Past Perf.	I had been thrown	we had been thrown
	you had been thrown	you had been thrown
	he (she, it) had been thrown	they had been thrown
Fut. Perf.	I shall have been thrown	we shall have been thrown
	you will have been thrown	you will have been thrown
	he (she, it) will have been thrown	they will have been thrown

IMPERATIVE MOOD
be thrown

SUBJUNCTIVE MOOD

Pres.	if I be thrown	if we be thrown
	if you be thrown	if you be thrown
	if he (she, it) be thrown	if they be thrown
Past	if I were thrown	if we were thrown
	if you were thrown	if you were thrown
	if he (she, it) were thrown	if they were thrown
Fut.	if I should be thrown	if we should be thrown
	if you should be thrown	if you should be thrown
	if he (she, it) should be thrown	if they should be thrown

to wake (active voice) *Principal Parts:* wake, waking, woke (waked), waked (wakened, woken)

Infinitive: to wake   *Present Participle:* waking
Perfect Infinitive: to have waked, wakened, woken   *Past Participle:* wakened, woken

INDICATIVE MOOD

Pres.	I wake	we wake
	you wake	you wake
	he (she, it) wake	they wake
Pres. Prog.	I am waking	we are waking
	you are waking	you are waking
	he (she, it) is waking	they are waking
Pres. Int.	I do wake	we do wake
	you do wake	you do wake
	he (she, it) does wake	they do wake
Fut.	I shall wake	we shall wake
	you will wake	you will wake
	he (she, it) will wake	they will wake
Fut.	I will wake *(P)*	we will wake *(P)*
	you shall wake *(C)*	you shall wake *(C)*
	he (she, it) shall wake *(C)*	they shall wake *(C)*
Past	I woke	we woke
	you woke	you woke
	he (she, it) woke	they woke
Past Prog.	I was waking	we were waking
	you were waking	you were waking
	he (she, it) was waking	they were waking
Past Int.	I did wake	we did wake
	you did wake	you did wake
	he (she, it) did wake	they did wake
Pres. Perf.	I have waked, wakened, woken	we have waked, wakened, woken
	you have waked, wakened, woken	you have waked, wakened, woken
	he (she, it) has waked, wakened, woken	they have waked, wakened, woken
Past Perf.	I had waked, wakened, woken	we had waked, wakened, woken
	you had waked, wakened, woken	you had waked, wakened, woken
	he (she, it) had waked, wakened, woken	they had waked, wakened, woken
Fut. Perf.	I shall have waked, wakened, woken	we shall have waked, wakened, woken
	you will have waked, wakened, woken	you will have waked, wakened, woken
	he (she, it) will have waked, wakened, woken	they will have waked, wakened, woken

to wake (active voice)

wake

SUBJUNCTIVE MOOD

Pres.	if I wake	if we wake
	if you wake	if you wake
	if he (she, it) wake	if they wake
Past	if I woke	if we woke
	if you woke	if you woke
	if he (she, it) woke	if they woke
Fut.	if I should wake	if we should wake
	if you should wake	if you should wake
	if he (she, it) should wake	if they should wake

(passive voice)

Infinitive: to be waked, wakened, woken

Perfect Infinitive: to have been waked, wakened, woken

Present Participle: being waked, wakened, woken

Past Participle: been waked, wakened, woken

INDICATIVE MOOD

Pres.	I am waked, wakened, woken	we are waked, wakened, woken
	you are waked, wakened, woken	you are waked, wakened, woken
	he (she, it) is waked, wakened, woken	they are waked, wakened, woken
Pres. *Prog.*	I am being waked, wakened, woken	we are being waked, wakened, woken
	you are being waked, wakened, woken	you are being waked, wakened, woken
	he (she, it) is being waked, wakened, woken	they are being waked, wakened, woken
Pres. *Int.*	I do get waked, wakened, woken	we do get waked, wakened, woken
	you do get waked, wakened, woken	you do get waked, wakened, woken
	he (she, it) does get waked, wakened, woken	they do get waked, wakened, woken
Fut.	I shall be waked, wakened, woken	we shall be waked, wakened, woken
	you will be waked, wakened, woken	you will be waked, wakened, woken
	he (she, it) will be waked, wakened, woken	they will be waked, wakened, woken
Fut.	I will be waked, wakened, woken *(P)*	we will be waked, wakened, woken *(P)*
	you shall be waked, wakened, woken *(C)*	you shall be waked, wakened, woken *(C)*
	he (she, it) shall be waked, wakened, woken *(C)*	they shall be waked, wakened, woken *(C)*
Past	I was waked, wakened, woken	we were waked, wakened, woken
	you were waked, wakened, woken	you were waked, wakened, woken
	he (she, it) was waked, wakened, woken	they were waked, wakened, woken

Past. *Prog.*	I was being waked, wakened, woken	we were being waked, wakened, woken
	you were being waked, wakened, woken	you were being waked, wakened, woken
	he (she, it) was being waked, wakened, woken	they were being waked, wakened, woken
Past. *Int.*	I did get waked, wakened, woken	we did get waked, wakened, woken
	you did get waked, wakened, woken	you did get waked, wakened, woken
	he (she, it) did get waked, wakened, woken	they did get waked, wakened, woken
Pres. *Perf.*	I have been waked, wakened, woken	we have been waked, wakened, woken
	you have been waked, wakened, woken	you have been waked, wakened, woken
	he (she, it) has been waked, wakened, woken	they have been waked, wakened, woken
Past. *Perf.*	I had been waked, wakened, woken	we had been waked, wakened, woken
	you had been waked, wakened, woken	you had been waked, wakened, woken
	he (she, it) had been waked, wakened, woken	they had been waked, wakened, woken
Fut. *Perf.*	I shall have been waked, wakened, woken	we shall have been waked, wakened, woken
	you will have been waked, wakened, woken	you will have been waked, wakened, woken
	he (she, it) will have been waked, wakened, woken	they will have been waked, wakened, woken

IMPERATIVE MOOD
be waked

SUBJUNCTIVE MOOD

Pres.	if I be waked, wakened, woken	if we be waked, wakened, woken
	if you be waked, wakened, woken	if you be waked, wakened, woken
	if he (she, it) be waked, wakened, woken	if they be waked, wakened, woken
Past	if I were waked, wakened, woken	if we were waked, wakened, woken
	if you were waked, wakened, woken	if you were waked, wakened, woken
	if he (she, it) were waked, wakened, woken	if they were waked, wakened, woken
Fut.	if I should be waked, wakened, woken	if we should be waked, wakened, woken
	if you should be waked, wakened, woken	if you should be waked, wakened, woken
	if he (she, it) should be waked, wakened, woken	if they should be waked, wakened, woken

to wear (active voice)   *Principal Parts:* wear, wearing, wore, worn

Infinitive: to wear   *Present Participle:* wearing
Perfect Infinitive: to have worn   *Past Participle:* worn

INDICATIVE MOOD

Pres.	I wear	we wear
	you wear	you wear
	he (she, it) wears	they wear
Pres. Prog.	I am wearing	we are wearing
	you are wearing	you are wearing
	he (she, it) is wearing	they are wearing
Pres. Int.	I do wear	we do wear
	you do wear	you do wear
	he (she, it) does wear	they do wear
Fut.	I shall wear	we shall wear
	you will wear	you will wear
	he (she, it) will wear	they will wear
Fut.	I will wear *(P)*	we will wear *(P)*
	you shall wear *(C)*	you shall wear *(C)*
	he (she, it) shall wear *(C)*	they shall wear *(C)*
Past	I wore	we wore
	you wore	you wore
	he (she, it) wore	they wore
Past Prog.	I was wearing	we were wearing
	you were wearing	you were wearing
	he (she, it) was wearing	they were wearing
Past Int.	I did wear	we did wear
	you did wear	you did wear
	he (she, it) did wear	they did wear
Pres. Perf.	I have worn	we have worn
	you have worn	you have worn
	he (she, it) has worn	they have worn
Past Perf.	I had worn	we had worn
	you had worn	you had worn
	he (she, it) had worn	they had worn
Fut. Perf.	I shall have worn	we shall have worn
	you will have worn	you will have worn
	he (she, it) will have worn	they will have worn

IMPERATIVE MOOD
wear

SUBJUNCTIVE MOOD

Pres.	if I wear	if we wear
	if you wear	if you wear
	if he (she, it) wear	if they wear
Past	if I wore	if we wore
	if you wore	if you wore
	if he (she, it) wore	if they wore
Fut.	if I should wear	if we should wear
	if you should wear	if you should wear
	if he (she, it) should wear	if they should wear

Infinitive: to be worn   *Present Participle:* being worn
Perfect Infinitive: to have been worn   *Past Participle:* been worn

INDICATIVE MOOD

Pres.	I am worn	we are worn
	you are worn	you are worn
	he (she, it) is worn	they are worn
Pres.	I am being worn	we are being worn
Prog.	you are being worn	you are being worn
	he (she, it) is being worn	they are being worn
Pres.	I do get worn	we do get worn
Int.	you do get worn	you do get worn
	he (she, it) does get worn	they do get worn
Fut.	I shall be worn	we shall be worn
	you will be worn	you will be worn
	he (she, it) will be worn	they will be worn
Fut.	I will be worn *(P)*	we will be worn *(P)*
	you shall be worn *(C)*	you shall be worn *(C)*
	he (she, it) shall be worn *(C)*	they shall be worn *(C)*
Past	I was worn	we were worn
	you were worn	you were worn
	he (she, it) was worn	they were worn
Past	I was being worn	we were being worn
Prog.	you were being worn	you were being worn
	he (she, it) was being worn	they were being worn
Past	I did get worn	we did get worn
Int.	you did get worn	you did get worn
	he (she, it) did get worn	they did get worn
Pres.	I have been worn	we have been worn
Perf.	you have been worn	you have been worn
	he (she, it) has been worn	they have been worn
Past	I had been worn	we had been worn
Perf.	you had been worn	you had been worn
	he (she, it) had been worn	they had been worn
Fut.	I shall have been worn	we shall have been worn
Perf.	you will have been worn	you will have been worn
	he (she, it) will have been worn	they will have been worn

IMPERATIVE MOOD
be worn

SUBJUNCTIVE MOOD

Pres.	if I be worn	if we be worn
	if you be worn	if you be worn
	if he (she, it) be worn	if they be worn
Past	if I were worn	if we were worn
	if you were worn	if you were worn
	if he (she, it) were worn	if they were worn
Fut.	if I should be worn	if we should be worn
	if you should be worn	if you should be worn
	if he (she, it) should be worn	if they should be worn

to weave (active voice)   *Principal Parts:* weave, weaving, wove, woven

Infinitive: to weave   *Present Participle:* weaving
Perfect Infinitive: to have woven   *Past Participle:* woven

INDICATIVE MOOD

Pres.	I weave	we weave
	you weave	you weave
	he (she, it) weave	they weave

Pres. Prog.	I am weaving	we are weaving
	you are weaving	you are weaving
	he (she, it) is weaving	they are weaving

Pres. Int.	I do weave	we do weave
	you do weave	you do weave
	he (she, it) does weave	they do weave

Fut.	I shall weave	we shall weave
	you will weave	you will weave
	he (she, it) will weave	they will weave

Fut.	I will weave *(P)*	we will weave *(P)*
	you shall weave *(C)*	you shall weave *(C)*
	he (she, it) shall weave *(C)*	they shall weave *(C)*

Past	I wove	we wove
	you wove	you wove
	he (she, it) wove	they wove

Past Prog.	I was weaving	we were weaving
	you were weaving	you were weaving
	he (she, it) was weaving	they were weaving

Past Int.	I did weave	we did weave
	you did weave	you did weave
	he (she, it) did weave	they did weave

Pres. Perf.	I have woven	we have woven
	you have woven	you have woven
	he (she, it) has woven	they have woven

Past Perf.	I had woven	we had woven
	you had woven	you had woven
	he (she, it) had woven	they had woven

Fut. Perf.	I shall have woven	we shall have woven
	you will have woven	you will have woven
	he (she, it) will have woven	they will have woven

IMPERATIVE MOOD
weave

SUBJUNCTIVE MOOD

Pres.	if I weave	if we weave
	if you weave	if you weave
	if he (she, it) weave	if they weave

Past	if I wove	if we wove
	if you wove	if you wove
	if he (she, it) wove	if they wove

Fut.	if I should weave	if we should weave
	if you should weave	if you should weave
	if he (she, it) should weave	if they should weave

Infinitive: to be woven   *Present Participle:* being woven
Perfect Infinitive: to have been woven   *Past Participle:* been woven

INDICATIVE MOOD

Pres.	I am woven	we are woven
	you are woven	you are woven
	he (she, it) is woven	they are woven
Pres. Prog.	I am being woven	we are being woven
	you are being woven	you are being woven
	he (she, it) is being woven	they are being woven
Pres. Int.	I do get woven	we do get woven
	you do get woven	you do get woven
	he (she, it) does get woven	they do get woven
Fut.	I shall be woven	we shall be woven
	you will be woven	you will be woven
	he (she, it) will be woven	they will be woven
Fut.	I will be woven *(P)*	we will be woven *(P)*
	you shall be woven *(C)*	you shall be woven *(C)*
	he (she, it) shall be woven *(C)*	they shall be woven *(C)*
Past	I was woven	we were woven
	you were woven	you were woven
	he (she, it) was woven	they were woven
Past Prog.	I was being woven	we were being woven
	you were being woven	you were being woven
	he (she, it) was being woven	they were being woven
Past Int.	I did get woven	we did get woven
	you did get woven	you did get woven
	he (she, it) did get woven	they did get woven
Pres. Perf.	I have been woven	we have been woven
	you have been woven	you have been woven
	he (she, it) has been woven	they have been woven
Past Perf.	I had been woven	we had been woven
	you had been woven	you had been woven
	he (she, it) had been woven	they had been woven
Fut. Perf.	I shall have been woven	we shall have been woven
	you will have been woven	you will have been woven
	he (she, it) will have been woven	they will have been woven

IMPERATIVE MOOD
be woven

SUBJUNCTIVE MOOD

Pres.	if I be woven	if we be woven
	if you be woven	if you be woven
	if he (she, it) be woven	if they be woven
Past	if I were woven	if we were woven
	if you were woven	if you were woven
	if he (she, it) were woven	if they were woven
Fut.	if I should be woven	if we should be woven
	if you should be woven	if you should be woven
	if he (she, it) should be woven	if they should be woven

to weep (active voice)   *Principal Parts:* weep, weeping, wept, wept

---

Infinitive: to weep   *Present Participle:* weeping
Perfect Infinitive: to have wept   *Past Participle:* wept

INDICATIVE MOOD

Pres.	I weep	we weep
	you weep	you weep
	he (she, it) weeps	they weep
Pres.	I am weeping	we are weeping
Prog.	you are weeping	you are weeping
	he (she, it) is weeping	they are weeping
Pres.	I do weep	we do weep
Int.	you do weep	you do weep
	he (she, it) does weep	they do weep
Fut.	I shall weep	we shall weep
	you will weep	you will weep
	he (she, it) will weep	they will weep
Fut.	I will weep *(P)*	we will weep *(P)*
	you shall weep *(C)*	you shall weep *(C)*
	he (she, it) shall weep *(C)*	they shall weep *(C)*
Past	I wept	we wept
	you wept	you wept
	he (she, it) wept	they wept
Past	I was weeping	we were weeping
Prog.	you were weeping	you were weeping
	he (she, it) was weeping	they were weeping
Past	I did weep	we did weep
Int.	you did weep	you did weep
	he (she, it) did weep	they did weep
Pres.	I have wept	we have wept
Perf.	you have wept	you have wept
	he (she, it) has wept	they have wept
Past	I had wept	we had wept
Perf.	you had wept	you had wept
	he (she, it) had wept	they had wept
Fut.	I shall have wept	we shall have wept
Perf.	you will have wept	you will have wept
	he (she, it) will have wept	they will have wept

IMPERATIVE MOOD
weep

SUBJUNCTIVE MOOD

Pres.	if I weep	if we weep
	if you weep	if you weep
	if he (she, it) weep	if they weep
Past	if I wept	if we wept
	if you wept	if you wept
	if he (she, it) wept	if they wept
Fut.	if I should weep	if we should weep
	if you should weep	if you should weep
	if he (she, it) should weep	if they should weep

(passive voice)

Infinitive: to be wept   *Present Participle:* being wept
Perfect Infinitive: to have been wept   *Past Participle:* been wept

INDICATIVE MOOD

Pres.	I am wept	we are wept
	you are wept	you are wept
	he (she, it) is wept	they are wept
Pres.	I am being wept	we are being wept
Prog.	you are being wept	you are being wept
	he (she, it) he being wept	they are being wept
Pres.	I do get wept	we do get wept
Int.	you do get wept	you do get wept
	he (she, it) does get wept	they do get wept
Fut.	I shall be wept	we shall be wept
	you will be wept	you will be wept
	he (she, it) will be wept	they will be wept
Fut.	I will be wept *(P)*	we will be wept *(P)*
	you shall be wept *(C)*	you shall be wept *(C)*
	he (she, it) shall be wept *(C)*	they shall be wept *(C)*
Past	I was wept	we were wept
	you were wept	you were wept
	he (she, it) was wept	they were wept
Past	I was being wept	we were being wept
Prog.	you were being wept	you were being wept
	he (she, it) was being wept	they were being wept
Past	I did get wept	we did get wept
Int.	you did get wept	you did get wept
	he (she, it) did get wept	they did get wept
Pres.	I have been wept	we have been wept
Perf.	you have been wept	you have been wept
	he (she, it) has been wept	they have been wept
Past	I had been wept	we had been wept
Perf.	you had been wept	you had been wept
	he (she, it) had been wept	they had been wept
Fut.	I shall have been wept	we shall have been wept
Perf.	you will have been wept	you will have been wept
	he (she, it) will have been wept	they will have been wept

IMPERATIVE MOOD
be wept

SUBJUNCTIVE MOOD

Pres.	if I be wept	if we be wept
	if you be wept	if you be wept
	he (she, it) be wept	if they be wept
Past	if I were wept	if we were wept
	if you were wept	if you were wept
	he (she, it) were wept	if they were wept
Fut.	if I should be wept	if we should be wept
	if you should be wept	if you should be wept
	he (she, it) should be wept	if they should be wept

to win (active voice)   *Principal Parts:* win, winning, won, won

---

Infinitive: to win   *Present Participle:* winning
Perfect Infinitive: to have won   *Past Participle:* won

INDICATIVE MOOD

Pres.	I win	we win
	you win	you win
	he (she, it) wins	they win
Pres.	I am winning	we are winning
Prog.	you are winning	you are winning
	he (she, it) is winning	they are winning
Pres.	I do win	we do win
Int.	you do win	you do win
	he (she, it) does win	they do win
Fut.	I shall win	we shall win
	you will win	you will win
	he (she, it) will win	they will win
Fut.	I will win *(P)*	we will win *(P)*
	you shall win *(C)*	you shall win *(C)*
	he (she, it) shall win *(C)*	they shall win *(C)*
Past	I won	we won
	you won	you won
	he (she, it) won	they won
Past	I was winning	we were winning
Prog.	you were winning	you were winning
	he (she, it) was winning	they were winning
Past	I did win	we did win
Int.	you did win	you did win
	he (she, it) did win	they did win
Pres.	I have won	we have won
Perf.	you have won	you have won
	he (she, it) has won	they have won
Past	I had won	we had won
Perf.	you had won	you had won
	he (she, it) had won	they had won
Fut.	I shall have won	we shall have won
Perf.	you will have won	you will have won
	he (she, it) will have won	they will have won

IMPERATIVE MOOD
win

SUBJUNCTIVE MOOD

Pres.	if I win	if we win
	if you win	if you win
	if he (she, it) win	if they win
Past	if I won	if we won
	if you won	if you won
	if he (she, it) won	if they won
Fut.	if I should win	if we should win
	if you should win	if you should win
	if he (she, it) should win	if they should win

(passive voice)

Infinitive: to be won   *Present Participle:* being won
Perfect Infinitive: to have been won   *Past Participle:* been won

INDICATIVE MOOD

Pres.	I am won		we are won
	you are won		you are won
	he (she, it) is won		they are won
Pres.	I am being won		we are being won
Prog.	you are being won		you are being won
	he (she, it) is being won		they are being won
Pres.	I do get won		we do get won
Int.	you do get won		you do get won
	he (she, it) does get won		they do get won
Fut.	I shall be won		we shall be won
	you will be won		you will be won
	he (she, it) will be won		they will be won
Fut.	I will be won *(P)*		we will be won *(P)*
	you shall be won *(C)*		you shall be won *(C)*
	he (she, it) shall be won *(C)*		they shall be won *(C)*
Past	I was won		we were won
	you were won		you were won
	he (she, it) was won		they were won
Past	I was being won		we were being won
Prog.	you were being won		you were being won
	he (she, it) was being won		they were being won
Past	I did get won		we did get won
Int.	you did get won		you did get won
	he (she, it) did get won		they did get won
Pres.	I have been won		we have been won
Perf.	you have been won		you have been won
	he (she, it) has been won		they have been won
Past	I had been won		we had been won
Perf.	you had been won		you had been won
	he (she, it) had been won		they had been won
Fut.	I shall have been won		we shall have been won
Perf.	you will have been won		you will have been won
	he (she, it) will have been won		they will have been won

IMPERATIVE MOOD
be won

SUBJUNCTIVE MOOD

Pres.	if I be won		if we be won
	if you be won		if you be won
	if he (she, it) be won		if they be won
Past	if I were won		if we were won
	if you were won		if you were won
	if he (she, it) were won		if they were won
Fut.	if I should be won		if we should be won
	if you should be won		if you should be won
	if he (she, it) does be won		if they should be won

to wind (active voice)

Principal Parts: wind, winding, wound, wound

Infinitive: to wind | Perfect Infinitive: to have wound
Present Participle: winding | Past Participle: wound

INDICATIVE MOOD

Pres.	I wind	we wind	
	you wind	you wind	
	he (she, it) winds	they wind	
Pres.	I am winding	we are winding	
Prog.	you are winding	you are winding	
	he (she, it) is winding	they are winding	
Pres.	I do wind	we do wind	
Int.	you do wind	you do wind	
	he (she, it) does wind	they do wind	
Fut.	I shall wind	we shall wind	
	you will wind	you will wind	
	he (she, it) will wind	they will wind	
Fut.	I will wind (P)	we will wind (P)	
	you shall wind (C)	you shall wind (C)	
	he (she, it) shall wind (C)	they shall wind (C)	
Past	I wound	we wound	
	you wound	you wound	
	he (she, it) wound	they wound	
Past	I was winding	we were winding	
Prog.	you were winding	you were winding	
	he (she, it) was winding	they were winding	
Past	I did wind	we did wind	
Int.	you did wind	you did wind	
	he (she, it) did wind	they did wind	
Pres.	I have wound	we have wound	
Perf.	you have wound	you have wound	
	he (she, it) has wound	they have wound	
Past	I had wound	we had wound	
Perf.	you had wound	you had wound	
	he (she, it) had wound	they had wound	
Fut.	I shall have wound	we shall have wound	
Perf.	you will have wound	you will have wound	
	he (she, it) will have wound	they will have wound	

IMPERATIVE MOOD

wind

SUBJUNCTIVE MOOD

Pres.	if I wind	if we wind	
	if you wind	if you wind	
	if he (she, it) wind	if they wind	
Past	if I wound	if we wound	
	if you wound	if you wound	
	if he (she, it) wound	if they wound	
Fut.	if I should wind	if we should wind	
	if you should wind	if you should wind	
	if he (she, it) should wind	if they should wind	

Infinitive: to be wound   *Present Participle:* being wound
Perfect Infinitive: to have been wound   *Past Participle:* been wound

INDICATIVE MOOD

Pres.	I am wound	we are wound
	you are wound	you are wound
	he (she, it) is wound	they are wound
Pres.	I am being wound	we are being wound
Prog.	you are being wound	you are being wound
	he (she, it) he being wound	they are being wound
Pres.	I do get wound	we do get wound
Int.	you do get wound	you do get wound
	he (she, it) does get wound	they do get wound
Fut.	I shall be wound	we shall be wound
	you will be wound	you will be wound
	he (she, it) will be wound	they will be wound
Fut.	I will be wound *(P)*	we will be wound *(P)*
	you shall be wound *(C)*	you shall be wound *(C)*
	he (she, it) shall be wound *(C)*	they shall be wound *(C)*
Past	I was wound	we were wound
	you were wound	you were wound
	he (she, it) was wound	they were wound
Past	I was being wound	we were being wound
Prog.	you were being wound	you were being wound
	he (she, it) was being wound	they were being wound
Past	I did get wound	we did get wound
Int.	you did get wound	you did get wound
	he (she, it) did get wound	they did get wound
Pres.	I have been wound	we have been wound
Perf.	you have been wound	you have been wound
	he (she, it) has been wound	they have been wound
Past	I had been wound	we had been wound
Perf.	you had been wound	you had been wound
	he (she, it) had been wound	they had been wound
Fut.	I shall have been wound	we shall have been wound
Perf.	you will have been wound	you will have been wound
	he (she, it) will have been wound	they will have been wound

IMPERATIVE MOOD
be wound

SUBJUNCTIVE MOOD

Pres.	if I be wound	if we be wound
	if you be wound	if you be wound
	if he (she, it) be wound	if they be wound
Past	if I were wound	if we were wound
	if you were wound	if you were wound
	if he (she, it) were wound	if they were wound
Fut.	if I should be wound	if we should be wound
	if you should be wound	if you should be wound
	if he (she, it) should be wound	if they should be wound

to work (active voice)
Principal Parts: work, working, worked, worked

Infinitive: to work
Perfect Infinitive: to have worked

Present Participle: working
Past Participle: worked

INDICATIVE MOOD

Pres.	I work	we work
	you work	you work
	he (she, it) works	they work
Pres.	I am working	we are working
Prog.	you are working	you are working
	he (she, it) is working	they are working
Pres.	I do work	we do work
Int.	you do work	you do work
	he (she, it) does work	they do work
Fut.	I shall work	we shall work
	you will work	you will work
	he (she, it) will work	they will work
Fut.	I will work *(P)*	we will work *(P)*
	you shall work *(C)*	you shall work *(C)*
	he (she, it) shall work *(C)*	they shall work *(C)*
Past	I worked	we worked
	you worked	you worked
	he (she, it) worked	they worked
Past	I was working	we were working
Prog.	you were working	you were working
	he (she, it) was working	they were working
Past	I did work	we did work
Int.	you did work	you did work
	he (she, it) did work	they did work
Pres.	I have worked	we have worked
Perf.	you have worked	you have worked
	he (she, it) has worked	they have worked
Past	I had worked	we had worked
Perf.	you had worked	you had worked
	he (she, it) had worked	they had worked
Fut.	I shall have worked	we shall have worked
Perf.	you will have worked	you will have worked
	he (she, it) will have worked	they will have worked

IMPERATIVE MOOD
work

SUBJUNCTIVE MOOD

Pres.	if I work	if we work
	if you work	if you work
	if he (she, it) work	if they work
Past	if I worked	if we worked
	if you worked	if you worked
	if he (she, it) worked	if they worked
Fut.	if I should work	if we should work
	if you should work	if you should work
	if he (she, it) should work	if they should work

Infinitive: to be worked   *Present Participle:* being worked
Perfect Infinitive: to have been worked   *Past Participle:* been worked

INDICATIVE MOOD

Pres.	I am worked	we are worked
	you are worked	you are worked
	he (she, it) is worked	they are worked
Pres.	I am being worked	we are being worked
Prog.	you are being worked	you are being worked
	he (she, it) is being worked	they are being worked
Pres.	I do get worked	we do get worked
Int.	you do get worked	you do get worked
	he (she, it) does get worked	they do get worked
Fut.	I shall be worked	we shall be worked
	you will be worked	you will be worked
	he (she, it) will be worked	they will be worked
Fut.	I will be worked *(P)*	we will be worked *(P)*
	you shall be worked *(C)*	you shall be worked *(C)*
	he (she, it) shall be worked *(C)*	they shall be worked *(C)*
Past	I was worked	we were worked
	you were worked	you were worked
	he (she, it) was worked	they were worked
Past	I was being worked	we were being worked
Prog.	you were being worked	you were being worked
	he (she, it) was being worked	they were being worked
Past	I did get worked	we did get worked
Int.	you did get worked	you did get worked
	he (she, it) did get worked	they did get worked
Pres.	I have been worked	we have been worked
Perf.	you have been worked	you have been worked
	he (she, it) has been worked	they have been worked
Past	I had been worked	we had been worked
Perf.	you had been worked	you had been worked
	he (she, it) had been worked	they had been worked
Fut.	I shall have been worked	we shall have been worked
Perf.	you will have been worked	you will have been worked
	he (she, it) will have been worked	they will have been worked

IMPERATIVE MOOD
be worked

SUBJUNCTIVE MOOD

Pres.	if I be worked	if we be worked
	if you be worked	if you be worked
	if he (she, it) be worked	if they be worked
Past	if I were worked	if we were worked
	if you were worked	if you were worked
	if he (she, it) were worked	if they were worked
Fut.	if I should be worked	if we should be worked
	if you should be worked	if you should be worked
	if he (she, it) should be worked	if they should be worked

to wreak (active voice)

Principal Parts: wreak, wreaking, wrought, wrought

Infinitive: to wreak	Present Participle: wreaking
Perfect Infinitive: to have wrought	Past Participle: wrought

INDICATIVE MOOD

Pres.	I wreak	we wreak
	you wreak	you wreak
	he (she, it) wreaks	they wreak
Pres. *Prog.*	I am wreaking	we are wreaking
	you are wreaking	they are wreaking
	he (she, it) is wreaking	
Pres. *Int.*	I do wreak	we do wreak
	you do wreak	they do wreak
	he (she, it) does wreak	
Fut.	I shall wreak	we shall wreak
	you will wreak	they will wreak
	he (she, it) will wreak	
Fut.	I will wreak (P)	we will wreak (P)
	you shall wreak (C)	you shall wreak (C)
	he (she, it) shall wreak (C)	they shall wreak (C)
Past	I wrought	we wrought
	you wrought	you wrought
	he (she, it) wrought	they wrought
Past *Prog.*	I was wreaking	we were wreaking
	you were wreaking	you were wreaking
	he (she, it) was wreaking	they were wreaking
Past *Int.*	I did wreak	we did wreak
	you did wreak	you did wreak
	he (she, it) did wreak	they did wreak
Pres. *Perf.*	I have wrought	we have wrought
	you have wrought	you have wrought
	he (she, it) has wrought	they have wrought
Past *Perf.*	I had wrought	we had wrought
	you had wrought	you had wrought
	he (she, it) had wrought	they had wrought
Fut. *Perf.*	I shall have wrought	we shall have wrought
	you will have wrought	you will have wrought
	he (she, it) will have wrought	they will have wrought

IMPERATIVE MOOD

wreak

SUBJUNCTIVE MOOD

Pres.	if I wreak	if we wreak
	if you wreak	if you wreak
	if he (she, it) wreak	if they wreak
Past	if I wrought	if we wrought
	if you wrought	if you wrought
	if he (she, it) wrought	if they wrought
Fut.	if I should wreak	if we should wreak
	if you should wreak	if you should wreak
	if he (she, it) should wreak	if they should wreak

Infinitive: to be wrought
Perfect Infinitive: to have been wrought

Present Participle: being wrought
Past Participle: been wrought

INDICATIVE MOOD

Pres. I am wrought
you are wrought
he (she, it) is wrought

we are wrought
you are wrought
they are wrought

Pres.
Prog. I am being wrought
you are being wrought
he (she, it) is being wrought

we are being wrought
you are being wrought
they are being wrought

Pres.
Int. I do get wrought
you do get wrought
he (she, it) does get wrought

we do get wrought
you do get wrought
they do get wrought

Fut. I shall be wrought
you will be wrought
he (she, it) will be wrought

we shall be wrought
you will be wrought
they will be wrought

Fut. I will be wrought *(P)*
you shall be wrought *(C)*
he (she, it) shall be wrought *(C)*

we will be wrought *(P)*
you shall be wrought *(C)*
they shall be wrought *(C)*

Past I was wrought
you were wrought
he (she, it) was wrought

we were wrought
you were wrought
they were wrought

Past
Prog. I was being wrought
you were being wrought
he (she, it) was being wrought

we were being wrought
you were being wrought
they were being wrought

Past
Int. I did get wrought
you did get wrought
he (she, it) did get wrought

we did get wrought
you did get wrought
they did get wrought

Pres.
Perf. I have been wrought
you have been wrought
he (she, it) has been wrought

we have been wrought
you have been wrought
they have been wrought

Past
Perf. I had been wrought
you had been wrought
he (she, it) had been wrought

we had been wrought
you had been wrought
they had been wrought

Fut.
Perf. I shall have been wrought
you will have been wrought
he (she, it) will have been wrought

we shall have been wrought
you will have been wrought
they will have been wrought

IMPERATIVE MOOD
be wrought

SUBJUNCTIVE MOOD

Pres. if I be wrought
if you be wrought
if he (she, it) be wrought

if we be wrought
if you be wrought
if they be wrought

Past if I were wrought
if you were wrought
if he (she, it) were wrought

if we were wrought
if you were wrought
if they were wrought

Fut. if I should be wrought
if you should be wrought
if he (she, it) should be wrought

if we should be wrought
if you should be wrought
if they should be wrought

to wring (active voice)   *Principal Parts:* wring, wringing, wrung, wrung

---

Infinitive: to wring   *Present Participle:* wringing
Perfect Infinitive: to have wrung   *Past Participle:* wrung

INDICATIVE MOOD

Pres.	I wring	we wring
	you wring	you wring
	he (she, it) wrings	they wring
Pres.	I am wringing	we are wringing
Prog.	you are wringing	you are wringing
	he (she, it) is wringing	they are wringing
Pres.	I do wring	we do wring
Int.	you do wring	you do wring
	he (she, it) does wring	they do wring
Fut.	I shall wring	we shall wring
	you will wring	you will wring
	he (she, it) will wring	they will wring
Fut.	I will wring *(P)*	we will wring *(P)*
	you shall wring *(C)*	you shall wring *(C)*
	he (she, it) shall wring *(C)*	they shall wring *(C)*
Past	I wrung	we wrung
	you wrung	you wrung
	he (she, it) wrung	they wrung
Past	I was wringing	we were wringing
Prog.	you were wringing	you were wringing
	he (she, it) was wringing	they were wringing
Past	I did wring	we did wring
Int.	you did wring	you did wring
	he (she, it) did wring	they did wring
Pres.	I have wrung	we have wrung
Perf.	you have wrung	you have wrung
	he (she, it) has wrung	they have wrung
Past	I had wrung	we had wrung
Perf.	you had wrung	you had wrung
	he (she, it) had wrung	they had wrung
Fut.	I shall have wrung	we shall have wrung
Perf.	you will have wrung	you will have wrung
	he (she, it) will have wrung	they will have wrung

IMPERATIVE MOOD
wring

SUBJUNCTIVE MOOD

Pres.	if I wring	if we wring
	if you wring	if you wring
	if he (she, it) wring	if they wring
Past	if I wrung	if we wrung
	if you wrung	if you wrung
	if he (she, it) wrung	if they wrung
Fut.	if I should wring	if we should wring
	if you should wring	if you should wring
	if he (she, it) should wring	if they should wring

Infinitive: to be wrung   *Present Participle:* being wrung
Perfect Infinitive: to have been wrung   *Past Participle:* been wrung

INDICATIVE MOOD

Pres.	I am wrung	we are wrung
	you are wrung	you are wrung
	he (she, it) is wrung	they are wrung
Pres.	I am being wrung	we are being wrung
Prog.	you are being wrung	you are being wrung
	he (she, it) is being wrung	they are being wrung
Pres.	I do get wrung	we do get wrung
Int.	you do get wrung	you are get wrung
	he (she, it) does get wrung	they do get wrung
Fut.	I shall be wrung	we shall be wrung
	you will be wrung	you will be wrung
	he (she, it) will be wrung	they will be wrung
Fut.	I will be wrung *(P)*	we will be wrung *(P)*
	you shall be wrung *(C)*	you shall be wrung *(C)*
	he (she, it) shall be wrung *(C)*	they shall be wrung *(C)*
Past	I was wrung	we were wrung
	you were wrung	you were wrung
	he (she, it) was wrung	they were wrung
Past	I was being wrung	we were being wrung
Prog.	you were being wrung	you were being wrung
	he (she, it) was being wrung	they were being wrung
Past	I did get wrung	we did get wrung
Int.	you did get wrung	you did get wrung
	he (she, it) did get wrung	they did get wrung
Pres.	I have been wrung	we have been wrung
Perf.	you have been wrung	you have been wrung
	he (she, it) has been wrung	they have been wrung
Past	I had been wrung	we had been wrung
Perf.	you had been wrung	you had been wrung
	he (she, it) had been wrung	they had been wrung
Fut.	I shall have been wrung	we shall have been wrung
Perf.	you will have been wrung	you will have been wrung
	he (she, it) will have been wrung	they will have been wrung

IMPERATIVE MOOD
be wrung

SUBJUNCTIVE MOOD

Pres.	if I be wrung	if we be wrung
	if you be wrung	if you be wrung
	if he (she, it) be wrung	if they be wrung
Past	if I were wrung	if we were wrung
	if you were wrung	if you were wrung
	if he (she, it) were wrung	if they were wrung
Fut.	if I should be wrung	if we should be wrung
	if you should be wrung	if you should be wrung
	if he (she, it) should be wrung	if they should be wrung